From Purpose to Impact

To meet the challenge of closing the gap between academic research and industry practice, we need a step change in how the business school and the business scholar engages with business. This book presents best practice in the methods of broadening successful academic–business engagement on a major scale. It presents concrete recommendations for setting programmes, creating incentives and structuring recruitment that will transform effective academic–business engagement.

Most universities claim to have significant links with industry and the professions, but, in reality, only a limited number of business scholars are engaged with industry. A focus on 'impact' presents an additional potential trap, confusing promotion of research and tactical tips and tricks, with genuine engagement. This book explores the increasing number of new and innovative partnerships and collaborative activities, and looks at how academics can adapt to and leverage these new opportunities. It focuses on the academic as the primary driver of the external relationship and outlines the skills and capabilities needed to proactively develop engagement. Finally, the book provides a number of examples of best practice from a range of countries.

Written by senior business scholars and leaders from around the world, and with examples of best practice included from leading universities, this book gives universities the insight needed to develop a broader range of relationships with businesses and to have genuine engagement and impact in practice.

Nicholas O'Regan is Professor in Strategy at Aston Business School. He is a Fellow of the Academy of Social Sciences and a Fellow of the British Academy of Management.

"In a world where humanity is at war with itself and its Home Planet, business education must evolve and consider its contribution to human society in very different ways. And I am not referring to tweaking the Capital Asset Pricing Model to account for the first ever downgrade of the US Government risk-free rate benchmark. As we move into a new Quantum World of unknown governance, Nicholas O'Regan's seminal work shows just how a cutting-edge business school can re-invent its relevance and significance to modern human society. How far can business innovation and enterprise go to mitigate the debilitating short-sightedness of human leadership?"

Xavier R. Rolet, KBE, Chairman of Shore Capital Markets, Harvard Fellow, and former CEO of the London Stock Exchange Group

"The contents of this book should interest all those concerned with economic development and organisational development in their cities and regions."

James Timpson, OBE DL, Chief Executive, Timpson Group

"A much-needed look by a wide range of contributors, at how business school academia must radically change to engage with real practice, real companies and graduates who need to be work-ready. As a devotee of 'what gets measured gets done', I particularly welcome the focus on Implementation and Impact – what in business we call execution and KPIs."

Leo Quinn, Group Chief Executive, Balfour Beatty

"Instead of resting on their laurels, this book stresses the need for change, reinvention and the professionalisation of the approach to business from our universities."

Ann Francke, OBE, Chief Executive, Chartered Management Institute

"A fascinating book, justifying why universities getting closer to business makes sense for them as institutions, and as a springboard for the brightest minds to become commercial success stories. Each chapter a compelling read."

Vis Raghavan, CEO, Europe, Middle East & Africa, J.P. Morgan

From Purpose to Impact

The University and Business Partnership

Edited by Nicholas O'Regan

Routledge
Taylor & Francis Group

LONDON AND NEW YORK

Designed cover image: Getty Images / shuoshu

First published 2025
by Routledge
4 Park Square, Milton Park, Abingdon, Oxon OX14 4RN

and by Routledge
605 Third Avenue, New York, NY 10158

Routledge is an imprint of the Taylor & Francis Group, an informa business

© 2025 selection and editorial matter, Nicholas O'Regan; individual chapters, the contributors

The right of Nicholas O'Regan to be identified as the author of the editorial material, and of the authors for their individual chapters, has been asserted in accordance with sections 77 and 78 of the Copyright, Designs and Patents Act 1988.

British Library Cataloguing-in-Publication Data
A catalogue record for this book is available from the British Library

ISBN: 978-1-032-60458-9 (hbk)
ISBN: 978-1-032-60363-6 (pbk)
ISBN: 978-1-003-45921-7 (ebk)

DOI: 10.4324/9781003459217

Typeset in Sabon
by SPi Technologies India Pvt Ltd (Straive)

Contents

Contributors

Nicholas O'Regan (Editor) is Professor in Strategy at Aston Business School, having held professorial appointments at Middlesex University and the University of the West of England (UWE). He has also held appointments as Associate Dean for Research at UWE and Deputy Dean for Research at Aston University

Nicholas has first-hand experience of both the public and private sectors. In the public sector, he was the youngest local authority chief executive in Ireland and held this distinction for nearly 8 years. He then undertook further post-graduate studies in the UK, after which he became one of the youngest chief officers in UK local government, heading departments ranging from economic development, industrial development and strategic planning.

In the private sector, he has worked as a consultant to a range of organisations, on themes such as strategic leadership development for the directors of an international blue-chip company.

Derrick M. Anderson is the Senior Vice President for Learning and Engagement at the American Council on Education and a professor of science and technology policy at Arizona State University.

Martha Arízaga is a PhD candidate at Arizona State University and the Director of Creativity, Memory and Heritage for the Municipality of Quito.

Jenny Bäckstrand is Associate Professor in Operations and Supply Chain Management at the School of Engineering, Jönköping University. She is also the initiator of the university's engagement accreditation.

Chris J. Barton works at Arizona State University and studies the politics of knowledge in mission-driven domains, such as development, conservation and sustainability.

Rebecca Beech is a lecturer in Marketing at Oxford Brookes University. She holds external affiliations at the British Academy of Management in the Marketing and Retail Special Interest Group, and is co-lead of the Early Career Academic Network, along with membership at the Academy of Marketing.

Carlos José Bello-Pérez is a researcher and professor of Operations Management and Head of the Capstone Project – Plan Padrinos – of the School of Management at the Universidad Externado de Colombia.

Ahmad Beltagui is Associate Professor at Aston Business School. As a member of the Advanced Services Group, his research involves businesses, large and small, in support of the transformation from product focus to a sustainable, digital and customer-centric strategy.

Alejandro Beltrán-Duque is a researcher and professor of strategy at the School of Management at the Universidad Externado de Colombia and former school dean for the 2008–2022 period.

Igor Campillo is the Executive Director of Euskampus Fundazioa (Basque Country, Spain). In the last three years, he has been the Impact Leader of the European University Alliance ENLIGHT. He has been recently acknowledged as one of the Spanning Boundaries Champions for university–industry–society cooperation by the UIIN – University Industry Innovation Network.

Candice Carr Kelman is an assistant research professor with the Center for Biodiversity Outcomes and teaches in the School of Sustainability at Arizona State University. She currently manages an NSF grant on actionable science in conservation, and co-directs the Conservation Solutions Lab as well as the Collab-Lab, which is focused on collaborative governance of social-ecological systems.

Joann Cattlin is a PhD candidate at the School of Global, Urban and Social Studies, RMIT University.

Jodie Conduit is a professor of Marketing, at the Adelaide Business School, Australia and visiting professor at EM Strasbourg Business School, France. Her research seeks to understand how to engage consumers and other stakeholders to achieve meaningful outcomes for society, particularly a circular economy.

Sandra Crocker is Associate Vice-President (Strategic Initiatives and Operations), Carleton University, Ottawa, Ontario, Canada. She was previously Assistant Vice-Principal (Strategic Planning and Partnerships) at McGill University and Associate Vice-Principal at Queen's University.

Timothy M. Devinney is Professor and Chair of International Business at the Alliance Manchester Business School. He is a Fellow of the AOM, AIB, EIBA, Academy of Social Sciences and the Alexander von Humboldt Stiftung.

Kevin J. Dooley is a Distinguished Professor of Supply Chain Management in the W.P. Carey School of Business at Arizona State University. He is also Chief Scientist of The Sustainability Consortium, a senior global futures scientist in the Julie Ann Wrigley Global Futures Laboratory, and Co-Director of the Complex Adaptive Supply Networks Research Accelerator.

Kelly Farrell has worked in universities for 25 years, across multiple disciplines, divisions and portfolios spanning a student union to the office of a Vice-Chancellor. She is now the Head of the Business Development team at the Australian National University, working with her team and colleagues across the university to build an ecosystem to support research partnering.

George Feiger was a junior fellow of the Society of Fellows and taught economics at Harvard, then finance at Stanford GSB. Subsequently, he was a senior partner at McKinsey&Co, Global Head of Investment Banking at SBC Warburg, Global Head of Onshore Private Banking at UBS and started and ran a wealth management company, Contango Capital Advisors, in the US. He was, most recently, Executive Dean of the College of Business and Social Sciences at Aston University in Birmingham.

Natalie Forde is a partnerships and innovation strategy practitioner who is passionate about the role innovation and social technical system shaping can play in transforming industries and societies to be more sustainable.

Leah R. Gerber is a professor of conservation science in the School of Life Sciences and founding director of the Center for Biodiversity Outcomes (CBO) at Arizona State University. Gerber's research, teaching and leadership advance the integration of science in decision processes to achieve biodiversity outcomes.

Lisa M. Given is Director, Social Change Enabling Impact Platform, and Professor of Information Sciences, RMIT University.

Judith Helmer is a research associate at the Science-to-Business Marketing Research Centre at the FH Münster University of Applied Sciences, Germany, and a PhD candidate at the University of Adelaide, Australia. Her research focuses on market shaping in times of digital transformation, specifically exploring the active role of digital technologies in shaping markets.

Michael A. Hitt is a University Distinguished Professor Emeritus at Texas A&M University. His research interests include corporate strategy (e.g., M&As) and international strategy (e.g., in different institutional environments) with emphasis on orchestration of resources and capabilities to gain and sustain a competitive advantage.

Andrew Jack is Global Education Editor, Financial Times. He oversees the free FT schools programme, business school rankings, and initiatives around academic impact and responsible business. He was a foreign correspondent in France and Russia, and is author of the French Exception and Inside Putin's Russia. He is a Companion of the British Academy of Management.

Rajagopalan Jayaraman is Head of Capstone Projects in the Executive Management Programme at the SP JAIN Institute of Management and Research, Mumbai, India. He is a recipient of the AIM Golden 'Best Professor – Operations Management (National)' award in 2021.

Paul Jones specialises in work psychology and human resource management. He has worked across the public, private and third sectors, and for the last decade, he has been applying his skills and experience within higher education. He is currently a lecturer for the Work and Organisation Department at Aston University.

Michel Kalika, emeritus Professor, is the President of the Business Science Institute. Previously, Michel was professor at IAE Lyon School of Management, University Jean Moulin, at University Paris Dauphine and Dean of EM Strasbourg Business School. He is the founder of the BSIS (Business School Impact System–EFMD–FNEGE).

Anita Kocsis is the Director of Design Factory Melbourne, Swinburne University's interdisciplinary innovation lab. Anita is a champion of the lab that creates the conditions for innovation by working on challenges beyond the scope of a single discipline or research practice.

Malin Löfving is Assistant Professor in Production Systems at the School of Engineering, Jönköping University. She has a long experience of working in industry and acting as an intermediate.

Jane McKenzie is Professor of Knowledge and Learning at Henley Business School. Her research interests focus on how connections and contradictions affect knowledge work and learning capacity in organisational life. Her most recent book examines the benefits, challenges and complexities of academic practitioner relationships.

Peter McKiernan is Professor of Management, University of Strathclyde. He is Distinguished Professor of Management, Brussels School of Governance at Vrije Universiteit Brussel, Adjunct Professor of Management at University of Notre Dame, Australia and Foundational Dean of the EURAM Fellows College.

Vadake K. Narayanan is the Deloitte & Touché Jones Stubbs Professor of Strategy and Entrepreneurship in Drexel University, Philadelphia, PA. He had formerly served as the founding Associate Dean for Research in the Le Bow College of Business, the Director of the Center for Management of Technology and the Associate Dean for Academic Affairs in the School of Business at the University of Kansas.

John A. Parnell is a Professor and Eminent Scholar in Management at the University of North Alabama. He is the author of over 250 basic and applied research articles, published presentations, and cases in strategic management and related areas. His current research interests include crisis management and nonmarket strategy.

Stephen Platt has worked in the French education system since 1990. His company, International Eyes, works with Business Schools and Universities to boost their international brand image, translating, copy-editing, and writing documents in authentic English. He is Quality Assurance and Accreditations Manager for the Business Science Institute.

Carolin Plewa is the Pro Vice-Chancellor (Researcher Education and Development) and Dean of Graduate Studies at The University of Adelaide, as well as Professor of Marketing and Stakeholder Engagement. She specialises in engagement and value co-creation across organisations and individuals, with a particular emphasis on university–business collaboration, service, and social contexts, as well as market shaping. She also co-edited the Future of Universities Thoughtbook series.

Iñigo Puertas is Impact Manager at Euskampus Fundazioa. Its work focuses on the methodological and strategic development of the entity's impact management. He is also a teacher and researcher at the University of Deusto.

Rafaela Costa Camoes Rabello was a postdoctoral researcher on the government-funded Science for Technological Innovation programme and currently the Projects and Innovations Leader for Peterson Projects and Solutions, South America

Einar Rasmussen is Professor at Nord University Business School, Norway. He has been a visiting scholar at the Universities of Nottingham, Strathclyde, Twente, Bologna and Ghent.

Erling Rasmussen has over 40 years of experience of employment relations research and public policy in private and public sectors in different OECD countries. He is the editor of NZ Journal of Employment Relations, the author of NZ's leading employment relations textbooks and has been advisor to governments, unions and employer associations.

Carlos Alberto Restrepo-Rivillas is the Business Environment Research Group Leader, directs the Business Environment and Sustainability area of the School of Management at the Universidad Externado de Colombia, and was recognized at the level of Associate Researcher by the Ministry of Science, Technology and Innovation.

Glória Nunes Rodrigues is International Manager at Euskampus Fundazioa and member of the Impact Task Force of the European University Alliance ENLIGHT. Previously, she worked as Research Advisor at the University of Deusto and as Policy Officer at the European Commission – Directorate General for Education and Culture.

Victor Schiller is a PhD researcher at Bayes Business School/City, University of London. He has seven AI-related patents and moved to academia after more than forty years as an entrepreneur, where he started, operated and sold five technology businesses.

Keith Schofield is an organisational psychologist and Deputy Dean in the College of Business and Social Sciences at Aston University. He leads international recruitment, partnership growth and programme development. His expertise has been particularly important for supporting and developing senior leaders through executive education.

David R. Seibold is Distinguished Professor Emeritus of Technology Management (College of Engineering) and of Communication (Division of Social Sciences), and former Director of the Graduate Program in Management Practice, at the University of California, Santa Barbara. He is a Fellow of the International Communication Association and a Distinguished Scholar of the National Communication Association.

Pamela Sharkey Scott is Professor of Strategy at Dublin City University, Pamela's research and teaching centre on how organizational leaders develop and implement strategic responses. As a former international corporate banker, Pamela maintains close links with leading global organizations on their responses to emerging challenges.

Lorraine Skelton is a principal lecturer at the Otago Polytechnic Auckland International Campus (OPAIC) Post Graduate Business School. She has a PhD in collaborative management practice, and is a member of the Institute of Directors and the Australasian New Zealand Academy of Management.

Howard Thomas is a 'serial dean' having held business school deanships in Asia (SMU), Europe (Warwick Business School), and North America (University of Illinois at Urbana-Champaign). He is a well-regarded and highly cited scholar in the fields of strategic management and management education. He is an Emeritus Professor and former Dean at LKCSB, Singapore Management University, and currently a Special Advisor at EFMD Global.

Katrin Uude is a research associate at the Science-to-Business Marketing Research Centre at the FH Münster University of Applied Sciences, Germany and a PhD candidate at the University of Adelaide, Australia. Her PhD focuses on the dynamic nature of engagement and her research interest centres on how actors can co-create to drive societal change.

Tim Vorley is the Pro Vice-Chancellor and Dean of Oxford Brookes Business School and University lead for Enterprise and Entrepreneurship. As a Professor of Industry and Innovation he has extensive experience of working with public, private and third sector partners, and leads the Innovation & Research Caucus funded by Innovate UK, ESRC and UKRI.

Paul J. Woodfield's research spans entrepreneurship and innovation, with specialty in the family business and traditional industries contexts. Alongside his position at AUT, New Zealand, Paul is a researcher on the government funded Science for Technological Innovation programme exploring ways to build New Zealand's innovation capacity.

Acknowledgements

I am sincerely grateful for the invaluable support extended to me by Aston University, without which the realization of this edited volume would not have been possible. My appreciation goes to Aston's visionary Vice-Chancellor Prof Aleks Subic for fostering an environment that encourages scholarly endeavours and academic–business engagement.

Special gratitude is reserved for Prof George Feiger, whose unwavering encouragement, support and countless stimulating discussions played a pivotal role in shaping the original proposal presented to Routledge. His insightful guidance was instrumental in navigating the complexities of the project, and I am indebted to him for his dedicated involvement.

I extend my deepest thanks to the esteemed academics who contributed to this edited collection. Their thoughtful chapters and profound insights have enriched the pages of this volume, transforming it into a comprehensive and enlightening resource. Without their scholarly contributions, this collection would remain a mere aspiration.

Finally, I express my gratitude for the collective commitment that has brought this project to fruition.

Part I

The Changing University/ Getting Impact on the Agenda

1 The New Priority for the New Academic Environment

Andrew Jack

When the *Financial Times* (*FT*) launched a responsible business education award in 2021 seeking the best academic research on societal issues with evidence of impact, there was both nervousness and scepticism.

Aside from wry smiles from cynics over how far "ethics", "purpose" and "responsibility" can be applied to business schools and their graduates at all, some raised practical and philosophical questions: the extent to which impactful research was taking place, how it could be meaningfully measured and whether academics should even be required to focus on in it at all.

The good news is that in the three years since, a strong series of entries has defied the critics and inspired many [www.ft.com/rbe]. The downside is continued widespread misunderstandings of the term by academics and the still relatively modest volume of such impactful work.

The awards provide broader lessons for those engaged on the topic, including some pointers on how to advance, with a focus on what might be called the "four Rs" to deliver meaningful impact: rigour (academic scrutiny including peer review); relevance (addressing societal needs such as the UN's global goals); resonance (dissemination beyond academia); and realisation (uptake in the world of practice).

The high quality of the *FT* winners bodes well for what can be achieved and acts as an inspiration to others. It also shows that while academic impact can be difficult to define in the abstract and challenging to achieve in practice, "you know it when you see it". Consider some of the top awardees in 2022, which also provide insights into the effort required:

1. Sendhil Mullainathan from the University of Chicago's Booth School of Business led a project with medical researchers and practitioners which scrutinised health insurance algorithms. But as he told the *FT*: "Papers are just the beginning of a conversation. If you want to have impact, you have to do a lot afterwards".

DOI: 10.4324/9781003459217-2

They not only identified large-scale racial bias and produced academic articles to describe it, but worked with the company studied to eliminate it and improve health outcomes; extended their analysis to other sectors; and produced a free algorithmic bias playbook online drawing on their insights for senior executives, policymakers and others to apply.

2. Fiona Marshall at the University of Sussex Business School worked with partners and civil society organisations in India to understand waste management practices, which highlighted how a policy of centralised incinerators was generating additional toxic emissions and undermining the traditional livelihoods of low-income waste-pickers.

"Impact takes a lot of time and effort and does not directly drive career trajectories," she cautions. But through blogs and policy outreach beyond the academic literature, they worked with the government and private contractors to develop alternative decentralised approaches working with waste-pickers to increase recycling, compost and biogas.

3. Shrihari Sridhar at the Mays Business School of Texas A&M University and colleagues used machine learning to analyse why screening rates for liver cancer were low for high-risk patients. They applied marketing techniques to develop more effective personalised prompts to increase uptake.

"Marketing is used in many bad ways to target customers but, if you channel the power of personalising messages to find when patients will respond, you can bring all the good aspects," he says. Beyond initial academic publications, they have worked with different medical centres in the US and Singapore, and are expanding their approach to colon cancer.

4. Erik Chavez at London's Imperial College Business School and colleagues analysed the risks and mitigating behaviours of farmers in Tanzania to encourage take-up of locally based agricultural insurance. "Getting your hands dirty with real-world problems allows you to formulate research questions that are not otherwise present in academia," he says.

They worked with the World Bank, reinsurance company Munich Re and local businesses to bundle bank finance and farmers' purchases with insurance, and are cooperating with the African Development Bank and regional reinsurers to expand the programme in other countries.

There were also dozens of impressive submissions in the following year, including these winners:

1. Gabriela Gutierrez-Huerter O at King's College London explored attitudes towards labour exploitation in the construction

industry, turning her published research into input into a revised British Standard on organisational responses to modern slavery.

2. Arijit Chatterjee at Essec examined how the Child in Need Institute in India successfully scaled up its work in child malnutrition, developing guidelines which have since been adopted by a number of other organisations.

3. Aaron Yoon at the Kellogg School of Management analysed the value the UN's Principles for Responsible Investment, concluding they attracted large fund inflows, but did not necessarily lead to improvements in environment, social and governance (ESG) practice. That helped reform how the organisation monitors all its signatories on disclosing funds.

4. Nicole Robitaille at the Smith School of Business at Queen's University explored why people do not follow through on their pledges to donate their organs. Their recommendations were adopted by Ontario's organ donation registration service and increased uptake. "It was the first time as an academic I cried. We are actually saving lives," says Robitaille.

Despite such impressive examples, the experience of the *FT* awards highlights the difficulties in engaging around impact. First, there is a problem of limited quantity. Despite the hundreds of eligible business schools in the world and thousands of academics, projects and publications, only a modest number enter.

Of course, only a subset of schools may even be aware of the awards or be motivated to apply. But the pattern suggests a gap between the volume of academic research being conducted in the discipline and the far smaller subset of truly impactful initiatives.

Second, even among those who submit, there is a widespread issue of "quality" – notably a misinterpretation of the definition of "impact". The awards explicitly state that the judges are seeking high-quality, peer-reviewed academic work on societal issues *with evidence of uptake in policy or practice*. In other words, the best entries will clearly demonstrate not only rigorous and relevant insights but also ones that resonate with and nurture realisation by business, government or the non-profit sector.

Yet many academics, instead, focus their own interpretation of successful impact far more narrowly on publication in "high-impact" academic journals. The sector has effectively "captured" the notion of impact with a reductive focus on bibliometrics. Publication marks an important first step: the need for dissemination of rigorous work underpinned by high-quality peer review. It is also fundamental to academic career progression.

The limitations of this system are well described. The growth in academic journals and ever greater stress on producing articles to fill them creates widespread scope for content with little fresh insight or applicability and few readers. The spiralling volume of content – and the lack of funding or even acknowledgement for peer reviewers – stretches to the limits the capacity of scrutiny.

Gaming strategies through self and mutual citations and social media shares fuel ways for articles to create nominal "impact", as measured by citation counts and more contemporary broader "altmetrics" alike.

These limitations sparked the Declaration on Research Assessment in 2012, and wider campaigns to critique bibliometrics and the rankings derived from them. They seek broader and fairer ways to assess academic achievement, but struggle to identify or stimulate broader alternative measures more focused on true impact.

If the rigour of such academically measured output is limited, so too is its relevance. It would be an inappropriate and dangerous threat to academic integrity and freedom to force all researchers to focus on particular topics beyond their interests or expertise, to influence their approach and methodologies, or to shift work into fields where the "returns" could be still more disappointing.

Yet, it seems regrettable that so many academics in business schools do not focus sufficiently on tackling the pressing issues of society, such as climate change and inequality – topics that their students demand and will seek to deploy as future citizens, employees and customers.

Nor do journal articles sufficiently focus on implementation and impact. It feels as though the pendulum has swung too far since the 1959 Carnegie and Ford Foundation reports criticised US business education for its low intellectual output as "trade schools" and argued for more theoretical research.

After all, business and management are *applied sciences* that study and engage with the world of practice beyond academia. Their primary field of activity is business and management, and their greatest direct source of impact is students, who will, in large majority, go into work in those sectors rather than in universities.

Many recent initiatives rightly reflect the demand for more academic research to be channelled towards such topics. That includes the Business School Impact System of Equis and the societal impact chapter of Association to Advance Collegiate Schools of Business (AACSB) respectively, the two leading accreditation agencies.

The appetite for relevance and realised impact is embedded in the collective commitments in the UN's Principles of Responsible Management Education network and the Responsible Research on Business and Management group, as well as numerous other associations of business schools engaged around societal purpose.

Governments including in the UK, France, Australia and Canada have similarly all sought ways to track impact, reflecting their priorities and needs as funders and overseers of higher education.

If rigour and relevance are essential, resonance is also important for impact. Given that most academic journals have a tiny readership largely designed for academia, their chance of being read by practitioners – let alone of their ideas being implemented – is negligible.

A first and primary type of impact through resonance of research should be dissemination to students. Yet the connection between high-quality researchers and teachers is vague. It is difficult to track how far the best and latest research filters systematically into the classroom. With the exception of a few schools, such as Harvard, which rewards faculty for writing cases, teaching is far less important to career progress than research.

A broader form of resonance is in reaching directly to those outside academia. Consider another *FT* initiative: in 2023, it launched a Business School Insights publication designed to identify and share the best research on sustainability. Yet many of the articles identified, through awards or recommendations from academics' networks, were too theoretical, small scale or tightly focused to replicate, or – especially given the urgency of action around climate change – already long out of date.

A parallel *FT* attempt to find the best academic insights was even more concerning. It polled thousands of business school alumni to ask which academic papers they had read and would recommend. Only a handful even replied with suggestions. The gulf between knowledge producers and practitioners is clearly vast. Few outside academia are reading academic journals, which are often framed in lengthy, jargon-ridden ways around theories of little apparent value to the general reader.

An alternative, frequently cited, category of "impact" goes further but remains reductive: the dissemination by academics themselves or by intermediaries signalling their research, whether at conferences, in blogs, popularising outlets for the general reader, such as The Conversation, practitioner journals, like Harvard Business Review, or opinion articles or news reporting in the mainstream media.

These should surely be essential tools for authors to share their ideas. But they are not ends in themselves. Impact happens when ideas are implemented and deliver positive results. The resonance of publication and dissemination of research to a broader audience is simply a necessary step along that journey.

Realisation requires persistent work with practitioners, and much will come through the work of intermediaries – whether "popularisers" of underlying research, external consultants who reframe and package insights or internal champions within organisations.

Uptake is not easy, nor without concerns. Some of the most widely circulated management concepts in books and articles have subsequently been criticised for lacking sufficient rigour, for example. Even some that began with peer review in academic publication may prove to be fads that are later shown to be ineffective or even counterproductive.

The time lag in research may also make many insights moot. The period between the date of any study data used and obtaining, analysing and publishing it can be many years, quickly rendering work on pressing issues, such as climate, outdated.

Such a holistic approach to resonance and realisation is not easy. The skills and temperaments of many academics may not be best suited to the four Rs. In the same way as the best researchers are not necessarily the best teachers, nor may they be confident and adept in communicating and implementing them with practitioners. Some have argued that if they were capable or motivated, they would have become consultants instead of academics.

Nonetheless, there is a clear appetite from many to have a greater impact. In a survey of social science academics undertaken by Sage in 2021,[1] four-fifths said it was either important or highly important that their research have value outside academics, and 94 per cent either agreed or strongly agreed that ultimately the goal of their research is to make a positive impact on society.

But only a third said their institutions rewarded efforts to apply research outside academia, with similar proportions saying external impact mattered for tenure, awards or funding. While 71 per cent said publication in a highly cited journal was important or very important for career advancement, 31 per cent said their institutions provided no rewards or acknowledgements for external impact of their research.

So how could the four Rs become more engrained in business schools? A first and essential step is structural: their leaderships – including deans and heads of individual faculties – need to commit to rewarding a wider set of skills and achievements in hiring, promotion and other incentives than citations.

That should mean efforts to identify, analyse and reward, not just high-impact journal articles, but colleagues with strong teaching, communication and outreach skills, who are engaged on external boards and advisory groups and can deliver results; as well the appointment of more practitioners or "clinical faculty".

Academic journal editors could also help shift incentives: in their selection criteria for articles that are published, they could prioritise topics and approaches that are more relevant and realisable. They could also systematically include taxonomies (such as the UN's sustainable development goals), lay summaries and blogs or videos outside their paywalls to flag up and ease discovery and readership by non-academics.

As for the general media, academics should explore more actively proposing ideas and being responsive to requests from journalists, who typically work on tight deadlines. If authors fail to swiftly respond, others will take their place and fill the gap despite their less insightful expertise and ideas.

Another reform concerns the design and conduct of applied research. That requires earlier and deeper engagement with colleagues from different academic disciplines and practitioners in identifying topics, structuring projects, testing, supporting and, ultimately, disseminating the results. It should naturally be accompanied by safeguards to maintain integrity and independence, with the ability to freely publish critical insights.

Paradoxically, one mechanism for change could come through the additional discipline of increased dependency on external funding sources, such as governments and philanthropists. The current business school finance model is far more reliant on tuition fees and donations from alumni, with limited pressure for accountability.

It should be no surprise that many of the best examples of business school research with societal impact are health-related and involve cooperation with faculties of medicine. These tend to harbour a far tighter, symbiotic relationship between researchers and their ultimate beneficiaries: doctors frequently practice as well as conduct research, and have a clear vocation to improve patient health.

Consider research around treatments including new medicines. It is typically targeted and focused on improved outcomes, with a strong focus on rapid development, rigorous testing, transparency and attribution in order to meet the scrutiny of drug companies, doctors, regulators and healthcare payers.

In business and management, this relationship is more problematic. There is greater opacity, including sometimes cosy relationships between academics and corporate partners in order to gain access to decision-makers or data. The competitive context means there is typically far less willingness to showcase and attribute ideas publicly rather than restrict them for the benefit of individual commercial partners. But a little more application of the medical approach would help considerably.

None of these steps are simple or guaranteed to succeed. But if business schools are to continue to attract, train and equip the coming generations of managers, leaders and entrepreneurs, they should surely be on the frontline of efforts to tackle the existential issues facing society – and their own organisations and customers. Otherwise, they are condemned to wither.

Note

1 SAGE (2023) *Measuring Societal Impact in Business & Management Research: From Challenges to Change*, Sage Publications, January 9, 2023. Accessed at: https://group.sagepub.com/white-paper-archive/measuring-societal-impact-in-business-amp-management-research-from-challenges-to-change

References

Jack, Andrew (2023) *Management research: why are so few of its ideas taken up?* https://www.ft.com/content/7cf1deb9-f8dd-498e-9cab-e8bf3a615ee9. Accessed February 5, 2023.
Jack, Andrew (2022) Business school rankings: The financial times' experience and evolutions. *Business & Society*, 61(4). https://doi.org/10.1177/000765032110167

2 A Radical Notion

Make Business Schools Useful to Businesses

George Feiger

A Strange Problem

Business school graduates should be immediately useful in workplaces. Business school engagement with enterprises and policy-makers should lead to improved enterprise performance, and improved policy for enterprises. But, too often, they aren't and, for the most part, it doesn't.

Employers find that they need to put newly hired business graduates into internal training programmes. They increasingly turn to Degree Apprenticeships to ensure students understand a real-work environment, as a complement to their university curriculum. Only a handful of the world's most prestigious business schools can effectively compete with entities like consulting companies in offering management education and support to senior business leaders. Commercial enterprises rarely turn to business school academics to help them create new opportunities and solve problems. Too rarely do policy-makers come knocking at the doors of business schools looking for advice. To use a particularly apt British expression, this product "doesn't do what it says on the tin".

No doubt business academics will disagree, strongly. They will claim that business school research is excellent and externally impactful, as demonstrated, for example, by the results of the UK's Research Excellence Framework (REF). But, notwithstanding multiple such REF outcomes, enterprises and governments still only rarely show up at the doors of business schools seeking advice that will improve their performance.

Conventional evaluations of research impact, like that in the REF, are misguided. Driven by today's academic metrics and incentive systems, they look only at the extent to which *new* research findings lead to measured external benefits. (I should add that only a small fraction of the research output of business school academics is subject to any such tests.) Even directly applicable new research constitutes only a very small part of the potential benefits business scholars could provide to the economy. Anyone with hands-on business and government experience knows the greatest need is not

DOI: 10.4324/9781003459217-3

new research, but understanding of approaches understood to be useful, and how to apply them. Indeed, offering these services is the basis of the management consulting industry, which, for all its flaws, is constantly used by enterprises and governments.

Business scholars will also say the employment and earnings success of their graduates demonstrates the value of what they learn. This claim doesn't pass the test of analysis. In the UK, business school graduates do earn more after a few years of work than in many other disciplines. However, this is primarily because they choose to work in industries that tend to pay more, the outstanding one being finance. As defenders of degrees in the humanities point out, when their graduates are hired into the same industries, they also earn more.

More fundamentally, earnings figures don't demonstrate the value of degree *content*. Higher education acts as a sorting mechanism for potential employers and potential employees. Attaining a degree is a sign that the graduate has been clever and hard-working enough to get it, not that the degree content is what makes the graduate likely to be productive. The programmes that are the hardest to get into attract the best students, who are hired by the best employers. This insight, into what he named *market signalling*, earned its author, Michael Spence, the Nobel Prize in Economics. It has been validated by abundant empirical investigation.[1]

The extreme extent to which business schools have become divorced from their natural enterprise and policy constituency is different from some other areas of professional education. Can we imagine needing to make teachers of mechanical engineering engage more often with machinery, or of medicine engaging more often with illnesses, or of dentistry engaging more often with teeth? Would we anticipate needing to pressure law schools to teach negotiation of contracts?

How Did It Come to This?

Schools teaching other professions have escaped this divorce from reality, because they are more directly assessed by measures of impact on their external constituencies. Licensing supervision by professional bodies keeps research and education more grounded in real needs. No such agreed licensing framework exists for business schools. Hence, too often in business schools one encounters social science and statistical research devoid of any linkage to how this will improve enterprise performance. Accounting academics talk about Foucault in research seminars. This time would be better devoted to discussing improving audit techniques for catching fraud.

Of course, other professional schools also integrate multiple disciplines into their work. Engineers use physics to design bridges and buildings, but they don't aspire to be physicists. Yet, for the most part, business schools treat the study and teaching of social sciences and statistics as a *mission* rather than as a *toolbox* for producing better business outcomes.

I am not the first observer to make these points, nor to explain the reason: the performance measurement and incentive systems of academia both create the problem and make it extraordinarily difficult to change direction.

Academic research is primarily manifested in a constantly increasing number of academic journal publications, because the quantity of published articles is a key criterion in academic career assessment. For this reason, the number of these journals has mushroomed as fields of study are divided into ever smaller and more specialised areas to provide places for academics to publish. The overwhelming majority of papers are never read after publication, because the fact of publication itself, rather than any measured consequence, is the performance indicator.

Of course, it is not only quantity of articles. There is a de facto hierarchy of journals, and publication in the "best" ones is deemed to evidence more skill. So, schools train their academics in techniques to achieve publication in higher-ranked journals. And the tastes of the editors and reviewers of the leading journals direct the nature of research, rather than agreement on which problems are the most important from an enterprise or policy perspective. The panels that make the REF assessments of research paper quality are composed of the editors and reviewers of those higher-ranked journals. Not surprisingly, they determine that the majority of business school research that they have published is internationally excellent and impactful. In another useful British phrase, they "are marking their own homework".

This system resists change by reproducing itself. Today's academics recruit and train doctoral students, the academic workforce of tomorrow, in their own image. Any academic operating differently than the measurement and incentive systems reward, would simply reduce their personal academic employment opportunities. Any business school trying to operate differently, would be told by its staff that following a different line would hinder them from making a job move to the overwhelmingly majority of schools operating in the current paradigm. Media and outside ranking bodies follow the current paradigm's assessments of programmes and schools. Who is going to be rewarded for turning the ship?

What Is to Be Done?

Business schools must learn from the engineers, doctors and dentists and reconnect fundamentally with the needs and perspectives of their external constituencies in everything that they do.

On the education side, this will require creation of external, user-driven accreditations for the skills – general management, marketing, talent management, supply-chain management and various others – being taught. There is already strong evidence that this works. It is, today, the de facto role of the Pathfinder Groups of industry employers that are assembled to create Degree Apprenticeship programmes in the UK. It is also validated by the success of Placement Year programmes, in enhancing the employability and earning power of graduates. The placement year is, de facto, an employer curriculum inserted into the university one. This mixing of end-user and academic input should be formalised and extended throughout the curriculum, and should be augmented by introducing public policy voices. Closer integration between these two curricula, and general adoption of multiple forms of integrated placement activities, can transform the productivity of students. It will also make employers strong supporters of universities.

Examples of productive interactions between academics and enterprises also exist. Through Knowledge Transfer Partnerships in the UK, academics work with businesses to define solutions to problems, then work together to implement them. The Goldman Sachs 10,000 Small Businesses programme identifies promising small and medium-sized enterprises (SMEs) and gives their leaders structured management education, effectively mini-MBAs, as well as creating a peer community for future support. But, in the business school world, these are a minority avocation, both in numbers of participating schools and in the proportion of participating academics.

However, we can identify initiatives that promise truly transformative change in the value business schools add to society, including:

- Widespread use of practitioner/teachers, as is the norm now in fields such as medicine;
- Establishment of advisory boards, composed of people currently in substantial business and policy positions, for all academic departments;
- Fostering secondment of academics to businesses and government entities for significant chunks of time, along with the expectation that *all* academics should take such secondments, as well as have ongoing close business relationships;

- Developing executive education programmes, not only as a funding source, but to build relationships between academics and external managers;
- Creation of joint programmes and certifications with large companies and with some government entities.

This goes against the grain of today's formidably entrenched academic career performance and measurement system, of course. However, the silver lining to the cloud of inadequate funding for universities may be that such reforms will attract students, and external partnerships and money, because there will be a direct and measurable payoff. And that would create a powerful and countervailing incentive for more and more schools to buck the current system.

Note

1 The reader could look, for example, at *The Case Against Education* by Bryan Caplan.

3 Business Schools and Business in the UK[1]

A Growing Success Story

Peter McKiernan

Introduction

It matters little what virtues they possess; business schools have an image of dark antiheros. Negative critique has come from many corners, from ministers to corporate magnates. Ironically, their own employees have fired some of the sharpest retorts. For example, in this collection of chapters, it is argued that their graduates are not immediately useful in workplaces; that their engagement with enterprises and policy-makers adds little value and that they have become divorced from their natural societal context to "an extreme extent" as outlined by Feiger in Chapter 2. This may have been true a decade or more ago, but it is now an ageing argument that takes little account of the recent impact of pan-global frameworks, national government initiatives, academy and association strategies and social movements driven by concerned scholars. In the United Kingdom of Great Britain and Northern Ireland (UK), more and more schools have adopted transformational agendas linked to the public good, integrating robust research tied to societal needs and thereby tightening the rigour–relevance knot, and thus, repositioning many business schools as a force for good. Outwardly at least, school deans are now talking up a creative and positively impactful story.

Inwardly, many systems, processes and associated key performance indicators (KPIs) in business schools are still wedded to a derelict mantra that plays to elite journals and metric counts, placing researchers in straightjackets that restrict freedoms and damage mental welfares – especially those of junior colleagues and doctoral students. Sadly, this is reinforced by academies, whose doctoral and early career programmes and plenary sessions still deify highly cited scholars and the war stories of how they 'made' it. It, whatever it may be, was achieved in a period dominated by a 'rush to publish' culture that mostly pandered to individuality in career progression, and that mostly tolerated poor science and irrelevance. Junior scholars, with little agency, are attempting to progress in a

DOI: 10.4324/9781003459217-4

new world of grand challenges and artificial intelligence that only remotely resembles the context that propelled their seniors to fame. Senior success stories have nothing meaningful to say about managing a career in such an alternate new world. Moreover, few internal systems are tuned to that new world. In Chapter 2, Feiger claims that these 'performance measurement and incentive systems of academia ... make it extraordinarily difficult to change direction'. *He may be right.*

With an outward display of righteousness and an inward strangulation of freedom, schools squeeze their own and their scholar's lives, making them more difficult than they need be. This chapter will examine the recent positive changes as business schools rectify prior anomalies in their economic and societal positions. It shows how a re-energising of the isomorphic forces that caused their 'global mimicry' has brought a U-turn in their purposing, bringing them closer to practice. It calls for the reward systems that incentivised past behaviours to be altered to reflect this new world of practice.

Business Schools and their Cyclical History

Business schools began as close partners with economy and society. For instance, the oldest 'government sponsored' commerce school, the Aula do Comércio in Lisbon in 1759 (closed in 1844), was inspired by English mercantilism (Rodriques et al., 2004). Additionally, Prussian *Cameralist*[2] chairs had already been set up at the Universities of Halle (Saxony) and Frankfurt-am-Oder (Brandenburg) in 1727 that shaped the training of administrators (Spender, 1989). The practice spread to Scandinavia in the mid 18th century (Engwall, 2004) where the Cameralist administration was admired by Joseph Wharton, who founded the Wharton School of Finance and Economics in 1881. This closeness to practice was followed by American and British management education in the 20th century, with many experienced managers lecturing in their schools and colleges. Essentially, many were still 'trade schools' where teaching was applied. In the United States of America (US), the Gordon and Howell report[3] (1959) noted the prominence of practice but advised on the strengthening of staff research and scholarship, forcing the US schools into becoming more like social science departments. Research-informed teaching curricula were born. Top journals, newly formed and modelled on traditional social science journals (Khurana, 2007), provided outlets for this fresh research (e.g., *Management Science* in 1954, *ASQ* in 1956, the *AMJ* in

1958). Arguably, a 'golden age' followed (McKiernan & Tsui, 2020) where business schools built a reputation in quantitative social science and produced concepts and models of high value to public audiences e.g., Burns and Stalker's contingency theory (1961); Galbraith's matrix organisations (1971); Jensen & Meckling's agency theory (1976); Porter's (2011) five forces and three generic strategies (1980); Locke and Latham's management by objectives (2002). Academics working alongside consultants produced innovative strategy grids, such as the BCG matrix, and others followed, e.g., Shell directional policy matrix and the GE business screen. This business school and practice partnership delivered a utility from the early 1960s to the late 1990s that informed teaching, consultancy and practice. From there, things began to stall.

As business researchers embraced a positivist research paradigm to enhance their legitimacy among social scientists, business school incentive systems followed suit, rewarding the published article, especially in elite journals. Career paths followed one express road to the top. Rigour in theory and method displaced relevance, and fast career advancement through article outputs and citations mostly eschewed slower, careful, multidisciplinary projects related to the issues of the day (Khurana, 2007). A focus on theory and method meant that business school research was silent on major societal issues, such as the global financial crisis (Starkey, 2015). Moreover, a lack of governance teaching meant that schools were blamed for training the 'hyper competitive and unethical agents' (Machold & Huse, 2010) at the heart of the toxic scandals that rocked the capitalist system. School's star product, the MBA, came under fire with students from Harvard and other major US schools being accused of being 'the masters of the apocalypse'[4] (see, also, Arjoon, 2010).

Ironically, there was no doubting the success of business academics in producing volumes of incremental knowledge in the most elite[5] peer-reviewed journals. Driven by incentives in internal school systems, which were copied from school to school, this number grew by nearly 4000 between 1990 and 2006 (see, Laing et al., 2021). Senior US academics estimated the total cost of this activity in the 780 AACSB accredited schools to be around $3.9bn (Glick et al., 2018). Costly though it was, a lot was scientifically weak, as corners were cut to get articles published quickly to advance careers. Many 'skirted at the edges of what was ethically acceptable' (Honig et al., 2014). Problems with positivism[6] related to the proliferation of HARKing (hypothesising after results are known) and p-hacking (repeatedly manipulating data to find a desired result); low replication rates; the reporting of only positive results to please reviewers and editors; and the emergence of citation groups referencing each other's work to increase personal citations and advance careers. Alas, practitioners or policy-makers were not the audience for much of this work. In a self-serving manner, other business school academics devoured and cited the work of their colleagues. Consumers wishing advice and support had to look elsewhere, for example, to management consultancy. This self-consumption reached such a pitiful state that government funding bodies (e.g., the UK Research Evaluation Framework [REF]) and senior academics called for an urgent change to 'end the pretence of science mimicry, heroic publishing and their support of an unsupportable system' (Harley, 2019). A return to relevance through 'impact' was demanded.

Clearly, business schools and their academics had lost their way: but why? Writing a decade or more ago, Wilson and McKiernan (2011) and McKiernan and Wilson (2014) used a series of neo-institutional arguments to explain this plight. Societal pressures, and rule-like patterns of action and behaviour driven by rankings, ratings, citations, accreditations, memberships, *inter alia*, became embedded in mental and business models within the institutions which then develop codified, standard operating procedures that their employees were expected to follow (Granovetter, 1985). These become quick set and, as Feiger (above) says, they became sticky to change. This significant isomorphic pressure could deny school leaders degrees of freedom in strategic choice, causing them to act in similar ways, and so their schools became reflections of each other – a process Wilson and McKiernan (2011) referred to as 'global mimicry'. Alone, this did not make business schools bad places, just places whose impact on their societies was limited as they were coerced into chasing goals and badges that preserved their legitimacy within their own strategic groups and for their own customer bases.

Moreover, business schools became 'business schools', whose revenue-generating abilities were gratefully welcomed within their universities. Hence, the model of teaching 'for-profit' material to MBA students at a high price became the norm for many schools, thus reinforcing strategic behaviours – a trap especially tight in university-based business schools with broad subject portfolios that required cross-subsidisation.

The focus on shareholder primacy and financial markets meant that longer-term thinking was a rare asset in the curricula. Many schools became captive of their own curricula content in their short-term strategic thinking, thus reinforcing their own prejudices at each three- or five-year strategic planning round. The pressures created a spiral which was difficult to stop, especially for lower-ranked schools who were mimicking the behaviour of their more famous brethren. It was hard to escape these pressures for conformity, but not impossible. Like most organisational change, the drivers came from outside the walls of academia. For instance, schools came under increasing criticism for their lack of voice on major societal events from their own stakeholders, e.g., staff and students. More, many external commentators, for example, investors and CEOs of organisations with long-term plans, called into question the consequences of shareholder primacy, pointing to its damaging ecological and social effects, such as deforestation and inequality. They called for organisations to pursue a more integrated role in their economies and societies, and to switch their thinking to issues around the public good, such as circular economies. The decade from 2010 to 2020 was to witness a series of subtle changes in the isomorphic pressures around schools that pushed and altered their strategies and changed individual behaviours. Ironically, the very pressures that coerced schools into mimicking each other were part of the solution in changing their fortunes. The following sections illustrate just some of the many initiatives that have fuelled this society-facing phenomenon.

Business Schools and the Responsibility Turn

The research crisis in academia[7] was so severe that it spawned a 'responsibility turn' targeted at reversing the scientific fault lines and turning the face of business schools, their academics and their research towards that of society once again. Clarion calls came from global institutions and across universities, as serious scholars feared the societal damage caused by erroneous scientific findings (Ioannidis, 2005). The ecosystem moved toward self-healing (Alberts et al., 2015). For instance, six principles of engagement were developed by stakeholders in the UN Global Compact during 2006/07 – the UN PRME. They quickly attracted hosts of signatory schools across the globe who promised to balance social, economic and environmental goals – especially the sustainability development goal.[8] Across the sciences, a raft of other initiatives followed, for example: San Francisco DORA which attacked the misuse of journal impact factors in assessing scientific output (Munafò et al., 2017); the Center for Open Science's efforts to increase the integrity of the science through the enactment of open sourcing in 2013; and the Leiden manifesto in 2014, besides developing ten guiding principles, emphasised the role of human judgement in assessing output. These change agents combined to help schools address good science and reposition their education. Though, business schools had to go further to address their public audience.

Consequently, in 2016, a group of 29 senior scholars comprising of editors, deans and academy leaders came together and, inspired by European Foundation for Management Development (EFMD), formed the community for responsible research in business and management (RRBM 2017 – www.rrbm.network – see Chapter 11 by Howard Thomas). They argued that it was not enough to develop good science, but that credible science had to deliver useful results to its societal stakeholders. Among its seven principles, an emphasis is placed on liaison with stakeholders throughout the research project, from start to finish, so bringing academics in line with managers and policy-makers as co-producers of knowledge. Further emphasis was placed on tackling pressing global issues, such as poverty, food and water security, inequality and migration, where it was believed that the knowledge and skill set of business school scholars could make vital contributions (see, for instance, Tsui & McKiernan, 2022). This social movement has had a significant impact on the profession and, particularly, on doctoral students and early career scholars. There are Honour Rolls for books and articles that reflect the RRBM principles; an annual symposium which has brought C-suite executives face-to-face with academics; a formidable array of special issues on grand challenges; annual education awards; dare-to-care scholarships for doctoral students; customised workshops for individual schools; and plentiful blog posts and webinars. Academies have adapted their doctoral programmes to situate RRBM initiatives (e.g., BAM, EURAM, ABIS). More, in 2021, AACSB altered their school accreditation criteria to incorporate RRBM principles. Business school science has improved by such positive initiatives and by pressure built from 'naming and shaming' dodgy research through retractions (see Retraction.watch. com). Clearly, some business schools[9] turned their back on their societies during the 2000s, but these external pressures for change meant a major volte face was in progress.

Business Schools and Repurposing

Evidence from the UK: Supportive Institutions, CABS and REF

Besides resetting their research agendas, schools turned to an examination of their organisational aims and consequently, their main curricula. They began to question their role in society over the longer term. The founders of RRBM had imagined a society in 2030, where business school research was actually useful and both governments and organisations of all kinds sought out the help of academics automatically; their advice seen as legitimate, and evidence-based. Now, schools were pressured by stakeholders, especially advisory boards, to re-think their purpose in this same society. But they were not alone in this task. In the US, a litany of Academy of Management (AoM) presidents (e.g., see Hambrick,

2007) had called for change at their annual meetings and many had started to lead it inside and outside their institutions (e.g., Tsui, in her founding of RRBM in 2015). Similarly in the UK, a prior dialogue and narrative had already emerged from academies (e.g., British Academy of Management [BAM], British Academy [BA]), and associations (e.g., Chartered Association of Business Schools [CABS]) and social movements (e.g., the Purposeful Company). Indeed, the BA, in its 'Future of the Corporation' Project in 2017, examined the role and purpose of business in society while CABS followed in 2021 with a Task Force of academics and business executives to report[10] on 'Business Schools and the Public Good'.

The main authors of the CABS Task Force (Kitchener and Levitt) noted that UK business schools were leading members of the UN PRME Champion School list (in 2023, 9 of the 47 champions were from the UK) and were possibly more advanced than other countries in engaging with a public good agenda. Their report provides evidence that 'there is a clear perception amongst UK business schools that delivering public good is rising up their strategic agenda, although not all schools are proceeding at the same pace" (Kitchener, Levitt & McKiernan, 2022). In their report, they classified schools as either purpose-led, emergent, planned development or traditional, based on the extent of their strategic engagement with a public-good agenda across four domains of teaching, research, internal operations and external engagement: the former two classifications were setting the pace, with purpose-led schools having initiatives across all four domains and emergent schools covering one or more in detail. Promising practices were identified across each domain, with far more in external engagement (70) than the others – teaching (51), operations (48) and research (32). That more promising practice was identified within the domains of external engagement and teaching helps dispel the persistent and obsolete view that schools are entirely dissociated from reality and signals that a repurposing was underway. In the domain of external engagement, promising practices included local business and law clinics (Northumbria and Brighton), long term engagements in hard social housing schemes (Napier) and, a 20-year activity in Ethiopia forming a coffee marketing cooperative (Huddersfield); in teaching, they included embedding responsibility into the curriculum (Leeds Beckett) and degree apprenticeships in social justice (Queen Mary, London); in operations, they included responsibility committees (Birmingham, Manchester), shadow management boards (Cardiff) and the development of a university strategy and identity for the common good (Glasgow Caledonian); and in research, they included a festival of research that showcases the work of junior faculty (Stirling), improving working conditions with the work foundation in London (Lancaster) and mapping sustainability issues in a 'Research4Good' initiative (Bath). The authors highlight,

> Our Report may not cover all the contributions to the public good provided by UK schools, but it shows an increasing commitment by many of them to rejecting traditional forms of purpose and replenishing the commonwealth through cooperation and purposeful scholarship.
>
> (Kitchener & Levitt, 2021, p. 120)

Although the overall findings of the CABS report are encouraging, the number count around promising practices in research may not be so impressive at first sight. Perhaps, research initiatives lag behind promising practices in the other domains because research projects take time to operationalise, conduct, report and disseminate – especially those involving multidisciplinary teams working on grand challenges where it can take years and not months to record a count. Also, the count does not register the gravity of a particular promising practice in terms of its importance or impact. The UK REF approach to impact is a better guide as to how UK schools have been persuaded to carry out more impactful research over the last decade.[11] Significantly, for the 2021 audit, the REF increased the weighting attached to impact case from 20 to 25 per cent to reflect the increasing importance of the element.

The REF is a UK audit assessing research quality over 157 UK universities and occurs every 5 years or so. The current version has run since 2014 but its predecessors (e.g., RAE, RSE) go back to the mid 1980s. Over those four decades, from an array of research outlets the focus now is almost entirely on the peer-reviewed article e.g., in the 2021 REF, 97 per cent of submissions were by article and only 1.4 per cent by books. This may be problematic for translating business and management research results to managers or policymakers as few, if any of them, read articles in those outlets. This barrier to accessibility can be eased as many academics are encouraged to disseminate their work in other ways e.g., blogs, webinars. But there is little evidence that these translate into practice. REF panels are prepared to assess policy advice reports, but few were submitted by the research community in the last two rounds.

On the plus side, the main REF panel were impressed by the business and management submission in 2021 with regards to *impact on economy and society*:

> the main and sub-panels were highly impressed by the range of types of impact ... by the extent of the beneficiaries, and by the

many ways that research is making a difference outside academia to a wide spectrum of organisations, groups, and individuals, within and beyond the UK.

(2021 REF Overview report
by Main Panel C and Sub-panels 13 to 24, p 29)

For the business and management sub-panel (17) in 2021 compared with 2014,[12] staff submissions were up 100 per cent, outputs rose by 31 per cent and, most importantly for this narrative, the impact cases were up 25 per cent to 539 – the largest across all the social sciences where the average increase was only 11 per cent. Clearly, business and management[13] academics provided strong evidence of their interaction with managers and policy-makers across the long audit period. Moreover, the quality of the impact cases increased with 84.5 per cent being judged as world leading (4*) or at international level (3*) compared with 80.2 per cent in 2014. The impact cases had a significant impact:

The impacts on public policy were widespread. These included, for example, impacts on policies for social inclusion, finance, policy, promoting sustainability, improved medical and health care systems, promoting business growth, the submission of highly influential evidence or advice on inquiries and the setting of standards within public bodies. Public policy impacts were seen across local, national, and international levels.

(Overview report by Main Panel C and
Sub-panels 13 to 24, p 87)

At the organisational level, impact cases spanned the 'for profit' and 'not for profit' sectors and covered, *inter alia*, strategic change, innovations, corporate social responsibility and professional practice, e.g., 'curricula and standards setting in Accounting and Finance'. The REF sub-panel remained impressed with the 'quality and reach' of UK business and management research worldwide. Clearly, when taken together with the CABS Task Force evidence, the REF data continues to highlight the increasing quality contributions from UK business and management academics to an external world.

Conclusion

These examples are part of a growing armoury of initiatives that have emerged over the last decade to bring schools closer to practice-policy, e.g., knowledge exchange initiatives, degree apprenticeships, the use of local counsellors and global practitioners as tutors. After a period in the doldrums, it is time to celebrate a strong reversal of fortunes for schools, much of it driven by tweaking the isomorphic forces that helped drive them to mimic each other in the first place, such as, changing AACSB[14] standards (some because of RRBM activities); the formation of the student-based, Positive Impact Rating;[15] EFMD's Business School Impact System (BSIS);[16] the production of Academy manifestos (e.g., CEEMAN); and the purposeful changes in weights and compositions of other rankings to improve impact e.g., FT. These tweaks are working, helping schools to contextually repurpose and so herald an enduring attention to societal utility. True, not all schools are so advanced (see the schools categorised as planned and traditional in the CABS report) and, some schools may be engaging only at the margins, using a few impact cases to cover a half-hearted commitment (impact washing). But for many, it is a stunning turnaround and a remarkable step in restoring legitimacy in their skills and knowledge capabilities. Businesses are awakening to the fact that business schools are useful places after all and integral to their strategic ecosystem. The gravity of this change is significant.

However, it is possible to accelerate this repurposing, if schools address some thorny internal issues of which Feiger speaks in Chapter 2. Scholars became used to a set of systems, processes and KPIs that reinforced behaviours around a particular publishing recipe, championing individual career progression over societal impact. According to the 2021 UK REF results, the rigour of the quantitative science is now at excellent levels and the relevance is as high as it has been for years. But those internal school systems show remarkable resilience as publishing in peer-reviewed, elite journals still rewards financial incentives and reduced teaching hours. This encourages productivity, while hoping for relevance. Perhaps the rewards should be redirected to reward relevance in any class of journal. Further, academics may have to consider whether or not they are producing too much incremental research at too high a cost because of those performance systems. Until change incentives are embedded within, then the full repurposing of business schools will remain incomplete.

Notes

1 Thanks to Wilfred Mijhardt (Erasmus) and Nicholas O'Regan (Aston) for comments on earlier drafts.
2 The study of administration and how science, especially measurement, could be used to serve the state functions to improve efficiency.
3 The Pierson report (1959) on management education, sponsored by the Carnegie Foundation, appeared in the same year, and mirrored a lot of the Gordon and Howell findings.

4 Broughton, P. 2009. 'Harvard's Masters of Apocalypse'. March 1. http://www.timesonline.co.uk/tol/news/uk/education/article5821706.ece

5 Defined in the Chartered Association of Business Schools (UK) academic journal guide as 4* and 4 star category. Articles in these categories are a small proportion (138) of all articles (1700) published e.g., in the 3, 2, 1 star and unclassified categories.

6 See, for instance, Schwab, A., & Starbuck, W. H. (2017). A Call for Openness in Research Reporting: How to turn covert practices into helpful tools. Academy of Management Learning & Education, 16(1), 125–141.

7 This was not limited to business schools but was a problem across academie; the sciences, in particular.

8 Erasmus has developed 'Sustainable Development Goal (SDG) metrics' that are aimed at stimulating dialogue among peers and institutional leaders and to help universities and business schools develop a better strategic understanding of SDG relatedness and to stimulate the design of data driven and evidence-based impact narratives. See: www.sdgmetrics.com

9 Notably, some university schools, e.g., French and Swiss schools of technology, did not or could not turn their back on their societies.

10 https://charteredabs.org/wp-content/uploads/2021/06/Chartered-ABS-Business-Schools-and-the-Public-Good-Final-1.pdf

11 The REF has been accused of 'marking its own homework' by employing business academics to evaluate business school submissions. The alternative is to have them evaluated by scholars in cognate social sciences (or others) – a pill that would not be swallowed easily by business school academics. To paraphrase Churchill (House of Commons, 11 November 1947), 'Indeed, it has been said that democracy is the worst form of Government except for all other forms that have been tried from time to time …'. The current REF system may be the best choice around.

12 The audit period for 2021 was longer than that for 2014 and there were some rule changes so direct comparisons between the two should be treated with caution.

13 Many of these will be from business schools but some will be from management schools.

14 See AACSB Standard 9 on engagement and social impact.

15 https://www.positiveimpactrating.org/

16 https://www.efmdglobal.org/assessments/business-schools/bsis/

References

Alberts, B., Cicerone, R. J., Fienberg, S. E., Kamb, A., McNutt, M., Nerem, R. M., & Zuber, M. T. (2015). Self-correction in science at work. *Science*, *348*(6242), 1420–1422.

Arjoon, S. (2010). Narcissistic behavior and the economy: The role of virtues. *Journal of Markets & Morality*, *13*(1), 59–82.

Burns, T., & Stalker, G. M. (1961). *The management of innovation.* Tavistock, London, 120–122.

Engwall, L. (2004). The Americanization of Nordic management education. *Journal of Management Inquiry*, *13*(2), 109–117.

Galbraith, J. R. (1971). Matrix organization designs: How to combine functional and project forms. *Business Horizons, 14*(1), 29–40.

Glick, W., Tsui, A. S., & Davis, G. F. (2018). The moral dilemma of business research. *AACSB BizEd*, May/June. https://bized.aacsb.edu/articles/2018/05/the-moral-dilemma-to-business-research

Gordon, R. A., & Howell, J. E. (1959). Higher education for business. *The Journal of Business Education, 35*(3), 115–117.

Granovetter, M. (1985). Economic action and social structure: The problem of embeddedness. *American Journal of Sociology, 91*(3), 481–510.

Hambrick, D. (2007). The field of management's devotion to theory: Too much of a good thing? *Academy of Management Journal, 50*(6), 1342–1356.

Harley, B. (2019). Confronting the crisis of confidence in management studies: Why senior scholars need to stop setting a bad example. *Academy of Management Learning & Education, 18*(2), 286–297.

Honig, B., Lampel, J., Siegel, D., & Drnevich, P. (2014). Ethics in the production and dissemination of management research: Institutional failure or individual fallibility? *Journal of Management Studies, 51*(1), 118–142.

Ioannidis, J. P. (2005). Why most published research findings are false. *PLoS medicine, 2*(8), e124.

Jensen, M. C., & Meckling, W. H. (1976). Theory of the firm: Managerial behavior, agency costs and ownership structure. *Journal of Financial Economics, 3*(4), 305–360.

Khurana, R. (2007). *From higher aims to hired hands: The social transformation of American business schools and the unfulfilled promise of management as a profession.* Princeton, NJ: Princeton University Press.

Kitchener M., & Levitt, T., (2021). *Business schools and the public good: A Chartered ABS Taskforce Report*, Chartered Association of Business Schools, London.

Kitchener, M., Levitt, T., & McKiernan, P. (2022). Business schools and the public good. *Global Focus, 16*(1). https://www.globalfocusmagazine.com/business-schools-and-the-public-good/

Laing, A., Richter, A., Mason, K., & Mijnhardt, W., (2021). A new future for research. *AACSB*, August 2021. https://www.aacsb.edu/insights/articles/2021/08/a-new-future-for-research

Locke, E. A., & Latham, G. P. (2002). Building a practically useful theory of goal setting and task motivation: A 35-year odyssey. *American Psychologist, 57*(9), 705.

Machold, S., & Huse, M. (2010). Provocation: Business schools and economic crisis - The emperor's new clothes – learning from crisis? *International Journal of Management Concepts and Philosophy, 7*(1), 13–20.

McKiernan, P., & Tsui, A. S. (2020). Responsible research in business and management: Transforming doctoral education. In D. C. Moosmeyer, O. Laasch, C. Parkes, & K. G. Brown (Eds.), *The Sage handbook of responsible management, learning and education*, London: Sage, ISBN 9781526460707

McKiernan, P., & Wilson, D. (2014). Strategic choice: Taking 'business' of B-schools. In A. M. Pettigrew, E. Cornuel, & U. Hommel, (Eds.), *The institutional development of business schools*, (pp. 248–269). Oxford: Oxford University Press.

Munafò, M. R., Nosek, B. A., Bishop, D. V., Button, K. S., Chambers, C. D., Percie du Sert, N., Simonsohn, U., Wagenmakers, E. J., Ware, J. J. & Ioannidis, J. (2017). A manifesto for reproducible science. Nature Human Behaviour, 1(1), 1–9. Pierson, F. (1959). *The education of American businessmen: A study of university-college programmes in business administration*. Carnegie Foundation.

Porter, M. E. (2011). *Competitive advantage of nations: Creating and sustaining superior performance*. Simon and Schuster.

Rodriques, L. L., Gomes, D., & Craig, R. (2004). The Portuguese school of commerce, 1759–1844: A reflection of the "Enlightenment". *Journal of Accounting History*, 9(3), 53–71.

RRBM. (2017). *A vision of responsible research in business and management; Striving for credible and useful knowledge*. www.rrbm.network

Spender, J-C. (1989). Meeting Mintzberg – and thinking again about management education. *European Management Journal*, 7(3), 254–266.

Starkey, K., (2015). The strange absence of management during the current financial crisis. *Academy of Management Review*, 40(4), 652–663.

Tsui, A. S. (2015). Reconnecting with the business world: Socially responsible scholarship. *EFMD Global Focus*, 9(1), 36–39.

Tsui, A. S., & McKiernan, P. (2022). Understanding scientific freedom and scientific responsibility in business and management research. *Journal of Management Studies*, 59(6), 1604–1627.

Wilson, D., & McKiernan, P. (2011). Global Mimicry: Putting strategic choice back on the business school agenda. *British Journal of Management*, 22(3), S457–S469.

4 Academics are from Pluto, Managers are from Mercury

Bringing Sense to the Management Science Versus Management Practice Debate

Timothy M. Devinney

It is interesting to what extent business school academics and business practitioners are at odds over the value that business schools provide to business practice and society (see, e.g., Bennis & O'Toole, 2005; Trkman, 2019). What is perplexing in the seemingly never-ending debate over the impact business schools have on practice is that the same debate is missing when it comes to medical schools, law schools, economics, psychology and sociology departments, arts schools, physics, biology and chemistry departments and most other science, engineering, technology and mathematics (STEM) and social science and humanities subjects.

The argument I will make in this essay is that this nearly pathological angst that business school academics have exhibited over the last several decades is misplaced. Indeed, the practical impact that business academics have is extraordinarily immense. It is just different from the practical impact that arises when, for example, a bio-geneticist discovers the underlying source of a disease. In addition, part of the difficulty faced by business school academics is a classic two-sided information and motivation problem. In the early 21st century two rom-com films came out. One entitled 'What Women Want' (2000) – about a sleazy advertising executive with the ability to hear what women think about him – and another 'He's Just Not That into You' (2009) – about a woman who consistently misreads romantic/non-romantic signals. Business academics and practitioners are reflected in these two films, in that one cannot have a problem – perceived or real – without both parties lacking the capability to understand one another and the ability to read the signals that are being sent. Relationships are always two-way streets and relationships are not saved, or don't exist for long, without

DOI: 10.4324/9781003459217-5

both parties to that relationship being respectful, adaptive and understanding. Finally, while academics may bemoan the science–practice gap that lies at the root of what I will be discussing, much of the problem is institutional rather than individual. As I will argue, it is an institution's choice regarding the portfolio of academics it hires and promotes, and what it rewards and punishes. Similarly, in the corporate world, the extent to which companies, as opposed to individuals, are involved in intellectual development of their most valuable assets, is key to whether that company is a good vehicle for meaningful interactions with academic institutions.

Yes, We Are Impactful – One Student at a Time

One of the keys to having a successful product is the degree to which the product has the potential for scalability. Consider, for example, medical schools versus business schools. There are approximately 2,600 medical schools in operation globally (World Directory of Medical Schools, 2022). While global numbers are hard to come by, it is estimated that there are approximately 14,000–15,000 new doctors graduating in the United States and between 9,000–10,000 in the United Kingdom of Great Britain and Northern Ireland (UK).[1] Compare these numbers to the number of business schools operating globally, which is estimated to be in the order of 16,000 (Collinson, 2017). The United States produces more than 150,000 MBA graduates[2] per year and nearly 400,000 undergraduate business majors (which amounts 19 percent of all undergraduates). Even by conservate estimation, there are believed to be approximately 250,000 MBA graduates worldwide[3] and well over 2 million undergraduate business graduates.[4] These numbers dwarf the number of medical professionals graduating each year by a substantial order of magnitude.

And this is where scalability comes in. Business school academics are responsible for more than 20 percent of all higher education graduates and bring their learning and knowledge to bear on an immense part of society at a particularly impressionable stage, in terms of development and maturity. In addition, this has flow-on effects. While most people interact with a doctor periodically (and a lawyer even less so and very rarely a physicist or psychologist or sociologist), nearly everyone in society deals with a businessperson multiple times every day. In this regard, business academics role in society is collectively extraordinary. No single subject in higher education has the opportunity and potentiality to drive change – either good or bad, which is a different debate from the science–practice gap – than academics in business schools. And I would maintain that this is a challenge that we take very responsibly, as evidenced by the degree to which new and societally important topics filter through the system via associations, journals, conferences and simply the need to ensure that our graduates are capable of operating effectively in an ever-changing society (see, e.g., Freeman, 2017; Future of the Corporation, 2022).

So, from the standpoint of our impact through pedagogy, I would contend that there is little doubt about the practical value of what we do. This is reinforced by the fact that business schools are probably the singularly most evaluated and monitored part of the university system globally (e.g., via schools, degrees and individual academics being ranked by groups such as the *Financial Times*, the *Wall Street Journal, the Economist, Business Week, Handlesblatt*, etc.) and are constantly in competition with one another over the employability of their graduates. Hence, whether (and to what degree) we view our ultimate stakeholder as the companies hiring the students or the students themselves or the publications engaging in ranking creation, we are closer to the market than any other part of the higher education system. If we didn't deliver something that was of value to these constituencies, we would never have been as successful as we have been over the last half century and companies would hardly be lining up to hire our graduates, enroll in our programs or seek out honorary and clinical professorships.

Varieties of Research and Scholarship: Science Versus Practice

One of the refrains that one hears commonly in the business press is 'why don't business academics do more research of relevance to business?' (e.g., Wylie, 2013). However, this is a one-sided, and rather naïve, view of what the role of research (or more appropriately, scholarship) is and how it can exist in varied forms (Devinney, 2013). To make this simple, Figure 4.1 presents a continuum that runs from 'Pure Science' through to 'Pure Consulting' with two axes representing the value to 'science' and the value to the 'corporate/policy' realm.

Pure Science (A) has high value to the academic community but much less (and perhaps even negative) value to the corporate/policy realm. At the other extreme, *Pure Consulting* has low value to the academic realm and high value to the corporate/policy arena. (Note that the ranges imply there is variance in the value.) Where there are potential areas of overlap is in the two intermediate forms of research/scholarship. *Applied Science* (B) still possesses considerable value to academia, with the added benefit that it can be seen as having some commercial or policy appeal – to a great degree, it amounts to the practical engineering of a scientifically supported

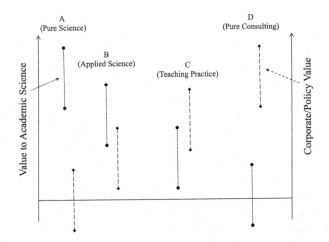

Figure 4.1 Varieties of Academic Inquiry

belief. This sort of work might best be seen in the development of HR reward systems, AI systems for supply chain or warehouse performance, financial risk monitoring algorithms, and so on. *Teaching Practice* (C) represents an area of work where the academic value might be low but with value to companies and policy-makers. This sort of work is seen with student field work (e.g., student consulting), the development of materials leading to case studies, industry association work, and so on. It can encompass the scalability of that engineered solution. Both B and C can fall into the area where collaborative contract work is done with companies and government bodies. What Figure 4.1 shows is that there are varieties of academic and consulting work and that this has different values distributed to various constituencies (I have left students out of this for simplicity).[5]

If we take this a bit further, we can articulate where there are fundamental differences at the extremes, in the sense that we can ask 'what is the difference between what academics (in the pure sense) and managers and policy-makers (again in a pure stylized manner) demand or need?' This is seen in Table 4.1.

In the academic world, a number of key things are valued. Academics want to develop models/theories that are causal and generalizable. The timeframe for the work is generally long (even ignoring reviewing times and publication cycles). Rigor is an uncompromising standard. In the end, Pure Science is about 'exploration' and 'discovery'. In addition, academics are usually subject-domain experts. Which means that their underlying capability is

Table 4.1 The Academic and Corporate/Policy-Maker

The Academic	The Corporate/Policy-Maker
Problems/phenomena: generalizable	Problems/phenomena: specific
Knowledge: specific and narrow	Knowledge: general and personal
Value: unclear or evolving; generally instrumental and indirect	Value: fits within specific corporate frameworks
Approaches: sometimes complex with long lead times and unclear lines of sight	Approaches: simple with definable times lines and limited lines of sight
Emphasis: on causality	Emphasis: on operationalization/workability
Rigor: cannot be compromised; rigor far more important than immediate value	Rigor: can be compromised for outcomes; value dominates rigor
Exploration valued more than Exploitation	**Exploitation valued more than Exploration**

their expertise about a specific topic area, and they tend to rely on past and current work in an area to buttress their value. While academics can be intellectually quite broad, their reputation and the incentives and rewards they face are for depth of specific knowledge. You don't get a PhD in everything but a PhD in something. This is why I characterize academics as from Pluto – they are small and far from the center of the solar system, and take a long time to get anywhere or for a cycle of work to be completed.

In the corporate and policy world (again at the extreme), there are differences in what matters. Managers are broadly focused on very specific (and, generally, very immediate) problems. These are usually reinforced by quite short and definable timelines, typically working within corporate or government budgetary windows. What matters is not generalizable theoretical insights or model structures, but what fits into the corporate structure and existing frameworks and systems they already have. Rigor may be important but is compromisable, in the sense that managers and policy-makers need something that works and can be operationalized within specific timeframes. It can be simply 'good enough', rather than perfect from a theoretical or methodological perspective. The policy-maker and manager are not subject domain experts. In fact, their expertise is simply being an expert with respect to their own experience and, hence, they tend to rely heavily on what they have seen and heard or done and share this in lessons learned via anecdotes, war stories or recent interactions with consultants and what may have appeared in popular books and magazines. In the end, the corporate/policy-maker is concerned about 'exploitation' and 'utilization'. This is why the Mercury analogy is material. Managers and policy-makers are close to the central mass of the solar system and are subject to immense heat. Their cycle is very short and quite repetitive.

Ultimately, if there is going to be meaningful and effective inter-action and collaboration between science and practice, it is unlikely to operate at the extremes. Pure Science (A) rarely fits into the cor-porate or government agenda except when it is a means to a more material end. Similarly, academics are not interested in or rewarded for Pure Consulting (D), except in financial terms and usually when doing it on private account (i.e., outside the university pay struc-ture). Hence, the sweet spots of interaction are in Applied Science (B) and Teaching Practice (C). It is here where there are clear oppor-tunities for knowledge and skills trading and relational capital building. Indeed, if one uses (B) and (C) as the entry point of a relationship, it is conceivable that it opens some opportunities for cooperation in (A) and (D) as well, but usually only as part of a bundled relationship. However, the main point is that, at the extremes, individual self-interest (as reflected in Table 4.1) takes over and it is unlikely that either party will be working with any degree of aligned incentives and outcomes.

Communicating to Different Audiences: Science Versus Practice

A third area that needs to be understood to have meaningful scholar–practice is that interaction is related to communication. We can look at this in two ways. The first is related to creating a mean-ingful narrative that relates to the importance and inspiration behind a piece of work or an interaction. The second is the process by which that is transformed into a communication for a specific audience.

Understanding and Creating the Core of a Narrative

In terms of creating the core of a meaningful narrative, the rules are similar across all audiences.

The first question to ask, and ensure that it is clearly articu-lated, is 'What is the inspiration?' The point is to look at how one brings something to life. Why is this an important issue? How am I going to motivate the reader to understand it easily? Inspiration that can be external, which is usually the case with more practice-driven issues or phenomenon, or internal, which can motivate a scholar to work on an obscure problem that is inspiring only to that individual or a small collection of like-minded intellectuals. Ultimately, that inspiration must be translated to others – either academics or practitioners – if it is ever going to have any intellec-tual or practice impact.

The second question is 'Why is it important to study this prob-lem/issue/phenomenon?' This can be a mixture of the practical need to solve the problem for any host of purposes (e.g., profitability, productivity, mental health, employee satisfaction), and the theoretical need – the problem appears to not have a clear identifiable logical theoretical link that guides decision-making. For the purely academic endeavor, it might amount to a theoretical gap or missing link or problem that is derived from failures in prior work. Work will, by definition, be important to the person doing it, which may naturally limit its impact, but, generally, we think of the most impactful work as resonating with others and the extent of that resonance will be a major driver as to its impact and uptake, either in terms of managerial/policy change or academic citations and influence.

The third question is 'How are you going to come to grips with the problem/issue/phenomenon?' The first part of this is to decompose and compartmentalize something that usually appears at first glance to be complex, unique and confusing into parts that can (a) be subjected to specific inquiry and (b) be related to similar (and previously examined) problems/issues/phenomenon, either via anecdote or background research. For academics, this is a natural process, but it is also part and parcel of simply bring closure to a story. Subject matter experts are quite good at seeing simplicity in complexity. Those with less experience or knowledge are more likely to fail to come to grips with the simplicity that is embedded within what appears to be a complex problem/issue/phenomenon.

The idea of narrative creation is well established in storytelling, from myths through to plays and movies (see, e.g., Campbell, 1949; Todorov, 1971) and what is discussed here is simply a variant. Usually, a story cycle starts with a protagonist (the academic or manager/policy-maker), that faces a challenge (e.g., something is not right or an external event has occurred or the academic has noticed that something important is missing), that becomes the motivation/inspiration for a journey (or a choice of where, metaphorically, to go for help), that leads to a search (which amounts to doing research of some variant), which has travails and challenges (that relate to problems and conflicts or confusion in the process discovery and learning), that leads to the protagonist returning home (back to the company or intellectually back to the original questions posed) and leading change (implementing something new or passing on the learnings from the journey and search).

The importance of understanding the basis of narrative creation is that it focuses on the story being presented to an audience. And it doesn't matter if it is a scholar communicating with a scholar, a scholar communicating with a student, a scholar communicating with a policy-maker or manager, or a manager wanting to communicate with a scholar.

Communicating the Narrative

In addition to having a narrative flow, communication requires specific targeting to specific audiences. One of the fatal flaws of bad communication is attempting to communicate to everyone via the same vehicle. In this regard, the narrative cycle discussed in the prior section may have some degree of universality, but the audience for different narratives requires tailoring and nuance that engages them. We can break the communicative aspect of the narrative into four inter-related parts.

The first and most critical is the 'To who' you are communicating. While this might appear to be obvious, most writers cannot articulate who, specifically, is their audience. We see this in academic articles where there is sometimes a section entitled 'Implications for Management', that is most assuredly not written to managers and has less chance of being read by a manager than a manager randomly being struck by lightning. And this is part of the usual practitioner complaint, that academic writing is obtuse and not meaningful or interesting to them. Going back to the four varieties of research and scholarship in Figure 4.1, a simple understanding that these four different variants will require at least four different narrative styles and communication outlets is critical. Managers/policy-makers do not need to waste their time reading work done in the Pure Science realm and, equally, those concerned with communicating with other scientists should not waste their time attempting to communicate to practitioners. Should a scholar want to communicate with a more public audience via a Teaching Practice approach, there are vehicles for that (e.g., *Psychology Today, New Scientist, Harvard Business Review, Forbes*, the *Conversation*) which require a different narrative style and alternative means of framing the inspiration, the importance and the means of coming to grips with the topic of the work.

The second critical question follows on from this, 'What do I have to say "to who?"' For academics speaking to academics, the 'what' is usually framed within the structure of a theoretical problem/conundrum. For a practice audience, the 'what' must be related to a problem that is critical to that quite specific group of people. And this relates to the third question, 'Why is what I am saying important/relevant to the "who"?' In essence, the importance to the author is of no relevance other than for their own personal inspiration. From the standpoint of communication, what matters is that what is being addressed is important and relevant to the reader or user.

Finally, the communication requires convincing proof. In other words, 'How are you going to convince the "who" of the appropriateness of your solution to the "what"?' This can be broken into two parts. The first is related to 'language'. Is the language I am using the language of the people with who I am communicating? For academics doing empirical Pure Science, the language is usually model-and method-based, framed in terms of hypotheses and tests, with statistical conclusions and contributions concentrated around improvements or conflicts with prior research. For managers, the language is very different – mainly couched around problems, frameworks and case studies or other examples. The conclusions would relate mostly to implementation and operationalization.

Ultimately, the narrative must align to the audience for which it is being created. The most common failure in scientific communication is a lack of recognition that the audience is not the writer. While it might be reflected in the opinions of the editors and reviewers of the publication being utilized, even then, they are only gatekeepers. The more audiences a communicator seeks to reach with one vehicle, the more likely it is that all of the audiences will be dissatisfied in some form. This can arise because the problem/issue/ phenomenon is simply of no interest or importance to them, or that the language used to communicate with them is inappropriate and not understood. It can also be the case that they are not inspired by what is being said or proposed. In one of my roles as an editor in the past, I would ask authors a very simple question that I wanted them to use to conclude their work: 'What do you want the reader to do differently (or think differently about) from what they have done in the past now that they have read your work?' It didn't matter who the targeted reader is. If they don't change their thinking or behavior, the 'what' is not going to be terribly impactful.

Horses for Courses

Few academics want their ideas to be restricted to the narrow realm of Pure Science. We all seek to have material influence in a variety of ways – through our academic publications, through our teaching and the development of teaching materials, through our interactions with executives and policy-makers and through communication with the public at large. However, as discussed throughout this chapter, these things cannot be achieved all at once or through common means. Each audience requires different communication vehicles with different styles, languages and evidence. And not every academic possesses the capabilities to span all of these domains (there simply are not a lot of Alexander von Humboldt's, Carl Sagan's, Richard Feynman's or Stephen Hawking's around). Indeed, few academics have either the capability or the time to be all things to all audiences. And nor should we expect them to be so.

This is why I said at the beginning of this essay that many of the issues with the science–practice gap are institutional. Business schools have a broad variety of stakeholders, and these vary considerably from school to school. In this sense, business schools are a dynamic construction project where there is a need for a wide variety of specialists and some degree of knowledge aggregators and generalists. Without the specialists doing things specialists do, the ability of the knowledge aggregator to aggregate and the generalist to generalize, simply would not exist. You may need architects to design buildings but without electricians, plumbers, roofers, and so on, the building devised by the architect is nothing more than non-functioning artwork. In this sense, it is meaningless to think about the practice value of any specific piece of scholarly work. Its value is in how it fits into the portfolio of an institution's proposition to its diverse set of stakeholders. Hence, one of the difficulties that many academics face is that their institutions simply do not know what the balance is of the varieties of scholarship they want in their portfolio. If all academics across all ranks and age groups are expected to do teaching and research, and the evaluation of that research is driven by the desire to publish in FT50 journals, then the definition of research is going to be institutionally limited. In the UK, if the unitary model of scholarship is the Research Excellence Framework (REF) and that has specific metrics, then the desires of scholars to do more pluralistic work will simply be crushed by the bureaucratic reward system imposed by government paymasters. If there is a failure in the nature of business scholarship being communicated today, the fault lies not with the academics doing the work, but with the institutions determining what is considered to be appropriate types of scholarship and research and what is rewarded. And by institutions, I mean not just the business schools, but the ancillary governance and monitoring system driven by our universities, our government funders and regulators, and self-appointed rating monitors, such as the *Financial Times*, QS, *Times Higher Education*, and so on. One of the great ironies, for me, is the fact that the *Financial Times* is one of the leading sources of complaints about the relevance of business research, yet they are one of the most significant factors in the choices that business school administrations make about how they operate their institutions, particularly with respect to research outlets (see, e.g., Jack, 2023).

As I pointed out earlier, all relationships have two sides. While business school academics have spent decades debating their relevance to practice, there is no apparent angst on the part of managers that they are fundamentally operating in a shallow anti-intellectual knowledge pool. Put more literally, 'Managers are just not into academics' while academics continue to try and seek out 'What managers want?' and are profoundly depressed when they discover there is no 'Field of Dreams' that can be built where academics and managers can play. There are two ways to try and address this. The first is to believe that, ultimately, we are the problem and unless we change to the benefit of the managers, who are inclined never to pay any attention to us, we have failed. For me, this is simply a path to perpetual existential angst that provides no value to anyone. The second is to focus on what we as academics want to achieve, through the varieties of different styles of science we can deliver and work to keep that portfolio flexible – but with the core understanding that without Pure Science, Applied Science is impossible, and without Applied Science, Teaching Practice is impossible, and without Teaching Practice, Pure Consulting is simply Astrology in another form. Our goal is to stoke the flames of knowledge creation and grease the wheels of its dissemination. However, the one task we can do well, that no-one else can, is Pure Science and Applied Science. Without us doing that, the value chain of scholarship breaks down.

So, What Do We Do?

From an individual perspective, it is valuable to avoid the resistance of the academic echo chamber. It is important to listen to our constituencies – students, policy-makers, managers, workers and everyday individuals doing their individual things – and utilize that in motiving and inspiring us in terms of what we do, and why we do what we do. However, we must remain scientific in our skepticism. While these groups can guide us to problems, issues, conundrums and phenomenon that inspire new work, they are not the source of the answers that require mixtures of domain-specific knowledge, methods and techniques that are beyond the capabilities of non-academics. We are specialists and technicians precisely to serve this purpose in society. We are, to some degree, the philosophical monitors of the social system, in that, part of our role is to ensure that logic, evidence and ethics be the key determinant and driver of decision-making from the individual to the societal level.

Additionally, individual scholars need a center of gravity in terms of the nature of their work. Given the constraints of capabilities and time, it is simply not possible to expect all academics to be all things, to all people. It is also not good to cave into reward systems that wants every academic to do, individually, everything that should be expected of an academic institution collectively. Hence, each scholar, at each point in the evolution of their career, needs to understand what their core is. Are they a mixture of Pure and Applied Scientist? Or Applied Scientist and Teaching Practice?

Or Teaching Practice and Pure Consulting? (Usually, adjacency of scholarly variety is better than non-adjacent pairings.) Typically, more junior scholars are more likely to concentrate more on their scientific and scholarly endeavors, while more senior scholars can spend more time devoted to engaging more with practice, as this is the standard process that generates promotion and tenure in most leading institutions. Yet, there is clearly societal benefit from the skills that go with Teaching Practice and Pure Consulting. Scholars concentrating on these areas need not have the hottest scientific skills, as their key capability is fundamentally one of aggregation, translation and application. This is the realm of textbooks, teaching cases, TED Talks, newspaper/blog articles and popular press books, populated by those represented in groups like Thinkers50, executive programs and speaking bureaus.

And this leads to the issue of what is the correct balance for different institutions, which has been the subject of considerable debate over the years. At one extreme, there are institutions that are very focused on the Teaching Practice and Pure Consulting model. These usually generate their income via Executive MBA or Executive Programs and many faculty are essentially key account managers (there are a considerable number in Europe). At the other extreme, are those that give lip service to the anything other than Pure and Applied Science and dabble a bit at the other varieties, but for very focused stakeholders. However, neither one nor the other is better, given that there is a distribution across and within institutions that embraces the variety. What is more important is not having variety but knowing, institutionally, why that variety is strategically and societally important to have; academia is a collective endeavor and there is little value in a collective endeavor that does not embrace variety. The school concentrating on Pure and Applied Science is made better by cooperation and competition with the school focusing on Teaching Practice and Pure Consulting, and vice versa. Ultimately, the inability to define this portfolio is a failure of business school leadership, not business school scholars.

Finally, from the corporate perspective, there needs to be a greater willingness to listen and seek out knowledge. In many ways the criticism that one hears about the science–practice gap assumes that the problem is with the academics. However, few managers and policy-makers read broadly, are uninterested and have no incentive to engage intellectually. The common refrain is 'why aren't you writing something I can understand?' – which I call prof-shaming. It is quite rare to find a manager be publicly introspective, question their willingness to seek out new knowledge and work to enhance their ability to understand more than what might be spoon-fed to them via an airport book, newspaper article or consulting firm. It might be fanciful to believe that highly compensated managers would want to waste their time on such activities (as they, too, are rewarded for a narrow vector of performance). However, a company can collectively work around the need to have their managers' noses to the grindstone rather than their heads in the ivory tower's clouds. A number of companies do use mixtures of academics to help them think beyond their confines. Some boards now use academic advisors to give them insights into critical issues and help give them advice on the research related to important topics for the company. In addition, it is become increasingly common for companies and governments to set up academic advisory groups around salient topics, to do something similar at a lower level. There is also a slew of academics who work with corporate training programs, or assist with corporate, government or independent think tanks. All of these are examples of how companies choose to insert a more scholarly and intellectual perspective into their corporate body.

To conclude, the science–practice gap is natural. Scholars are intellectually, culturally, and motivationally different from practicing managers and policy-makers. However, rather than this being a problem, I see it as an opportunity for gains from intellectual and experiential trade. The fact that there is a 'gap' should not be viewed as anything more than a reflection that academics operate on a different planet from managers and policy-makers. However, in the end, we all live, work and play in the same solar system.

Notes

1 This information is available through Statista; e.g., https://www.statista.com/markets/412/topic/452/health-professionals-hospitals/#overview. Accessed 21 October 2023.
2 This information is from the AACSB (https://www.aacsb.org) and published in Poets & Quants (2022; https://poetsandquants.com/2022/04/29/how-many-students-are-studying-for-an-mba/). Accessed 21 October 2023.
3 This information is available through Statista; e.g., https://www.statista.com/statistics/185334/number-of-bachelors-degrees-by-field-of-research/. Accessed 21 October 2023.
4 This is the authors estimate given the ratio of the number of degree granting institutions in the US versus the rest of the world. However, the sheer size of the number of graduates is supported by the fact that there are nearly 800,000 business school graduates in China (https://www.statista.com/statistics/610758/china-management-undergraduate-graduates/), nearly 1 million in the EU (https://ec.europa.eu/eurostat/web/products-eurostat-news/-/edn-20201117-1) and 175,000 in the UK (https://www.hesa.ac.uk/news/16-01-2020/sb255-higher-education-student-statistics/qualifications)

5 I am ignoring, for simplicity and focus, the casual interactions between practitioners and academics via panels and public interactions that are common throughout all universities. The point of Figure 4.1 relates to varieties of scholarly practice.

References

Bennis, W., & O'Toole, J. (2005). How business schools lost their way. *Harvard Business Review*, 83(5): 96–104.

Campbell, J. (1949). *The hero with a thousand faces*. Princeton: Princeton University Press.

Collinson, S. (2017). *Are business schools fit for the future?* Chartered Association of Business Schools. https://charteredabs.org/business-schools-fit-future/. Accessed 21 October 2023.

Devinney, T. M. (2013). What is the role of scholarship in business schools? *Financial Times*, 14 November 2013. https://www.ft.com/content/3ba9551e-4898-11e3-8237-00144feabdc0. Accessed 6 October 2023.

Freeman, R. E. (2017). The new story of business: Towards a more responsible capitalism. *Business and Society Review*, 122(3): 449–465. https://doi.org/10.1111/basr.12123

Future of the Corporation. (2022). https://www.thebritishacademy.ac.uk/publications/future-of-the-corporation-teaching-purposeful-business-in-uk-business-schools/

Jack, A. Management research: Why are so few of its ideas taken up? *Financial Times*, 6 February 2023. https://www.ft.com/content/7cf1deb9-f8dd-498e-9cab-e8bf3a615ee9. Accessed 7 October 2023.

Todorov, T. (1971). The 2 principles of narrative. *Diacritics*, 1(1): 37–44. https://doi.org/10.2307/464558

Trkman, P. (2019). The value proposition of business schools: More than meets the eye. *International Journal of Management Education*, 17(3): 100310. https://doi.org/10.1016/j.ijme.2019.100310

World Directory of Medical Schools. (2022). *World Director of Medical Schools*. https://www.wdoms.org. Accessed 21 October 2023.

Wylie, I. (2013). Research? Most people can't understand it. *Financial Times*, 7 April 2013. https://www.ft.com/content/cde6163c-7f4a-11e2-97f6-00144feabdc0#axzz2PzNmhAFx. Accessed 6 October 2023.

5 Research, Impact, and Institutional Actors

Where are the Leaders?

Vadake K. Narayanan

In recent years, there has been significant interest in the impact of business school research, an interest that has been stimulated by debates within the academy and impromptu assessments made by various vocal and influential practitioners. Under the umbrella of "impact," this interest has also metamorphosed into ways of *assessing* the impact of business school research, especially the work done by *individual* faculty members, as they are being considered for appointments, tenure, promotion and related human resource decisions.

Although the concept of impact has had a long history in industrial research, in business schools this topic has been of recent interest. In this chapter, I will argue that while an interest in impact is useful, if not inevitable, the topic of impact is truly a meeting point for several widely different political interests, and much of the contemporary discussion fails to acknowledge the underlying differences in the conceptualization of "impact", among those participating in its measurement. To some, perhaps a large, extent, the differences can be traced to the subset of stakeholders whose interests undergird any conceptualization. Second, I would argue that unless we are careful about managing this process, we will wind up privileging some constituencies over others, to the detriment of knowledge creation or research in the traditional academic sense of the term.

This chapter is organized as follows. First, I will provide a short history of the evolution of the concept of impact in business education to highlight the wide diversity of conceptualizations. Second, I will identify three representative stakeholder groups, who have an interest in impact and sketch their widely differing characteristics. I will venture to make some predictions about the immediate future and what we can expect in the domain of impact research. And finally, I will conclude by pointing out some ways forward making the case for collaborative research with industry.

DOI: 10.4324/9781003459217-6

Evolution of the Concept of Impact

Although the assessment of research utility has had a long history in the academy, especially in chemistry and engineering, the concept of impact in business schools has had a checkered history. This history reflects the challenges of establishing business as a discipline – a field that sits uneasily at the border of science and practice – subsequent internal criticism and developments in the current context where external stakeholders have begun to scrutinize the operation of business schools.

Early Years

Business schools were among the newer "species" to appear in the academy, and although, because of their applied focus, they resembled schools of engineering, law and medicine (ELM), their evolutionary path in the academy has been quite distinct. Whereas by the turn of the twentieth century, ELM had managed to carve out an autonomous scholarly existence within the academy and developed licensing requirements for their graduates, thereby erecting a barrier to anyone desiring to enter the profession, business schools were not accorded the lofty designation of a profession. Indeed, many thought leaders in the early years spent their time and energy on establishing business as a profession. As Khurana (2007) stated so elegantly,

> The very ambitiousness of the professionalization project in American business education required strong institutional foundations and the effort to create them required business schools to turn the institutional logics they had appropriated into stable structures.
>
> (p. 136)

Indeed, the early success of business education in the United States of America (US) was measured by number of graduates, and, during the first half of the twentieth century, the undergraduate business degree awards grew impressively (see Khurana, 2007, p. 13). MBA programs were also launched during this period with remarkable success in graduation rates.

Building Social Science Foundations

Post World War II, institutional players, especially the Ford Foundation, played a significant role in the development of business school curriculum in the US, where significant "improvements" in business education took place. Partly as result of falling academic standards, and unwillingness of American Assembly of Collegiate Schools of Business (AACSB),[1] to sanction marginal players, Ford Foundation undertook several initiatives, which resulted in, among other things, the famous Gordon-Howell report that recommended reshaping business school curriculum and doctoral education. Gordon and Howell have often been credited with recommending that business schools adopt a model tied to basic social science (Bottom, 2009), and hire faculty from social science-based disciplines (Kieser, 2011; Miner, 1997; Mitroff, 2008; see also McLaren, 2019).

In this second stage, business schools, then still a young discipline, set themselves the task of establishing their scholarly credentials within the academy. In practice, this meant that they sought intra-institutional legitimacy ('intra' here meaning within the academy), a concept that was understood to mean winning the hearts and minds of other academics (in social sciences, primarily in economics, psychology and to a lesser extent sociology). And, in this search for legitimacy, there was a well understood metric of impact – publications and citations. Several journals devoted to management fields (e.g., *Management Science* or the *Academy of Management Journal*) appeared and many rose in prominence welcoming submissions from social science theorists. Although influential scholarly books also appeared, over time they seem to have receded in importance in the evaluation of individual faculty members.

Thus, this period witnessed the quest for academic legitimacy by business schools as they sought to entrench themselves in the academy. Impact was interpreted in scholarly terms (read citations), with limited attention to either organizational relevance or business practice.

Soul Searching

The protracted search for academic legitimacy also led to the charge that the business schools had lost touch with organizational realities. These strains of criticism, which have always been there, focused both on students and research.[2]

On the student side, whereas the number of graduates was a metric during the early phase, critics were now more concerned with the value added to the students by a business education. Armed with then sophisticated statistical analysis, they were able to marshal support for the conclusion that the degree has at best marginal effects on students' future income (e.g., O'Reilly & Chatman, 1994), thus questioning the value added by MBA education. The second strain focused on research, suggesting that business research had little impact on management practice. Here the criticism was fierce, although confined to a select group of scholars. Pfeffer & Fong (2002) noted,

> Why has there been such a modest effect of business scholarship on practice, in spite of the tremendous expenditure of resources by intelligent and motivated people? One possible answer comes from a reflective essay by Paul Lawrence. Lawrence argued that "the better work in our field has come from problem-oriented research rather than from theory-oriented research" (1992:140) but many institutional pressures conspired to ensure that there was not very much problem-oriented research being done. Sutton and Staw questioned whether theory in the organizational sciences was useful and wrote that "the field needs more descriptive narrative about organizational life" (1995: 378). Pfeffer (1997), in a similar vein, argued that research should be anchored in important phenomenon. So, perhaps the emphasis on theory rather than observation, problems, or phenomenon explains part of the problem.
>
> (p. 88)

Although these critics were listened to, they were not as well heard, leading Khurana (2007) to lament,

> Inside business schools, quantitative analysis increasingly came to be seen as the most legitimate form of research. In fields from organization behavior to marketing to operations, sociology and psychology also claimed many adherents oriented more to their discipline than to the study of business per se, further weakening the claim that either scholarship or teaching in these institutions represented any genuine engagement with the realm of "professional practice." As the research and instruction taking place in business schools came to have less and less to do with practice, these core activities came to be more and more loosely coupled with the ostensible purposes for which business school existed.
>
> (p. 333)

The debate between (academic) legitimacy seekers and their critics was primarily an *internal* affair, conducted within the academy.

The Current Context

During the last decade, discussions of impact have been broadened by the appearance of players other than the scholarly community.

This development is attributable to numerous interrelated factors, including technological developments, funding sources and the involvement of profit-motivated press and media. The internet revolution and the relentless march of digitalization are making it possible to imagine and create new forms of quantifiable data that can then serve as metrics of impact measurement. Because technology somewhat freed us from geographic constraints, academic institutions, especially in the emerging economies, are finding it useful to create their own impact measurements to showcase their value.

While globally, technological development has bestowed feasibility on many untried approaches, the influence of funding sources has varied across regions. In the US, business research was financed primarily through private funding – endowments, tuition dollars or executive education. Government agencies, which contributed a significant share of research dollars in engineering and medicine, played a limited role in financing business research. The private donors in the US looked less to peer-reviewed articles; they viewed students (Narayanan, 2005), consulting projects and popular books as ways to judge business school research impact. The situation was different in some other countries, especially Australia and the United Kingdom of Geat Britain and Northern Ireland (UK), where the governments (in both countries) wanted to phase in accountability in research funding. Because impact evaluation funding was substantial, the effort now seems to be to control the costs of evaluation. As concluded by Williams and Grant (2018),

> For future evolution of policy, this paper suggests we are likely to see a continued political commitment to research impact assessment in both countries. The core debate going forward is likely to centre around reducing the perceived costs and burden of impact assessment through the use of metrics.

Another set of actors has emerged in recent times – the media. The rankings game was initiated in around 1988 by *Business Week* when it started publishing b-school rankings in the US. By 2001, *Financial Times* pioneered the FT 50 list for journals (Rodenburg et al., 2022), and became increasingly used in business schools, although other rankings had already been available. Though profit motivated, *FT* collaborated with scholars to assess research impact which was primarily operationalized as publications in highly ranked journals. Because of their potential influence on aspiring MBA applicants, these rankings and the research impact measures have mustered some influence in the business schools.

In Table 5.1, I have caricatured the history of "impact" in business schools.

Table 5.1 Evolution of the Concept of Impact in Business Schools

Eras	Key Task	Objectives	Key Actors	Metrics	Triggers
1. Early Years	Legitimacy for the business profession	Founding of Business School in the university	Institutional players and enlightened societal leaders	Programs and number of students	The need for executives for status
2. Establishing Business Scholarship	Gaining academic credibility	Business knowledge as credible	Business faculty	Publications increasing in scholarly journals	Ford foundation initiatives
3. Soul Searching	Bringing research closer to organizational realties	Relevance	Business faculty	No clear criteria	Dominance of social science research
4. Current Context	External legitimacy	Demonstrating accountability for resources spent on research	External entities and institutional actors	Unclear	Government funding of university research

Diverse Conceptions of Impact

Understanding of the term impact differs between users and audiences (Penfield et al., 2014) and our discussion of the evolution of the concept of impact over the years has also illustrated how the meaning of the term has shifted over the years. Partly based on Narayanan et al. (2021), I offer a simple framework to organize various conceptions to bring some clarity to the underlying dynamics. In what follows, I put forth two dimensions of divergence: focus of conceptualization and locus of interest.

Focus of Conceptualization

The first dimension captures the debates between social science theorists and their critics.

Phenomenon based or context driven. In one category of this dimension, we can place advocates of theories, topics or phenomena unique to business contexts (e.g., problem solving, opportunity recognition, strategy process, etc. see also [Narayanan and Zane, 2011]) that require theory construction, perhaps testing and application.

Social science based or theory based. In the second category, we place researchers who have attempted to invoke the strategy of "knowledge growth by extension" (Weick, 1989, p. 518), where new contexts are assimilated by extending the boundaries of already available social science theories. For example, as Narayanan and Zane (2011) illustrate, "while identity and sensemaking are researched in other literature domains, entrepreneurial cognition researchers explored how ethnic and entrepreneurial identities intersect (Barrett & Vershinina, 2017), and examined cultural views of venture failure through the lens of sensemaking (Cardon et al., 2011)."

Although these two categories may be considered complementary, few researchers have either bridged the two or simultaneously advocated for both.

Locus

A second major component of diversity, less talked about, is the target of impact: just who or what is influenced by what a business school does. The organic evolution of the discussion around impact has illustrated at least three positions:

- The classical academic view focuses almost exclusively on *research* and assesses impact by the degree to which a scholars' research influences ensuing research.
- The critics of the approach also primarily focus on research but address the degree to which research influences managerial *practice*.
- Another group, primarily the industry leaders in the US, are more interested in the business school's ability to turn out effective and successful leaders through education.

The issue of locus pertains to the perspective that informs the discussion of impact, whether it is internal to the academy or extrinsic to it.

In Figure 5.1, we have juxtaposed these two dimensions to illustrate two major points:

1. The *rigor versus relevance* debate to date has primarily been an *incestuous* debate within the academy between advocates different foci of research. As we have sketched in the evolution of the concept, this debate has been present for a long time even before the arrival of new players in the current context. It has begun to

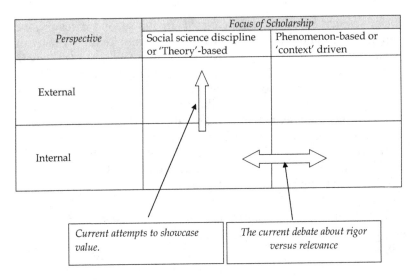

Figure 5.1 A Categorization of the Meanings of Impact

intensify partly as the relevance advocates felt pushed to the sidelines by social science-oriented scholars who have come to dominate the business schools.

2. *Level of analysis.* The rigor versus relevance debate has obfuscated the differences in the level of analysis. This debate has been confined to a function within the business school – research; however, other conceptions focus on the totality of the business school operations, including the teaching (and service) functions performed by it. An *institutional* conception of business school, which is concerned with legitimacy in external fields in addition to intra-institutional legitimacy, has often been missing.

Summary

This short trip down the memory lane was intended to remind us of a simple conclusion: The topic of impact has begun to attract the attention of a wider array of players than before. What was once a matter for debate and discussion within the academy, motivated by creating a business discipline and winning its legitimacy *within* the academy, is now attracting other interested parties, many of whom are external to the academy. In the following discussion of impact, I suggest we also examine the powerful stakeholders who participate in the process by which some meanings of impact are privileged over others.

Stakeholders in the Debate About Impact[3]

Shifting the analysis to a more macro level enables us to address the covert forces that influence the notion of impact among business schools. For the sake of simplicity, I focus on three major players: knowledge fields (business school level), institutional players and the broader external resource controllers. In Table 5.2, I have summarized the key distinctions among these actors for this discussion of impact.

Knowledge Fields. These represent domains where like-minded *scholars* pursue a shared interest reinforcing each other's work but distinguishing their work from other domains. At a somewhat broad level, they could be social science disciplines, such as psychology or sociology, but, in reality, they tend to be much narrower in focus. As they have evolved, they compete among themselves for prestige, visibility, editorial positions and, of course, journal space. The knowledge fields control scholarly production: what gets to be accepted as valid scholarship or knowledge. However, they are dependent on the institutional system in at least three ways. First, professional associations have a *parasitic* relationship to the institutional system, being significantly financed by the latter for their operations (typically, the membership fees and conference attendance expenses by individual scholars are borne by the institution). Second,

Table 5.2 Macro Level of Analysis

Characteristic	Macro Levels		
	Knowledge Fields	Institutional Level	Resource Controllers
Key Task	Creation of valid knowledge	Maintenance of legitimacy and ensuring flow of resources	Sensible allocation of resources and ensure appropriate outcomes
Involved Constituencies	Academics and professional associations	Regulatory, markets and academic constituencies	Political constituencies, players with specific agendas
Resources and Capabilities	Human capital	Managerial capabilities, industry relations and social capital	Resource provision, access to media and popular opinion
Control Over	Process of production	Management of business school	Oversight and resource control
Dependence	Quasi autonomous, but dependent on institutional level	Dependence on resource controller	Broad legitimacy

decisions with respect to the human capital needed in knowledge fields are partly determined by institutional actors. Third, scholars' access to infrastructure and resources somewhat depends on the approval of the institutional actors.

Institutional Actors. These actors mediate between resource controllers and knowledge fields and operate as the managerial system of the academic enterprise. Of course, the institutional players can exert their influence on the knowledge creation process: witness the actions of Derek Bok in shaping the evolution of Harvard Business School (for a more detailed description, see Khurana, 2007 pp. 308–310). The institutional actors' influence on knowledge creation is indirect: by the creation of appropriate infrastructure, choice of human capital and systems of evaluation (including metrics), certainly acquiring resources from external sources (including tuition and executive program revenues) and by simply having a "bully pulpit." In many institutions, they are the primary "fund raisers;" while they may use individual scholars as instruments, these same scholars are often forbidden from raising money on their own, except from designated sources (such as competitive grants). Thus, the institutional players exert significant influence on an individual scholar's career through decisions related to resource allocation and indirect control of knowledge creation. They are, however, dependent on external actors, impersonal ones, such as markets, and personal ones, such as powerful donors.

Resource Controllers. They are a diffuse set of actors in the case of business schools – regulators, students thorough their ability to pay tuitions and big doners to name a few. Some, like the regulators, may be outcome focused, primarily to demonstrate to their taxpayer constituencies their performance as prudent caretakers for taxpayers. Although any one of them may contribute only a small percentage of resources needed by the business schools, their access to media and levers of political power gives them significant leverage over the business schools. However, with a few exceptions, they are less knowledgeable about business schools and their views can be shaped by appropriate interactions by the institutional players.

It is to be expected that, because the meaning of impact is advocated by all the three actors above, the power of the actors will privilege some meanings over others. Thus, in the US, where the government regulators have little influence on the operation of business schools, actors in the knowledge fields category have been most influential. Historically, as we have seen earlier, the dominance of the social science-trained faculty has been an outcome emanating from the initiatives undertaken by external funding sources, such as the Ford Foundation. In the current context, because of the many forces acting on higher education in the US – shifting demographics, technological change brought about digitization, cost pressures and lifestyles of students to name a few – the institutional actors in charge of business schools, which significantly subsidize many operations of a university, are likely to look for revenue opportunities rather than overhauling research. Thus, in most business schools, the "rigor versus relevance" debate is likely to remain a fashionable topic of discussion among senior faculty with little or no effect on the research conducted.

In some other countries, such as the UK and Australia, the government regulators may have significant influence the meanings of the term impact. For example, Penfield et al. (2014) attributed part of the reason why impact has become "the term of choice for research influence beyond the academia" to "accountability," that is "to demonstrate to government stakeholders and the wider public the value of research." Australia, while different, appears closer to the UK than US in this regard, demonstrating how a resource controller, such as government, can influence the notion of impact. I have also noted that going forward, there will be pressures to reduce the cost of assessment (see the quote from Williams and Grant, 2018 above) in these countries. It is likely that regulators will look for a technologically enabled, inexpensive, standardized tool that can perform the assessment quickly, without instituting elaborate committees or hierarchical layers. If a frequently observed institutional response asserts itself, the institutional actors are likely to opt for the least "inconvenient option." In practice, this means that the burden will fall on individual faculty members to show that they have made speeches, tv appearances or done consulting work – easily quantified metrics of impact performance.

Although metrics of performance are easily available for the US response and will soon (if not already available) be for the UK and Australian systems, I maintain that both the above responses are missed opportunities. In what follows, I make the case for a collaborative approach, a true partnership between academy and industry at the institutional level.

Toward a Partnership with Industry

In this paper, I have implicitly suggested that (see Figure 5.1) the current frenzy to adopt metrics for showcasing impact based on journals and faculty appearances in public forums are founded on a mode of research that Narayanan and Fahey (1983) had characterized as belonging to the "scientific conclave." In this model, the researchers are in full control of the phenomena to be studied and data collected, and the role of the subject, participants in the industry, is to learn from them. Indeed, the converse "a brokerage conclave," most commonly practiced then in Harvard Business School, relegates researchers to the role of scribes documenting what the industry participants have done. To be truly relevant and impactful, we had argued we needed a third way, which we had labeled as "collaborative." In collaborative research, the focus is on *novel* problems to be solved in industry, the qualifier "novel" distinguishing research from consulting[4]. Collaborative research thus dissolves the distinction between rigor and relevance, under the assumption that industry will not finance "irrelevant" problems. Table 5.3 shows the differences among the three models.

Currently, several forces are conspiring to move us toward this third model. First, there has been dissatisfaction with the use of theories that are five decades or so old for meeting contemporary problems. Second, many "grand challenges" are not addressed in "prestigious research streams." Third, the growing tide of digitization, with its potential to alter the form and design of organizations, calls for field engagement. Finally, many developing nations with their own aspirations are uneasy with models of business incubated in the developed world.

Just how do we address these forces? At a minimum, the collaborative model requires engagement with the field, but business schools are currently *ill equipped at the institutional level* to facilitate the process. Most schools are currently structured around a "functional" model, with departments (accounting, marketing finance, operations and/or management information systems) mimicking the organizational structures of single industry firms. These inherited structures may have served us well in the past, but they

Table 5.3 Critical Distinction among the Three Conclaves

	Conclaves		
	Scientific	**Collaborative**	**Brokerage**
Relation to Utilization	Dominant	Mixed degrees of dominance	Low dominance
Methods	Experimentation	"Action research"	Observation of organizational elites
Focus of Inquiry	Scientifically valid knowledge	Valid knowledge and organizational effectiveness	Diffusion
Criteria of Usefulness	Cumulative law-like postulates	Affirmative of certain values	Past success

Reproduced from Narayanan & Fahey, 1983

stand as barriers to holistic problem-focused research that is needed in the current altered context of businesses.

If we are serious about industry engagement and about dissolving the tension between rigor and relevance, that is, if we are serious about collaborative research, the institutional level actors in business schools need to rethink the characteristics of the institutions they are building. At a minimum, four characteristics will need to be nurtured:

Capabilities. Field engagement requires significant institutional capabilities: social networks, supportive firms and industries. They require time for development, and, in turn, commitment of resources whose outcomes are not immediate or visible (Narayanan, 2019).

Structures. Although functional structure, currently popular in business schools, may still be necessary, interdisciplinary units should be created within business schools, drawing on the broader expertise of the institutions to couple deep specialization with equally deep integration (Ghobadian & Narayanan, 2014).

Culture. Problem-focused research requires a different culture from the ones that have emerged in business schools. Indeed, business schools have inherited the key facets of social science fields, and this culture has served them well in their pursuit of internal legitimacy.

Human Resource Management (HRM) Systems. Critical in the endeavor is the designing of HRM systems – the choice of faculty members, their formal and social reward systems, career progression and especially their continued training and development.

Building these characteristics is likely to take time, effort and resources. Just like in any major change, these efforts are likely to face significant resistance from the entrenched political interests within the academy and will, thus, require individuals with unique skill sets to *lead* them, and to *ensure* that their imprints live way past their tenure. So, the real question for us is: Where are such leaders?

Notes

1 American Assembly of Collegiate Schools of Business was later known as the American Association of Collegiate Schools of Business and as the International Association for Management Education.
2 There was criticism of teaching as well, which I do not address here.

3 This paper is built on a political conception of knowledge creation, ideas that had been put forth in a paper by Narayanan and Fahey (1983).
4 The boundary between research and consulting under this category is blurred.

References

Barrett, R., & Vershinina, N. (2017). Intersectionality of ethnic and entrepreneurial identities: A study of post-war polish entrepreneurs in an English city. *Journal of Small Business Management*, 55(3), 430–443.

Bottom, W. (2009). Organizing intelligence: Development of behavioral science and the research-based model of business education. *Journal of the History of the Behavioral Sciences*, 45(3), 253–283.

Cardon, M. S., Stevens, C. E., & Potter, D. R. (2011). Misfortunes or mistakes?: Cultural sensemaking of entrepreneurial failure. *Journal of Business Venturing*, 26(1), 79–92.

Ghobadian, A., & Narayanan, V. K. (2014, July 24). The vital role of management education, *Financial Times*, https://www.ft.com/content/1858250a-0b6f-11e4-9e55-00144feabdc0

Khurana, R. (2007). *From higher aims to hired hands: The social transformation of American business schools and the unfulfilled promise of management as a profession*. Princeton University Press.

Kieser, A. (2011). Between rigor and relevance: Co-existing institutional logics in the field of management science. *Society and Economy*, 33(2), 237–247.

Lawrence, P. R. (1992). The challenge of problem-oriented research. *Journal of Management Inquiry*, 1(2), 139–142.

McLaren, P. G. (2019). Stop blaming Gordon and Howell: Unpacking the complex history behind the research-based model of education. *Academy of Management Learning & Education*, 18(1), 43–58.

Miner, J. B. (1997). Participating in profound change. *Academy of Management Journal*, 40(6), 1420–1428.

Mitroff, I. I. (2008). Knowing: How we know is as important as what we know. *The Journal of Business Strategy*, 29(3), 13–22.

Narayanan, V. K. (2005). Paper presented at the *Futures conference in Strathclyde Business School*.

Narayanan, V. K. (2019). Using institutional knowledge to answer puzzling questions about novel challenges and opportunities. *Strategy & Leadership* 47(6), 15–23.

Narayanan, V. K., & Fahey, L. (1983). High priests, disciples, and disbelievers: A political conception of knowledge generation and utilization. In Ralph H. Kilmann, Kenneth W. Thomas, Dennis P. Slevin, Raghu Nath, & S. Lee Jerrell (Eds.), *Producing Knowledge for Organizations*. Jossey-Bass.

Narayanan, V. K. & Zane, L. J. (2011). Current theoretical debates in management research: Epistemological analysis in strategic management. In B. Lee & C. Cassell (Eds.), *Challenges and controversies in management research* (pp. 211–227). Routledge.

Narayanan, V. K., Zane, L. J., & Liguori, E. (2021) Critical methodological considerations for entrepreneurial cognition research. *Journal of Small Business Management 59*(4), 756–793.

O'Reilly III, C. A., & Chatman, J. A. (1994). Working smarter and harder: A longitudinal study of managerial success. *Administrative Science Quarterly, 39*(4), 603–627.

Penfield, T., Baker, M. J., Scoble, R., & Wykes, M. C. (2014). Assessment, evaluations, and definitions of research impact: A review. *Research Evaluation, 23*(1), 21–32.

Pfeffer, J. (1997). *New directions for organization theory: Problems and prospects*. Oxford University Press.

Pfeffer, J., & Fong, C. T. (2002). The end of business schools? Less success than meets the eye. *Academy of Management Learning & Education, 1*(1), 78–95.

Rodenburg, K., Rowan, M., Nixon, A., & Christensen Hughes, J. (2022). The Misalignment of the FT50 with the Achievement of the UN's SDGs: A Call for Responsible Research Assessment by Business Schools. *Sustainability, 14*, 9598.

Sutton, R. I., & Staw, B. M. (1995). What theory is not. *Administrative Science Quarterly, 40*(3), 371–384.

Weick, K. E. (1989). Theory construction as disciplined imagination. *Academy of Management Review, 14*(4), 516–531.

Williams, K., & Grant, J. (2018). A comparative review of how the policy and procedures to assess research impact evolved in Australia and the UK. *Research Evaluation, 27*(2), 93–105.

6 Collaboration

Why Getting It Right is the Key to Academic Success

Lorraine Skelton

Introduction

In its most basic form, academic collaboration involves working with peers on research projects and providing knowledge transfer to industry through education. It can involve academics from the same or different disciplines, institutions, or countries. Lambovska and Yordanov (2020), found the primary motivation for collaboration is research funding, financial assets, promotion, contribution to society, and researcher reputation. They also found collaboration, material support, research funding, promotion, and time have the potential to influence a researchers path.

Of the many reasons to collaborate, amplifying the impact of academic research is possibly the most compelling (Larivière et al., 2015; Thelwall & Maflahi, 2019), along with generating innovative solutions (Perkmann & Walsh, 2007), and the ability to position academics at the forefront of their field (Bozeman & Corley, 2004). It also enables a collective effort to tackle complex global challenges and drive positive change for society (Leydesdorff & Wagner, 2019).

As Larivière et al. (2015) note, the potential to increase the impact of research, is a much sought after measure. By pooling their resources, expertise, and perspectives, academics can conduct larger and more complex studies that would not be possible individually. When academics from different disciplines work together, they bring new ideas and perspectives leading to creative and unexpected solutions to complex problems. Academic collaborations assist the need to stay current in their fields and maintain a competitive edge (Bozeman & Corley, 2004). By collaborating with others, there is the ability to learn about new developments and trends, and stay at the forefront of their research areas.

Academic collaboration is not without its challenges, Wicks and Etzkowitz (2003) observe that developing and maintaining relationships with academic and industry partners entails the ability to identify and connect with potential partners, and build trust and rapport. There is also a need to negotiate and manage contracts,

DOI: 10.4324/9781003459217-7

and ensure their research interests are aligned with the partners. With a partner also comes the potential for conflicts of interest (Etzkowitz & Dzisah, 2007). When academics work with industry partners, there is also a need to ensure their research remains objective and unbiased, including being transparent around funding sources and potential conflicts of interest. Despite the inherent challenges, the benefits to collaboration are numerous.

Collaborative research teams can make faster progress by pooling resources and knowledge, leading to quicker publications, grants, and, ultimately, greater academic recognition. Integrating real-world challenges into academic projects through industry collaborations can enhance the curriculum and provide students with a more well-rounded and relevant education. Academics can engage in discussions with policymakers to influence regulations and policies that impact both academia and industry positively. This can create an environment conducive to collaboration and innovation. Overall, industry collaboration is a valuable tool for academia, industry, and government to achieve their goals. By understanding the mutual benefits involved and working together to address potential challenges, the partners can create a more innovative and prosperous future.

Academic As Influencers and Drivers

Perkmann and Walsh (2009) note that academics are able to take on the role of the primary driver in developing engagement and collaboration. Proactively establishing and nurturing relationships, as well as playing a significant role as influencers, bringing expertise, credibility, and an ability to generate new knowledge (Etzkowitz & Leydesdorff, 1995, 2000; Leydesdorff, 2006). Academics can leverage their expertise to shape the future direction of research, promote best practice, advocate for the importance of academic rigor and integrity, serve on advisory boards or steering committees, mentor and train industry researchers, and share findings through co-authored publications and presentations. By effectively leveraging their expertise and influence, academics can drive impactful collaborations and contribute to advancements in both areas. By sharing insights and perspectives, researchers can help to shape research agendas, promote responsible research practices, and advocate for the use of research findings to address real-world problems.

Being trained in research methodologies, critical thinking, and data analysis, academics also become a valuable asset for both conducting research projects and facilitating data-driven decision-making, which is becoming more and more relevant with the advent of big data (Perkmann & Walsh, 2007). A key component of the academics skills are the design and execution of complex studies using a variety of data analysis tools and techniques to extract insights from large datasets. With a remit of continuous learning and staying current with the latest developments in their fields, academics make ideal partners for innovation. The academic contribution to collaboration plays a fundamental role in advancing knowledge, including the ability to publish their findings in reputable journals, presenting their work at conferences, and preparing reports and white papers that are relevant to industry, all of which develops the reach of their influence and disseminates this knowledge to a wider audience, including industry leaders and policymakers which in turn helps to gain recognition within their fields.

Through the rigor of scientific research design and methodology, academics also add credibility to research. A well-designed research study with robust methodologies and appropriate data analysis techniques enhances the credibility and validity of the findings, leading to greater recognition for all partners. Adhering to research ethics and maintaining academic integrity also helps in building trust in the research community with academics playing a vital role in ensuring that research is conducted in an ethical and responsible manner.

Collaboration between academia and industry brings benefits to both parties. For academics, collaboration can provide access to resources, increased research impact, and opportunities to influence industry research agendas. For industry partners, collaboration can provide access to cutting-edge research expertise, new ideas and perspectives, and innovative solutions to real-world problems. Collaborating with partners can be a rewarding experience, both professionally and personally. By working with others, academics can impact both their specialized areas and society.

Interdisciplinary and Transdisciplinary Collaboration

Pohl and Hadorn (2008) define interdisciplinary research as a form of coordinated and integration-oriented collaboration among researchers from different disciplines, but without non-academic stakeholders in the research process. Whereas transdisciplinary research projects bring together diverse perspectives and include the participation of non-academic stakeholders to address an issue. Many real-world challenges are complex and multifaceted, requiring both interdisciplinary and transdisciplinary solutions. By collaborating with experts from various fields, academics can address complex issues more effectively and produce comprehensive research outcomes.

Collaborating with diverse partners opens up new research opportunities that may not exist within the confines of their own discipline, and external partners, specifically, may have unique research questions, datasets, or projects that academics can contribute to. This allows researchers to explore new areas of study, expand their research portfolio, and diversify their expertise. Wider collaborations often involve multidisciplinary teams comprising researchers from various academic backgrounds, as well as industry professionals. This fosters interdisciplinary collaboration and knowledge exchange, enabling academics to gain insights from different perspectives. This cross-pollination of ideas can lead to innovative research approaches and breakthroughs and can lead to the ability to tackle grand challenges, such as climate change, sustainable development, and global health. These challenges are too complex to be solved by a single discipline, and require a collaborative approach that draws on the expertise of researchers across different fields.

There are a number of ways that academics can promote interdisciplinary and transdisciplinary collaborations. Academics can actively seek partnerships with industry organizations and companies in their area of interest. Initiating dialogue and finding common research interests will lay the foundation for fruitful collaborations. They may also engage in joint research projects with external partners that bridge the gap between theory and application. These collaborations allow academics to gain real-world insights while helping industry professionals benefit from academic expertise. Academics can also offer their services as consultants or advisors to industry projects. These roles allow academics to provide valuable guidance while gaining practical experience.

Industry and Government Collaborations

While collaborations come in many forms, interdisciplinary being the most common, both transdisciplinary and collaboration with industry can bring greater benefits. Particularly, collaborations with industry and government can provide access to much-needed resources, such as funding, research facilities, data sources, and specialized equipment. This can mean a wider impact, reaching a more diverse audience, and have a greater impact on the world. Academics' commitment to academic freedom, objective research, and ethical considerations can also assist in ensuring that results are credible, reliable, and provide beneficial outcomes.

Universities and other academic institutions need funding to function, and often face challenges related to budget constraints, resource allocation, and financial sustainability. With research that develops practical applications and the potential for commercialization, collaborations can strengthen research quality where collaborative efforts undergo rigorous peer review from multiple perspectives, which helps ensure the validity and reliability of findings. Industry and government partners may also provide funding for academic research, helping to reduce the financial burden and lead to the access of additional resources and expertise.

Students may also gain hands-on experience with real-world problems and develop skills that are in high demand in the workforce, improving their job prospects after graduation. Academics guide the next generation of researchers and professionals. In collaborative research, they can mentor and nurture young researchers and industry professionals, fostering a culture of innovation, curiosity, and intellectual growth. By transferring their knowledge and skills, academics can have a lasting impact on the development of talent within industry settings.

Academics often have a broad network of contacts, including industry professionals, government officials, and community leaders. This diverse set of individuals, with diverse backgrounds, can bring together experts from various fields to tackle multifaceted problems effectively. Such external engagement can help industry partners to connect with new stakeholders, identify new opportunities, and build relationships that can lead to future successful collaborations. By collaborating with academics, industry partners can gain access to cutting-edge knowledge and expertise, helping them to stay ahead of the competition and develop new products and services that meet the needs of their customers. Along with this, new innovation can drive economic growth, create jobs, and enhance competitiveness in global markets.

As academics are trained to think critically and approach problems from diverse angles, they have the ability to contribute innovative thinking, challenging conventional wisdom, and pushing boundaries. With the ability to generate novel ideas and propose alternative solutions, academics can inspire industry and government partners to explore new avenues and take risks, leading to breakthrough innovations and competitive advantages.

Successful collaborations also enhance the recognition and credibility of academics. Working with reputable industry partners can validate the quality and impact of their research, increasing visibility within both academic and industry circles. Such collaborations can also lead to joint publications or awards, further establishing the academic's reputation in their field. Industry collaborations also provide researchers with practical experience and exposure to real-world challenges, which can enhance their professional skill set and increase their marketability. Industry collaborations can also provide academics with the opportunity to demonstrate their skills and expertise to a wider audience, which can lead to new job opportunities and promotions.

Collaboration also plays a vital role in bridging the gap between academia and industry. Academics excel in theoretical understanding, while industry professionals are experienced in implementing solutions and dealing with real-world challenges, which also help to break down barriers and foster a culture of knowledge exchange between academia and industry, leading to more fruitful partnerships and innovations. They are also able to focus on long-term goals and solutions rather than immediate profitability. This long-term vision can lead to creative sustainable and ethically responsible innovations. By working together, university, industry, and government can accelerate innovation, solve complex problems, and make a positive impact on the world.

Collaboration Skills and Capabilities

Academics who are willing to explore the potential of their research, identify opportunities for knowledge transfer or commercialization, and actively seek out industry partnerships that can accelerate the impact of their work require a proactive and innovative approach to research and a willingness to step outside the traditional academic comfort zone. Miller (2018) defines the entrepreneurial academic, as those who engage with industry with a view of demonstrating the application of their research to the wider society, despite often not having contractual obligations. These academics engage more frequently with consultancy and contract research, collaborative research, and training with industry, rather than with commercialisation activities, such as patents licences or spin out activities, and this more informal mode of collaboration is often driven by research-related aims. Academic entrepreneurs, in contrast, are faculty members who undertake commercialization using formal modes of engagement, capitalizing on specific market opportunities. Key motivations and challenges can be identified depending on the type of engagement each academic adopts. Whichever term is utilized, both styles require specific skills and capabilities for collaboration.

In order for academics to connect with industry and government professionals and build meaningful relationships, they require effective communication and active listening skills, and the ability to establish rapport. Academics also need to stay informed about industry and government trends, challenges, and opportunities in their field of expertise. Understanding the business and administrative landscape, market dynamics, and industry and government needs enables academics to identify areas of potential collaboration and align their research interests with industry priorities. This awareness helps in crafting compelling proposals that resonate with industry partners. Engaging with industry and government also requires flexibility and adaptability to accommodate the practical constraints and timelines of collaborations. Academics should be open to adjusting research plans, methodologies, and project timelines to meet requirements. This flexibility helps to build trust and fosters a collaborative environment.

Academics need to be able to articulate their research interests and potential areas of collaboration to industry partners in a clear and concise manner, with the ability to negotiate project objectives, resource allocation, and intellectual property rights effectively. It is beneficial for an academic to possess project management skills to effectively plan, execute, and oversee projects, including clear goal setting, project milestones definition, resource management, and results delivery. Strong leadership skills are also valuable in coordinating interdisciplinary teams and driving the collaborative effort forward.

Collaborating with external partners often involves bridging the cultural gap between academic and industry cultures first termed by Kirkland (2010). Academics should strive to understand the culture, language, and practices of the industry partners they engage with. This understanding helps in establishing effective working relationships, fostering trust and navigating potential differences in expectations and priorities. In addition, they must maintain regular communication with industry partners to keep them updated on relevant research developments and explore new opportunities for collaboration. Academics that take the lead in driving engagement with industry, result in mutually beneficial collaborations that enhance the impact of their research.

Summary

Collaborations play a vital role in academic success, however academics need to ensure that the institute to which they belong, has appropriate policies and guidelines in place to govern collaborations, while upholding academic integrity and independence. Collaboration enriches research by bringing practical relevance, access to resources, and interdisciplinary expertise. It also offers career development opportunities, enables knowledge transfer and commercialization, and enhances the financial sustainability of academic institutions. By fostering effective collaborations, academics can maximize the impact of their work and contribute to the advancement of society.

It is worth noting that academics should ensure that industry collaborations align with their academic goals, values, and research integrity, and establish clear agreements, communicate expectations, and maintain the independence and objectivity of their research. However, with proper management and strategic partnerships, academics can leverage collaborations to advance their research, increase their impact, and contribute to the advancement of society.

Bibliography

Bozeman, B., & Corley, E. A. (2004). Scientists' collaboration strategies: Implications for scientific and technical human capital. *Research Policy, 33*(4), 599–616.

EEA (European Environment Agency). (2016). Sustainability transitions: Now for the long term.

Etzkowitz, H., & Dzisah, J. (2007). *Universities and the global knowledge economy: A triple helix of university-industry-government relations.* Edward Elgar Publishing.

Etzkowitz, H., & Leydesdorff, L. (1995). The triple helix – university, industry, government relationships: A laboratory for knowledge based economic development. *EASST Review, 14*(1), 11–19.

Etzkowitz, H., & Leydesdorff, L. (2000). The dynamics of innovation: From national systems and "mode 2" to a triple helix of university-industry-government relations. *Research Policy, 29*(2), 109–123.

Jahn, T., Bergmann, M., & Keil, F. (2012). Transdisciplinarity: Between mainstreaming and marginalization. *Ecological Economics, 79,* 1–10.

Kirkland, J. (2010). The Management of University Research. In, *International Encyclopedia of Education,* (pp. 316–321). The Association of Commonwealth Universities, London, UK.

Lambovska, M., & Yordanov, K. (2020). Motivation of researchers to publish in high-quality journals: A theoretical framework. *TEM Journal, 9*(1), 188–197.

Larivière, V., Sugimoto, C. R., & Gingras, Y. (2015). Team size matters: Collaboration and scientific impact since 1900. *Journal of the Association for Information Science and Technology, 66*(7), 1323–1332.

Leydesdorff, L. (2006). The triple helix model of innovation: An introduction. *Research Policy, 35*(3), 293–303.

Leydesdorff, L., & Wagner, C. S. (2019). Global university-industry collaboration: A bibliometric analysis of patent data. *Journal of Informetrics, 13*(3), 100973.

Miller, A. (2018). The role of creative coursework in skill development for university seniors. *Global Education Review, 5*(1), 88–107.

Perkmann, M., & Walsh, K. (2007). *University-industry relationships and open innovation: Towards a new paradigm.* Oxford University Press.

Perkmann, M., & Walsh, K. (2009). University-industry relations and innovation: Evidence from the UK. *Journal of Economic Policy Research, 11*(1), 1–16.

Pohl, C., & Hadorn, G. H. (2008). Core terms in transdisciplinary research. In, *Handbook of transdisciplinary research,* pp. 427–432.

Slaughter, R. A. (2012). Welcome to the Anthropocene. *Futures, 44*(2), 119–126.

66 Lorraine Skelton

Thelwall, M., & Maflahi, N. (2019). Academic collaboration rates and citation associations vary substantially between countries and fields. *Journal of the Association for Information Science and Technology, 70*(10), 1033–1042.

Wicks, D., & Etzkowitz, H. (2003). Industry collaboration with universities: Lessons learned from the US experience. *Science and Public Policy, 30*(6), 423–435.

7 'Nothing ill can dwell in such a temple'

Internal Partnering for External Success[1]

Kelly Farrell

It's a bit strange, isn't it? The title of this chapter. Quirky maybe; eccentric, even. Using a Shakespeare quote in a piece about internal partnering in universities? And what in heaven's name does it *mean*, anyway: 'Nothing ill can dwell'?

Your reading of this chapter's title – not to mention your tolerance for it – will very much depend on who you are and where you come from. In this context, when using 'where', I am not referring to your latitude and longitude. I don't mean your geographical location, I mean your *disciplinary* one. Your knowledge background. Who you consider your intellectual family to be. The tribe you belong to. *That* 'where'.

The title of this paper reflects my own disciplinary tribe and my own territorial knowledge boundaries that exist to this day, despite the fact that I have not worked in my 'home' discipline (English and Cultural Studies) for more than 20 years. You see, it was *de rigeur* in the late 1990s, in those disciplines, to title your paper with a catchy phrase or quote and then to follow with a clever explanation of what the paper was about so for me, there is an easy naturalness to the title. If you have a degree from, let's say, the sciences – and perhaps particularly the 'hard' sciences – you may well regard the title as either adorably twee or downright ridiculous.

In the early 2000s, I was at the Centre for the Study of Higher Education at the University of Melbourne and, as an early-career academic at the time, I was delivering professional development for academic staff in teaching and learning while doing a small study on the experience of PhD students at universities. In the course of the literature review, I came across a book by Tony Becher and Paul Trowler called *Academic Tribes and Territories: Intellectual Enquiry and the Culture of Disciplines*.[2] I didn't stay in academe but the Becher and Trowler work stayed with me. It was – and remains – a formative brick in the wall of my approach to getting

DOI: 10.4324/9781003459217-8

things done in universities and working with and alongside researchers: work that I love and have been lucky enough to remain in in the intervening years since.

While the roles I have served in across three universities during my career have been many and varied and have been in both the teaching and learning and research portfolios, in the last six years or so I have had increasing exposure to working with external entities, to the point that, at the time of writing, I find myself Head of Business Development at the Australian National University (ANU). At ANU, I am privileged to lead an exceptionally talented and passionate team of 'boundary spanners': Business Development Managers working in a 'matrix' structure – reporting to my role but embedded in each college. They do incredible work connecting themselves both inside and outside of the university and, then, connecting the inside and outside together.

Even now, more than twenty years later, the understanding of academic discipline that Becher and Trowler gave me, the tacit ways discipline guides knowledge-creation, culture and behaviour continues to help me navigate the complex 'small worlds'[3] that universities are. It also serves to remind me that, with the constant and rapid technological advancement with which we live, we are sometimes seduced into thinking that if we just get this *process* right, if we just roll out *that* system or implement *this* app, we will solve all the problems of working in a highly complex environment.

And when it comes to complexity, working as a 'boundary-spanner' in a university pretty much takes the cake. It can be challenging enough to operate internally within these institutions that are inherently and historically inward-looking (and whose internal workings frequently seem to have been explicitly designed to repel external partnering) but throw in an impatient partner with a deadline to the mix and you've pretty much served up the aforementioned cake delicately iced and with a cherry on top.

What I have learned from many years of working in these complicated, beautiful and important organisations is that it isn't the *things* – the processes, the policies, the systems and now the apps – that determine whether the ecosystem works well. It's the people. The *humans*. The expensive customer relationship management (CRM) that promised salvation from all relationship-management woes loses its sheen pretty quickly when the novelty wears off and no one makes time to update it.

When it comes down to it, you can have all the shiny stuff and all the beautiful software in the world, but it is only as good as the people who use it and, critically, *the culture that supports them to do that well*. And, in this case, when it comes to creating and maintaining a healthy ecosystem of process and culture that supports and then elevates the capacity to partner externally, the people involved tend not to be academic staff, but what we in Australia call their 'professional staff' colleagues. It is this cohort of people who are doing their best to create an environment for this to happen, but they are, more often than not, trying to do it within institutional behemoths where multiple internal portfolios and their key performance indicators (KPIs) are in a constant and competitive flamenco, jostling for supremacy and attention.

Becher and Trowler are specifically talking about academic communities in *Tribes and Territories*. However, in this chapter, I want to look at how their work can be applied to give us nearly as much insight into the people who work shoulder-to-shoulder with academics in these highly complex organisations. I want to look at the ways in which *we* also belong to internal tribes and territories and how, in some ways at least, these tribes are enabling and productive of an ecosystem that supports external partnering. But I also want to argue that, more often than not, they are also regressive, obstructive and downright inimical to building relationships with external partners: relationships that, in today's environment, are critical sources of impact and research funding for most universities across the world.

Ultimately, I want to suggest that some of our most strategic partnerships are not external at all and that they are, in fact, the ones that we build internally, *with each other*.

So how do Becher and Trowler define academic 'tribes and territories'? For them, tribes are academic communities while territories are the academic ideas across which a particular tribe will range. Each of these tribes has its own culture made up of 'sets of taken-for-granted values, attitudes and ways of behaving' (23) and these are 'articulated through and reinforced by recurrent practices among a group of people in a given context.' (23) They acknowledge that the two are inextricable from each other, that the relationship between them is 'mutually infused: disciplinary knowledge forms are to a large extent constituted and instantiated socially' (23) but at the same time they seek to separate the social aspects of these knowledge communities from the ways that knowledge is formed, in order to understand how each influences the other.

For our purposes it is enough to understand that being inducted as a member of a disciplinary community – which is effectively what happens when your PhD is passed – means that you identify with and are personally committed to that community. You pick up the same kinds of 'gatekeeping' responsibilities and behaviours that already-inducted members have. You guard the accepted values, traditions, forms of linguistic and symbolic communication and codes of conduct that characterises that particular tribe (remember the title of this chapter and whether you had tolerance for it or not?) along with your fellow tribe-mates – who are likely spread across the globe. You won't know each other by name and you will have never met, but you are so socialised into that disciplinary tribe that if you did meet it would not take long before you recognised each other as belonging to one of these 'imagined communities'.[4] Conversely, dialogue with those outside that discipline can sometimes result in the distinct feeling that you are undertaking a form of cross-cultural communication.

How territories are created and maintained – how knowledge is formed and accepted and what it's objects and boundaries look like – differs widely across the disciplines. As Becher and Trowler explain, the sciences can be characterised into 'hard' (e.g., physics) and 'soft' (e.g., biology); mechanical engineering is concerned with how mechanical principles can be applied to technical devices, but it is also about how people use them. Academic law has as its central subject a body of rules while sociology uses both 'hard' and 'soft' data and it is generally accepted that theories are always contestable. As Becher and Trowler traverse the discipline spectrum, it becomes clear how social knowledge is, how hierarchical academic tribes are and how tribes and the marking of their territories are shot through with power dynamics.

There is, of course, an enormous body of work that examines group dynamics in workplaces, but Becher and Trowler bring a lens to those interested in developing industry–university partnerships that others can't: an understanding of the esoteric way that universities function. Many workplaces would say they experience 'siloing' but those of us who have experienced life in a university know that absolutely nowhere does tribalism and territorialism better than higher education institutions.

It is my contention that tribes and territories are far from confined to the academic cohort in universities and that they extend to the essential group of people who power internal university business: professional staff. An awareness of the concept of silos is common for most of us, as is an understanding that faculties – and often also the schools within them – are more often than not effectively small and medium-sized enterprises (SMEs) working to the beat of their own separate drums, with their own cultures and ways of doing things and that these do not necessarily bear any relation or alignment to each other or to how central university units, such as finance, HR and, most certainly, industry engagement/business development, works.

What is less common is an awareness of how we, like our academic colleagues, create and gatekeep our own tribes and how the nature of the work we do – our territories – will often dictate who we see as 'in' and who we see as 'out'. This is, of course, tacit knowledge developed almost by osmosis, a product of our exposure to culture and people who pass 'the knowledge' down to us via a range of social interactions, where certain behaviours and values are sanctioned and others are rebuffed. No one has sat down and told us 'the rules'. Our experiences mean we just have it 'in our heads' and rarely – if ever – do we take it out, put it on a table and interrogate it.

I don't mean to suggest that having our own tribes is inherently 'bad'; it's a human trait that has, after all, meant the survival of our species for millennia. Even taking into account the complex, comfortable, highly technological first world that most of us are lucky enough to operate in, our brains remain primitive and built for survival: they know that belonging to a tribe can literally keep us alive.

Seeking a sense of belonging is thus wired deeply within us. While it may be true that in the modern workplace we don't need to belong to a group to keep ourselves fed and protected from being eaten alive by other hungry beasts (at least in the literal sense!) we still experience a number of emotional and practical pay-offs from being – *and being seen as* – part of a 'tribe'. These include emotional safety, the development of loyalty, trust and a sense of shared goals and, on the practical side, a hierarchy to exploit when we need assistance getting something done. Tribalism in contemporary organisations like universities effectively boosts our social capital. It makes us both safer and more powerful.

Which all sounds great, and is, in some respects, wholly necessary to the effective working of our institutions as it offers so much clarity: clear identification of which work is mine and which is yours. This is perfect for the *traditional* model of a university: after all, it makes us all 'stay in our lanes'.

However, for those whose role is literally to breach boundaries and take university research outside and bring industry 'outsiders' in, staying in a neat, well-defined lane just isn't an option. Even if it were, the fact is, there *isn't* a clear lane to stay in. Each potential industry partner brings a unique set of needs that generally unfold along a unique pathway that utterly refuses to adhere to internal university procedure, workflows and timelines: no matter how diligently we may map these out. For better or worse, to get the job done people working in these areas in universities must, to some extent or other, disrupt the internal system and, to some degree, break down those tribal boundaries.

This is also where 'territories' come in. By way of example, let's take two colleagues working in the same research services unit but in different teams. First, a grants team member whose work revolves primarily around checking compliance with requirements set by funding bodies and, second, an industry-engagement team member charged with developing partnerships with external organisations.[5] One is likely to work with clear process, pre-set timelines and a relatively high degree of certainty. Good administration, a methodical approach and a high level of detail is valued and rewarded by the team leader. For their industry-partnerships colleague working across the room, the opposite may be true: their work is likely characterised by a high level of uncertainty, no clear path to 'finished' and a relative need for agility and rapid turnaround. Both roles are essential. Both colleagues are skilled, motivated and committed. Both may even acknowledge that they are essentially trying to reach the same outcome. Yet, often, the complexity of their environment will render them one or all of: frustrated by their colleague's lack of understanding of their pressures; a sense that people are 'overstepping' (or conversely, being overly officious and obstructive); and the perception that the other does not adequately value or respect the work they do.

This is an example where colleagues are in the same team. Toss in working across administrative divisions and/or schools and the level of complexity goes through the roof. While there may be times when we despair at how difficult it can all be, there are ways we can change our mindset and our practice around working internally that can help to improve our networks, our own effectiveness and contribute to building a healthier, more impactful internal ecosystem to support our researchers to partner more often and to greater effect.

1. Apply a Partnering Lens Internally

By referring to the colleagues and units we work with as 'internal partners', we can bring an external partnering approach to those inside the university. When targeting a new external partner to grow a potential relationship, we will work hard to understand their objectives, their people and their business. When working with colleagues internally, we can sometimes go in with the mindset of 'I just need to get them to do this. It's their JOB to do this for me'. In contrast, when dealing with external partners, we are always trying to build sustainable rather than transactional partnerships, ones that can be grown, expanded and deepened for greater impact. By taking time to understand and get to know our partner-colleagues – and not just their names and contact details, but what is important to *them* and *their* business – we play the long game. When under pressure to get something done, it can be tempting to push and push our colleagues in other areas for that one piece of work to get through their workflow as soon as possible – after all, having made a promise to an external partner to get something to them by a particular date, all we can think about is not missing the deadline. Applying a partnering lens would help us see that while we may get a quick win this time, we may also burn some bridges that may make it harder to get subsequent work through the same person. Sacrificing rapidity for quality may just be the best way forward in terms of preserving relationships that you will need in future.

2. Recognise our own Tribal Biases

This is harder and more confronting than it might at first seem; like our socially acquired knowledge the tribes we belong to are also tacit: we just know we're part of something without really thinking about it. When you actively acknowledge your membership of particular groups, you're suddenly confronted with the fact that you yourself contribute to tribalism, gatekeeping and boundary-setting around who is 'in' and who is 'out'. To help recognise where your tribal lines lie, where they are helpful and where they are obstructive, you can ask yourself a few simple questions:

- Which tribes do you belong to?
- Which ones do you need to be part of to increase ease and effectiveness and help build a healthier ecosystem for partnering?
- How might you muffle the borders of your own tribe(s) to let others who need access to get in? What might be the benefits and how willing are you to do this?

This is not a process of self-flagellation; rather, it will help you map out where you currently have influence and connection and where – if anywhere - you need to build it.

3. Encourage Cross-cultural Communication

There are ways we can open our borders and introduce others to our territories in informal ways that boost our networks and springboard understanding of our colleagues as people, the nature of their work, their challenges and what they consider to be success. Opportunities to do this need to be architecturally designed, however, or heavy workloads and other priorities will otherwise always take precedent. At ANU, we have had good success with the establishment of Communities of Practice (CoP): at time of writing the Industry Engagement CoP is an active group of cross-divisional and cross-college colleagues working in engagement and partnering who meet on a monthly basis. Sometimes speakers present at these but, at heart, the CoP provides an informal platform for people to bring their challenges and successes, to share information and experience and to build internal understanding and capacity around partnership and business development. On a team level, I have also had some success introducing what I call 'Celebrity Morning Tea' where we will invite another team from within the university to visit, so we can meet the people who were previously just an email address face-to-face and learn more about what they do. We feed them, of course, and while some people break out in hives at the thought of doing an 'icebreaker', I generally find that throwing a fun activity in to lighten the 'vibe' is a good idea.

These are just a few ideas. They are anecdotal, not rocket science, but they provide a starting point for thinking about how to build an 'internal partnering' mindset.

The quote that forms part of the title of this chapter comes from *The Tempest*, 1611, a play that can itself be read as an exploration of tribes and territories, those who belong and those who do not. The short version is that Prospero, the exiled Duke of Milan (who has magic powers and now lives on an island with his daughter, Miranda) has conjured a violent storm to shipwreck his treacherous brother Antonio (now the Duke of Milan). Also on the boat is the handsome Ferdinand who Miranda falls in love with at first sight. After Prospero accuses Ferdinand of being a spy and a traitor, Miranda exclaims in protest that:

> There's nothing ill can dwell in such a temple:
> If the ill spirit have so fair a house,
> Good things will strive to dwell with't.

Miranda is, of course, talking about Ferdinand's body, but her words could be a metaphor for our institutions where if we only made them temples of positivity, where boundaries came down and tribal lines miraculously dissolved, then only 'good things will strive to dwell' within them.

It is just not realistic for university boundary spanners to expect that we can ever have Miranda's 'temple': our complex context forbids it. But what we *can* do is operate with a mindset that helps us understand ourselves and others more clearly, improves our capacity and willingness to partner internally and allows us to operate more effectively in complexity. And when we are talking about 'strategic partners', we need to expand our definitions to include the people alongside us, our internal colleagues, who are some of our most strategic partners of all.

Notes

1 With apologies to Mr Shakespeare.
2 Anthony Becher and Paul Trowler, *Academic Tribes and Territories: Intellectual Enquiry and the Culture of Disciplines*, (Second Edition). The Society for Research into Higher Education and Open University Press, 1989.
3 This references David Lodge's 1984 Booker-shortlisted satirical campus novel *Small World: An Academic Romance*.
4 Benedict Anderson, *Imagined Communities: Reflections on the Origin and Spread of Nationalism*. Verso: London, 2016. Arnold's influential argument about nationalism can be applied to any community. As he writes communities are '*imagined* because the members of even the smallest nation will never know most of their fellow members, meet them, or even hear of them, yet in minds of each lives the image of their communion.' (p. 14) So, too, it is true of academic communities or 'tribes'.
5 For the purposes of this exercise, some stereotyping may need to take place.

8 Engagement as Strategy

Tim Vorley

Introduction

Universities are changing. In fact, they have been in constant evolution although the nature of this change has often been more radical than incremental. That said, there is a tendency to identify key points of transition, such as the shift from Newman's conception of universities as teaching institutions to the coupling of teaching and research embodied in the Humboldtian vision of the university. Clark Kerr, while Chancellor of the University of California system, identified another point of transition in the emergence of what he called the 'Multiversity', to more accurately depict the growing range of activities in which universities are engaged (Kerr, 2001).

The notion of universities engaging with industry and society is not new, and, in many instances, the relationships between universities and industry are as old as universities themselves. However, as universities have evolved and increasingly more is demanded of them, roles beyond teaching and research, embodied in their relationships beyond the academy, have become both more visible, prominent and emphasised in policy. As engines of innovation and civic anchors, universities have been positioned as key place-based institutions within the economies and communities of which they are a part.

Early in my career, I made well-intended, but, on reflection, partially informed, contributions to the academic debate on the then so-called 'Third Mission' of the university (see Vorley & Nelles, 2009). The Third Mission refers to the broader socio-economic engagement through mechanisms such as knowledge exchange, commercialisation and partnerships. The introduction of several neologisms, such as the 'Entrepreneurial University' (Etzkowitz, 1993), the 'Enterprise University' (Marginson & Considine, 2000) and the 'Corporate University' (Aronowitz, 2001) all sought to capture the evolving form of universities, and each with a different emphasis on the nature and forms of engagement. While I started researching the entrepreneurial university as an early career researcher, my career path has seen me become Pro Vice-Chancellor

DOI: 10.4324/9781003459217-9

and Dean of a business school, and my academic insights on the field still serve to inform my approach in practice.

Despite the heterogeneous nature of universities and business schools therein, the shift toward engagement is a common trend in the sector, in the UK and internationally. However, what engagement looks like and the ways in which it is delivered differs significantly between institutions. This is often as a result of their profiles for teaching and research, as well as their position within their respective ecosystems, and the characteristics of the places where they exist. It is also a reflection of the individual academic, technical and professional service staff who comprise the university. It is this variation which presents both the opportunity and challenge for engagement as strategy.

While engagement has become part of the everyday lexicon in universities, it remains only partially understood and, consequently, its potential benefits are only partially realised. Business schools should be crucibles of engagement, where engagement is not a by-product of the business school but is intrinsic to it. As such, engagement should be considered as an outcome of deliberate design and purposive strategy. Given the ways in which engagement crosses portfolios, there is a need to be more strategic in identifying and leveraging opportunities. This is about more than implementing strategies to enable engagement, but rather positioning engagement as the foundation upon which business schools are built.

Given the importance of engagement to business schools, reliance on an unstructured or organic approach is too high risk. As Thomas and Ambrosini (2021) highlight, there is a need for business schools to develop a more strategic focus, which reinforces the argument to pursue engagement as a strategic imperative. To achieve this, the remainder of the chapter is organised in three sections: the first discusses the scope of engagement; the second introduces engagement as strategy; and, the third situates the importance of leadership over management in enabling engagement. The chapter concludes by reflecting on the importance of pursuing an engagement-led strategy for the business of business schools.

Openness to Engagement

It is important to put our preconceptions of engagement aside. Whether a teacher, researcher or administrator, chances are that most colleagues working in business schools have only a limited perspective on and experience of engagement. This is not to underplay the value or importance of that experience, but rather to emphasise the scale and opportunity of the matter at hand. Across different portfolios, with different partners, in different ways and to different ends, the possibilities for engagement are limitless. The National Co-ordinating Centre for Public Engagement (NCCPE) depicts the engaged university as one incorporating engagement into their research, knowledge exchange, teaching and social responsibility as shown in Figure 8.1.

As a career research academic, engagement for me has by and large been something associated with research – both in terms of the research process as well as being a precursor to impact, as captured through case studies for the Research Excellence Framework (REF) in the United Kingdom of Great Britain and Northern Ireland (UK). Yet, as a leader in a university, I have needed to re-examine my own assumptions and biases around engagement, and it is this which has ultimately seen my thinking evolve in terms of engagement as strategy.

Engagement, and impact, are about more than research, and are certainly about more than the REF. Upon deeper reflection, as a teacher I have always drawn upon insights and expertise beyond the academy to bring real-world relevance into the classroom. I have participated in the policy process regionally and nationally to provide insight and evidence, worked with businesses to understand and implement changes and deliver growth. And it is recognising that the work of an academic, while grounded in their position as a researcher or teacher, is rarely constrained to that domain alone. So, the strategic challenge for business school leaders is in how to enable and scale engagement, with a view to realising the broader benefits to the individual, the institution, the partner and society.

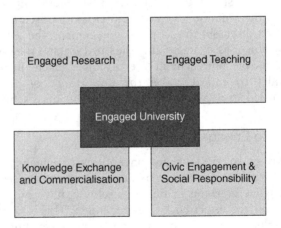

Figure 8.1 Types of Engagement

Source: Adapted from NCCPE, 2022

Business schools are engaged in a broad portfolio of activities with partners, that can vary by the type of engagement. The concepts of engaged research and teaching are perhaps better understood; the former being associated with working with partners to co-produce insights, while the latter is associated with engaging partners in teaching and learning in different ways. In their report, 'The Changing State of Knowledge Exchange', Hughes et al. (2016) identify four categories of activities, as shown in Table 8.1. While not exhaustive, the table serves to highlight the breadth of activities relevant to an engaged business school or university. Much engagement activity is organic and reflects the pursuits of individual academics, with less engagement driven as the product of business school strategy.

Table 8.1 Types of Knowledge Exchange Activities

People-based activities	• Student placements • Participation in networks • Standard setting forums • Enterprise education • Attending conferences • Giving invited lectures • Employee training • Sitting on advisory boards • Curriculum development
Problem-based activities	• Joint publications • Consultancy services • Joint research • Prototyping and testing • Research consortia • Hosting personnel • Contract research • Informal advice • External secondment • Setting of physical facilities
Community-based activities	• Social enterprises • Heritage And tourism • Museums and art galleries • Public exhibitions • Performing areas • Community-based sports • Lectures for the community • School projects
Commercialisation activities	• Formed/run consultancy • Patenting • Licenced research • Spin out companies

Adapted from Hughes et al., 2016

The types of engagement also transcend different domains involving different partners as highlighted in Box 8.1. While this list is not exhaustive, it highlights some of the key domains of engagement with different kinds of partners; this is not to presuppose the various modes of engagement or their outcomes. At the heart of reimagining engagement is rethinking who, as business schools and business school academics, we engage with and how we engage with them; as well as the outcomes and impacts of engagement. There is an important question as to the strategic objectives associated with engagement from a business school perspective, as distinct to the objectives that individual academics might pursue independently. For the contemporary business school, the sum of individual engagement activities cannot and should not be assumed to meet the needs for institutional engagement.

It is also important to view engagement as multifaceted, and move away from thinking about engagement on a transactional basis. Instead, the focus should be looking at the difference that relationships and partnerships make rather than reducing them to individual initiatives and activities. Such a transactional view of engagement rarely yields mutually beneficial outcomes. Again, the motivations for and outcomes of engagement need to be shared, and without a genuine commitment to engagement activities they are unlikely to be successful.

Depending on the size and orientation of a business school, it may be involved in multiple domains, almost always including business engagement. Yet the nature of business engagement can

---

Box 8.1 Domains of Engagement

Public engagement brings academics and the public together by raising awareness of and encouraging involvement with higher education where the benefits are shared with the public.

Business engagement involves academics working and collaborating with businesses on organisational and commercial ideas and opportunities, helping businesses to thrive, innovate and grow.

Third sector engagement sees universities engaging with a range of charities and not-for-profits in different ways, around the services they deliver.

Policy engagement refers to many ways that academics and policymakers connect around policymaking processes, working in a range of areas on different issues.

Activist engagement describes the engagement of academics with activist organisations working in areas of politics of human rights, justice and civil society.

range from working with the largest multinationals to small businesses and start-ups, in a variety of different ways as noted in Figure 8.1. In reality, many business schools are often engaged in other domains as well, often driven in a bottom–up organic way, according to the interests and activities of individual academics. However, as positive as this is, it represents a challenge to scaling engagements as academics move institutions or change roles – leaving an 'engagement gap'. The answer, therefore, is in the pursuit of engagement as strategy, to see it become embedded across the business school.

Pursuing Engagement as Strategy

The discussion to this point is not to suggest that such engagement has not figured in the strategy of universities. Indeed, the very notion of the civic university which has seen a revival over the past decade underpinned the creation of many redbrick universities and post-1992 universities that have a rich history of engagement. But the centrality of that engagement has been forgotten, and the benefits lost for a time. The renewed prominence of the civic agenda is now seeing many universities reavow their commitment to working with government and strategic partners to realise the geographic role and responsibility of the university to drive positive societal change.

The international orientation of universities has also seen the emergence of a new global civic university agenda, where engagement is not constrained to their immediate geography but extends nationally and internationally. Working across scales and through the excellence of their teaching and research portfolios, universities are increasingly leading and convening the debate around global environmental and societal challenges that lie ahead. The challenge moving forward is to rethink what engagement as strategy means and how to realise the opportunities it presents.

The focus of many universities pre- and post-pandemic has, for many valid reasons, been on their own security and resilience (Nandy et al., 2021). However, at a time when talk of ecosystems, collaboration and co-creation dominate the discourse around higher education, the strategy needs to better reflect this. While for the majority, engagement is no longer considered as an 'add on' or fringe activity, in the absence of a coordinated and coherent approach, it has seen engagement become fragmented and *ad hoc*. Again, this is not bad, and is arguably a phase in the evolution towards engagement, but without coordination and coherence, there are undoubtedly opportunities forgone.

The rallying cry of this chapter is not to manage engagement top–down, but rather recognise the value of engagement that has come to be articulated in the mission and visions of universities and their constituent schools and faculties as *a point of departure* rather than an outcome or endpoint. Situating engagement at the heart of the strategy recognises the value of partners and stakeholders to teaching and research as the core missions of universities, and sees this as a two-way relationship where there are shared, but not always common, interests and values. Pursuing engagement as strategy is a key way to develop this shared understanding.

An important related point is recognising that engagement has costs as well as benefits; investment is needed to ensure that the capacity and capabilities are in place to realise the benefits. This is more likely to occur if engagement is in the strategy, but thinking of engagement as strategy with a longer term perspective demands rethinking the resourcing model. It also requires key partners and stakeholders to contribute to the development of the strategy itself, recognising that engagement is a two-way process and regarding engagement with partners as a core component of a university's overall approach.

For business schools, engagement as strategy revolves around building and maintaining meaningful and productive relationships with partners and stakeholders to realise the vision of the business school and achieve long-term success. The nature of engagement may or may not align with or build upon the interests and work of colleagues, but the outcomes of such engagement activities will further the interests of the institution as much, if not more, than individual members of staff involved. This is in contrast to the outcomes of more organic engagement activities that may further the interests of particular individuals. Of course, those engagement opportunities that fulfil the interests and needs of both the individual and the institution are highly desirable and are likely to attract greater buy-in and support.

Delivering an engagement-led strategy, and for it to be effective, requires a responsiveness and agility to continuously refine and develop the relationship and associated activities. Relationships between business schools and their partners are likely to evolve, and be more stable where the relationships are multidimensional. In all cases, there are five principles that need to underpin engagement with partners as identified in Box 8.2. These principles serve to guide the development of engagement as strategy, and a good strategy is about being different. In the case of engagement as strategy, this demands that business schools choose different sets of activities to deliver value in a range of ways. Delivering the business of business schools often demands trade-offs, and these trade-offs are often necessary to sustain our work. However, an engagement-led approach can better leverage

> **Box 8.2 Five Principles of Engagement as Strategy**
>
> **Purpose**: Meaningful engagement will only occur when the strategy is aligned with the mission and vision. This ensures that engagement is authentic and resonates with staff, students and stakeholders who share similar values.
>
> **Authenticity**: A fundamental aspect of engagement is authenticity. Without intent and meaning engagement can be reduced to activity and outcomes. Partners, stakeholders and wider society are more likely to engage where engagement is underpinned with integrity.
>
> **Trust**: A critical component for successful engagement is trust. Universities need to work to establish and maintain trust with their partners, stakeholders and wider society by ensuring transparency and consistency in their actions and communications.
>
> **Adaptability**: Strategies for engagement need to be sufficiently agile and adaptable in order to respond to changing contexts and circumstances, as well as the evolving needs of partners and stakeholders. This can mean being prepared to adjust the approach as necessary.
>
> **Communication**: By its nature, engagement demands effective communication. This starts with dialogues around co-creation, listening to feedback, appreciating concerns and incorporating views into the design and decision-making.

synergies across domains in ways that more siloed approaches struggle to realise. Fundamentally, it is about understanding how domains of engagement and the engagement activities therein relate, and more importantly may be coordinated, combined and consolidated. Where there is a good 'strategic fit' or complementarity of engagement activities across different domains, this can serve to reinforce the strengths of a business school and, with it, the school's performance. Yet, as good and clear as the strategy might be, its implementation depends on leadership – and increasingly bold leadership given the challenges facing the higher education sector.

Engaged Leadership and Enabling Engagement

As a leader in a business school, like many others, I am often preoccupied with laying the foundations to deliver for the next assessment or accreditation exercise. However, such a culture – whether driven by compliance or competition – is one that can detract from the essence of leadership. As a once self-proclaimed 'engaged academic', I have since become invested in the concept of engaged leadership, which is premised on the active involvement, commitment and connection between leaders and their teams.

In this way, engaged leadership is about fostering a highly collaborative way of working, in the case of universities, between the leadership team and academic and professional services colleagues. Creating a supportive work environment, by aligning the institutional interests of universities and the individual interests of colleagues, working together towards shared goals. To achieve this, many of the same principles identified in Box 8.2 apply, and, in addition, engaged leaders need to create the environment to empower colleagues to engage with partners, stakeholders and civic society.

As discussed above, the foundations and focus of engagement can be wide ranging, and transcend research and knowledge exchange, education and student success, and societal contributions. Adopting an 'engagement as strategy' led approach can be unifying, especially since the major assessment or accreditation exercises have come to increasingly value the importance of engagement. In the UK, this is true of the REF, which explicitly values engagement and impact; the Teaching Excellence Framework (TEF), that values engagement through various student experience measures; and the Knowledge Exchange Framework (KEF), that values working with business as well as public and community engagement.

In the world of business schools, engagement is again valued by the main accrediting bodies in different ways. The latest standards of the Association to Advance Collegiate Schools of Business, better known as the AACSB, have introduced an explicit focus on thought leadership, engagement and societal impact. The two relevant standards focus on the 'impact of scholarship' on external stakeholders and 'engagement and societal impact' that contributed to the betterment of society (see AACSB, 2023). Likewise, the European Foundation for Management Development, better known as the EFMD, emphasises the connections with practice across its standards across all areas of the business school.

Such assessment and accreditation frameworks do, as Wilson (2015, cited in Kitchener et al., 2022) suggests, provide a means to manage elements which are essential for high performance. However, I would suggest that leading an engaged business school is about more than managing performance. Recognising the strategic value of engagement requires business schools to assume a more inclusive and adaptive approach. In this way, such frameworks are less about managing performance than evaluating performance and demonstrating success as intended.

The challenge for business school leaders is to move beyond the constraints of stewardship and build a vision for the future. As higher education and wider society continues to face challenging times, the future of business schools are as purpose-driven agents of change. Delivering an engagement-led strategy requires maintaining a broad perspective, and having confidence in making the shift from engagement as activity to engagement as culture. Achieving this cultural change is contingent on understanding, and while this starts with a strategy co-created with partners, stakeholders and civic society – its success is dependent on colleagues across the business school understanding the value and importance of engagement.

Conclusion

Business schools should, and can be crucibles of engagement, but engagement is a strategic choice. In describing the 'business of business schools' Peters et al. (2022) note the need for business schools to be managed in a business-like manner. The essence of engagement as strategy is to ensure that engagement across different domains both aligns with and augments the mission, vision and business objectives of business schools. Engagement serves to add value to business schools by creating a positive and collaborative environment that benefits staff and students as well as external partners, stakeholders and civic society.

Engagement is not new, but thinking about engagement as strategy requires business school leaders to make choices about what matters both to and beyond the business school. In this respect, engagement isn't about a formula or set of activities, but, if developed with the mission and vision, can serve to reinforce the purpose of the business school and provide a source of competitive advantage. Ultimately, this will see engagement become an intrinsic part of the business school and integral to its success, but will always by its nature be subject to continuous improvement.

Considering engagement as a strategy requires business school leaders to decide what matters. Not just for the school, but for the broader context in which the business school operates. To this end, engagement is more than a prescribed formula or a set of activities. When aligned with the school's mission and vision, it can strengthen the school's purpose and offer a competitive edge. Ultimately, engagement as strategy sees engagement an intrinsic part of the business school and engagement is integral to its success, but will always be subject to continuous improvement.

References

AACSB. (2023). *2020 Guiding principles and standards for AACSB business accreditation,* https://www.aacsb.edu/-/media/documents/accreditation/2020-aacsb-business-accreditation-standards-june-2023.pdf?rev=d31cfbe864e54792816ff426fe913e65&hash=33A159779F107443A64BDACBBB7000C5

Aronowitz, S. (2001). *The knowledge factory: Dismantling the corporate university and creating true higher learning.* Beacon Press.

Etzkowitz, H. (1993). Technology transfer: The second academic revolution. *Technology Access Report,* 6, 7–9.

Hughes, A., Lawson, C., Kitson, M., Salter, A., Bullock, A., & Hughes, R. (2016). *The Changing State of Knowledge Exchange: UK Academic Interactions with External Organisations 2005–2015.* National Centre for Universities and Business. https://www.ncub.co.uk/index.php?option=com_docman&view=download&alias=429-the-changing-state-of-knowledge-exchange&category_slug=reports&Itemid=2728

Kerr, C. (2001). *The uses of the university* (Vol. 29). Harvard University Press.

Kitchener, M., Levitt, T., & Thomas, L. (2022). Towards purposeful business schools: Deepening and broadening external engagement. *Futures,* 144, 103042.

Marginson, S., & Considine, M. (2000). *The enterprise university: Power, governance and reinvention in Australia.* Cambridge University Press.

Nandy, M., Lodh, S., & Tang, A. (2021). Lessons from Covid-19 and a resilience model for higher education. *Industry and Higher Education,* 35(1), 3–9.

NCCPE (National Co-ordinating Centre for Public Engagement). (2022). 'What does an engaged university look like?'. NCCPE. Accessed 19 September 2023. https://www.publicengagement.ac.uk/aboutengagement/what-does-engaged-university-look

Peters, K., Thomas, H., & Smith, R. (2022). *The business of business schools in the value & purpose of management education* (pp. 86–93). Routledge.

Thomas, L., & Ambrosini, V. (2021). The future role of the business school: A value cocreation perspective. *Academy of Management Learning & Education,* 20(2), 249–269.

Vorley, T., & Nelles, J. (2009). Building entrepreneurial architectures: A conceptual interpretation of the third mission. *Policy Futures in Education,* 7(3), 284–296.

Wilson, C. (2015). *Designing the purposeful organization: How to inspire business performance beyond boundaries* (1st. ed.). Kogan Page.

9 From Purpose to Impact

From Partnerships to Shaping Systems

Carolin Plewa, Judith Helmer, Katrin Uude,
Jodie Conduit, and Natalie Forde

Introduction

Since their inception, universities have been important anchor points for the communities in which they exist. Independent of their distinctive missions, roles or circumstances, universities have demonstrated unique contributions to the social, cultural and economic fabric of society. The ability of universities to make a difference to society has commonly been linked to university–industry engagement as a central pathway to achieving such impact. Universities create a rich environment for discovery through fundamental and cutting-edge research and innovation solving today's social challenges. They drive economic growth by generating new or advancing the competitiveness of current business or industries, develop human capital in line with current and future needs, and develop pathways for talent. Over the years, universities have transformed from isolated institutions with a focus on human capital development and/or a research-focused mission, to actors in a quadruple helix system, with multiple connections to engaged actors across science, policy, industry and society (Carayannis & Campbell, 2009). It is this collective engagement that creates a pathway to impact, through the collaborative efforts of universities and actors across all corners of society.

Recent years and decades have seen prolific research into university–industry engagement, as evidenced, for example, in the bibliometric review of fifty years of research on university–industry collaboration conducted by Bastos, Sengik and Tello-Gamarra (2021). In particular, we have seen an increase in the discourse on the diversity of interactions and mechanisms through which universities and other actors may engage (Galan-Muros & Davey, 2017), along with a recognition of the importance of strong relationships or partnerships as compared to transactional approaches or the simple one-way transfer of knowledge (Clauss & Kesting, 2017; Davey et al., 2018). However, there is still little known about

DOI: 10.4324/9781003459217-10

the role of universities in the transformation of the societies at scale. In an era where society is eager to adopt sustainable development goals and embrace new technologies, there is a need for universities to be part of a transformation agenda.

This chapter adopts the perspective that understanding and advancing university–industry engagement from the view of partnerships, and the individuals and organisations that drive such partnerships, is not sufficient to achieve the transformative impact society needs. While building an important foundation, it is now that we need to understand how we jointly design the system in which impact can thrive. How we generate and advance the collective or shared engagement towards a clear vision and purpose, is what will enable the impact and transformation needed to address opportunities and challenges of modern society. Drawing on contemporary thinking on market shaping and collective engagement, this chapter aims to instigate a discussion that takes purpose to impact beyond the university–industry partnership and will lead to tangible actions and developments in the future.

From Purpose to Impact

With the positive impact of universities on the prosperity of their cities and regions well documented, attributed commonly to related advances in human capital and innovation (Valero & van Reenen, 2019), universities and, in turn academics, are increasingly asked to explain and evidence their positive contribution to society. Such impact is commonly understood to be "mobilized" (Watermeyer, 2012) by engagement with a diverse range of stakeholders, a reason for the significant policy, practice and academic discourse on university–industry engagement or collaboration over many years (Bastos et al., 2021).

Along with significant emphasis on the role of strong and long-standing relationships and partnerships for the realisation of mutual benefits (Boehm & Hogan, 2013), much focus to date has been given to the roles of individuals who support both the diversity of engagement activities and the development and advancement of strong and lasting partnerships. In particular, research has investigated what motivates academics to engage (Lam, 2011; Orazbayeva and Plewa, 2020), and the skills and identity of staff required to effectively span cross-institutional and sectoral boundaries (Martin & Ibbotson, 2019; Prysor & Henley, 2017). Indeed, discussions increasingly emerge on academic identity and on what it means to be an open or impactful academic (Kelly, 2022; McCarthy & Bogers, 2023); a focus area of this book, and a critical area of development for the future.

A similar discourse has emerged at the institutional level, with extensive conversations across researchers, practitioners and policymakers on the identity, role and future of universities (e.g. Orazbayeva et al., 2020), including, but not limited to, specific types of universities, may they be entrepreneurial (Guerrero & Urbano, 2012; Meissner, D., 2018), civic (Goddard et al., 2016), engaged (Breznitz & Feldman, 2012; Thomas & Pugh, 2020), or purpose driven (Haski-Levelnthal, 2020). Yet, to date, much of the discourse remains at the level of the partnership, the individual or the institution. Despite an early recognition of triple and quadruple helix (Leydesdorff, 2012; Miller et al., 2018) and of the university–industry ecosystem (Galan-Muros & Davey, 2017), our understanding of how we proactively encourage systemic change remains amiss. Yet, while changes to the individual and institutional mechanisms will allow for incremental, and significant, improvement of engagement and, in turn, impact, the urgency of many global challenges facing humankind requires a transformative and systemic change.

By drawing on the marketing literature that increasingly stresses markets as malleable, complex adaptive systems (Nenonen & Storbacka, 2020a) which are not given but become (Vargo & Lusch, 2004), we seek to instigate a discussion on how to design a system that facilitates transformative impact through universities' engagement with other actors. Actors, such as individuals or organisations, as part of these systems can take advantage of their malleability and shape them through purposive or purposeful actions (Hawa et al., 2020; Nenonen & Storbacka, 2020b). Changes to a market can relate (a) to the exchange processes in markets, such as in products, prices or methods of transaction, (b) to its actor network, such as in interactions with suppliers, customers and other providers, and (c) to institutional transmitters, such as the appearance of representations of the market and its norms (Nenonen et al., 2019). For example, with the emergence of ride sharing apps like Uber or Grab, they not only offer an alternative transportation option but have done so by re-thinking and re-designing who is involved, how the services are delivered, priced and offered, and what the nature of the experience should be.

Although market change happens in multiple or even all categories simultaneously as well as sequentially, we specifically focus here on institutional changes. Changes to institutional arrangements can reflect in habits, norms, routines, rules and laws which guide interactions of individual and collective actors (Lawrence & Suddaby, 2006). In fact, the existing literature on market change outlines that the institutional perspective is helpful to understand market change on a system level while linking to market shaping activities

(Storbacka, 2019). This perspective involves actors being able to understand existing institutional arrangements, such as norms, while being able to envision future institutional arrangements to shape markets.

As the university context is highly institutionalised, with specific norms and regulations, impactful changes will often require a change through institutional transmitters (Rybnicek & Königsgruber, 2018). Such changes most commonly arise in response to megatrends, such as digitalisation (Chubb et al., 2022) or the increasing relevance of societal challenges and impact (Bayuo et al., 2020). However, universities should critically examine these institutional transmitters and look to proactively modify them to achieve their transformative purpose. For example, clear norms exist regarding what it means to be an academic, and the roles that academics take in the university, such as education and/or research specialists. While some boundary positions, such as "industry professors" have emerged, future visions of a broader diversity of academics would require a shift of not just institutional, sectoral or national interpretation but an international one, given the global nature of the market for such talent. Indeed, with many calls for porous boundaries between academia, industry and government, and thus for fluid career pathways for scientific talents across sectors, recognised global indicators of performance may have to change. For example, we may see movement from individual, highly quantifiable, metrics-driven approaches to performance measurement to those focused on teams, on leadership and a portfolio of qualitative and quantitative short-term and long-term measures. Efforts to shape such norms on research assessment are visible in actors facilitating collective understanding and commitment, for example the San Francisco Declaration on Research Assessment.[1]

If we accept that universities operate and engage in a broader system, any efforts to change the institutions (norms, routines, habits and regulations) would require the efforts of multiple actors. Efforts to shape a market are rarely limited to one sole market actor but are the efforts of multiple actors (Sprong et al., 2021). In the university context, these actors go well beyond universities or higher education institutions. As also reflected in the quadruple helix model, at a high level, relevant actors also include firms, policymakers and society (Miller et al., 2018), and thus, a highly diverse range of individuals, collectives and organisations. To successfully shape a market, these actors can individually, as well as collectively, initiate shaping activities (Hawa et al., 2020), but to achieve institutional change, engagement among multiple actors in the market shaping process would be required (Kleinaltenkamp et al., 2021).

Initiating Impactful System Changes

While market shaping can take diverse forms and unfold in diverse possible pathways (Möller et al., 2020), there are three key steps that should occur in the process. First, multiple, relevant actors should be mobilised to be involved; second, a shared vision should be created among these actors; and third, these actors need to be collectively and meaningfully engaged to enact the shared purpose. We will now explore each of these steps using an example of energy transition as one of the greatest challenges that our society has ever faced.

Mobilising multiple actors and developing a shared vision. Making this happen requires the collaboration of multiple actors towards "market work" (Fehrer et al. 2020, p. 2). As "market-shaping is very much a collective endeavour" (Nenonen & Storbacka, 2020a, p. 267), the institutional change that is required relies on the collaboration of multiple actors, and thus collective actions towards market shaping. Successfully navigating a transition to new forms of energy requires intensive, long-term collaboration across a variety of stakeholders involved in the current energy system. This will include governments, industry leaders, niche industry players and disrupters, policymakers, the community and research institutions. Given the speed at which the energy landscape is evolving, if universities are not central to these collaborative efforts and do not assert their relevance and contributions, they risk being marginalised. Active participation ensures that their vast intellectual resources, diverse range of research endeavours – from fundamental to applied research – and academic insights remain integral to shaping and implementing effective transition strategies.

A principal first step in market shaping is the development of an impactful protovision (Nenonen & Storbacka, 2020a). This requires questioning the status-quo of a market and envisioning (an) alternative state(s) that would solve current problems, engaging market-shapers inside an organisation as well as other actors. In addition to understanding the market system and actors' value drivers, engaging multiple actors will help anticipate alternative visions for the market, and translate a favourable vision to other stakeholders. Through interaction with and the authoring of meaning for multiple actors, the initial protovision, initiated by a market-shaper, develops into a shared market vision. In this context, an important aspect is to guide the interaction towards a scalable market vision which focuses on long-term value creation and is supported by a critical mass. Ultimately, this establishes a clear purpose to achieve impactful change that is viable and durable in the market.

For example, in 2022, the Government of South Australia became the first state parliament in Australia to declare a Climate Emergency (South Australia (SA) Department for Environment and Water, 2022), reaffirming the urgent need to decarbonise South Australia and continue to grow renewable sources of energy (SA Government, 2022). One of their first activities was to mobilise key stakeholders, with a roundtable workshop that brought together over 100 industry, government, research and consumer stakeholders, representatives included householders, small to medium enterprises (SMEs), commercial and industrial (C&I) customers, energy industry participants, investors, producers, market bodies, peak bodies and research institutes (SA Department for Energy and Mining, 2023). Such activities were complemented by a range of initiatives shaped by various actors, such as university workshops and roundtables as well as large-scale research and translation activities, to name a few. Ongoing developments aimed at shaping the next steps of a systems transition included an open invitation to everyone to engage in shaping South Australia's Energy Future through consultation of a green paper, noting that "All South Australians are central to this consultation" (SA Department for Energy and Mining, 2023), generating a foundation for a shared vision.

Collective engagement. To better understand collective actions, researchers have drawn on actor engagement (Fehrer et al., 2020) and collective engagement (Kleinaltenkamp et al. 2019). Actor engagement is understood as a "dynamic and interactive process that reflects actors´ disposition to invest resources in their interaction with other connected actors in a service system" (Brodie et al. 2019, p. 2), and thus reflects engagement, for example with a new market vision or purpose, at the individual level. Whereas collective engagement reflects the manifestation of engagement across multiple actors and is defined as a "multiple actors´ shared cognitive, emotional, and behavioral disposition, as manifested in their interactive efforts devoted to a focal object" (Kleinaltenkamp et al. 2019, p. 12). The definition of collective engagement describes engagement as a shared phenomenon, pointing out that it presents not the sum or average of the engagement of the individual actors (Storbacka, 2019), but an emerging phenomenon that is more than the sum of the individual parts (Kleinaltenkamp et al., 2019).

In considering how universities engage with the energy sector (as our example), most commonly noted are those activities that are easily visible; jointly developing curriculum, collaborative research, a joint event, or discussions facilitated by co-location. While this behavioural focus on engagement behaviour is most visible in the engagement literature, it is important to note that engagement is a multi-dimensional construct, as agreed upon in recent business literature (Conduit et al., 2019). Consumer and actor engagement is commonly understood to comprise the dimensions of cognitive (thought-based), emotional (feeling-based) and behavioural (activity-based) engagement (Hollebeek & Andreassen, 2018; Kleinaltenkamp et al. 2019), describing different kinds of resources invested by an actor. These resources are devoted to a focal object, describing a real object, an activity, another actor or an idea, an actor can be engaged with. In the context of the energy transition, and indeed in many other market shaping initiatives, the focal engagement object is often an idea, or indeed the protovision. For example, if we think about someone's engagement with a new vision for energy transition, cognitive engagement reflects their knowledge investment, thoughts about and reflection on that vision. Emotional engagement, and thus the invested feelings, signal the emotions they feel regarding the vision, may that be excitement or pride that we are creating a better society, or in the case of negative engagement, anxiousness or fear. Behavioural engagement may be reflected in the voluntary investment of, for instance, participation, effort or monetary resources to make the vision a reality. In fostering collective engagement, universities need to be cognisant and manage for each of these dimensions of engagement, ensuring positive investments across cognitive, emotional and behavioural aspects.

Impacting system change through engagement. Importantly, for universities to significantly shape their societal impact through university–industry engagement, engagement at the collective level is required. Engagement needs to go beyond individual partners and individual actors jointly engaging with a future-focused vision. Collective engagement requires all parties working in unison with a concerted and aligned approach to achieve impactful, systematic change. For collective-level engagement, there are two pathways: either the actors commence the innovation project with shared understandings and similar contextual conditions (Bakker et al., 2006), or engagement evolves from contagion: as one actor engages, this influences the engagement of a "nearby" actor (Torrente et al., 2013). In the latter scenario, the transition to a collective is more probable when a larger number of actors are involved and when individual engagement is particularly intense. Focusing on actors demonstrating high engagement with the protovision becomes instrumental in kickstarting the contagion effect, and thereby stimulating the emergence of collective engagement. Additionally, possessing a robust and compelling protovision is essential to achieve collective cognitive and emotional engagement. Such collective engagement is indispensable for generating a sufficiently robust and impactful engagement that drives systemic change and delivers tangible outcomes. Recognising the importance of collective engagement becomes crucial to the academic–business context.

For instance, in the pursuit of transitioning to renewable energy sources, all actors can work together providing knowledge to conduct research on economic feasibility, environmental impact assessments and innovative technological solutions. This knowledge exchange aids in informed decision-making and policy formulation for a sustainable energy shift. This collective engagement necessitates structured and frequent interactions. Regular meetings serve as platforms for exchanging progress updates and aligning strategies. A shared language, common understanding and storytelling based on successful case studies from other regions ensure a cohesive approach towards energy transition. To ensure success, a co-design methodology, involving active participation from all parties, fosters joint ownership and commitment to formulated strategies. Continuous dialogue and discussions enable swift adaptation to changing circumstances and emerging challenges. This approach not only ensures the development of a robust protovision and strategy, but perhaps, more importantly, it fosters and maintains the collective engagement among all actors.

Conclusion

There is no doubt that universities can continue to enhance the way they partner with a variety of external stakeholders, how they support their staff and students in their efforts to generate impact and the way they design institutional structures, processes and cultural facets to improve their positive impact on society; changes universities globally appear committed to engage in, with support from policymakers and partners. However, for us to truly address the global challenges of our time, and to significantly advance global prosperity and peace through progress in the United Nations Sustainable Development Goals, we need change at the system level.

This chapter is positioned as a conversation starter, by introducing the underpinnings of market shaping and collective engagement to university–industry engagement. We hope that it will instigate a discussion on what comes next; a discussion that takes us beyond a focus on individual universities, individual partnerships or even partnership clusters, to visions of systems, fostering not just behavioural but emotional and cognitive engagement of a large group with such vision, and the ways in which various actors influence changes in the habits, norms, routines, rules and laws necessary to move towards such vision.

Note

1 https://sfdora.org and the Coalition for Advancing Research Assessment (https://coara.edu/).

References

Bakker, A. B., Emmerik, H. V., & Euwema, M. C. (2006). Crossover of burn-out and engagement in work teams. *Work and occupations*, 33(4), 464–489.

Bastos, E. C., Sengik, A. R., & Tello-Gamarra, J. (2021). Fifty years of university–industry collaboration: A global bibliometrics overview. *Science and Public Policy*, 48(2), 177–199.

Bayuo, B. B., Chaminade, C., & Göransson, B. (2020). Unpacking the role of universities in the emergence, development and impact of social innovations – A systematic review of the literature. *Technological Forecasting and Social Change*, 155, 120030.

Boehm, D. N., & Hogan, T. (2013). Science-to-business collaborations: A science-to-business marketing perspective on scientific knowledge commercialization. *Industrial Marketing Management*, 42, 564–579.

Breznitz, S. M., & Feldman, M. P. (2012). The engaged university. *Journal of Technology Transfer*, 37, 139–157.

Brodie, R. J., Fehrer, J. A., Jaakkola, E., & Conduit, J. (2019). Actor engagement in networks: Defining the conceptual domain. *Journal of Service Research*, 22(2), 173–188.

Carayannis, E. G., & Campbell, D. F. (2009). 'Mode 3' and 'Quadruple Helix': Toward a 21st century fractal innovation ecosystem. *International Journal of Technology Management*, 46(3/4), 201.

Chubb, J., Cowling, P., & Reed, D. (2022). Speeding up to keep up: Exploring the use of AI in the research process. *AI & Society*, 37(4), 1439–1457. https://doi.org/10.1007/s00146-021-01259-0

Clauss, T., & Kesting, T. (2017). How businesses should govern knowledge-intensive collaborations with universities: An empirical investigation of university professors. *Industrial Marketing Management*, 62, 185–198.

Conduit, J., Karpen, I. O., & Tierney, K. D. (2019). Volunteer engagement: Conceptual extensions and value-in-context outcomes. *Journal of Service Theory and Practice*, 29(4), 462–487.

Davey, T., Meerman, A., Galan-Muros, V., Orazbayeva, B., & Baaken, T. (2018). *The state of university–industry cooperation in Europe: Final report*. ©European Union, accessible online: Final_report_14_05_2018.indd (ub-cooperation.eu)

Fehrer, J. A., Conduit, J., Plewa, C., Li, L. P., Jaakkola, E., & Alexander, M. (2020). Market shaping dynamics: Interplay of actor engagement and institutional work. *Journal of Business & Industrial Marketing*, 35(9), 1425–1439.

Galan-Muros, V., & Davey, T. (2017). The UBE ecosystem: Putting together a comprehensive framework for university–industry cooperation. *Journal of Technology Transfer*, 10, 1–36.

Goddard, J., Hazelkorn, E., Kempton, L., & Vallance, P. (2016). *The Civic University: The policy and leadership challenges*. Edward Elgar Publishing Limited.

Guerrero, M., & Urbano, D. (2012). The development of an entrepreneurial university. *Journal of Technology Transfer*, 37, 43–74.

Haski-Levelnthal, D. (2020) *The purpose-driven university: Transforming lives and creating impact through academic social responsibility*. Emerald Publishing.

Hawa, J., Baker, J., & Plewa, C. (2020). Composing markets: A framework of intentionality in market-shaping. *Journal of Business Research*, 121, 47–57.

Hollebeek, L. D., & Andreassen, T. W. (2018). The SD logic-informed "hamburger" model of service innovation and its implications for engagement and value. *Journal of Services Marketing*, 32(1), 1–7.

Kelly, W. (2022). The impactful academic: Building a research career that makes a difference. Emerald Publishing.

Kleinaltenkamp, M., Conduit, J., Plewa, C., Karpen, I. O. and Jaakkola, E. (2021). Engagement-driven institutionalization in market shaping: Synchronizing and stabilizing collective engagement. *Industrial Marketing Management*, 99, 69–78.

Kleinaltenkamp, M., Karpen, I. O., Plewa, C., Jaakkola, E., & Conduit, J. (2019). Collective engagement in organizational settings. *Industrial Marketing Management*, 80, 11–23.

Lam, A. (2011). What motivates academic scientists to engage in research commercialisation: 'Gold', 'ribbon', or 'puzzle'? *Research Policy*, 49(10), 1354–1368.

Lawrence, T. B., & Suddaby, R. (2006). Institutions and institutional work. In S. Clegg, C. Hardy, T. Lawrence, & W. Nord (Eds.), *The SAGE Handbook of Organization Studies* (pp. 215–254). SAGE Publications Ltd.

Leydesdorff, L. (2012) The Triple Helix, Quadruple Helix, …, and an N-Tuple of Helices: Explanatory models for analyzing the knowledge-based economy? *Journal of the Knowledge Economy*, 3, 25–35.

Martin, L., & Ibbotson, P. (2019) Boundary spanning as identity work in the university business engagement roles. *Studies in Higher Education*, 46(7), 1272–1284.

McCarthy, I. P., and Bogers, M. L.A.M. (2023). The open academic: Why and how business academics should use social media to be more 'open' and impactful. *Business Horizons*, 66(1), 153–166.

Meissner, D. (2018). Entrepreneurial universities: Towards a revised paradigm. In D. Meissner, E. Erdil, & J. Chataway (Eds), *Innovation and the Entrepreneurial University* (pp. 37–55).

Miller, K., McAdam, R., & McAdam, M. (2018). A systematic literature review of university technology transfer from a quadruple helix perspective: Toward a research agenda. *R&D Management*, 48(1), 7–24.

Möller, K., Nenonen, S., & Storbacka, K. (2020). Networks, ecosystems, fields, market systems? Making sense of the business environment. *Industrial Marketing Management*, 90, 380–399.

Nenonen, S., & Storbacka, K. (2020a). Don't adapt, shape! Use the crisis to shape your minimum viable system – And the wider market. *Industrial Marketing Management*, 88, 265–271.

Nenonen, S., & Storbacka, K. (2020b). On the marketness of markets and actor clout: Market-shaping roles. *Journal of Service Management Research*, 4(2–3), 170–184.

Nenonen, S., Storbacka, K., & Frethey-Bentham, C. (2019). Is your industrial marketing work working? Developing a composite index of market change. *Industrial Marketing Management*, 80, 251–265.

Orazbayeva, B., Meerman, A., Galan-Muros, V., Davey, T., Plewa, C. (Eds). (2020). *The future of universities thoughtbook – During times of crisis edition*, University-Industry Innovation Network, ISBN 9789491901508.

Orazbayeva, B., & Plewa, C. (2020). Academic motivations to engage in university–industry cooperation: A fuzzy set analysis. *Studies in Higher Education*, 47(3), 486–498.

Prysor, D., & Henley, A. (2017). Boundary spanning in higher education leadership: Identifying boundaries and practices in a British university. *Studies in Higher Education*, 43(12), 2210–2225.

Rybnicek, R., & Königsgruber, R. (2018). What makes university–industry collaboration succeed? A systematic review of the literature. *Journal of Business Economics*, 89, 221–250.

SA [South Australia] Department for Environment and Water South Australia (2022, 1 June). *Australia declares climate emergency*, accessible online https://www.environment.sa.gov.au/news-hub/news/articles/2022/06/south-australia-declares-climate-emergency#:~:text=%E2%80%9CSouth%20 Australia%20will%20be%20the,hydrogen%20plant%20in%20 South%20Australia

SA Department for Energy and Mining (2023). *South Australia's Energy Future*, accessible online https://yoursay.sa.gov.au/energytransition#:~:text= The%20Government%20of%20South%20Australia,the%20people%20 who%20regulate%20it

SA Government (2022, 31 May), *Climate emergency declaration passes in Parliament*, accessible online https://www.premier.sa.gov.au/media-releases/ news-items/climate-emergency-declaration-passes-in-parliament

Sprong, N., Driessen, P. H., Hillebrand, B., & Molner, S. (2021). Market innovation: A literature review and new research directions. *Journal of Business Research*, 123, 450–462.

Storbacka, K. (2019). Actor engagement, value creation and market innovation. *Industrial Marketing Management*, 80, 4–10.

Thomas, E., & Pugh, R. (2020). From 'entrepreneurial' to 'engaged' universities: Social innovation for regional development in the Global South. *Regional Studies*, 54(12), 1631–1643.

Torrente, P., Salanova, M., & Llorens, S. (2013). Spreading engagement: On the role of similarity in the positive contagion of team work engagement. *Revista de Psicología del Trabajo y de las Organizaciones*, 29(3), 153–159.

Valero, A., & van Reenen, J. (2019). The economic impact of universities: Evidence from across the globe. *Economics Education Review*, 68, 53–67.

Vargo, S. L., & Lusch, R. F. (2004). Evolving to a New Dominant Logic for Marketing. *Journal of Marketing*, 68(1), 1–17.

Watermeyer, R. (2012). From engagement to impact? Articulating the public value of academic research. *Tertiary Education and Management*, 18, 115–130.

10 Not Just Academic

Strategies to Keep Rigorous Research Relevant

Ahmad Beltagui and Michael A. Hitt

Introduction

In an address to the Academy of Management in 1997, the audience were invited to consider how the world would look 13 years into the future, in the year 2010. Looking back at that imagined future, another 13 years on, is fascinating. It is hard to argue that the pace of technological change has accelerated, that information systems and the internet have grown in importance nor that the development, diffusion and use of knowledge lies at the heart of competition. With smart phones and machine learning, we do indeed *"expect machines that learn, diagnose, adapt, reconfigure and recreate themselves...largely driven by...the sound and touch of humans"* (Hitt, 1998, p. 220). Yet, although mobile connectivity means we *"expect people to be continuously online while traveling or moving around"* have we really removed the *"boundary between training and doing"*? Technology is drastically different but is what we teach and how we teach in business schools so different in 2023 from 2010 or even 1997? And is the knowledge developed and diffused in business schools any more useful or relevant? The relevance of business and management research has consistently been questioned over several decades (Carton & Mouricou, 2017; Hambrick, 1994; Palmer et al., 2009; Starkey & Madan, 2001). Articles published in the top management journals between 1960 and 2010 have been found to have declining practical value for managers (Lambert, 2019). Thus, critics have characterized academic research as being of little practical value and the ultimate criticism of something irrelevant is often to say it is academic (Toffel, 2016).

High quality (rigorous) scholarly research is important for developing new knowledge thereby providing a foundational base for the continuing development and understanding of critical topics in the management field (Hitt & Greer, 2012). Such research also offers the basis for textbooks and teaching in business schools. The best textbooks integrate research and practice, explaining concepts

DOI: 10.4324/9781003459217-11

derived from rigorous research through cases and examples that demonstrate relevance (Hitt et al., 2020; Johnston et al., 2020). Yet, there is also a case to be made that insisting on relevance can prevent new knowledge creation. For example, James March argues that researchers should focus on new concepts. He suggests *"the primary usefulness of management research lies in the development of fundamental ideas that might shape managerial thinking, not in the solution of immediate managerial problems"* (March, in Starkey & Madan, 2001). Meanwhile the best practices, "passing fads" and "management gimmicks" (ibid) can be left to management consultants. According to this logic, management research can be seen as analogous to R&D, creating the products and services of the future, as opposed to operations and marketing, making and selling those available today. Thus, some believe the focus on rigor in scholarly research, without a corresponding focus on relevance, is justified. Taken too far, this logic leads some to view engaging with specific business problems with suspicion as a moral dilemma. As the main character in the business novel, Critical Chain suggests:

> *"Consulting for me is almost equal to prostitution. But maybe I'm just affected by people who didn't dare go out in the real world. People who prefer producing worthless articles to being judged by tangible results"*

(Goldratt, 1997, p. 131)

The author's cynicism is clear, and the character's opinion changes due to the realization that engaging with MBAs on their real struggles helps to generate original theory. The novel describes the perspective of a struggling academic in search of tenure, in a struggling business school, who develops the Critical Chain project management approach by applying Theory of Constraints to innovation projects. It perhaps offers a template for developing research and theory in an engaged manner, such that its relevance stems from being informed by real problems and its rigor comes from applying theory to inform real decisions. It is, however, a fictional story; can the same results be achieved in reality?

Here it helps to reflect on how academics responded to the COVID-19 pandemic. Given the unprecedented nature of the events, decision-makers were largely unprepared and therefore much more open than usual to insights and support from any perspective. Management scholars responded very rapidly, both by bringing existing knowledge to bear on the problems and by studying events to generate new insights. For example, the rapid repurposing of technologies and reconfiguration of organizations offered a perfect opportunity to apply prior research on innovation ecosystem formation (Adner & Kapoor, 2016; Ansari et al., 2016; Beltagui et al., 2020). Prior studies had examined ecosystems over years or decades, deriving theoretical insights from historical data or participants' recollections. In this case, an ecosystem formed to produce medical ventilators, designed a new product, created a supply chain, produced large volumes and then reached the end of its life within a few months (Liu et al., 2021b). Academics applied the concept of exaptation (the discovery of latent functionality in existing technologies), which had previously been applied only to historical cases, to understand what was happening (Liu et al., 2021a). And used the pandemic as an opportunity to test and develop knowledge on entrepreneurship (Kuckertz et al., 2020), crisis management (Rodríguez-Espíndola et al., 2020), digital transformation (Kunovjanek & Wankmüller, 2020; Rapaccini et al., 2020) and open innovation (Chesbrough, 2020; McGahan et al., 2021).

This chapter looks at what lessons can be learned and how to make rigor and relevance reinforcing rather than conflicting objectives for business schools and management research. It identifies three key capabilities that academics should seek to develop and deploy, stakeholder engagement, agility and resource orchestration. In doing so, it draws on the recommendations of research for firms, which can be applied to the way that research is conducted and knowledge is generated.

The Challenges

Easy access to big data and powerful analytical tools means it has never been easier to conduct highly sophisticated analysis without ever having to interact with people. In the past, gathering data could be a laborious process, whereas today researchers can rapidly access company data, from annual sales figures to greenhouse gas emissions, or individuals' opinions, perspectives, likes and dislikes. It is no longer necessary to directly interview or survey people because their perspectives are widely and publicly shared through official documents and social media posts. And, we can apply traditional statistical tools along with automated natural language processing and machine learning, to analyze everything from the overall positive or negative sentiment of online reviews to the specific words and phrases that might attract investors to a business venture. With little or no statistical training, researchers can use a host of software packages and analytical tools to perform increasingly sophisticated statistical work. Without experiencing the practical challenges of collecting data, we can therefore split our time evenly between rigorous analysis and theoretical framing to explain the results we find.

Theory, of course, is vital in order to publish rigorous research in the top journals. In the past, many observations could be considered as novel contributions because they had not yet been written and published. Today, it can be difficult to demonstrate an idea is truly novel because so much more has been communicated in some form, by so many people. As a result, we must use and develop more sophisticated concepts and theories to frame and explain what has been observed. Clearly, explaining rather than simply describing, is incredibly useful. However, the management field's

> *"theory fetish ... prevents the reporting of rich detail about interesting phenomena for which no theory yet exists. And it bans the reporting of facts – no matter how important or competently generated – that lack explanation, but that, once reported, might stimulate the search for an explanation".*
>
> (Hambrick, 2007, p. 1346)

While academics, driven by the publish-or-perish mentality, focus attention on theory and methodological rigor, words such as impact have become ominously ubiquitous. Policymakers and funding bodies are concerned with a triple helix (Etzkowitz & Leydesdorff, 2000) to bring the benefits to industrial and political concerns to the fore. Research funding increasingly requires a theory of change, often expressed in a model, that explains the logic underlying the expected benefits arising from the research. In this context, academic outputs, i.e., journal publications, are not viewed as the end but rather the beginning of the story. Researchers are challenged to show not only the relevance of their work but also the actions and mechanisms they plan to use to make the world a better place. They must not only create new knowledge, nor merely communicate it to the expected beneficiaries but also help those beneficiaries to understand and implement this knowledge.

The Solution

Herbert Simon (1996) distinguished between natural sciences, whose aim is to discover the rules governing the world we find ourselves in, and artificial sciences, which focus on designing and redesigning the world. With this distinction in mind, the nature and role of theory should differ between, for example, understanding the fundamental rules of biology that explain natural ecosystems and developing guidelines for business ecosystems. Yet, a major concern is that the design sciences are often understood and taught as though they were natural sciences (Simon, 1996). Business schools and management scholars have a need for legitimacy that leads to 'physics envy' (Thomas & Wilson, 2011). They seek ever more sophisticated theories and rigorous methodologies to demonstrate the intellectual legitimacy of management research and to show that the business school is more than just a cash cow. In doing so, it is possible that some researchers lose sight of the practical problems their research can and should address. As Mentzer (2008) argues, rigor is *"the constant examination of whether research can actually support and justify the claims it makes ... not ... the use of increasingly complex methodologies just to prove we can use them"* (Mentzer, 2008, p. 72). Yet too often, we equate the use of references or the use of methodologies with genuine theory development (Sutton & Staw, 1995; Weick, 1995).

If we assume natural sciences, like (theoretical) physics, focus on analysis and explanation, design sciences, like management, should focus on synthesis and action (Starkey et al., 2009). Design has been defined as any act of changing the world to shape current situations into preferred ones (Evans et al., 1982; Simon, 1996). Just as firms can choose to adopt an adaptive or shaping strategy (Rindova & Courtney, 2020), so can academics choose analysis or synthesis. An adaptive strategy involves reactively changing an organization in response to changes in the external environment. A shaping strategy proactively changes the competitive landscape, institutional environment and technology (Hitt et al., 2023a). Similarly, management researchers can choose to study and seek to explain what exists, or else proactively set out to influence and shape the environment they study. They may choose to advance knowledge by testing preconceived theories. Alternatively, they can choose a strategy of intervention seeking to learn the reasons reality does not confirm to theory (Oliva, 2019). This is, perhaps, even more important when we consider the educational role of business schools. Students can be directed to develop deep knowledge of theories and expertise in the rigorous application of methods. They could also be supported in learning by doing and gaining the ability to shape the organizations they create and lead. The value of focusing solely on theory is limited and continues to decline as generative AI develops. What matters more may be understanding and applying theory and methods to make decisions and shape the world.

Three capabilities are needed. First, the ability to engage deeply with stakeholders and beneficiaries. Second, the ability to act in an agile manner, being open to experimentation, action and course-correction. Third, the ability to combine and recombine networks, resources, methods and theories in support of the research strategy.

Stakeholder Engagement

Barney (2018) argues that a more complete understanding of how managers create value requires stakeholder engagement be integrated into the management of resources (resource-based view). This is true for scholarly research in business schools as well. Thus, engagement with stakeholders is critical, or the relevance of research may be lost. If practitioners are viewed merely as data points, the "managerial implications" section of an article is likely be superficial. Instead, there should be a regular meaningful interaction with practitioners that allows researchers to better understand and, hopefully, influence managers' decisions. For example, when studying the context of a new technology or specific market, researchers can attend relevant meetings, trade shows and events. These will allow a first-hand appreciation of the language these stakeholders use and the issues that concern them most. Toffel (2016) suggests setting up a sounding board of practitioners, who may be acquaintances or former students but who can help to validate the work being done. Without such engagement, there is often a risk of spotting gaps in knowledge that are meaningless beyond a narrow academic audience. Instead, examining the extent to which academic theories stand up to real-world problems can help to frame research questions through problematization (Alvesson & Sandberg, 2011). When theory does not fully explain observed phenomena, there is an opportunity to develop alternative explanations and thereby advance knowledge. While this must be carried out in a rigorous manner, taking managers' problems as the starting point can keep the research relevant. For example, the theory of disruptive innovation (Christensen, 1997), developed in part through the inability of existing theories to explain or inform practice. Christensen reported conversations with managers who had the latest technologies literally sitting on a shelf but needed a new perspective to understand the unseen opportunities and threats facing them.

> these companies did not fail because the technology wasn't available. They did not fail because they lacked information about hydraulics or how to use it; indeed, the best of them used it as soon as it could help their customers. They did not fail because management was sleepy or arrogant. They failed because hydraulics didn't make sense – until it was too late.
>
> (Christensen, 1997, p. 73)

The research on mergers and acquisitions has produced multiple, and often conflicting, explanations for their success and lack thereof. Hitt et al., (2023b) identified four different types of mergers which entailed different combinations of capabilities and their performance outcomes (large dataset of more than 3000 mergers). To better understand the why some of these mergers performed better than others, they identified the ten highest and lowest performing mergers in each group and then collected all published data (e.g., company press releases, CEO interviews, business media accounts) available on each of these mergers. This information was used to develop case descriptions of the mergers in which reasons for the performance outcomes were identified. These case data showed that the integration process was critical to gain the most value from the acquired firm's capabilities. For example, RCM Technologies was unable to build synergy with, and gain value from, the different "solutions" firms it acquired. RCM developed a new solutions unit, integrating all of the firms acquired into it. The top executives of the acquired firms were required to remain with RCM and in the management of the solutions unit for at least two years. However, this policy was ineffective. The former CEOs of the acquired firms were now two levels below the CEO, all grouped into a solutions division. Several of the managers of the acquired firms departed after their contracts were completed. The case data also showed that, even in the category of mergers with the lowest average performance, some mergers produced high value. For example, using a targeted acquisition strategy, Symantec transformed from competing only in the antivirus product market to competing in the much broader corporate security market. In the integration process, Symantec depended greatly on the managers in the acquired firms, treating them as stakeholders and thereby managing the acquired business as a part of Symantec's product portfolio. The data on actual practices provided a richer understanding of why some mergers succeeded and others failed, that the statistical analyses of the 3000+ mergers was unable to identify.

Agility

Terms such as agile and resilient may be fashionable but should not be viewed as passing trends. At its heart, an agile approach is one based on collaboration, learning and adapting to changing circumstances. Agile practices are often associated with software development, in which changing customer requirements, continual developments in technology and increased understanding of the task at hand mean plans must be continually adapted. Yet the concept initially emerged from research in product development, which sought to explain the success of Japanese automobile manufacturers (Takeuchi & Nonaka, 1986). The practices observed were described in a seminal article as akin to rugby, with its scrums, in which teammates physically support each other and move as one unit. This contrasted strongly with the relay race approach of passing the baton from one runner to the next with no interaction between them. The agile concept is increasingly valued as a means to manage businesses in the face of fast-moving and uncertain environments (Rigby et al., 2016). Responding to unprecedented and unexpected demands required firms to collaborate in an agile manner, including empowering teams drawn from different organizations to make rapid decisions and solve problems as they arose (Liu et al., 2021a). The example of agile practices is relevant because it demonstrates how influential research can be when it is relevant as well as rigorous. Takeuchi and Nonaka's (1986) description of scrums and sprints has become the basis for practices that are widely applied and taught four decades later. The example is also relevant because it points the way to academics who seek to combine rigor and relevance. An agile mindset and approach encourage the overall direction to be adjusted in a continuous conversation with the situation (Suchman, 1987). Plans can and should be informed by prior knowledge and theory. Yet, there should also be room to adjust the plans in order to maintain the relevance of the research. The recent global pandemic, which created massive disruptions in the conduct of business, the delivery of quality education in colleges and universities and in the conduct of research, produced a need for major adjustments by managers and by researchers. For example, the disruption caused by the pandemic heightened the importance of some theories (e.g., stakeholder theory) and reduced the relevance of others (e.g., agency theory) to understand the actions of managers in dealing with the major disruptions during the pandemic and beyond (Hitt et al., 2021). So, both managers and researchers must demonstrate agility to change as the environment dictates and the interactions between the two will help researchers develop more relevant theory which will translate into better research and higher quality instructional content.

Orchestration

Finally, the complexity of real-world problems makes it very difficult for highly specialized knowledge and methods to be applicable to every problem. It is therefore vital to be flexible in bringing the right theory and the right methods, as well as the right academics to the problem. It has long been argued that the scope of competition has moved beyond individual companies. First, supply chains competed with other supply chains, meaning focal firms that coordinated their suppliers and partners would succeed over more insular rivals. More recently, operations have become distributed among entire ecosystems of loosely coupled collaborators, coordinated through digital platforms (Cennamo & Santalo, 2013; Eisenmann et al., 2011). Similarly, academics must work across knowledge boundaries, pool their talents and work together if they are to address real-world problems. This requires not only having knowledge but knowing how to use it. And, not only having networks of potential collaborators to call on but also knowing how to orchestrate them. Resource orchestration refers to a strategy of deciding which resources to acquire, combine and divest (Sirmon & Hitt, 2009). Orchestration can also refer to the role that platform leaders play in coordinating ecosystems of actors that offer their resources to deliver a value proposition to stakeholders (Mukhopadhyay & Bouwman, 2019; Parker et al., 2017). Researchers can enact a similar strategy by seeking to reconfigure their teams and recombining their expertise in theory and methods to respond to management challenges. In doing so, they can apply their knowledge and find new opportunities to refine and develop theory.

Illustrative Example – Advanced Services Group

This chapter argues that the key to integrating rigor and relevance may lie in stakeholder engagement, agility and orchestration. Methodological guidance on ensuring rigor is beyond the scope of this chapter but we focus on maintaining relevance, to ensure rigorous work that is not just academic. To illustrate, we present the example of the Advanced Services Group (ASG), which is based at Aston Business School, in Birmingham, England. ASG was established in 2012 as a research center focused on the topic of servitization. It is led by Professor Tim Baines, who is among the most highly cited scholars in the area. ASG has a mission to "accelerate the adoption of Servitization and Advanced Services within businesses". It does so through partnership and collaboration with academic and business partners in a manner that exemplifies the three strategies. In the following section, we first explain the topic and the academic research before explaining the operating model, with examples of stakeholder engagement, agility and orchestration.

Servitization and Advanced Services

Servitization refers to the transformation of businesses from a focus on the manufacture, distribution and sale of goods to an emphasis on how value is created through these goods. The term was first used in the 1980s to describe the increasing focus on services as a differentiator and value creating mechanism (Vandermerwe & Rada, 1988). Subsequently servitization has been a short-hand for the growing interdependence, leading to value creation through integrated product–service systems (Baines et al., 2007; Pawar et al., 2009), that combine physical goods, service processes, digital technology, skills and resources that jointly deliver outcomes. The transformation seen in business is conceptualized through various academic concepts. Service dominant logic (Vargo & Lusch, 2004) defines a philosophical shift from focusing on economic value embedded in, and exchanged through, goods to value-in-use, when goods are doing something for people or organizations. Co-creation (Ceccagnoli et al., 2012; Prahalad & Ramaswamy, 2004; Spohrer & Maglio, 2008) describes the emphasis on customers as active participants in value creation, rather than passive consumers that destroy the value created by manufacturers. This echoes the argument that selling things without acknowledging the needs they fill and the "jobs" they do for customers (Christensen et al., 2016) is short-sighted (Levitt, 1960). It also resonates with arguments that customers seek experiences over commoditized goods and services (Beltagui et al., 2012; Beltagui & Candi, 2018; Pine & Gilmore, 1998) and that owning goods has become less important than accessing value or achieving outcomes through services and platforms. In this context, the academics in ASG have published extensively in operations, marketing, innovation and information systems journals. For example, their research has explored the nature of Advanced Service business models, such as Heat-as-a-Service (Wasserbaur et al., 2023), the nature of the transformation process (Baines et al., 2020), the challenges of organizational transformation (Beltagui, 2018; Bigdeli et al., 2021), partnerships and ecosystems (Kapoor et al., 2021) and use of digital technologies to enable servitization (Naik et al., 2020; Schroeder et al., 2020).

Stakeholder Engagement

The above section illustrates some of the research outputs and publications generated by ASG and should indicate the rigor, recognized by peer reviewers of leading journals. The mechanism by which the research knowledge is created, however, is also important. Academics are typically trained to focus on publication and then 'translation' of research results for businesses or students. Instead, ASG seeks co-creation over translation. The Advanced Services Partnership comprises a number of large businesses, from a variety of industry sectors and geographical locations, that are not direct competitors and have a strategic focus on Servitization and Advanced Services. The membership of the partnership changes but most members remain involved for years. They benefit from quarterly roundtable events and regular interactions with a specific ASG relationship manager, as well as other events, such as webinars and conferences. University administrators may see the partnership model principally as a source of revenue, yet its value for the researchers comes in the potential for co-creation and relevance. The Advanced Services Partnership enables a synergistic relationship between the generation and application of knowledge. Its members act not only as a sounding board, but as early adopters of the models, frameworks and tools created through research. Moreover, their perspectives and inputs help to shape the research direction and to inform the research, ensuring relevance. For instance, observing the challenges and changes in direction over a period of time helped to create a "roadmap" for servitization. Identification of digital platforms as an important topic, prompted research on the topic of platform ecosystems. These partners do offer opportunities for data collection, but by building a long-term relationship, they contribute far more. On the other hand, benefiting from the relationship requires considerable effort and coordination on the part of the academics. Regular interactions are not viewed solely as a pathway to publishing, but as a means of understanding the partner, their problems and how research might be relevant to their needs. Applying the lessons of service management, ASG therefore co-creates research that is relevant by building relationships rather than through transactions.

Agility

Engaging with stakeholders is challenging if researchers are rigid in their focus and direction. Or alternatively, if operating within a very large organization such as a university makes rapid changes in direction challenging. Large businesses enable agility by creating spinout companies that can respond quickly to new needs. Similarly, the strategic foresight of Aston University has enabled agility through a spinout company that enables the knowledge created by ASG to form the basis of advisory services. A dedicated team draws on the intellectual property captured within academic publications and which is generated through the Advanced Services Partnership. Joining the partnership represents a large commitment in time and resources. Alternatively, bespoke interactions can be delivered to businesses, for example workshops or training, from introducing the concepts and benefits of Advanced Services to supporting the design of business models and value propositions. To do so, considerable effort is invested by ASG into the creation of resources, including mini-guides, outlining how to conduct processes such as empathy mapping, value proposition design and segmentation for services. These documents can be purchased and could easily be viewed as a source of revenue. Yet their value lies in offering a structure, around which bespoke interactions can be built. By understanding the specific objectives and commitment of any stakeholder, the most appropriate tools can be applied in the most appropriate sequence and method. The connection between research and application is always clear. The tools result from (rigorous) research that is guided by interaction with stakeholders (for relevance), but their application raises new questions or opportunities to understand the phenomena in greater detail.

Orchestration

Being agile and open to adapt to changing stakeholder inputs is challenging. As the previous section demonstrates, it can be enabled by a stock of resources, including the knowledge captured in frameworks and strategic tools. It also requires networks of potential collaborators that can help to address needs as they arise. ASG is at the heart of the servitization research community because it hosts a leading academic conference, the Spring Servitization Conference, held annually and attracting many of the leading academics. The conference has helped to develop a relatively small but close-knit community of academics for over a decade. And, drawing on this community has helped in generating research outputs, as well as collaborative research funding. Meanwhile, working closely with industry stakeholders generates a community of businesses that can be mobilized to respond to grant funding opportunities; ASG has received several large collaborative research grants and is viewed as a center of excellence in research on outcome-based Advanced Services business models and the servitization transformation process. The relevance of these topics is increasingly recognized by businesses, by fellow academics and, crucially, by funding bodies as an integral component of addressing societal challenges. By aligning commercial incentives of various stakeholders around a business model focused on value, servitization can be a means to enable decarbonization of heating, digital transformation in industry, or addressing the health needs of an ageing population. Such challenges can be characterized as wicked problems (Rittel & Webber, 1973), which can only be addressed by involving multiple stakeholders and drawing on multiple perspectives. Orchestrating these stakeholders involves bringing the required capabilities online at the right time, while maintaining the network of potential partners at other times. For a specific project, the appropriate academic partners are brought onboard to provide the needed rigor in the specific topic, method or approach required. Similarly, the appropriate industry partners are brought onboard to provide the required access and advise the academics with a view to maintaining ongoing relevance.

Conclusion

Academics are preoccupied with how to ensure rigor in research, while external stakeholders increasingly push for relevance. Should we really see these as competing objectives?

> It is hard to understand why we continue this debate, when the answer is right in front of us: Why would we choose only one? How can research be considered "good" if it is not relevant to the discipline under study? How can research be useful if our methods are not rigorous enough to allow us to be confident in our results?
> (Mentzer, 2008, p. 72)

New technologies make it easier to access and process data and allow incredibly sophisticated analysis to be conducted and theories to be generated. Taken out of context, however, we risk this work being undervalued, because it is not of concern to those who could use it. Building on Mentzer's argument that rigor and relevance are mutually supportive and reinforcing, we identify three strategies, which are illustrated by example. Stakeholder engagement helps to set the direction of research and increase the chances that the rigorous analysis will be relevant. Agility enables changes in direction since what was relevant at first may no longer be so. Orchestration allows complex problems to be examined and distributes the problem of rigor among the most suitable partners, since relevant problems are likely to be complex ones. These strategies may sound simple but, as the examples above illustrate, they require conscious effort. Short-term sacrifices may be required to develop a better long-term position. And crucially, we suggest that rigorous, relevant research must be a team sport, built on collaborative relationships with academic and non-academic partners.

References

Adner, R., & Kapoor, R. (2016). Innovation ecosystems and the pace of substitution: Re-examining technology S-curves. *Strategic Management Journal*, 37(4), 625–648. https://doi.org/10.1002/smj.2363

Alvesson, M., & Sandberg, J. (2011). Generating research questions through problematization. *Academy of Management Review*, 36(2), 247–271.

Ansari, S. S., Garud, R., & Kumaraswamy, A. (2016). The disruptor's dilemma: TiVo and the U.S. television ecosystem. *Strategic Management Journal*, 37(9), 1829–1853. https://doi.org/10.1002/smj.2442

Baines, T., Bigdeli, A. Z., Sousa, R., & Schroeder, A. (2020). Framing the servitization transformation process: A model to understand and facilitate the servitization journey. *International Journal of Production Economics*, 221, 107463.

Baines, T. S., Lightfoot, H. W., Evans, S., Neely, A., Greenough, R., Peppard, J., Roy, R., Shehab, E., Braganza, A., Tiwari, A., & Alcock, J. R. (2007). State-of-the-art in product-service systems. Proceedings of the Institution of Mechanical Engineers, Part B. *Journal of Engineering Manufacture*, 221(10), 1543–1552.

Barney, J. B. (2018). Why resource-based theory's model of profit appropriation must incorporate a stakeholder perspective. *Strategic Management Journal*, 39, 3305–3325.

Beltagui, A. (2018). A design-thinking perspective on capability development: The case of new product development for a service business model. *International Journal of Operations & Production Management*, 38(4), 1041–1060.

Beltagui, A., Candi, M., & Riedel J. C. K. H. (2012). Design in the experience economy: using emotional design for service innovation. In S. Swan, & S. Zou, (Eds.), *Interdisciplinary Approaches Top Product Design, Innovation and Branding* (pp. 111–135). Emerald.

Beltagui, A., & Candi, M. (2018). Revisiting service quality through the lens of experience-centric services. *International Journal of Operations & Production Management*, 38(3), 915–932.

Beltagui, A., Rosli, A., & Candi, M. (2020). Exaptation in a digital innovation ecosystem: The disruptive impacts of 3D printing. *Research Policy*, 49(1). https://doi.org/10.1016/j.respol.2019.103833

Bigdeli, A. Z., Kapoor, K., Schroeder, A., & Omidvar, O. (2021). Exploring the root causes of servitization challenges: An organisational boundary perspective. *International Journal of Operations & Production Management*, 41(5), 547–573.

Carton, G., & Mouricou, P. (2017). Is management research relevant? A systematic analysis of the rigor-relevance debate in top-tier journals (1994-2013). *M@n@gement*, 20(2).

Ceccagnoli, M., Forman, C., Huang, P., & Wu, D. J. (2012). Cocreation of value in a platform ecosystem! The case of enterprise software. *MIS Quarterly*, 36(1), 263–290.

Cennamo, C., & Santalo, J. (2013). Platform competition: Strategic trade-offs in platform markets. *Strategic Management Journal*, 34(11), 1331–1350.

Chesbrough, H. (2020). To recover faster from Covid-19, open up: Managerial implications from an open innovation perspective. *Industrial Marketing Management*, 88, 410–413. https://doi.org/10.1016/j.indmarman.2020.04.010

Christensen, C. M. (1997). *The innovator's dilemma: When new technologies cause great firms to fail*. Harvard Business School Press.

Christensen, C. M., Hall, T., Dillon, K., & Duncan, D.S. (2016). Know your customers' jobs to be done. *Harvard Business Review*, 94(9), 54–62.

Eisenmann, T., Parker, G., & Van Alstyne, M. (2011). Platform envelopment. *Strategic Management Journal*, 32(12), 1270–1285.

Etzkowitz, H. & Leydesdorff, L. (2000). The dynamics of innovation: From national systems and "Mode 2" to a triple helix of university–industry–government relations. *Research Policy*, 29(2), 109–123.

Evans, B., Powell, J. A., & Talbot, R. (1982). *Changing design*. Wiley.

Goldratt, E. M. (1997). *Critical Chain*. Gower.

Hambrick, D. C. (1994). 1993 Presidential Address: What if the academy actually mattered? *Academy of Management Review*, *19*(1), 11. https://doi.org/10.2307/258833

Hambrick, D. C. (2007). The field of management's devotion to theory: Too much of a good thing? *Academy of Management Journal*, *50*(6), 1346–1352.

Hitt, M. A. (1998). Twenty-first century organizations: Business firms, business schools, and the academy. *Academy of Management Review*, *23*(2), 218–224.

Hitt, M. A., Arregle, J.-L., & Holmes, R. M. (2021). Strategic management theory in a post-pandemic and non-ergodic world. *Journal of Management Studies*, *58*: 259–264.

Hitt, M. A. & Greer, C. R. (2012). The value of research and its evaluation in business schools: Killing the goose that laid the golden egg? *Journal of Management Inquiry*, *21*(2), 236–240.

Hitt, M. A., Holmes, R. M., & Mistry, S. (2023a). Agility, meta capabilities, dynamic capabilities, stakeholders and strategic leadership in the new normal environment. In S. J. Zaccaro, N. J. Hiller & R. Klimoski, (Eds.), *Senior Leadership Teams and the Agile organization*. Routledge. https://doi.org/10.4324/9780429353161-13

Hitt, M. A., Ireland, R. D., & Hoskisson, R. E. (2020). *Strategic management: Competitiveness and globalization*. Cengage Learning.

Hitt, M. A., Lim, S., Sirmon, D. G., & Xu, K. (2023b). *A resource orchestration perspective on 'who brings what' to M&As: Heterogeneous market evaluations of different capability configurations*. Working paper. Texas A&M University.

Johnston, R., Shulver, M., Slack, N., & Clark, G. (2020). *Service Operations Management* (5th ed.). Pearson.

Kapoor, K., Bigdeli, A. Z., Dwivedi, Y. K., Schroeder, A., Beltagui, A., & Baines, T. (2021). A socio-technical view of platform ecosystems: Systematic review and research agenda. *Journal of Business Research*, *128*, 94–108.

Kuckertz, A., Brändle, L., Gaudig, A., Hinderer, S., Morales Reyes, C. A., Prochotta, A., Steinbrink, K. M., & Berger, E. S. C. (2020). Startups in times of crisis – A rapid response to the COVID-19 pandemic. *Journal of Business Venturing Insights*, *13*(April). https://doi.org/10.1016/j.jbvi.2020.e00169

Kunovjanek, M., & Wankmüller, C. (2020). An analysis of the global additive manufacturing response to the COVID-19 pandemic. *Journal of Manufacturing Technology Management*, *32*(9), 75–100. https://doi.org/10.1108/JMTM-07-2020-0263

Lambert, D. M. (2019). Rediscovering relevance. *International Journal of Logistics Management*, *30*(2), 382–394. https://doi.org/10.1108/IJLM-02-2019-0059

Levitt T. (1960). Marketing Myopia. *Harvard Business Review*, *38*(July–August), 57–66.

Liu, W., Beltagui, A., & Ye, S. (2021a). Accelerated innovation through repurposing: Exaptation of design and manufacturing in response to COVID-19. *R&D Management*, *51*(4), 410–426. https://doi.org/10.1111/radm.12460

Liu, W., Beltagui, A., Ye, S., & Williamson, P. (2021b). Harnessing exaptation and ecosystem strategy for accelerated innovation. *California Management Review, 64*(3), 78–98. https://doi.org/10.1177/00081256211056651

McGahan, A. M., Bogers, M. L. A. M., Chesbrough, H., & Holgersson, M. (2021). Tackling societal challenges with open innovation. *California Management Review, 63*(2).

Mentzer, J. T. (2008). Rigor versus relevance: Why would we choose only one? *Journal of Supply Chain Management, 44*(2), 72.

Mukhopadhyay, S., & Bouwman, H. (2019). Orchestration and governance in digital platform ecosystems: A literature review and trends. *Digital Policy, Regulation and Governance, 21*(4), 329–351.

Naik, P., Schroeder, A., Kapoor, K. K., Bigdeli, A. Z., & Baines, T. (2020). Behind the scenes of digital servitization: Actualising IoT-enabled affordances. *Industrial Marketing Management, 89,* 232–244.

Oliva, R. (2019). Intervention as a research strategy. *Journal of Operations Management, 65*(7), 710–724.

Palmer, D., Dick, B., & Freiburger, N. (2009). Rigor and relevance in organization studies. *Journal of Management Inquiry, 18*(4), 265–272. https://doi.org/10.1177/1056492609343491

Parker, G., Van Alstyne, M., & Jiang, X. (2017). Platform ecosystems. *Mis Quarterly, 41*(1), 255–266.

Pawar, K. S., Beltagui, A., & Riedel, J. C. (2009). The PSO triangle: Designing product, service and organisation to create value. *International Journal of Operations & Production Management, 29*(5), 468–493.

Pine, B. J., & Gilmore, J. H. (1998). The experience economy. *Harvard Business Review, 76*(6), 18–23.

Prahalad, C. K., & Ramaswamy, V. (2004). Co-creation experiences: The next practice in value creation. *Journal of Interactive Marketing, 18*(3), 5–14.

Rapaccini, M., Saccani, N., Kowalkowski, C., Paiola, M., & Adrodegari, F. (2020). Navigating disruptive crises through service-led growth: The impact of COVID-19 on Italian manufacturing firms. *Industrial Marketing Management, 88,* 225–237. https://doi.org/10.1016/j.indmarman.2020.05.017

Rigby, D.K., Berez, S., Caimi, G., & Noble, A. (2016). *Agile innovation.* Bain & Company Brief.

Rindova, V. P. & Courtney, (2020). Shape or adapt: Knowledge problems, epistemologies and strategic postures under Knightian uncertainty. *Academy of Management Review, 45*(4). https://doi.org/10.5465/amr.2018.0291

Rittel, H. W., & Webber, M. M. (1973). Dilemmas in a general theory of planning. *Policy Sciences, 4*(2), 155–169.

Rodríguez-Espíndola, O., Chowdhury, S., Beltagui, A., & Albores, P. (2020). The potential of emergent disruptive technologies for humanitarian supply chains: The integration of blockchain, artificial intelligence and 3D printing. *International Journal of Production Research, 58*(15), 4610–4630. https://doi.org/10.1080/00207543.2020.1761565

Schroeder, A., Naik, P., Bigdeli, A. Z., & Baines, T. (2020). Digitally enabled advanced services: A socio-technical perspective on the role of the internet of things (IoT). *International Journal of Operations & Production Management, 40*(7/8), 1243–1268.

Simon, H. A. (1996). *The sciences of the artificial*. MIT Press.

Sirmon, D. G., & Hitt, M. A. (2009). Contingencies within dynamic managerial capabilities: Interdependent effects of resource investment and deployment on firm performance. *Strategic Management Journal*, *30*(13), 1375–1394.

Spohrer, J., & Maglio, P.P. (2008). The emergence of service science: Toward systematic service innovations to accelerate co-creation of value. *Production and Operations Management*, *17*(3), 238–246.

Starkey, K., Hatchuel, A., & Tempest, S. (2009). Management research and the new logics of discovery and engagement. *Journal of Management Studies*, *46*(3), 547–558. https://doi.org/10.1111/j.1467-6486.2009.00833.x

Starkey, K., & Madan, P. (2001). Bridging the relevance gap: Aligning stakeholders in the future of management research. *British Journal of Management*, *12*(s1). https://doi.org/10.1111/1467-8551.12.s1.2

Suchman, L. A. (1987). *Plans and situated actions: The problem of human-machine communication*. Cambridge University Press.

Sutton, R. I., & Staw, B. M. (1995). What theory is not. *Quarterly*, *40*(3).

Takeuchi, H., & Nonaka, I. (1986). The new new product development game. *Harvard Business Review*, *64*(1), 137–146.

Thomas, H., & Wilson, A. D. (2011). 'Physics envy', cognitive legitimacy or practical relevance: Dilemmas in the evolution of management research in the UK. *British Journal of Management*, *22*(3), 443–456.

Toffel, M. W. (2016). Enhancing the practical relevance of research. *Production and Operations Management*, *25*(9), 1493–1505. https://doi.org/10.1111/poms.12558

Vandermerwe, S., & Rada, J. (1988). Servitization of business: Adding value by adding services. *European Management Journal*, *6*(4), 314–324.

Vargo, S. L., & Lusch, R. F. (2004). Evolving to a new dominant logic for marketing. *Journal of Marketing*, *68*(1), 1–17.

Wasserbaur, R., Schroeder, A., & Beltagui, A. (2023). Heat-as-a-Service (HaaS): a Complex Adaptive Systems perspective on servitization. *Production Planning & Control*, 1–15.

Weick, K. E. (1995). What theory is not, theorizing is. *Quarterly*, *40*(3).

Part II

The Impact University

11 The Responsible Research in Business and Management (RRBM) Community

Responsible Management Education and Impactful Research

Howard Thomas

Introduction

In the first half of the 20th century, business school models typically followed the strategies of leading US business schools, such as Harvard and Wharton, and European schools of commerce in aiming to develop a class of well-trained professional managers for business organisations. This approach was criticised for producing 'wastelands of vocationalism' – in essence 'trade schools' – by Professor Herbert Simon (1991, p. 139) and others. They argued that business schools lacked academic identity and legitimacy. Books funded by the Ford and Carnegie foundations in the late 1950s (Gordon and Howell, 1959; Pierson, 1959) advocated the adoption of a 'logical positivist' business school model, which proposed a value objective for a responsible business as the maximisation of shareholder wealth (Friedman, 1970) and a business school model focused on building rigorous, credible research and academic scholarship alongside curricula anchored firmly in the core disciplines of the economic and social sciences. This model quickly became the dominant business school paradigm globally and favoured a strong, analytical approach based more on the functional aspects of business than the processes of managing.

Over the last 50 years both as a business school academic and a 'serial' dean, it has been clear that there have been a number of phases in the evolution of business schools. The first, stretching from the 1960s (using the logical positivist approach) until the Global Financial Crisis (2008–2010), was described by Augier and March (2011) as the 'golden age of business schools'. In that period, business schools were formally ranked in league tables by media publications,

DOI: 10.4324/9781003459217-13

such as *Business Week*, the *Financial Times* and US News & World Report, and their faculty, increasingly PhD (doctorally trained), were judged primarily in quality terms using citation counts and impact assessments of their publications, mainly in prestigious academically oriented journals. Hence, in this period business schools became businesses judged on their reputations, quantified by media league table rankings and assessments of research quality based on counts of faculty publications in the leading academic journals.

However, this very specific and narrow set of impact assessments was increasingly subject to criticism around the time of the Global Financial Crisis and following the catastrophic financial engineering collapse of companies, such as Enron. Indeed, the late Sumantra Ghoshal, a prominent business school business strategy academic (along with others, e.g., Locke and Spender, 2011) pointed out that business schools, in their desire to be considered as legitimate academic players, had taught and propagated amoral theories that destroyed sound managerial practices and, hence, had contributed to the lapses in managerial behaviour that may have, in turn, led to business failures in, and around, the financial crisis (Ghoshal, 2005).

Therefore, following the Global Financial Crisis, academics and business school leaders began to rethink and re-evaluate the mission and purpose of a business school, noting that the Global Financial Crisis and its subsequent ramifications had been a 'turning point' or perhaps a 'tipping point' towards a second curve (Handy, 2022) in the evolution of the business school. Handy's sense, in drawing from detailed evidence in the research sponsored by EFMD on the 'future of management education' (Thomas et al., 2013, 2014), was that business schools had, in fact, moved well beyond the first phase of their strategic development.

He argued that this meant a new role for business schools in intellectual terms as being 'the "think tanks" exploring the future of business, of capitalism, of organisation structures and the role of regulation, and so on". The EFMD study on the future of management education also gained support from two other sources. First, the growing evidence from business school students and faculty in Europe and the US (e.g., the Aspen Institute surveys [Thomas, 2017]) that they wanted more emphasis on socially responsible 'people and the planet' issues of moral and ethical management concern, including corporate social responsibility, inequality, sustainability and inclusive growth, in their business school curricula frameworks. This led to the creation of new, more balanced management education models based upon a broad stakeholder perspective (Freeman, 2010) involving greater business, government and civil society collaborations in order to address the re-evaluation of the role of capitalism (Henderson, 2020; Mayer, 2016) given the presence of many social democratic forms of capitalism in the European Union (EU). These concerns suggested the adoption of more nuanced forms of capitalism in business school models which would involve stakeholder maximisation objectives rather than just wealth maximisation for shareholders.

Second, the early evidence on the findings of the EFMD future research study led the board of EFMD to produce their own manifesto on the future of management education (EFMD, 2012) advocating five clear principles for the future direction of business school strategy and operations. These principles were grounded in terms of a more European-style of management education. In particular, the manifesto proposed a purposeful shift towards multiple stakeholder perspectives in programme design and research activities. As a consequence, this would require the development of sound principles for responsible management education, involving frameworks for cross-disciplinary thinking and approaches for handling issues of ethics, moral responsibility and sustainability in a more comprehensive fashion.

It is also very important to acknowledge the leading role of EFMD and its president Eric Cornuel (2023) (co-operating with other professional organisations in the field) in recognising the need for establishing sound principles for responsible management education and strengthening linkages between business schools and their stakeholders, in such areas as environmental, social and governance issues, sustainability management and societal impact, in the growth and evolution of business schools following the turmoil arising from the financial crisis and the COVID-19 pandemic.

Indeed, the European culture and social democratic character strongly encourages greater social empathy and more direct trisector (business, government and civil society) collaboration which can, in turn, improve socio-economic growth.

The Emergence of Responsible Management Education

Hence, the belief in socially responsible management education is embedded not only in EFMD's Manifesto on the Future of Management Education (2012) but in the DNA of its partner organisations and members. This belief is shared, in particular, by agencies such as the GLRI (Globally Responsible Leadership Initiative), ABIS (Academy of Business in Society), PRME (Principles of Responsible Management Education) and RRBM (Responsible Research in Business and Management). All of these agencies have been carefully nurtured and supported by EFMD as they all endorse the 17 Sustainable Development Goals (SDGs) of the UN Global Compact (https://sdgs.un.org/goals). In 2013, EFMD also introduced its BSIS – Business School Impact System – to assess the impact of business schools on society (Kalika & Cornuel, 2023).

More recently, Eric Cornuel reflected on the much broader influence that EFMD and academics should have on the growth of responsible management education in the period from 2020 to the present day (Cornuel, 2023). He notes that following the COVID pandemic, and resulting social and geopolitical disruptions, there has been a noticeable rise of nationalism and populism which serves to entrench poverty, inequality and insecurity, and stalls inclusive growth in society across generations. Therefore, he champions the concept of engaged academic scholarship (Hoffman, 2021), drawing upon the writings of Professors Andrew Pettigrew and Andy Van de Ven on co-production of knowledge, as an approach for researching many of the current societal growth challenges. He quotes from Hoffman to capture the spirit, purpose and meaning of academic scholarship as follows, 'I want my research, teaching and outreach to have positive impact on the world around me".

Echoing the spirit of these 'engaged scholars', the next section discusses the value and impact of Anne Tsui's RRBM community (https://www.rrbm.network) on the growth of responsible management education.

Anne Tsui and the RRBM Community: Its Creation and Evolution

Introduction and Inception

Anne Tsui is the legendary and inspiring founder of the RRBM community. In her articles entitled 'Reconnecting with the Business World' (2015) and 'Celebrating Small Wins and Calling Bold Actions' (2022), she describes the genesis and growth path of RRBM. Her clear vision at the outset is expressed in a quote from the 2015 paper, namely, 'all parties in the research enterprise can contribute to the pursuit of socially responsible scholarship by remembering the goal of science in the discovery and application of true knowledge to improve the human condition".

Thus, in 2015, a global team of business academic scholars (I was one of the 24 scholars) representing five major disciplines, met alongside a number of institutional leaders in management education to craft an RRBM Position Paper. This was aimed at bridging the so-called 'rigour-relevance' gap in existing academic research with a renewed attack on purpose and responsibility to society through addressing societal grand challenges and achieving positive societal impact. Table 11.1 shows the five topics that were considered as most important research topics in the original RRBM Position Paper.

They also proposed seven principles of responsible research, which along with the vision statement and Position Paper, would constitute the *raison d'être* of RRBM. These principles were a call to action to achieve 'responsible research for better business and a better world'. The seven principles were service to society backed by three credible research criteria – basic and applied research, pluralistic and multi-disciplinary collaborations and sound methodology; and three 'relevance' criteria – stakeholder involvement, impact on stakeholders and broad dissemination (specific definition of these criteria can be reviewed in Table 11.2).

Table 11.1 RRBM Position Paper: Relevant Topics of Research Importance

1	Understanding the broader impact of firms and their roles in society, beyond the creation of shareholder value
2	Understanding the changing nature of work and the workforce, as well as the changing nature of consumers and their role in co-creating value
3	Examining the social sustainability of business organisations, including their impact on the health and wellbeing of employers, customers and community
4	Enhancing environmental sustainability, managing the use of natural resources, and reducing negative environmental impact
5	Alleviating poverty, creating greater prosperity, and reducing economic inequality, both locally and globally

Table 11.2 Seven Principles for Responsible Management Education

1	Service to society: Development of knowledge that benefits business and the broader society, locally and globally, for the ultimate purpose of creating a better world
2	Valuing both basic and applied contributions: Contributions to both the theoretical domain to create fundamental knowledge and in applied domains to address pressing and current issues
3	Valuing plurality and multi-disciplinary collaboration: Diversity in research themes, methods, forms of scholarship, types of inquiry and interdisciplinary collaboration to reflect the plurality and complexity of business and societal problems
4	Sound methodology: Research that implements sound scientific methods and processes in both quantitative and qualitative or both theoretical and empirical domains
5	Stakeholder involvement: Research that engages different stakeholders in the research process, without compromising the independence of inquiry
6	Impact on stakeholders: Research that has an impact on diverse stakeholders, especially research that contributes to a better business and a better world
7	Broad dissemination: Diverse forms of knowledge dissemination that collectively advances basic knowledge and practice

Update on What Has Been Achieved (2015–2023) by RRBM

From a population of 28 founders and 85 co-signers of the RRBM declaration and vision document, the RRBM Vision Statement has gained support from well over 100 universities and 2000 academics who have endorsed the RRBM Position Paper. This was achieved without any significant marketing campaign, and it continues to grow exponentially in the current volatile socio-economic environment. Anne Tsui also catalogues the 'small wins and bold actions' over the first seven years in her *Global Focus* article (Tsui, 2022). In an important first step, RRBM established awards for responsible research and, since 2018, it has reviewed many nominations for these awards for responsible research written in books and academic journals on management. These nominations are critically reviewed by a judging panel and, to date, there have been 108 award-winning research articles and 15 book awards, across the core disciplines of management, marketing and operations management. An analysis of the themes in the award-winning articles follows (see also website www.rrbm.network/taking-action/awards).

Analysis of the Award-winning Themes in the Responsible Research Awards Since Their Inception

A thorough analysis of the major themes in the RRBM award-winning articles and books is provided in the article by Tsui, Bitner and Netessine (2023). They highlight five major themes (and relevant UN SDGs) in the award-winning articles, namely, *wellbeing* (SDGs 1, 2, 3, 8); *justice/equity* (SDGs 5, 10); *sustainability* (SDGs 6, 7, 12, 13); *institutions of infrastructure* (SDGs 9, 11, 16) and *organisational outcomes*. They also point out where award papers can be further reviewed in detail via the RRBM website. The book awards have tended to focus on broader topics. For example, books by Rebecca Henderson (2020) on reimagining capitalism, Marquis (2020) on how the B Corp movement is rewriting capitalism, and Gray and Purdy (2018) reflect different attempts to examine alternative stakeholder models of capitalism. On the other hand, others such as London (2016) examine how to alleviate poverty through building sustainable enterprises and Thomas and Hedrick-Wong (2019) examine, with clear theoretical frameworks and a range of case studies, issues of inclusive growth and social/financial inclusion in developing economies. From a managerial perspective, Bazerman (2020) examines how by being better – and not necessarily behaviourally, ethically and morally perfect – we can achieve as leaders, maximum sustainable goodness in the world we inhabit.

Andy Hoffman's (2021) book on engaged scholarship, discussed earlier, encourages us to extend the impact of research on problems in today's world, to research on how we would like it to be in the future.

Thus, the RRBM Responsible Research Awards have clearly demonstrated the impressive volume of quality academic outputs, in terms of both academic articles and books. Indeed, it has perhaps come much closer than other awards in achieving increased focus and attention on the meaningful, impactful outputs of business school research. However, there is an important issue and ongoing problem with many of the academic articles because, while they describe very thoroughly the potential pathways to achieve impact, they rarely provide commentary about the actual, or even potential, impact of the article. (Note that this may well be the result of the policies of many journals in the academic field, which while requiring sound methodology and high-quality research as the key criteria, often do not require impact – statements addressing potential areas of application. This is because academic legitimacy is the *raison d'être* of most top academic journals and they typically do not require or even encourage impact statements.) A notable exception was the award-winning article by Bone, Christensen and Williamson (2014) which showed clearly that US banks had changed their loan criteria following their study on minority access to bank loans.

It is important also to note the comment Renate Meyer (2023) writes about impact. She argues that research impact is hard to determine because 'it unfolds in a non-linear way', often over a number of years, and that allocating causality is a very difficult activity. Perhaps attempts should be made to persuade the editors of leading journals to adopt impact statements as a key criterion in the article submissions process. And, a further suggestion might be the addition of a short conclusions section outlining the research impact together with a reflection on how the research findings might be applied. Such impact statements and conclusions/reflections would surely enhance the objectives of responsible societal management practice.

However, books provide a more longitudinal definitive and positive lens on impact. For example, Henderson's work on capitalism and Bazerman's work on a better, but not perfect moral and ethical compass in management offer a range of purposeful ideas and insights for meaningful and successful change in practical management situations.

In the future, it is inevitable that governments, businesses and research agencies will increasingly require clear impact and value statements in their review of different research projects that they have either funded or sponsored. They will increasingly expect to receive well-argued policy and strategy implications from projects as well as demonstrations of how managerial capabilities and skills have been successfully developed.

Other Research Activities Championed by RRBM

There have been a number of special issues (55 in total) in leading academic journals, such as the *Academy of Management Discoveries*, and Annual Best Paper Awards for Responsible Research on Marketing Applications in the *US Journal of Marketing*, and the European Finance Association in the area of responsible finance research.

There have also been a series of Responsible Management research seminars and summits since the first Global RRBM Summit, held at Rotterdam School of Management in 2019,with over 60 participants from 13 countries. The aim of each summit has been to foster personal interactions between professors, young faculty and doctoral students,and group commitment to endorse and promote RRBM research projects and principles. Despite pandemic challenges, further meetings have been hosted by schools, such as Imperial (UK), Wharton (US) and most recently in the Summit held in Summer 2023 at INSEAD. The INSEAD seminar brought together journal editors, thought leaders and doctoral researchers to explore, even further, how more impactful research can be promoted by RRBM advocates. Further, it should also be noted that RRBM has sponsored a number of doctoral candidates through its 'Dare to Care' dissertation fellowships. Currently, these are held at schools, such as Cranfield and Strathclyde in the UK, and in US schools, such as Berkeley, Michigan, NYU, Oregon and Washington. Thus, it has created 'cradle to grave' pathways for both young and well-established scholars to push forward the RRBM community through its advocacy awards, websites and regular newsletters (called RRBM 'Voices'). Much has been achieved but what is the ongoing vision?

Where is RRBM Going Now?

As of the current date, RRBM has stable governance structures, including a working board which meets regularly and an inaugural Distinguished Fellows group, led by its dean, Anne Tsui, who are jointly charged with growing the community – from its current strong growth, with well over 2,000 academic endorsers and over 130 institutions as signatories.

The aim over the coming five years, through the leadership of the Chair of the RRBM Board, Andrew Karolyi, Dean of the Cornell S. C. Johnson Business School in the US, is to set up a number of task forces to grow the impact of RRBM in the business school research domain. These task forces will attack a number of challenges, and goals, for the community including:

- Raising funds for RRBM activities, including research summits, dissertation fellowships, webinars, further initiatives for responsible management research and growing its reputation in the field
- Changing the criteria for promoting business school faculty to include all dimensions of impact – through teaching, research and service
- Persuading leading journals to address broader impact measurements, particularly in the area of societal impact
- Encouraging leading journals to request authors to provide societal impact statements for their research articles, thus emphasising relevance and reach as well as rigour and relevance.

Needless to say, RRBM welcomes the involvement and support of academics and scholars from all disciplines to build upon the inspiring, energising and relentlessly effective and continuing leadership of its founder, Professor Anne Tsui.

References

Augier, M. and J. March (2011) *The Roots, Rituals and Rhetorics of Change: North American Business Schools after the Second World War*. Stanford: Stanford Business Books.

Bazerman, M. H. (2020) *Better not Perfect: A Realist's Guide to Maximum Sustainable Goodness*. New York: Harper Collins.

Bone, S. A., Christensen, G. L. and Williams, J. D. (2014) Rejected, shackled, and alone: The impact of systemic restricted choice on minority consumers' construction of self. *Journal of Consumer Research*, 41(2), pp. 451–474.

Cornuel, E. (2023) Positive impact: An important role for business school leadership in a changing precarious world, pp. 9–12. In E. Cornuel, H. Thomas and M. Wood (eds) *Perspectives on the Impact, Mission and Vision of the Business School*. Abingdon: Routledge Publishing.

EFMD (2012) *Manifesto on the Future of Management Education*. 24th January 2012. Brussels: EFMD Publications.

Freeman, R. E. (2010) *Strategic Management: A Stakeholder Approach*. Cambridge: Cambridge University Press.

Friedman, M. (1970) The social responsibility of a business is to increase its profits. *New York Times Magazine* 33(30) pp. 122–125.

Ghoshal, S. (2005) How management theories are destroying good management. *Academy of Management, Learning and Education 32*, pp. 178–186.

Gordon, R. A. and J. E. Howell (1959) *Higher Education for Business*. New York: Columbia University Press.

Gray, B. and J. Purdy (2018) *Collaborating for Our Future: Multi-stakeholder Partnerships for Solving Complex Problems*. Oxford: Oxford University Press.

Handy, C. (2022) The past is not the future, pp. 166–174. In E. Cornuel, H. Thomas and M. Wood (eds) *The Value and Purpose of Management Education: Looking Back and Thinking Forward*. Abingdon: Routledge Publishing.

Henderson, R. (2020) *Reimagining Capitalism in a World on Fire*. New York: Public Affairs.

Hoffman, Andrew (2021) *The Engaged Scholar: Expanding the Impact of Academic Research in Today's World*. Stanford: Stanford University Press.

Kalika, M and E. Cornuel (2023) The search for meaning: BSIS and its role in promoting business schools and societal impact, pp. 20–25. In E. Cornuel, H. Thomas and M Wood (eds) *Perspectives on the Impact, Mission and Vision of the Business School*. Abingdon: Routledge Publishing.

Locke, E. R. and J.-C. Spender (2011) *Confronting Managerialism: How the Business Elite and Their Schools Threw Our Lives Out of Balance*. London: Zed books.

London, T. (2016) *The Base of the Pyramid: Building Business with Impact and Scale*. Stanford: Stanford University Press.

Marquis, C. (2020) *Better Business: How the B Corp Movement is Remaking Capitalism*. New Haven: Yale University Press.

Mayer, C. (2016) *Prosperity: Better Business Makes the Greater Good*. Oxford: Oxford University Press.

Meyer, R. E. (2023) How might societal impact be recognized within an FT top 50 journal, pp. 5–6. In U. V. C. Haley and A. Jack, *Measuring Societal Impact in Business and Management Studies*. Sage Business White Paper. London: Sage Publications.

Pierson, F. C. (1959) *The Education of American Businessmen*. New York: McGraw-Hill.

Simon, H. (1991) *Models of my Life*. New York: Basic Books.

Thomas, H. (2017) Rethinking and Re-evaluating the purpose of the business school, in *Rethinking Business Education: Fit for the Future*. Chartered Association of Business Schools, London.

Thomas, H. and Y. Hedrick-Wong (2019) *Inclusive Growth: The Global Challenges of Social Inequality and Financial Inclusion*. Bingley: Emerald Publishing.

Thomas, H., M. Lee, L. Thomas and A. Wilson (2014) *Securing the Future of Management Education*. Bingley: Emerald Publishing.

Thomas, H., L. Thomas and A. Wilson (2013) *Promises Fulfilled in Management Education*. Bingley: Emerald Publishing.

Tsui, A. S. (2015) Reconnecting with the business world, pp. 152–158. In E. Cornuel, H. Thomas and M. Wood (eds) *The Value and Purpose of Management Education: Looking Back and Thinking Forward*. Abingdon: Routledge Publishing.

Tsui, A. S. (2022) Celebrating small wins and calling bold actions. *Global Focus Magazine*, EFMD.

Tsui, A. S., M. J. Bitner and S. Netessine (2023) What topics should business school research focus on, pp. 25–33. In E. Cornuel, H. Thomas and M. Wood (eds) *Perspectives on the Impact, Mission and Vision of the Business School*. Abingdon: Routledge Publishing.

12 Third Space Innovators

Boundary Spanning for University–Industry Collaboration

Anita Kocsis, Joann Cattlin, and Lisa M. Given

Introduction

The co-innovation mandate for universities and government to foster research, and to drive applied research translation, diffusion, and commercialisation is a transdisciplinary (Gibbons, 2000) and human-centred activity. While research is acknowledged as core university business, in the last 15 years, the triple helix agenda (Halilem, 2010) – which positions universities, industry/community, and government in a single ecosystem – has influenced an increase in focused innovation spaces (e.g., precincts, hubs, labs) that facilitate engagement with a wide range of external organisations (Nnanna et al., 2023; Halilem, 2010). There are calls, globally, for "increased collaboration, both within and between different research areas and with industry" (Australian Government, 2021, p. 16; OECD, 2019). The intention is for universities to solve societal problems and close the gap between concept and outcome for societal impact as collective and collaborative pursuits. This requires work across sectors, and across institutional and disciplinary silos, using specific methods to synthesise diverse research and development. The success of these initiatives relies on the capacity of those involved for building and sustaining relationships across sectoral, organisational, and professional boundaries and for this work to be validated and recognised within the institution (Björklund et al., 2019; Cinar & Benneworth, 2021). While an investment in innovation hubs has increased, there are scant details on the skill sets, mindsets, and roles of the staffing complements and organisational approaches needed to drive innovation capability (Nnanna et al., 2023). Additional research is needed to identify the attributes that define cross-functional teams, and that produce design-driven, translational, and novel methods that support mission-led, socially relevant challenges.

In this chapter, we highlight the growth of capability within innovation infrastructures, such as platforms, hubs, living labs,

DOI: 10.4324/9781003459217-14

etc., and explore how these roles are shaping both infrastructural and organisational activities. We discuss the case of the 10-year evolution of an innovation hub, known as Design Factory Melbourne (DFM), that functions across diverse disciplinary and geographically distributed units and organisations situated in a university. DFM is part of the international network of design factories that originated at Aalto University (Björklund et al., 2019).

We present this case example by deploying theories on the crossing of boundaries and "boundary infrastructures" (Star, 2010; Wenger, 1999), and on operators in "third spaces" (Whitchurch, 2008); these theories, combined, provide an analytic lens to explore the practical challenges of organisations seeking to resource and manage this work. The improvisations and adaptations required of staff working in innovation roles, and shaped by the demands of innovation infrastructures and the increasing trend in novel, hybrid, in-between academic and professional activities, are explored using the theory of the bricoleur (Lévi-Strauss, 2021). These theoretical frameworks demonstrate the boundary infrastructure and the boundary spanners who shape experiences in between, within, and across innovation organisations. We theorise the *third space innovator* to highlight both academic and professional staff ingenuity in response to innovation challenges, requiring novel methods and processes beyond those typically used in either role. We identify DFM as a boundary infrastructure (Bowker & Star, 2000), and profile the academic and professional staff as boundary spanners (Bowker et al., 2016). We interrogate case examples of individuals who have developed transversal expertise, transdisciplinary research practice, coaching in innovation education, and managing complex stakeholder arrangements. We demonstrate how these projects exemplify boundary objects, with the intra-and extrarelationships serving as boundary networks in the context of the DFM hub.

What can we learn about the professionals and academics in innovation hubs like DFM, who work across sectors, disciplines, and professional boundaries? Given the mandate for innovation, how have academics and professional staff traversed the boundaries across university organisational silos and traditional university teaching, research, and service practices? Does this diverse community of practitioners constitute a third space of professionals (Whitchurch, 2008) and, if so, what are the attributes of these roles (Whitchurch et al., 2023)? By exploring who works within these innovation spaces (and who is not represented), we can better understand future needs, potential gaps, and areas requiring workplace adaptations for co-creation, at scale.

The Case of Design Factory Melbourne, an Innovation Hub

The concept of the Design Factory (DF) originated at Aalto University and now comprises a Design Factory Global Network of 40 design factories, worldwide. The DF model is one example of the types of organisations that form the broader innovation ecosystem, which features various types of platforms and infrastructures, such as living labs, technology parks, research centres, innovation hubs, and experimental spaces, that enable collaboration between universities, government, industry, non-profit organisations, community groups, and research organisations (Minguillo & Thelwall, 2015; Youtie & Shapira, 2008). DF and other innovation organisations provide education and applied innovations for various workplace contexts. Such knowledge economy generators engage with enterprise, government, and businesses to translate research and other codified knowledge, with a diverse remit. Depending on the host organisation, this ranges from the commercialisation of fundamental research to transversal learning skills for students. Many organisations provide mentoring and specialist expertise for collaboration and problem-solving, seed and/or start-up funding, commercialisation support to accelerate research adoption, and co-working spaces to facilitate inter-institutional exchange and development (Nnanna et al., 2023).

DFM, located at Swinburne University of Technology in Australia, illustrates boundary roles, capabilities, and solutions derived from the remit of the innovation hub (Coddington et al., 2016). The DFM hub purpose is twofold:

1. To provide a place, a culture, and programmes (Björklund et al., 2017) for applied formative innovation (Gregor & Hevner, 2015); and,
2. To offer international experiential innovation education.

(Joore et al., 2022; Kolb, 1984)

Over a ten-year period, DFM shifted from a learning programme situated within a School of Design to become a centrally situated, cross-university, problem-solving, experimentation and learning generator. Over time, the DFM infrastructure shifted in and out of organisational units, being situated at various points in school, faculty, research office, and central innovation precinct units, to its current portfolio within Swinburne's Innovation and Enterprise division. The first group of staff consisted of academics from the disciplines of design and engineering, and a professional manager. These individuals were tasked with building the initiative while balancing multifaceted modes of operation; this meant managing traditional academic work expectations alongside the generative, ambiguous, and risk-taking practices that are common to problem-solving for innovation efforts. Academic and professional staff activities in the hub included what Buijs (2007) refers to as forming–storming–norming–performing–adjourning (p. 204) in the pursuit of problem scoping, ideation, and the development of shared meaning for knowledge translation.

The Challenge of Innovation Roles, Tasks, and Recognition

DFM's innovation processes and methods formed out of the needs of the innovation challenge and were contingent on individuals' practices and approaches, not necessarily linear, nor always agreed on, and sometimes conflicting and diverse. Individuals in the DFM formed creative approaches at the front end of innovation (Matthews, 2017; Rekonen & Björklund, 2016), with interdisciplinary teams deploying prototypes to improve communication (Dow et al., 2009; Wensveen & Matthews, 2014) and knowledgeability (Kocsis, 2020; Wenger-Trayner et al., 2019). Academic and professional staff leveraged design thinking and design innovation methods (Brown, 2009; Buchanan, 2019; Dalsgaard, 2010; Hanington & Martin, 2019; Norman, 1999; Wrigley, 2016; Wylant, 2008). Co-design practices (Bφdker et al., 1995; Council, 2018; Sanders & Stappers, 2008; Van der Bijl-Brouwer & Dorst, 2017) were employed by bringing together scholars from diverse disciplines, alongside students and industry sponsors. This approach required novel methods for legitimate peripheral participation (Wenger-Trayner et al., 2014) to codify the motivation, purpose, and potential outcomes of collaboration.

Intrinsic motivation and passion for the innovation challenge for both academics and professionals enabled tolerance of competing demands, work that was integrated across roles and disciplines, and an increasing blurring of roles. The roles evolved rapidly, and the importance of extrinsic recognition for the rapidly evolving capability and role types was underestimated, with outcomes being largely tacit and not measured formally. Agility to respond to intra- and international problem-solving in innovation hubs and labs, and with industry partners ranging from start-ups, small to medium enterprises (SME), government, and non-profit and commercial multinationals, saw both professional and academic staff extending their cognate expertise by radical and creative co-innovation methods (Leifer & Steinert, 2011; Leifer, 2000; Verganti, 2008, 2009). The activities, priorities, and evolution of key roles at the inception of DFM also underestimated the complexity of the work, which did not fit neatly into either academic or professional port-folio position descriptions. As the DFM evolved, it was challenging to hire staff for existing positions because the roles had evolved and required a mixture of skills, responsibilities, and ambitions beyond the norms that existed in the university infrastructure.

To meet these challenges, the DFM and the Design Factory Global Network (DFGN) community of practice described and identified roles by their capabilities and tasks. However, staff often referred to roles by various colloquial descriptors, such as *janitor, cleaner, unicorn, prototyping superman, El Capiton, Sailor, digital fabrication wizard, swiss army knife, octopus, innoCoach*, and *expectation manager*. These descriptors made clear that there was often a mismatch between capability, tasks, and expertise and the university role designations available, requiring DFM staff to stretch beyond traditional roles. For example, a designation as an academic *research fellow* or a professional *manager* were not suffi-cient to recognise the skills, responsibilities, or activities undertaken in each role. Nor did these titles provide recognition and career opportunities commensurate with the work involved or future requirements. For those employed on academic contracts, a *research fellow* designation came with expectations to publish peer-reviewed publications to meet performance requirements; yet the nature of the DFM work often extended beyond research work, leaving staff with little time to produce sufficient research outputs. For those on professional contracts, a *manager* role did not bring with it any opportunities to engage in research activities, with limited opportu-nities for promotion.

Looking to the Future of Innovation Roles: The DFM Model

To address the complexities of role definitions, boundaries, and rec-ognition, DFM provides a useful case example in the evolution of roles within innovation ecosystems. Here, we present an overview of three key roles that were successfully deployed within DFM:

1. First Impressions Manager;
2. Innovation Coach; and,
3. ProtoCoach.

These roles were held interchangeably by both academics and pro-fessional staff in DFM. Regardless of role, all DFM staff have a minimum master's degree (in such fields as business, architecture, design, and engineering), with a small percentage holding PhDs. People employed in DFM engage in various types of tasks born out of the passions they hold for a project. Yet, this approach is not easily captured or documented in traditional academic and/or professional position descriptions, which are lodged with the university's human resources division during the hiring process, subject to change only through formalised processes for role review, and governed by negotiated enterprise agreements. Thus, institutional requirements add another layer of complexity to navigating the content and boundaries of innovation work within university settings.

The DFM First Impressions Manager

The role of the *first impressions manager* was designed to be the DFM interface, with engagement responsibilities within the university and across international hubs in the DF network. The role of *first impressions manager* had three different role configurations in the ten years:

1. An academic who understood the national research model and moved into a professional role;
2. A professional staff member with experience as an executive, and with diverse experience in research, business development, student co-design, and product development; and,
3. A person experienced in arts management, with an academic background in arts and psychology, who managed DFM strategy and operations.

These individuals responded to the push of organisational leadership and the pull derived from the demands of DFM's projects. Daily tasks included fielding enquiries, stakeholder management, assisting with scoping projects, developing business models, resourcing diverse materials, operationalising recruitment of staff and interns, organising events for culture building, supporting staff and student operational needs, coaching strategic partnerships, participating in, or coaching student experiential learning, and leading and participating in workshops and interventions. An array of partner, academic, and student engagement daily, required experience of the DFM mission and the operations of research and academia, generally.

The DFM Innovation Coach

The DFM innovation coach was an academic with expertise in engineering who led strategy development and supported practices to foster innovation culture. Coaching (or being a "guide on the side") included curating serendipitous engagements to increase the incidents for ideation, and facilitating project teams to improve knowledge sharing across disciplinary differences. The *innovation coach* engaged with innovation curriculum development, led scoping exercises for large and diverse disciplinary research opportunities, taught in user-centred product development projects, and liaised with other international coaches in the DF global network to promote change culture. Coaching is employed in various ways in DFM, including in the curriculum as a tactic for experiential learning, for facilitation of programmes, through activities to normalise innovation culture, and to empower individual and team behaviours and tools to communicate tacit to explicit knowledge (Thong & Mattila, 2017).

The *innovation coach* was required to dedicate large portions of time to this role due to the high human interaction touchpoints of innovation work. This included investigating practices for socio-psychological negotiation skills and facilitating workshops that drove cross-institutional research scoping initiatives with research centres and internal and external institute initiatives. Work included formative ideation, across disciplines, including space research, social sciences, medtech, allied health, business, and law. The scoping tasks included developing use cases and customer identification with industry partners. Development work and stakeholder management in an interdisciplinary curriculum proved more time consuming than first estimated. The *innovation coach* was integral to strategic research and innovation initiatives, but their outputs were invisible in the university ecosystem, as research metrics and professional workloads did not include the type of work required for this role.

One *innovation coach* hired as professional staff, who had a degree in architecture (and without prior medical or health expertise), devised a novel innovation fellows programme to include design-led problem-solving for medical and allied practitioners. Another, academic *innovation coach*, brokered relationships across faculties to design distributed modes of engagement that would improve experiential learning through interdisciplinary transversal skills programmes. The role of the *innovation coach* acted as an institutional entrepreneur (Hasanefendic et al., 2017), instigating novel approaches for strategic action. For example, these staff enabled development of the first Bachelor of Applied Innovation by gaining buy-in from Deans and negotiating differing agendas, challenges, expectations, and opportunities across units and disciplinary silos in health, science, business, design, social sciences, law, and engineering.

The DFM ProtoCoach

The *protoCoach* was hired to develop skills for learners to think, to communicate complex concepts in diverse disciplinary student and research teams, and to demonstrate working proofs of concept. The *protoCoach* works through prototyping to help to translate researchers' and businesses' ideas, irrespective of disciplinary expertise, to solve or challenge a social, scientific, and/or technical problem.

The *protoCoach* was initially employed based on technical skills to operate equipment, such as routers, laser cutters, robots, and 3D printers, but expanded the role by developing new interior cues for innovation activity. The *protoCoach* extended their expertise to reconfigure the interior space as a tool to encourage modes of interaction; for example, they developed protocols to use equipment alongside novel methods to prototype fast, to materialise concepts for user testing, and to drive novel digital solutions for remote work. The *protoCoach*, while supporting academic teams, did not typically lead as a formal investigator for a programme of research. The *protoCoach* used prototyping to demonstrate to students, academics, and industry partners the viability, desirability, and feasibility (Brown, 2009) of problem-solving. During the initial phases of the Covid-19 pandemic, for example, Melbourne and other parts of Australia were locked down for significant periods of time over two years. The *protoCoach* and other team members designed a *ProtoKit* that was sent to students to continue their hands-on method training while working exclusively online, from home. This creative, demand-driven ingenuity resulted in a responsive solution due to the "all in" willingness of the team to achieve the impact irrespective of the academic, professional binary, or traditional expectations of university roles.

The *protoCoach* skill set facilitated modes of exploration that were hybrid and involved unlikely pairings of research and development (R&D) as a technical *service*, rather than only being identified as a core contributor of experimental prototyping approaches that *assisted* R&D.

These three DFM roles evolved to meet the demands of the innovation projects, regardless of formalised position descriptions that were normalised within the university. Today, the *innovation coach* is a ratified position description within the university and is also a common nomenclature in the international DF network. All roles in DFM require aspects of an institutional entrepreneur mindset to manage, mediate, and broker across otherwise unconnected groups and teams (see Figure 12.1). Innovation challenges and project types are boundary objects that drive team behaviours, needs, and outcomes, requiring collaborative structures that respond to and work across multiple partners, businesses, universities, and sectors. The DFM boundary-crossing infrastructure is an exemplar of the institutional challenges involved in undertaking innovation work.

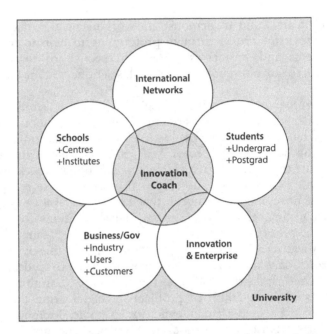

Figure 12.1 Innovation coach-boundary spanning across silos, organisational units, disciplines, and expertise, building new practices for innovation

Investigation of the individuals, the capability required, and the roles themselves, point to the emergence of a role we have identified as a *third space innovator*. Academics and professional staff in DFM extended their core knowledge to others, experimenting with untried and experimental practices to advance innovation, and crossing normalised boundaries that would otherwise have limited what DFM could achieve.

Theorising the Third Space Innovator Through the Lens of Bricoleur and Boundary Spanning

DFM's experience demonstrates that while institutional entrepreneurs are acknowledged, even if only informally, it is less well understood how individuals navigate the binary of academic vs. professional roles, disciplinary allegiances, organisational responsibilities, and key performance indicators. We employ theories of boundary spanning and boundary objects (Star, 2010; Lave & Wenger, 1991), third space professionals (Whitchurch, 2008, 2009, 2012, 2023), and bricolage (Lévi-Strauss, 2021) to consider the evolution and challenges of innovation roles and identify them as *third space innovators*. We describe DFM as a boundary infrastructure through Star's (2010) three dimensions of boundary objects: 1) interpretive flexibility, 2) material/organisational structure, and 3) scale of project and collaborative reach. We focus on the boundary spanners (Wenger, 1998, 1999), who shape the boundary infrastructure by legitimate professional participation (Lave & Wenger, 1991) in diverse disciplinary communities of practice (Wenger, 1998) and geographical networks. We position boundary objects (Wenger et al., 2011) as projects in response to the multiple, abstract, and ill-defined challenges, wicked and tame (Rittel & Webber, 1973) in the pursuit of innovation.

Boundary spanning "is the act of searching for knowledge from outside the current domain ... categorization of search behaviour underlying the innovation processes" (Nerkar & Miceli, 2016). Levina and Vaast (2013) characterise boundary spanners as "institutional entrepreneurs" who work as "translators" and "negotiators", which are hard to fill and "require legitimate peripheral participation in multiple fields, the legitimacy to represent and negotiate on behalf of these fields, and the symbolic, cultural, economic, and social capital endowments to help create new fields" (p. 302). While collaborative practices can result in a new joint field of practice (Levina & Vaast, 2005), the legitimation of this relies on the negotiation of capital with existing fields (Kislov et al., 2017). Boundary objects and infrastructures are crucial in supporting the practices of boundary spanning (Star, 2010; Levina & Vaast, 2013) providing a means of traversing, but also connecting, silos. Boundary work can be difficult to identify and classify within organisations where it is "invisible to the whole group and how a shared representation may be quite vague and at the same time quite useful" (Star, 2010, p. 607). The traversing of boundaries is also a learning opportunity and supports development of identity, where moving between fields of practice is characterised by what Lave and Wenger (1991) refer to as "legitimate peripheral participation".

Lévi-Strauss' concept of bricolage and the bricoleur is used in organisational studies to explore how new organisational practices are formed and found to be more prominent in times of change (Davis et al., 2005, p. 57). The bricoleur uses alternate means in comparison to a craftsperson or an engineer where tools, methods, and systems are ready made, well-understood, and defined by the parameters of the discipline, sector, and task at hand. The bricoleur's approach is not perfect, not exact, and arrives at the solution with multiple possible outcomes; they make do with what is available, being adept at finding tools and materials suitable for the purpose at the time, which may vary in the next challenge and be refined and developed over time. The tools, materials, and procedures may be constrained by an array of considerations, such as financial, environmental, social, and regulatory, so the bricoleur adapts, refines, and possibly retools. They, therefore, learn a new repertoire of practice to communicate or build something entirely new, with successive projects and tasks.

The Role of the Third Space Innovator

The concept of third space professionals originated from socio-cultural theories of the impact of context and experiences on identity (Bhabha, 2012); the concept is now used to explain the experiences of many staff in higher education working across traditional boundaries (Enders & Naidoo, 2019; Whitchurch, 2008, 2009). The third space is characterised as a location "beyond the traditional bounds of individual scientific disciplines … to other relevant stakeholder domains" (OECD, 2020, p. 15) involving hybridised roles, tasks, and motivations (Whitchurch, 2008, p. 378). Emerging "third space professionals" blur the lines between professions and organisational boundaries, morphing of career paths, roles, and identities, but are often invisible within organisational structures (Whitchurch, 2008), which presents challenges for formal role recognition and career paths (Akerman, 2020; Berman & Pitman, 2010; Dunleavy et al., 2019).

Following on the DFM experience, we developed the concept of the *third space innovators* as boundary spanners, who shape innovation outcomes beyond the remit of single fields of practice or disciplines, working across professional and academic roles, and challenging traditional organisational structures. We extend on third space theory, arguing that the pace and diversity of university–industry innovation traverses both academic and professional boundaries, creating new hybrid identities and practices assembled by an intellectual bricoleur (Lévi-Strauss, 2021; Whitchurch, 2008). *Third space innovators* facilitate translation across communities of practice, connecting different disciplines, and generating novel practices and expertise (Lave & Wenger, 1991; Whitchurch, 2015). Their ingenuity, resilience, and disciplinary ambidexterity reflects the approach of the bricoleur, as these innovators respond to, and successfully navigate, the requirements of projects, stakeholders, and their own institutions (Lévi-Strauss, 2021), even when these are not well-aligned and/or work in opposition to one another. The adoption of the bricoleur methodology in exploring the constituent skills, mindsets, and motivations of the *third space innovator* finds parallels in the political bricoleur, acknowledging that when "bits and pieces from several institutional and ideational legacies are blended to answer the continual stream of challenges" (Carstensen, 2011, p. 164), new concepts emerge. *Third space innovators* are resilient, creative, and design-integrated players in innovation eco-systems; they inhabit Levi-Strauss' theory of the bricoleur (Berry, 2015; Carstensen, 2011; Stinchfield et al., 2013) and bring this approach to the activities and policies shaping innovation spaces.

An innovation ecosystem includes many actors whose organisational structures are built on the canons of scholarship, fundamental research, learning practices, and service to society at large. Innovation hubs, labs, and experimental platforms require the evolving expertise of the third space innovator to navigate these structures, including through brokering relationships, creating solutions from disparate knowledge, and supporting implementation of emerging ideas. In the DFM, over 10 years, third space innovators, who began their careers as professionals or academics (or both), and who then developed transversal expertise, including transdisciplinary research practices, coaching expertise in innovation education, and strategies for managing complex stakeholder arrangements, were able to thrive. These innovators "build the plane as they fly it" through improvisation, creativity, and by responding to the challenge at hand. Yet, there are scant criteria to benchmark roles in a university system that has developed over centuries. To coach others to achieve innovation outcomes is not equivalent to sharing research outcomes by publishing in an academic journal. While both tasks are important, value is not weighted or acknowledged equally within our institutions. As universities continue to embrace an innovation mindset, and as they expect academics and professional staff to adopt and deploy the skills needed for innovation work, they must also acknowledge and recognise this work, formally, in position descriptions, promotion requirements, and performance measures.

Implications and Discussion

The DFM experience demonstrates that institutions must acknowledge the human factor in understanding and rewarding university triple helix collaboration. Currently, there is little attention or detail provided for the complexities of the roles and tasks needed for innovation success, despite the increasing demand for capability related to fostering university–industry collaboration. The *Australian Universities Accord Interim Report* (Australian Government, 2023) exchanges the term *collaboration* for *interaction* as the document reiterates the evidence of mission-focused initiatives to codify and diffuse innovations in a knowledge economy. Managing, operationalising, and rewarding intra-and extra-university–industry interactions is contingent on acknowledging a burgeoning capability found in innovation platforms, driven by *third space innovators* and their R&D capacity. DFM has led the way over more than a decade; yet, the experience of this one innovation hub demonstrates that significant support is needed within and across institutions to drive success of the type required by innovation work. This is complex work that requires complex role development; yet many universities and the organisations with whom they interact continue to focus on traditional roles, bounded tasks, and understandings of workload that are not fit for purpose for innovation work.

Innovation hubs require agility and ongoing disciplinary flexibility. Yet, their hosts (such as universities and research organisations) are not well-equipped to recognise, reward, or provide career progression and advice for *third space innovators*. Currently, this leads to career disruptions for staff who do not "fit the mould" and cannot attain traditional measures of success, due to competing work demands. We need to move beyond the academic vs. professional binary if we are to fully realise the promise of innovation work. The challenges tackled by innovation hubs like DFM, which have the potential to drive innovation outcomes and socio-economic impact, provide a sandbox to mitigate risk and engage in novel R&D. In practice, this includes high levels of ambiguity, failure, and experimentation, where no criteria for success exist; this makes the work difficult to measure and recognise, particularly when traditional key performance indicators (such as publications and research funding amounts) continue to drive university rankings and staff expectations for promotion (Kelly & Given, 2023).

While one may argue that research on innovation, entrepreneurship, and institutional entrepreneurship is its own field, creating a new silo for innovation work and the experience of the third space innovator is not the solution. The type of bricoleur ingenuity experienced in DFM affects all disciplines and individuals with varied educational and experiential backgrounds. Critical mass for exploration and resolution of the problems of working in the third space must be achieved across disciplines, and across sectors, providing a holistic view of the benefits and challenges of innovation work. Beyond universities, other types of innovation labs, start-ups, and the like in the commercial sector also rely on *third space innovators*. However, in many of these contexts, innovative work behaviours are rewarded and remunerated, measured against exploration, generation, and championing and implementation of ideas (De Jong & Den Hartog, 2010). Universities have much to gain by partnering with these innovation organisations, to explore how *third space innovators* can be better integrated into the university workforce and reward schemes. This also aligns to global future workforce demands for the top 15 skills for 2025, which include analytical thinking and innovation, creativity, originality and initiative, complex problem-solving, reasoning, problem-solving and ideation, emotional intelligence, troubleshooting and user experience, persuasion, and negotiation (World Economic Forum, 2020, p. 36). Innovation demands new practices, skills, and ingenuity, and universities cannot afford to maintain the status quo in the design and implementation of traditional academic and professional role descriptions.

Conclusion

Third space innovators are a burgeoning innovation workforce comprising academic and professional staff that respond to the speed of the knowledge economy and are responsive to ambiguity and disruption. As a result, these staff devise novel methods, strategies, and approaches by problem-solving to advance innovation efforts. We theorise the multifaceted, transdisciplinary, and transversal skills of *third space innovators*, like the bricoleur, have no existing set of resources or defined practices. Traditional academic and professional roles, responsibilities, and associated position descriptions were developed over time and became deeply entrenched in university structures, performance expectations, and disciplinary ways of being. As innovation work requires new and diverse expertise and abilities, alongside traditional skills and knowledge, these roles are currently invisible, unrecognised, and unrewarded within the standard university bureaucracy.

We depict activities, roles, and levels of expertise in the DFM innovation hub narrative that (like the bricoleur) are shaped not out of an existing repertoire of practice or well-worn sets of tools and systems; rather, *third space innovators* forge new modes of operation, research, development, and innovation to advance the urgent socio-technical and environmental challenges of our time. The task of connecting disparate areas of knowledge to focus on a challenge and codify solutions requires novel and untested approaches, both of which are precursors to innovation. Despite the ten years of evolution in the DFM, innovation roles remain challenging to classify as visibility beyond the classical organisational criteria for role types in universities and industry are abstract. Criteria are dominated by long-standing measures and slow to recognise *third space innovator* expertise.

Universities and other research organisations are yet to catch up on the human factors reflected in the work of *third space innovators*, despite the investment in innovation capital. DFM's approach recognises that third space workers are typically situated in variable environments; they adapt to tasks, manage ambiguity, explore multiple possible outcomes, and work with what is available rather than with prescriptive tools designed to meet other needs. *Third space innovators* in hubs define the boundary infrastructure, that is, the space and community of practice that affords innovation. The challenges remain for identifying roles, responsibilities, and expertise to attract and foster a growing innovation ecosystem that impacts careers, relationships, and activities in universities and research infrastructures. Innovation can only be realised with holistic approaches that account for both the infrastructural and human needs within the ecosystem. As long as we expect academics and professional staff in "traditional" roles to embed innovation practices on top of traditional measures of success – and without acknowledging or rewarding the unique aspects of innovation work – we cannot fully realise the promise of innovation to transform either our institutions or society at large.

References

Akerman, K. (2020). Invisible imposter: Identity in institutions. *Perspectives: Policy and Practice in Higher Education, 24*(4), 126–130.

Australian Government. (2021). *National Research Infrastructure Roadmap.* Canberra: Department of Education, Skills and Employment. https://www. dese.gov.au/national-research-infrastructure/resources/2021-national-l research-infrastructure-roadmap

Australian Government. (2023). *Australian Universities Accord Interim Report.* Australian Universities Accord Review Panel. https://www.education.gov.au/ australian-universities-accord/resources/accord-interim-report

Berman, J. E., & Pitman, T. (2010). Occupying a 'third space': Research trained professional staff in Australian universities. *Higher Education, 60*(2), 157–169.

Berry, K. S. (2015) Research as bricolage: Embracing relationality, multiplicity and complexity. In K. Tobin and S. R. Steinberg (Eds), *Doing Educational Research: A Handbook* (Second Edition) (pp. 79–110). Sense Publishers.

Bhabha, H. K. (2012). *The Location of Culture.* Routledge.

Björklund, T. A., Keipi, T., Celik, S., & Ekman, K. (2019). Learning across silos: Design Factories as hubs for co-creation. *European Journal of Education, 54*(4), 552–565.

Björklund, T., Laakso, M., Kirjavainen, S., & Ekman, K. (2017). *Passion-based co-creation.* Aalto University.

Bødker, S., Grønbæk, K., & Kyng, M. (1995). Cooperative design: Techniques and experiences from the Scandinavian scene. In R. M. Baecker, J. Grudin, W. Buxton & S. Greenberg (Eds.), *Readings in Human–Computer Interaction* (pp. 215–224). Morgan Kaufmann.

Bowker, G. C., Timmermans, S., Clarke, A. E., & Balka, E. (Eds.). (2016). *Boundary Objects and Beyond: Working with Leigh Star.* MIT Press.

Bowker, G. C., & Star, S. L. (2000). *Sorting Things Out: Classification and its Consequences.* MIT Press.

Brown, T. (2009). *Change by design: How design thinking transforms organizations and inspires innovation*. Harper Collins.

Buijs, J. (2007). Innovation leaders should be controlled schizophrenics. *Creativity and innovation management, 16*(2), 203–210.

Buchanan, R. (2019). Surroundings and environments in fourth order design. *Design Issues, 35*(1), 4–22.

Carstensen, M. B. (2011). Paradigm man vs. the bricoleur: Bricolage as an alternative vision of agency in ideational change. *European Political Science Review, 3*(1), 147–167.

Cinar, R., & Benneworth, P. (2021). Why do universities have little systemic impact with social innovation? An institutional logics perspective. *Growth and Change, 52*(2), 751–769.

Coddington, A., Giang, C., Graham, A., Prince, A., Mattila, P., Thong, C., & Kocsis, A. (2016) Knowledgeability culture: Co-creation in practice. In P. Lloyd, & E. Bohemia (Eds.), *Future Focused Thinking – DRS International Conference 2016*, 27–30 June, Brighton,United Kingdom. https://doi.org/10.21606/drs.2016.134

Council, D. (2018). *The design economy 2018: The state of design in the UK*. Design Council.

Dalsgaard, P. (2010, November). Research in and through design: An interaction design research approach. In *Proceedings of the 22nd conference of the computer–human interaction special interest group of Australia on computer–human interaction* (pp. 200–203).

Davis, G. F., McAdam, D., Scott, W. R., & Zald, M. N. (2005). *Social Movements and Organization Theory*. Cambridge University Press.

De Jong, J., & Den Hartog, D. (2010). Measuring innovative work behaviour. *Creativity and Innovation Management, 19*(1), 23–36.

Dow, S. P., Heddleston, K., & Klemmer, S. R. (2009, October). The efficacy of prototyping under time constraints. In *Proceedings of the seventh ACM conference on Creativity and cognition* (pp. 165–174).

Dunleavy, K., Noble, M., & Andrews, H. (2019). The emergence of the publicly engaged research manager. *Research for All, 3*(1), 105–124.

Enders, J., & Naidoo, R. (2019). Audit-market intermediaries: Doing institutional work in British research-intensive universities. *Studies in Higher Education, 44*(7), 1290–1301.

Gibbons, M. (2000). Mode 2 society and the emergence of context-sensitive science. *Science and Public Policy, 27*(3), 159–163. doi:10.3152/147154300 781782011

Gregor, S., & Hevner, A. R. (2015). The front end of innovation: Perspectives on creativity, knowledge and design. In *New Horizons in Design Science: Broadening the Research Agenda: 10th International Conference*, DESRIST 2015, Dublin, Ireland, May 20–22, 2015, Proceedings 10 (pp. 249–263). Springer International Publishing.

Halilem, N. (2010). Inside the triple helix: An integrative conceptual framework of the academic researcher's activities, a systematic review. *Journal of Research Administration, 41*(3), 23–50.

Hanington, B., & Martin, B. (2019). *Universal Methods of Design Expanded and Revised: 125 Ways to Research Complex Problems, Develop Innovative Ideas, and Design Effective Solutions*. Rockport Publishers.

Hasanefendic, S., Birkholz, J. M., Horta, H., & van der Sijde, P. (2017). Individuals in action: Bringing about innovation in higher education. *European Journal of Higher Education, 7*(2), 101–119. https://doi.org/10.1080/21568235.2017.1296367

Joore, P., Björklund, T., Thong, C., & Zancul, E. D. S. (2022). Co-creating the future through design-based education in innovation hubs. *CERN IdeaSquare Journal of Experimental Innovation, 6*(2), 1–3.

Kelly, W. B., & Given, L. M. (2023). The community engagement for impact (CEFI) framework: An evidence-based strategy to facilitate social change. *Studies in Higher Education*, DOI: 10.1080/03075079.2023.2238762

Kislov, R., Hyde, P., & McDonald, R. (2017). New game, old rules? Mechanisms and consequences of legitimation in boundary spanning activities. *Organization Studies, 38*(10), 1421–1444.

Kocsis, A. (2020). Prototyping: The journey and the ripple effect of knowledgeability. *Fusion Journal*, (18), 60–70.

Kolb, D. A. (1984). *Experience as the source of learning and development.* Prentice Hall.

Lave, J., & Wenger, E. (1991). *Situated learning: Legitimate peripheral participation.* Cambridge University Press.

Leifer, L. J., & Steinert, M. (2011). Dancing with ambiguity: Causality behavior, design thinking, and triple-loop-learning. *Information Knowledge Systems Management, 10*(1–4), 151–173.

Leifer, R. (2000). *Radical Innovation: How Mature Companies Can Outsmart Upstarts.* Harvard Business Press.

Lévi-Strauss, C. (2021). *Wild Thought: A New Translation of "La Pensée Sauvage".* University of Chicago Press.

Levina, N., & Vaast, E. (2005). The emergence of boundary spanning competence in practice: Implications for implementation and use of information systems. *MIS Quarterly, 29*(2), 335–363.

Levina, N., & Vaast, E. (2013). A field-of-practice view of boundary-spanning in and across organizations: Transactive and transformative boundary-spanning practices. In J. L. Fox & C. Cooper, *Boundary-Spanning in Organizations* (pp. 295–317). Routledge.

Matthews, J. (2017). Experimenting and innovation: Purposes, possibilities and preferred solutions. *CERN IdeaSquare Journal of Experimental Innovation (CIJ), 1*(1), 17–20.

Minguillo, D., & Thelwall, M. (2015). Which are the best innovation support infrastructures for universities? Evidence from R&D output and commercial activities. *Scientometrics, 102*, 1057–1081.

Nerkar, A., & Miceli, K. A. (2016). Boundary Spanning. In M. Augier & D. J. Teece (Eds.), *The Palgrave Encyclopedia of Strategic Management* (pp. 1–7). Palgrave Macmillan UK. https://doi.org/10.1057/978-1-349-94848-2_333-1

Nnanna, J., Charles, M. B., Noble, D., & Keast, R. (2023). Innovation hubs in Australian public universities: An appraisal of their public value claims. *International Journal of Public Administration, 46*(2), 133–143.

Norman, D. A. (1999). Affordance, conventions, and design. *Interactions, 6*(3), 38–43.

OECD. (2019). *University–Industry Collaboration: New Evidence and Policy Options.* OECD Publishing. https://doi.org/10.1787/e9c1e648-en

OECD. (2020). *Addressing Societal Challenges Using Transdisciplinary Research*. OECD Science, Technology and Industry Policy Papers, No. 88, OECD Publishing. https://doi.org/10.1787/0ca0ca45-en

Rekonen, S., & Björklund, T. A. (2016). Adapting to the changing needs of managing innovative projects. *European Journal of Innovation Management*, 19(1), 111–132.

Rittel, H. W., & Webber, M. M. (1973). Dilemmas in a general theory of planning. *Policy sciences*, 4(2), 155–169.

Sanders, E. B. N., & Stappers, P. J. (2008). Co-creation and the new landscapes of design. *Co-design*, 4(1), 5–18.

Star, S. L. (2010). This is not a boundary object: Reflections on the origin of a concept. *Science, technology, & human values*, 35(5), 601–617.

Stinchfield, B. T., Nelson, R. E., & Wood, M. S. (2013). Learning from Levi-Strauss' legacy: Art, craft, engineering, bricolage, and brokerage in entrepreneurship. *Entrepreneurship Theory and Practice*, 37(4), 889–921.

Thong, C, & Mattila, P. (2017). Coaching for an innovation culture. In T. Björklund, M. Laakso, S. Kirjavainen, & K. Ekman (Eds.), *Passion-Based Co-Creation* (pp. 102–109). Aalto Design Factory. https://designfactory.aalto.fi/for-media/#publications

Van der Bijl-Brouwer, M., & Dorst, K. (2017). Advancing the strategic impact of human-centred design. *Design Studies*, 53, 1–23.

Verganti, R. (2008). Design, meanings, and radical innovation: A metamodel and a research agenda. *Journal of Product Innovation Management*, 25(5), 436–456.

Verganti, R. (2009). *Design driven innovation: Changing the rules of competition by radically innovating what things mean*. Harvard Business Press.

Wenger, E. (1998). Communities of practice: Learning as a social system. *Systems Thinker*, 9(5), 2–3.

Wenger, E. (1999). *Communities of Practice: Learning, Meaning, and Identity*. Cambridge University Press.

Wenger, E., Trayner, B., & De Laat, M. (2011). *Promoting and Assessing Value Creation in Communities and Networks: A Conceptual Framework*.

Wenger-Trayner, E., Fenton-O'Creevy, M., Hutchinson, S., Kubiak, C., & Wenger-Trayner, B. (Eds.). (2014). *Learning in Landscapes of Practice: Boundaries, Identity, and knowledgeability in Practice-Based Learning*. Routledge.

Wenger-Trayner, B., Wenger-Trayner, E., Cameron, J., Eryigit-Madzwamuse, S., & Hart, A. (2019). Boundaries and boundary objects: An evaluation framework for mixed methods research. *Journal of Mixed Methods Research*, 13(3), 321–338.

Wensveen, S., & Matthews, B. (2014). Prototypes and prototyping in design research. In *The Routledge Companion to Design Research* (pp. 262–276). Routledge.

Whitchurch, C. (2008). Shifting identities and blurring boundaries: The emergence of third space professionals in UK higher education. *Higher Education Quarterly*, 62(4), 377–396.

Whitchurch, C. (2009). The rise of the blended professional in higher education: A comparison between the United Kingdom, Australia and the United States. *Higher Education*, 58, 407–418.

Whitchurch, C. (2012). *Reconstructing Identities in Higher Education: The Rise of 'Third Space' Professionals*. Routledge.

Whitchurch, C. (2015). The rise of third space professionals: Paradoxes and dilemmas. In U. Teichler, W. Cummings, (Eds.), *Forming, recruiting and managing the academic profession*, (pp. 79–99). Springer.

Whitchurch, C. (2023). Rehabilitating third space professionals in contemporary higher education institutions. *Workplace: A Journal for Academic Labor, 33*, 23–33.

Whitchurch, C., Locke, W., & Marini, G. (2023). *Challenging approaches to academic career-making*. Bloomsbury Publishing.

World Economic Forum. (2020). *The Future of Jobs Report 2020*. https://www.weforum.org/publications/the-future-of-jobs-report-2020/

Wrigley, C. (2016). Design innovation catalysts: Education and impact. *She Ji: The Journal of Design, Economics, and Innovation, 2*(2), 148–165.

Wylant, B. (2008). Design thinking and the experience of innovation. *Design Issues, 24*(2), 3–14.

Youtie, J., & Shapira, P. (2008). Building an innovation hub: A case study of the transformation of university roles in regional technological and economic development. *Research Policy, 37*(8), 1188–1204.

13 The Two Imperatives of Business School Impact

Michel Kalika and Stephen Platt

Introduction

Since the 2008 financial crisis, which notably called into question the teaching of finance in business schools, there has been a growing interest in matters relating to impact. If there is one word that has come to the fore over the past decade, it is clearly impact! Beyond the financial crisis, two phenomena may help us to understand the growing role of impact in the management of business schools. First, the limits of traditional accreditations focused exclusively on processes (it is telling that AACSB has made impact one of its three pillars and that AMBA has focused its Business Graduates Association [BGA] accreditation on impact), and second the growing role of stakeholders in holding schools to account. Today's climate change challenges raise the question of how future business managers will deal with sustainability issues. But beyond the virtuous rhetoric and the haphazard use of the word "impact", we believe that there are two things that schools need to do in terms of impact. First, it should be properly measured, and second, research that truly generates impact should be encouraged, particularly in the context of Doctorates of Business Administration (DBAs).

The Need to Measure Impact Properly

Beyond the traditional formula attributed to Peter Drucker, "what gets measured gets managed", impact measurement is essential for several reasons. First, because without indicators, it is impossible to set objectives in terms of impact and to engage teams internally. Second, because measuring impact provides the institution with a powerful communication tool, particularly for its stakeholders.

If we accept that impact measurement is essential, and that we no longer need to answer the question of why impact should be measured, five questions remain, and business schools have a duty to provide the answers.[1]

DOI: 10.4324/9781003459217-15

1. Who are the stakeholders we want to convince about the impact? Are they local, regional, national or international? The answers to this question, which can be many and varied, will determine both the indicators and the areas of impact taken as a reference.

2. Which impact(s) do we want to measure? Is it the impact of programmes? At bachelor's, master's or doctoral level? Is it the impact of executive education? Is it the impact of research (a topic we will come back to later in this chapter)? Or, is it the impact of activities related to entrepreneurship, entrepreneurship programmes or incubators?

3. Then there is the tricky question of the zone (or zones, as there may be several) where the impact is to be assessed. It should be noted here that impact zones are directly linked to the stakeholders we want to convince about the impact, but also to the school's mission. For example, a school that sets itself the objective of running international programme provision might take the whole world as its zone of impact. The question also arises for multi-campus schools, where it is useful to study the impact of each campus in its own specific location.

4. There is also the question of impact on whom or on what. When talking about impact, it is important not only to specify (see point 2) which impact we are talking about, but also to specify what this impact relates to. Are we interested in the individual impact of undergraduate and graduate education, or of executive training? Are we interested in the impact of programmes or research on businesses or public or voluntary organisations? Are we focusing on the societal impact of the school, particularly through education or research?

5. Finally, there is the delicate question of the timeframe over which the impact will be assessed. When we talk about financial impact, we generally consider the impact over a period of one year. But this makes no sense when we are studying the entrepreneurial impact of a school, for example. In this case, we need to take a longer period as a reference (a decade, for example), and to include in financial terms a proportion representing the school's role in the development of revenue, fundraising or job creation. The same question arises when considering the impact of training students in sustainable development. Here, we need to consider deferred impacts and conduct surveys of alumni.

As with any study, it will be necessary to decide whether to use an outside organisation to provide methodology and human resources, whether to strengthen the accreditation team internally or create a team to focus specifically on questions of impact. This last option has the advantage of making the tools your own and monitoring the indicators over time.

These different questions, to which the answers are contingent and specific to each institution, explain why impact measurements do not lend themselves well to the comparisons and rankings favoured by magazines and newspaper league tables.

Once the answers to these five preliminary questions have been provided, we need to specify which dimensions of impact should be selected. Some consultancies specialising in the evaluation of universities limit their approach to calculating the impact in financial terms, particularly over one year. In our view, these approaches are simplistic, and it would be more appropriate to adopt a multi-dimensional approach to impact, which genuinely incorporates the various facets and the overall impact of a school on its different ecosystems. In the Business School Impact System[2] (BSIS) approach mentioned below, we have selected seven dimensions of impact. They are not independent of each other, but they do allow us to understand impact from a holistic perspective.

1. The financial impact, which is probably the easiest to calculate. A distinction is made between direct and indirect financial impact. The direct financial impact is assessed on the basis of the school's budget, the entities that would not exist if the school did not exist (student and alumni associations), and a proportion of the budget of outlying organisations to which the school contributes (incubators, associations, etc.). The difficulty sometimes lies in defining the institutional perimeter to be taken into account and in assessing the percentage of expenditure made in the zone under consideration. The indirect financial impact mainly includes student spending in the local region (excluding enrolment fees, which are already included in the school's budget).

2. The educational impact, which is of course one of the most important, must include the number of students enrolled in the various programmes, as well as the attraction rates for students from other regions or countries and the retention rates in the regions concerned. Employment rates are, of course, also taken into account. But beyond the quantitative impact, there is the question of the immediate and delayed qualitative impact of the programmes on students. What remains of courses in ethics and sustainable development when the students have become alumni in charge of businesses? We should consider that measuring the delayed educational impact of an institution on its former students must involve alumni surveys. This is not easy, but it is the only way to measure the educational impact, particularly in terms of sustainable development.

3. The economic development impact of a school should be assessed in three main ways: Internships or placements, whose contribution to companies and organisations can be measured by taking recruitment salaries and applying a weighting based on the students' year of study; consultancy assignments or projects carried out for companies as part of the curriculum; business start-ups created by students and alumni, taking into account the impact on employment and turnover generated.

4. The school's intellectual impact is linked to its research activity. Traditionally, when we talk about the impact of research, we think of "A-ranked journal", "impact factor", "H index". Today, it is more and more widely accepted that the analysis of the impact of research cannot be limited to its academic dimension, as managers, and even consultants, rarely read the academic journals cited by academics. We therefore need to add educational, managerial and societal dimensions to the perspective of academic impact. In terms of pedagogical impact, it is important to identify the research used in teaching both in undergraduate/postgraduate training and in executive education. Measuring the managerial impact of research is more difficult, except in the case of intervention research where the link between research and practice can be clearly identified. For mainstream research, we need to use proxies and look at professional or general public publications, dissemination videos and conferences held for practitioners in particular. In terms of societal impact, measurement is even trickier, except in the case of research that directly inspires legislators. In order to avoid contradictory injunctions, schools should clearly specify to their faculty the objectives and indicators for measuring academic, managerial and societal impact.

5. The impact on the ecosystem is too often ignored. But in fact, a business school interacts to varying degrees with other entities in the academic world, professional organisations, chambers of commerce, companies, public organisations, associations, etc. By its very DNA, a business school is open to its environment. It may, therefore, be advisable to draw up an ecosystem map showing the different types of stakeholders (academic, private, public, etc.) and to specify the nature and intensity of the relationships. As there is a great deal of information to be included, an interactive online version may be useful.

6. The societal impact includes the full range of activities carried out by the school and its students, and especially their clubs and societies. This dimension, which is not independent of the educational and intellectual dimensions, is increasingly taken into

account through the 17 United Nations Sustainable Development Goals (SDGs). The contribution of the business school's activities is therefore measured in terms of the link with each SDG.

7. Finally, the impact of the school's brand image is also too often ignored or underestimated. Some schools or universities bear the name of the town or region in which they are located. All the school's communications, as well as the presence of students and the organisation of events, benefit the region's reputation.

To conclude this discussion on the need to measure the impact of business schools, we would like to highlight the dilemma that these institutions have to overcome in terms of measuring impact. Because of the influence of accreditation, schools focus on publishing academic articles, regardless of their impact on managers, companies and society. It is common knowledge that the impact of the vast majority of so-called academic publications is limited to bonuses for professors and meeting accreditation standards. Academic impact is, therefore, reduced to impact within academia. There is an urgent need to change the way we measure the impact of research, so that research that has a managerial and societal impact is valued. This is particularly true of DBA research, for example, where managerial recommendations are generated specifically for the benefit of business.

The Need to Develop More DBA Programmes

Doctorate of Business Administration (DBA) programmes, as defined by EQUAL[3] or the Executive DBA Council (EDBAC),[4] are doctoral programmes designed for managers who, in three to four years,[5] prepare a thesis under the supervision of a university professor.

According to a recent survey[6] of some one hundred business schools, conducted by the European Foundation for Management Development (EFMD) and EDBAC, 86 per cent of respondents believe that the DBA market will grow in the near future. Moreover, 23 per cent of institutions that do not currently run a DBA, are planning to launch one. Among the main factors driving growth are career transformation objectives, the quest for a doctorate qualification that can make a difference in a market where the MBA has become commonplace, and the need for research that generates impact.

What DBA programmes have in common with traditional PhD programmes is that they include seminars on research design, epistemological positioning, literature reviews and data analysis methodologies. The main differences are threefold:

1. First, the thesis topic comes from the practitioner and is directly linked to their experience and the managerial concerns they face in their professional life. The role of the faculty is to enable them to transform their managerial concerns into research questions and conceptual problems.
2. Second, DBA theses are generally very closely linked in terms of data collection to the country and/or business sector in which the manager operates. This leads many DBA candidates to use qualitative methodologies grounded in rich professional contexts.
3. Finally, and this is the characteristic of DBA theses that gives them such a high impact potential, they systematically include managerial recommendations that are directly linked to the research results. In this way, the loop is closed and the virtuous circle of impact is initiated: the topic comes from the field, the conceptual framework comes from the literature, the data comes from the research field and its processing produces results that are useful to managers and their organisations.

Based on an interview survey conducted with 80 of our alumni[7] in 2022–23, we were able to identify several types of impact from their accounts. First, the impact of the DBA must be differentiated according to the phases of the doctoral process. During the first phase, i.e., enrolment in the programme, some doctors already report a different attitude from their professional entourage. During the second phase, preparation for the DBA, which lasts three to four years on average, the doctors point to a real process of intellectual transformation, which they illustrate by talking about the ability to stand back from their practice and manage complexity. The third phase closes the formal process with the viva and generates impacts in terms of credibility, legitimacy, image and prestige. The fourth phase, after the defence, concerns the publications and conferences contributed to by the doctors (Figure 13.1).

Second, the impact of the DBA needs to be differentiated according to the parties involved. The first stakeholder is, of course, the doctor. Alumni cite a large number of changes that impact them personally. They emphasise the impact of the DBA on their personal attitude. They talk of pride, but also of humility and self-confidence. They also note profound changes in their working methods, in terms of rigour and their ability to put things into perspective. In terms of skills, the DBA had a positive influence on their cognitive abilities (analytical and summarising abilities) and

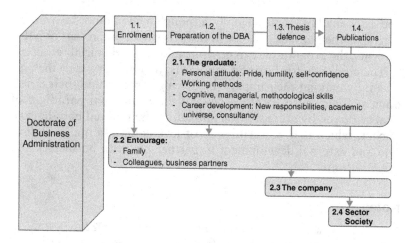

Figure 13.1 Impact of the DBA
Source: 80 Tales of DBA Impact 2013–2023, p. 21.

on their managerial and methodological skills. Finally, the doctors note the impact of the DBA on their career direction. Access to new responsibilities, to the academic world and to the consulting profession are very frequently mentioned as results of the DBA. The second stakeholder concerned by the impact of the DBA is the company where the doctor is employed. The results of the doctoral process lead to the implementation of managerial recommendations that bring about changes in the organisations where the doctors work. Finally, the impact on the sector and on society at large should be highlighted. In the case of Business Science Institute, the doctors have published 26 books, available online or in hard copy, and they also generate an impact by virtue of the responsibilities they hold (CEO, ministers, consultants). As around half of them teach in universities, this is also a factor in disseminating the impact.

For a university, the benefit of a DBA programme is far-reaching, helping to open the institution to its professional and social environment and leading to multiple impacts.

In terms of research, a DBA programme gives researchers access to fields of investigation and data that are very valuable in qualitative terms. It also enables the institution to forge research partnerships with companies and professional organisations. At the same time, it helps to change the internal culture of research centres, by linking academic impact (publications) with managerial and societal impact. Indeed, some professors have made it clear to us that supervising DBA theses has helped them develop their approach to supervising and assessing PhD theses. Finally, although it should not be overestimated, as the number of DBA students is smaller than that of MBA students, the programme can generate additional financial resources.

The challenge for business schools is, therefore, to shift the paradigm by making their impact the driving force behind their development. They need to move beyond the traditional paradigm of quality driven by accreditation and adopt the internal paradigm of impact, which is a powerful way of leveraging internal mobilisation and external development in partnership with businesses and organisations.

Notes

1 Michel Kalika, *BSIS, a Decade of Impact* (Paris: EMS, 2022).
2 BSIS: https://www.efmdglobal.org/assessments/business-schools/bsis/
3 EQUAL: https://www.equal.network/wp-content/uploads/2016/11/161110-EQUAL_Guidelines_Doctoral.pdf
4 EDBAC: https://edbac.org/
5 AMBA accreditation for DBAs requires a minimum duration of 4 years.
6 https://www.efmdglobal.org/knowledge/report-the-future-of-dba-market-perceptions-of-business-schools/
7 Frédéric Branger, Aline Closse, Michel Kalika and Stephen Platt, *80 Tales of DBA Impact 2013–2023* (Paris: EMS, 2023).

14 Leveraging Academic Structures and Resources to Impact Non-Academic Organizations

David R. Seibold

Introduction

In this chapter, I discuss eight ways that university faculty members can leverage academic structures and resources on their campuses, and on others, to impact non-academic organizations – especially businesses. I do so from the perspective of a social scientist with a specialty in organizational and team communication. During 38 years of full-time employment, I was a faculty member in the communication departments at three major universities in the United States (U.S.) (Purdue University, University of Illinois at Urbana-Champaign [UIUC], and University of California Santa Barbara [UCSB]), as well as the multidisciplinary Technology Management Department in the College of Engineering at UCSB.

I also was privileged to serve as a Visiting Professor at the University of Southern California, University of Nebraska, Ohio University, and Kent State University. Before then, I completed graduate degrees at the University of Michigan and at Michigan State University. Throughout my years as a faculty member, I participated on teams of external reviewers for a half dozen programs at other major universities in the United States. Furthermore, nearly two-thirds of my 22 doctoral advisees accepted tenure-leading positions at prominent universities, other than those I have noted in my career biography (e.g., University of Texas, Rutgers University, University of Georgia, University of Wisconsin), and their opportunities to bridge between their institutions and businesses mirrored mine in most ways. I mention all these institutions because the totality of my appointments and theirs enhanced my awareness of structures and resources that full-time academics can leverage to impact businesses. A UCSB emeritus faculty member for the past five years, I have continued to publish works for other scholars and for practitioners, to teach graduate-level courses on a "callback"

DOI: 10.4324/9781003459217-16

basis, and to consult actively with businesses. All three of these post-retirement commitments also inform the eight proposals below, each of which I illustrate with examples from campuses on which I was a faculty member at the time.

Although I have lectured at universities internationally, have collaborated with faculty from outside the U.S., and have advised international graduate students studying in the U.S. (and served as a member of examining committees at universities in other countries), I simply do not know enough about the structures and resources at non-U.S. universities that faculty members there can appropriate to impact businesses. Therefore, this chapter, regrettably, is written from only an American perspective (and mainly major public universities in U.S. states). I trust that non-U.S. academics will see similarities and differences between what I propose and their local circumstances in order to impact business, and that they will identify still other structures and resources at their campuses that they can appropriate.

1. Personal Consulting: Leveraging Academic Expertise and Academic Policies

Within the scope of creating, disseminating, and applying knowledge for the betterment of the global society, all U.S. universities' missions include an institutional goal (and expectation for faculty) of "service". For example, my current institution (UCSB) pledges that "our commitment to public service is manifested through the creation and distribution of knowledge that advances the well-being of our state, nation, and world". Academic personnel policies have been developed to encourage and set boundaries for faculty members' consulting with other organizations, including businesses. Leveraging areas of personal academic expertise, together with university policies that encourage sharing that expertise with businesses, is an important way that faculty members can impact those organizations, while also indirectly strengthening relationships between the university and them.

As discussed in Seibold (2005) and elaborated in Seibold (2016), my own commitment as an academic researcher has been to theoretical studies that are methodologically rigorous and socially relevant. Being engaged in socially relevant research and practice also has entailed consulting with organizations when appropriate. Over the course of now 47 years (including graduate studies), I have consulted with 95 organizations at over 140 locations. Approximately 65 percent of these consultations were with for-profit organizations, ranging from family-owned and-managed companies, to minority-owned small enterprises, to Fortune 500 corporations.

They have been in diverse sectors: energy, technology, telecommunications, hospitality, retail, professional services, transportation, consumer goods, agriculture, financial services, insurance, and entertainment. Roughly 30 percent of the consultations were with government and non-profit organizations in numerous areas: education, philanthropy, environmental protection, international development, health, human services, and professional associations. The last five percent have been projects in which colleagues and I offered services to organizations unable to undertake them on their own (e.g., charitable and civic organizations). For nearly 25 years, during the heart of my career, I committed roughly a day each week, part of most vacations, and the majority of summer recess with at least 4000 persons from nearly 50 countries. These consultations included serving as content expert, facilitator, executive coach, technical advisor, program evaluator, trainer, curriculum designer, process consultant, and featured speaker. The consulting relationships lasted from one-day/one-time speaking engagements to 21 years of work with a Fortune 500 energy company. I reviewed these experiences to demonstrate that there are widespread opportunities for faculty members to similarly serve and impact businesses.

2. Consulting Partnerships: Leveraging Collaborations Among Academics

Collaborations are natural for faculty members used to partnering on research projects and coauthoring papers. Consulting to businesses, as discussed in (1), need not imply that those engagements are done *alone*. Indeed, efforts to bridge between universities and business are arguably more plentiful and potentially more impactful if they involve *collaborations* among multiple faculty members. The faculty may be in the same discipline and from the same department or similar departments at different universities. The collaborations may involve faculty from two or more disciplines, again from the same university and/or from more than one campus. In addition, collaborations between one or more faculty members and one or more practitioners (especially from the client business) are not only possible but may provide rich experiences for both parties. They proffer impactful engagements, and they may even foster co-created academic research (Simpson & Seibold, 2008).

Quite a few of my consultations involved collaborations with many other faculty and with several practitioners. The most fruitful and effective collaborative consultations were with what is now a major consulting firm in the eastern U.S. that specializes in executive leadership and strategic communications. Its managing partner founded the company nearly 40 years ago when he was a faculty member at the University of Illinois. He fostered collaboration with two other faculty there (myself included) and with another at Temple University. All of us were active in consulting besides being established scholars. Our aim was to collaborate with one or more of the other three faculty members to deepen our work with our own clients, and to increase impact through leveraging others' expertise, skills, and availability. In a short time, these synergistic collaborations led to more varied – yet integrated – engagement with client businesses, more new clients who were intrigued by the potential of working with a *team* of top research faculty, and a broader base of academics/consultants who could be invited to collaborate as needed. The firm was affiliated with several dozen communication and management faculty members from universities around the U.S.

3. Class Projects in Organizations: Leveraging the Teaching Mission with Service

Within universities' teaching mission of offering students an educational journey of discovery that stimulates learning, independent thought, creativity, and application – and conjoined with universities' aims to serve citizens and other stakeholders, faculty may have opportunities in some of their classes to fashion class projects with local organizations that aid them and foster student application and learning.

For many years, I taught an undergraduate course in organizational communication that included a project in which groups of students conducted communication "audits" of non-profit and for-profit organizations. Using interview protocols, on-site observations, and self-report surveys, students helped those organizations (including many small-to medium-sized businesses) to determine communication climate, information flow in formal and informal networks, communication load (especially roles in which members felt they had too much or too little information and interaction), and other communication strengths and weaknesses unique to the organization. With my advising, students conducted these audits for more than 60 business and non-profit organizations in Illinois and California. Nearly half of them led to independent study classes the next term in which subsets of those teams continued their involvement and their impact with the organization. We sought to redress the problematic issues identified in the audit by collaborating with key organizational members to make recommendations and intervene when appropriate.

At the graduate level, while at the University of Illinois, I occasionally taught the department's required course on field methods of research. Given my experience as a program evaluator for nationwide allied health projects of two U.S. federal agencies, I expanded the course to include evaluation principles and methods. Students also collaborated on evaluations of programs for local businesses and agencies, including an innovative technical leader program implemented in a local manufacturing plant of a major corporation (Lewis & Seibold, 1993), the effectiveness of a communication training program in a large company (Seibold et al., 1993), and causes of turnover among volunteer oncology nurses in a hospice (Seibold et al., 1987). Not only were we of considerable service to these organizations, but our efforts led to the publications noted that were intended for scholars in some instances and practitioners in others.

4. Embedded Internships: Leveraging Graduate Degree Requirements and Student Career Goals

At least two master's degree programs at UCSB secure field internships in which teams of students are required to be embedded for periods up to a year. The Technology Management Department, in which I monitored the teams' progress, placed a cohort of 50 students – nested in teams of 5–7 members with as many as ten years of work experience prior to returning to graduate school – into one of as many as eight technology firms for two terms each. Placements were based on students' ranked requests, rankings that were often driven by their career goals and the organizational internship they felt would most help them secure employment (including by some of the sponsors). Each project was advised by a faculty member with a specialty in that area (especially strategy, marketing, finance, product development, operations, and engineering).

The project teams and their reports/recommendations were usually quite helpful to the businesses – enough so that several sponsors requested a team year after year. Project foci included developing an algorithm for planning decisions and allocation of resources to multiple projects simultaneously underway; evaluating a real estate technology firm's opportunities for increasing energy management efficiency in clients' buildings; strategic analysis of entering a new vertical market; improving business unit collaboration in an education technology firm; lean engineering optimization and quantification in an aerospace business; developing a data-driven approach to enhancing the customer experience with a complex software; analyzing a new marketing platform; assessment of a firm's investment effectiveness, among many others.

Securing these business sponsorships is time consuming, at least until successful projects become known within executives' networks.

Then, firms begin inquiring about the university program, and wish to make a presentation concerning whether their business needs are suitable for an embedded project. When that occurs at a scale the program can manage, the university–business partnership moves well beyond intent and to impact.

5. Multidisciplinary Centers: Leveraging Structures Promoting Innovation to Impact Business

Most universities encourage interdisciplinary collaboration; mine (UCSB) places a special emphasis on it. One structure that promotes interdisciplinary research and application, and is an outcome of it, is the multidisciplinary "centers" on campus that draw together faculty members with common interests but different disciplinary perspectives to pursue external funding, collaborate on research projects, and coauthor academic publications and public dissemination. UCSB has fostered the creation of 40 multidisciplinary centers and institutes.

One of these is the Institute for Energy Efficiency (IEE), for 15 years an interdisciplinary research enterprise dedicated to the development of cutting-edge science and technologies that support an efficient and sustainable energy future. Formed with input from faculty in engineering, sciences, social sciences, environmental sciences, economics, and technology management, its members have produced award-winning research that has been the foundation for numerous energy-saving innovations, including energy-saving white light LED lighting, more energy-efficient data-center communications and interconnects, and software that reduces energy usage in buildings worldwide. In addition to hosting policy conferences and offering testimony to legislative bodies, IEE members have worked closely with businesses regarding their own research into relevant technologies, planning, and resource allocation. Multidisciplinary institutes and centers are another powerful way in which university faculty members can impact business.

6. Industry Research Partnerships: Leveraging Sponsored Research to Impact Business

According to the *Times Higher Education World University Rankings 2022*, UCSB's College of Engineering (CoE) ranks in the top 3 percent globally (of 1,188 universities) in industry income for research. In 28 years of full-time employment at UCSB, the last 8 years of which were in the Technology Management Department in CoE, I witnessed CoE nurture its relationships with business and industry. A principal initiative is the Industry Center, which accelerates corporations' access to faculty and labs in order to augment the research capabilities of each firm and to investigate novel technologies.

Before that, I witnessed communication departments at Michigan State University and the University of South Florida develop partnerships with businesses to aid with message design and testing in media campaigns, network analyses as part of mapping communication dissemination, and assessments of needs for training programs. I share these examples of sponsored research in partnerships with firms as another way in which university faculty members can impact business directly.

7. University Outreach: Leveraging Professional Education Programs

Public universities in the U.S. have developed multiple structures to provide education and to support professional development of citizens, including members of businesses. These include "outreach" efforts, such as course-based certificates in Extension Programs for the public in general and professionals in particular. Sometimes individual colleges on campus have their own outreach programs for professionals in their purview. During my 14 years at UIUC, I delivered just under 50 one-day trainings, one-week sessions, and facilitated-retreats for the outreach arms of the College of Business and Commerce, the Labor and Industrial Relations Institute, and the campus umbrella Division of Extended Learning. Often these activities occurred on campus, but about 15 times I traveled to one of the organization's sites. Participants ranged from first-line supervisors to senior executives. Sometimes these engagements led to longer-term consulting with the firm (with the approval of the UIUC outreach administrator), including a 21-year long relationship with a Fortune 500 energy company.

8. Conferences Bridging Research and Practice: Leveraging Academic–Practitioner Bonds

In the spirit of collaboration among academics from the same discipline who consult together (point 2), academics with shared expertise, and shared commitments to bridging from their universities to assist organizations, can leverage support from their institutions to create conferences for interacting with each other and practitioners. One such conference in one discipline is the Aspen (CO) Engaged Communication Scholarship Conference, held nearly annually since 2002 and dedicated to dialogue among academics and practitioners concerning engaged scholarship in

organizations and making a difference to them. As documented by
Seibold (2022), the conference evolved to include speaker panels
and dialogue sessions with practitioners; consulting with organizations – including an insurance firm and technology corporation – at
and after conferences. Themes included organizational change, crisis communication, organizational design, and ways that academics' engagement with practitioners has made a difference. In 20
years, the hundreds of participants have included more than 75 of
the top scholars in organizational communication who are actively
engaged with organizations. They discussed multiple methods and
best practices for their work – including collaborations with
practitioners.

Conclusion

There are myriad *other* ways in which faculty members routinely
strengthen the university–business partnership: mentoring students
who seek careers in business; inviting speakers from business and
industry to classes and colloquia; fostering Corporate Affiliates
relationships with firms seeking to recruit students for internships
and employment; creating new venture competitions; encouraging
students to participate in industry prize initiatives; hosting state of
the discipline conferences for alumni who now work in business;
participating in business-sponsored summer programs for faculty
to experience the latest trends in a sector; creating management
education certificates for graduate students in STEM disciplines
seeking careers in business and industry (as with the UCSB Graduate
Program in Management Practice). In my experience, however, the
eight university structures discussed in this chapter have the potential to produce the *greatest* impact on businesses: personal consulting by faculty, consulting partnerships among them; class projects;
embedded internships of graduate student teams; campus multidisciplinary centers with businesses as stakeholders; industry–university research partnerships; university outreach programs; and
conferences aimed at bridging research and practice.

References

Lewis, L. K., & Seibold, D. R. (1993). Innovation modification during intra-
organizational adoption. *Academy of Management Review*, *18*, 322–354.
Seibold, D. R. (2005). Bridging theory and practice in organizational communication. In J. L. Simpson & P. Shockley-Zalabak (Eds.), *Engaging communication, transforming organizations: Scholarship of engagement in action*
(pp. 13–44). Cresskill, NJ: Hampton.

Seibold, D. R. (2016). The communication scholar's unique perspective on organizational consulting: Personal reflections and a design approach. In J. A. Waldeck & D. R. Seibold (Eds.), *Consulting that matters: A handbook for scholars and practitioners* (pp. 11–30). New York: Peter Lang Publishing.

Seibold, D. R. (2022, July). *Recollections of the emergence and evolution of the Aspen conference.* Presentation to the annual *Aspen Engaged Communication Scholarship Conference.* Aspen, CO.

Seibold, D. R., Kudsi, S. O., & Rude, M. W. (1993). Does communication training make a difference? Evidence for the effectiveness of a presentation skills program. *Journal of Applied Communication Research, 21,* 111–131.

Seibold, D. R., Rossi, S., Berteotti, C., Soprych, S., & McQuillan, L. (1987). Volunteer involvement in a hospice care program. *American Journal of Hospice Care, 4,* 43–55.

Simpson, J. L., & Seibold, D. R. (2008). Practical engagements and co-created research. *Journal of Applied Communication Research, 36,* 265–279.

15 Innovative Pedagogical Strategies Through University–Firm Dynamics
Transforming Practices and Mindsets

Carlos Alberto Restrepo-Rivillas, Alejandro Beltrán-Duque, and Carlos José Bello-Pérez

1. Introduction

Achieving more effective learning processes and research that is more relevant to the environment demands changing how academics and business schools relate to companies. Educational institutions are looking for new strategies to bring teachers and students closer to the business world. Forming teams of people who work together to carry out projects in companies and solve real problems is an increasingly popular approach (Cárcel, 2016). So, new teaching methodologies are necessary to expand the involvement of academics in the corporate world. To do this, schools must overcome pedagogical models that privilege passive learning strategies (Michel et al., 2009), in which the student conceives himself as a receiver of information and the teacher as a transmitter. Achieving this objective poses essential challenges to business schools, in terms of the design of teaching strategies and how they operate. Recent studies show that academics' perceptions of learner–teacher relationships are changing (Dai & Matthews, 2023). Therefore, this research analyzes an educational initiative implemented by a management school in an emerging country, in which companies and academia are integrated. Beyond a superficial impact on companies, the strategy described in this research illustrates how universities can achieve the involvement of the different actors in the educational process by engaging students, teachers, and managers in the processes. The research analyzes the stages, evolution, challenges, and obstacles the school faced during the twenty-five years it took to implement the initiative. However, mainly, it shows the changes in the mindset of the teachers and in the way the school operates. Likewise, this research provides important lessons for

DOI: 10.4324/9781003459217-17

other schools that wish to implement new programs and ways to engage their academics with the business environment.

2. Origins and Context of the Initiative

Since its founding,[1] the School of Management at Externado de Colombia University implemented a training model that allowed it to respond to the training needs of business people and managers of the leading companies in Colombia, an emerging economy.[2] For more than 57 years, the school has changed its program offerings to adapt to the conditions and needs of its environment. In the design of this portfolio, teaching–learning processes were privileged with traditional methodologies, such as master classes, conferences, and exhibitions. In these designs, the student became the recipient of the knowledge taught by the teachers, and the classroom was the main training space. During this period, the school was recognized as one of the five best in the country, within a landscape of nearly 150 management schools. Its graduates stood out for occupying management positions in medium and large companies in the country.

3. Operation and Methodology of the initiative

Although the perceived performance of the school was positive, its managers were aware of the need to offer even more relevant programs connected to the country's business reality. So, in 1998, the School of Management decided to implement educational spaces and courses characterized by using learning-by-doing approaches (Chang et al., 2014; Dewey, 1910; Guest & Riegler, 2017) and based on constructivist proposals (Jakobsen et al., 2019; Piaget, 1952; Sioukas, 2022; Vygotsky, 1962). At that time, an interest arose in using learning strategies in business contexts of small and medium-sized companies (SMEs) (Fullan, 2001), in which the integration of knowing, being, and doing was sought, involving, in addition to the teacher and the student, other actors, such as companies and their managers, graduates, unions and governmental agencies that promoted business development in the country.

One of the initiatives was Plan Padrinos® (Do in Context), which consisted of a free consulting program for companies that required strategic direction and the development of an improvement plan that would allow them to increase their competitive performance. Under this new training scheme, companies and their needs became the central axis of the learning process. There, interactions were generated between the different actors in the educational process, where each one assumed specific roles in the initiative. In particular, the School of Management carried out intervention projects in small and medium-sized enterprises, and to do so, it formed teams with students from the undergraduate and graduate programs, junior consultants and professors who were experts in different management topics, and senior consultants. The company managers actively participate in the project, providing information and support to the university team. Government institutions that promote business development in the country and other organizations that provide help to SMEs joined the program, and their role was to support the call and the monitoring of projects.

In the first part of this program, teachers invite and select companies and students who will participate. They study the reality of functioning as an SME and receive training on interacting with managers and their teams in each company. Subsequently, the companies are assigned to each program team, and the students and professors visit the companies and hold meetings with managers and their collaborators to diagnose the company's situation and identify areas in which intervention and improvement are required. In this phase, students and teachers apply the program's methodologies and use instruments developed by the school's researchers. Then, teachers conduct management dialogues in which students, businesspeople, and professors participate in workshops with other experts from each area to analyze the company's main problems and identify good management practices. Based on this evaluation, junior consultants design the company's strategic planning. Likewise, they must propose improvement action plans for the most critical areas, with the most significant impact on the assigned companies. Finally, the junior consultants make a presentation supporting the proposals to the senior consultants and managers.

4. Transforming Practices and Mindsets

Although the initiative was initially very well received, it also faced resistance to change from the actors in the educational process, as well as restrictions of various kinds. Some obstacles came from the teachers' mindset; others originated in the students' resistance and the rigidities in the functioning of processes in the school.

Mindsets are people's beliefs about some human attributes, including abilities (Dweck, 2015). In this case, some teachers stated that they could not assume this new role and, therefore, did not continue in the program; other teachers stated that the initiative forced them to completely change the sequence of the course's content and structure that they traditionally taught, which is why they decided not to continue with the process and were assigned to other subjects. Some teachers believe that their abilities and those of their students cannot be changed (Dweck, 2015). Therefore, this shows that when educational strategies that involve modifying old practices are implemented, it is sometimes difficult for some teachers to adapt.

At that moment, it became clear that implementing the initiative would require a change in the teachers' mindset, since they had to assume functions, attitudes, and roles different from the traditional ones. The proposal required, for example, abandoning the master class format, where the teacher's knowledge was central and where the their role was to transmit information. The initiative demanded that the teacher assume a facilitating and connecting role between the company's needs and the student's capabilities to design solutions, in an agreed process with businesspeople and students. The initiative also involved a new approach to the training process, in which teachers and students faced challenges that companies posed, for which they needed to leave the classroom, visit the companies, and develop work sessions for the managers of each company and their teams of collaborators. These new activities required additional competencies and a change in how to view the learning dynamic. For this reason, the school decided to expand teacher training in pedagogical innovation issues, promote the participation of teachers in executive education, and recognize the work teachers did with companies.

For their part, the master's and undergraduate students, at first, expressed their disagreement about having to assume a new role during the learning process. The responsibility of providing solutions to the participating companies broke with the traditional role, in which the student was limited to presenting reports, essays, and exams to the teacher. Others stated that they felt tremendous pressure, as they knew that the solutions they designed for companies would directly impact the performance of these organizations.

From the point of view of the school's operation, the initiative contemplated that the work sessions on the university campus should be at most 30 percent of the total course and that the remaining time should be used to carry out activities in the facilities of the participating companies. At first, this generated resistance from the school's administrative staff and the program, who wanted to maintain the organization of the activities. Added to this was that, at that time, there was little availability of physical infrastructure of classrooms with the capacity and arrangement of chairs and tables adapted to a more participatory methodological process. Likewise, there was difficulty in controlling attendance and managing grades within the structure of the subject, given that many activities took place in the facilities of the assigned companies. The school had to change how class schedules were defined to facilitate the physical movement of teachers and students to the companies' facilities, some of which were located outside the city. This increased the course's operating costs compared to others using only a board and a video projector.

As a result of these learnings, and to ensure the continuity of the initiative, not only the actors in the educational process, but also actors external to the university, understood the need to make changes. These adjustments allowed the initiative to continue and to generate different benefits for all participants in the educational process.

Internally, the school created new positions in the staff team to guarantee the connection of companies with the appropriate characteristics. As it is a free program for managers, it was evident that some companies had sufficient resources to hire consulting services through the school's extension area. This was an opportunity for the school to strengthen links with the business sector and expand the services portfolio to these companies. The changes also allowed the school to adapt its operating model, regarding the design of schedules and curricular structure of the programs, among others. For students, it represented the opportunity to learn by doing. Through this methodology, the student could apply what they learned, address a need of the company, and help it improve its performance. The school also proposed that companies issue certificates of participation to students, who could include them in their curriculum vitae as part of their professional experience. For the teacher, it was the opportunity to provide solutions to an organization and accompany the student in the learning process in real application contexts.

Actors external to the school found benefits from the initiative. School graduates, who were business owners, expressed their satisfaction with the implementation of this initiative and requested that their companies be considered to enter the program. The country's financial entities, that focused their credit lines on strengthening SMEs, found that the school could be a valuable ally since the companies benefiting from the credits could improve their performance thanks to the program. The same occurred with government entities focused on developing SMEs through training processes.

5. Consolidation and Growth of the Initiative

Starting in 2001 came a period of growth for the initiative. At the same time, there was a gradual change in the mentality of teachers, students, school managers, businesspeople, graduates, and other actors involved in this initiative, regarding acceptance of the proposal and recognition of its benefits.

The results allowed the initiative to become the support and central axis of a business support program promoted by the School of Management. The school directors and teachers considered that this type of program should be carried out in collaboration with other universities and government entities that promote the development of SMEs. Therefore, collaborative work began with the Colombian Association of Micro, Small and Medium Enterprises (ACOPI), the only association of this type in Colombia. The school designed a particular program for affiliated companies. Likewise, to improve the program's performance and strengthen teachers' skills in using this type of approach, the school carried out training with international institutions that were pioneers in using active methodologies. So, the school developed projects with the Foundation for Sustainable Development (FUNDES) of Swiss origin and the University Tecnológico de Monterrey in Mexico.

Another organization that entered the initiative was the Banco de Comercio Exterior de Colombia S.A. (Bancoldex), a mixed economy entity linked to the Ministry of Commerce, Industry and Tourism, which operates in Colombia as a second-tier bank, is responsible for the development of the business sector, and is a promoter of the country's foreign trade. They sought to support the development of SMEs that accessed the country's financial sector and had to strengthen their management processes. Likewise, to expand the program's scope to cities, other than the school's headquarters, the teachers developed diagnostic methodologies and improvement plans that business people throughout the country could use.

Another type of ally was large companies or organizations in Colombia. This is how Sociedades Bolívar, one of the five leading conglomerates in the country, became involved and has been an active part of the program for more than 20 years. In that case, the purpose was to strengthen the relationship with large companies in the region and develop cooperation agreements so that the suppliers of these companies were linked to the program. Today, large companies in the country are an integral part of the program through the participation of their suppliers.

6. Conclusion and Discussion

The constant progress in management practices and technical resources makes it necessary to create links between the university and the company and connect teachers and students with how companies currently carry out activities (Arancibia & Pino, 2022). Likewise, it is necessary to make people more aware of the realities they will face in the workplace (Hernández, 2014). This research analyzes an experience in which a management school successfully integrates teachers, students, and companies to promote two-way knowledge transfer.

Teachers' characteristics, such as their mindset, are critical when implementing these initiatives since they affect their pedagogical practices (Toding et al., 2023). In this sense, the results show how an educational strategy has allowed academics to modify conceptions of their role in the training process of students in higher education, in which students act as partners (Dai & Matthews, 2023) that contribute to the design of solutions to real problems of companies. Likewise, this study shows that it is possible to generate learning dynamics that help students and teachers understand that they can improve skills through continuous effort (Sahagun et al., 2021). This experience shows that teachers can change their mindset and accept that collaborative work with students carried out directly in the company can also be a source of learning for them (Dweck, 2015).

The importance of students carrying out activities outside the educational center, in other spaces that allow them to apply and acquire knowledge, skills, and abilities, is increasingly recognized (Fandos et al., 2017). However, at the same time, teachers have a conception of the educational process in which the classroom is the center of the learning process and that only the teacher and the student should be there. Therefore, another way in which this initiative contributed to changing the mindset of teachers was in terms of helping them understand that the company can also be a valid learning space, in which there are learning objects and resources that can be useful for facilitating the teaching process.

Teachers' beliefs about teaching, learning, and student characteristics influence their teaching style (Vermote et al., 2020). The experience analyzed in this research made it possible to change teachers' beliefs, for whom the center of the learning process is knowledge itself, and their job as trainers is solely to transmit that knowledge. The results showed that the initiative managed to make teachers change this vision and understand that more than knowledge, what is important is what students can do with said knowledge and the applications that the students can make; therefore, their work is that of facilitating and guiding the process of appropriation of said knowledge by the student.

Notes

1 The School of Management at Externado de Colombia University was founded in 1965.
2 Currently, the School has about 1,500 students and offers a doctorate program, 13 master's programs, an undergraduate degree, executive education,

and consulting programs. The school recently received accreditation from the AssoEciation of MBAs (AMBA), the Education Quality Accreditation Agency (EQUAA), and the Association to Advance Collegiate Schools of Business (AACSB).

References

Arancibia, M. L., & Pino, B. (2022). Articulación de la empresa y la universidad: experiencia de formación de profesores en Mecánica Automotriz. *Revista Educación en Ingeniería, 18*(35), 1–6. https://doi.org/10.26507/rei.v18n35.1246

Cárcel, F. J. (2016). El método de proyectos como técnica de aprendizaje en la empresa. *3 C Empresa, 5*(1), 16–28. DOI: http://doi.org/10.17993/3cemp.2016.050125.16-28

Chang, J., Benamraoui, A., & Rieple, A. (2014). Learning-by-doing as an approach to teaching social entrepreneurship. *Innovations in Education and Teaching International, 51*(5), 459–471. DOI: http://doi.org/10.1080/14703297.2013.785251

Dai, K., & Matthews, K. (2023). 'Students as partners rather than followers but …': understanding academics' conceptions of changing learner–teacher relationships in Chinese higher education. *Higher Education Research & Development, 42*(6), 1362–1376. https://doi.org/10.1080/07294360.2022.2135690

Dewey, J. (1910). *How We Think.* Lexington, MA: Heath and Company.

Dweck, C. (2015). Teachers' mindsets: "Every student has something to teach me". *Educational Horizons, 93*(2), 10–14.

Fandos, M., Renta, A., Jiménez, J., & González, A. (2017). Análisis sobre el aprendizaje y la aplicación de las competencias generales en el contexto laboral. Estrategias de colaboración entre la formación profesional, la universidad y la empresa. *Educar, 53*(2), 333–355. https://doi.org/10.5565/rev/educar.889

Fullan, M. (2001). *The new meaning of educational change.* Jossey-Bass.

Guest, J., & Riegler, R. (2017). Learning by doing: Do economics students self-evaluation skills improve? *International Review of Economics Education, 24*, 50–64.

Hernández, R. (2014). Training in companies, permanent training and adult learning: An epistemological approach. *Procedia. Social and Behavioral Sciences, 139*, 434–440. http://doi.org/10.1016/j.sbspro.2014.08.035

Jakobsen, M., Mitchell, F., Nørreklit, H., & Trenca, M. (2019). Educating management accountants as business partners. Pragmatic constructivism as an alternative pedagogical paradigm for teaching management accounting at master's level. *Qualitative Research in Accounting & Management, 16*(4), 517–541. http://doi.org/10.1108/QRAM-10-2017-0099

Michel, N., Cater, J., & Varela, O. (2009). Active versus passive teaching styles: An empirical study of student learning outomes. *Human Resource Development Quarterly, 20*(4), 397–418. DOI: http://doi.org/10.1002/hrdq.20025

Piaget, J. (1952). *The origins of intelligence in children.* New York: International Universities Press.

Sahagun, M., Moser, R., Shomaker, J., & Fortier, J. (2021). Developing a growth-mindset pedagogy for higher education and testing its efficacy. *Social Sciences & Humanities Open* (4), 100168. https://doi.org/10.1016/j.ssaho.2021.100168

Sioukas, A. (2022). Constructivism and the student-centered entrepreneurship classroom: Learning avenues and challenges for US college students. *Industry & Higher Education*, *37*(4), 473–484. http://doi.org/10.1177/09504222221135311

Toding, M., Mädamürk, K., Venesaar, U., & Malleus, E. (2023). Teachers' mindset and attitudes towards learners and learning environment to support students' entrepreneurial attitudes in universities. *The International Journal of Management Education*, *21*, 100769. https://doi.org/10.1016/j.ijme.2023.100769

Vermote, B., Aelterman, N., Beyers, W., Aper, L., Buysschaert, F., & Vansteenkiste, M. (2020). The role of teachers' motivation and mindsets in predicting a (de) motivating teaching style in higher education: a circumplex approach. *Motivation and Emotion*, *44*, 270–294. https://doi.org/10.1007/s11031-020-09827-5

Vygotsky, L. (1962). *Thought and Language*. MIT Press.

16 The Sustainability Consortium as Action Research

Kevin J. Dooley

Engaged Scholarship and Action Research

There is increased call for scholarship to be engaged with practitioners, helping to drive change in real systems (Van de Ven, 2018). Management scholar Andrew Van de Ven was a leading proponent of the "engaged scholar" (Van de Ven, 2007). He started his research career working on community-based decision making, which is where he invented the Delphi process for collaborative decision making (Dooley, 2021). He saw engaged scholarship as a means by which to integrate knowing through theory versus knowing through experience.

He stated, "engagement is a relationship that involves negotiation and collaboration between researchers and practitioners in a learning community; such a community jointly produces knowledge that can both advance the scientific enterprise and enlighten the community of practitioners" (Van de Ven, 2007, p. 7). Van de Ven links the concept of engaged scholarship to other akin concepts, such as service learning, community, outreach, extension services, and participatory research. He defines four types of engaged scholarship dependent on the research perspective and question: basic science with stakeholder advice, policy evaluation research, co-produced knowledge, and action research.

Hoffman (2021) details the numerous challenges there are for business school scholars to be engaged in the manner described. Engaged scholarship generally takes more time, as relevant stakeholders need to be identified and recruited, and trust needs to be developed. The engaged scholar must not only attend to research rigor, but the practicalities of delivering value to stakeholders in a manner that they can appropriate. Communication of the research results outside of journal publications is essential to engaged scholarship, but incentives and rewards for tenure and promotion do not usually recognize such efforts to diffuse knowledge into practice.

In this chapter, we shall discuss The Sustainability Consortium (TSC) as an example of engaged scholarship, specifically, action

DOI: 10.4324/9781003459217-18

research. Argyris and Schon (1989) defined participatory action research as,

> a form of action research that involves practitioners as both subjects and coresearchers. It is based on the Lewinian proposition that causal inferences about the behavior of human beings are more likely to be valid and enactable when the human beings in question participate in building and testing them. Hence it aims at creating an environment in which participants give and get valid information, make free and informed choices (including the choice to participate), and generate internal commitment to the results of their inquiry.
>
> (1989, p. 613)

In TSC's use of action research, participants were not research subjects, but rather subject matter experts, akin to a standards development process (ANSI, 2021). The role of TSC was to create or synthesize the relevant science to the question at hand and use stakeholder engagement to develop business tools or solutions derived from that science.

Using cases from TSC, I suggest a process model of multi-stakeholder action research. First, a critical problem must be identified. Next, engaged scholars must identify and convene relevant stakeholders. Third, a co-governance structure is formed. In this collaboration, engaged scholars provide value to the collective by either creating new science or translating existing science into applications. Because stakeholders may not agree with one another, engaged scholars may need to be an arbiter and mediator; because stakeholders have expectations of progress and view their own contributed efforts as valuable, engaged scholars need to provide effective project management for the effort. Finally, learnings need to be communicated to stakeholders, practitioners, and the academy. This process is depicted in Figure 16.1.

The Sustainability Consortium (TSC)

TSC was created in 2009 as a joint effort between the University of Arkansas and Arizona State University (Dooley, 2014). Walmart and other consumer goods companies, producing products such as food, beverages, home and personal care items, electronics, clothing, and general merchandise, came together to form TSC. The charge for TSC was for the universities and corporate, non-governmental organization (NGO), and government stakeholders to create a way to measure the sustainability of the consumer products that they sold. TSC's efforts were funded by membership fees

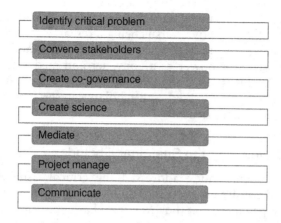

- Identify critical problem
- Convene stakeholders
- Create co-governance
- Create science
- Mediate
- Project manage
- Communicate

Figure 16.1 Process Model of Action Research

paid by the participating stakeholders. However, TSC also had to reach far beyond its paid membership to secure the necessary scientific expertise and business perspective needed to create the so-called Walmart Sustainability Index (Dooley & Johnson, 2015) (now called THESIS).

TSC wanted to create sustainability information that a consumer could understand and use to make purchasing decisions (Friedberg, 2013). Over time, it was realized that most consumers were not ready to do that, and that instead retailers and consumer goods companies should concentrate on trying to improve the sustainability of all the products they sold. To that end, TSC created a governing structure and process to perform the materiality assessment on different consumer goods categories, and then develop key performance indicators that the consumer goods companies could use to assess the sustainability of their products and share that information with their downstream retailers.

Any retailer or a consumer goods company can do their own proprietary identification of critical issues in their supply chains and create ways to measure their performance. The benefit of creating such a system in a collective manner is that stakeholders across a sector's value chain come to common agreement on what the critical and environmental and social issues are, to address and measure progress on, and agree on how to measure performance. This allows a single measurement to be efficiently communicated to multiple retailers at once.

This type of effort could have been done without academic researchers or universities. Research skills and effort would still have had to have been performed, either by the participating corporations or through outsourcing of those research activities to third parties, such as universities. The benefit of the university being the leader of the collective, versus being a research service provider alone, is that a university can act as a trustworthy and legitimate institution, giving it power as a convener and mediator (Johnson et al., 2018). This is especially true when science is essential to the critical issue being addressed, and scholars can serve as the trusted judges of scientific evidence.

Case 1: Developing the Sustainability Index

The Sustainability Index addressed the critical issue that both retailers and consumers needed to understand the relative sustainability of the products that they were purchasing. At that time, there were hundreds of eco certifications and other labels that made sustainability claims to consumers; however, consumers did not easily understand whether a particular eco certification was of good quality and believable, or if it was an example of greenwashing. For merchants within retailer organizations, they similarly had no systematic way to evaluate the overall sustainability of one product over another. There was also a recognition that if each retailer were to create their own sustainability information reporting system, that that would lead to significant inefficiencies and additional, unnecessary costs. Thus, when Walmart approached Arizona State University and the University of Arkansas to organize a collective, pre-competitive effort to develop the index, it brought other competitor retailers into the effort as well and insisted that competitors selling the same types of products (e.g., computers, shampoo, soda) were also involved and working together.

Because so many different types of stakeholders were needed to create the index and give it legitimacy, there were many differences that emerged during the discussion of specific environmental or social issues, and how to practically measure the associated impacts. NGOs would tend to be more progressive than corporations, retailers would tend to be more progressive than manufacturers, and academic researchers tended to be less sensitive to measurability issues than the corporate participants who would have to make such measures. A governance structure was needed to provide fair and broad input into decision making. The governance structure had to absorb and mediate conflicts that arose because of the diversity of stakeholders. The structure also had to ensure that the 400+ projects that were needed to create the index could be managed effectively and on tight timelines.

In this structure (Figure 16.2), the Executive Director and their management team worked with a Board of Directors on strategic issues and with a smaller Executive Board on university compliance

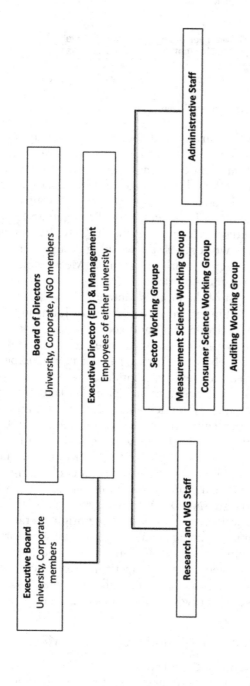

Figure 16.2 TSC Governance Structure

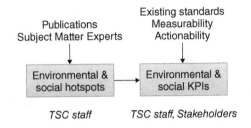

Figure 16.3 Sustainability Index Governance

issues and executive hiring. Both Boards were set up so that representation from universities and NGOs was one person larger than representation from corporations. To ensure effective project management and stakeholder engagement, the index development work was organized into Sector Working Groups (Clothing, Footwear, and Textiles; Electronics; Food, Beverage, and Agriculture; General merchandise; Home and Personal Care; Packaging; Toys). Standardization of work across the working groups were facilitated by several cross-sector working groups: Measurement Science, Consumer Science, and Auditing.

The development of the index's content followed a standardized process, as depicted in Figure 16.3 (Dooley & Johnson, 2015). The identification of environmental and social hot spots was done by TSC staff via their interpretation of peer reviewed publications, identified by themselves, and other subject matter experts. After hotspots were identified, existing standards were considered in the construction of key performance indicators (KPIs) that would track a brand's performance on reducing impacts related to the hotspots. For each product category, the process of developing hotspots and KPIs went on over an 8-to-12-week period. Drafts of work were shared with stakeholders to gather feedback, and the next draft always included explicit responses to all stakeholder input.

There were significant efforts to communicate TSC's work, primarily to industry and NGOs. A brand identity was created, and a marketing team was created as part of the original staff structure, which is uncommon in an academic center. Equally important, TSC provided a communication setting for the corporate and NGO stakeholders, and even among competitors, constructive conversations could be had. The focus on scientific evidence allowed TSC to mediate what were otherwise contentious decisions.

Case 2: Developing the Priority Chemicals KPIs

Within the Sustainability Index, several product categories, especially in the home and personal care sector, had hotspots related to human health, i.e., product safety hotspots. For formulated goods like shampoo or laundry detergent, there already existed many state and federal regulations regarding chemical safety, indicating chemicals that could be used only in limited amounts or not at all. The broader scientific evidence about product safety was hard to interpret without expert knowledge. TSC hired a scientist who had expertise in chemical testing for product safety.

The challenge came when creating the KPIs for so-called priority chemicals, stakeholders had very different opinions. One group favored a hazard-based approach, aligned with the precautionary principal where one assumes a product is not safe unless proven to be (Scott et al., 1999). The other group believed that a risk-based approach was more scientifically sound than a hazard-based approach because it considered exposure pathways and probabilities. The tension between the hazard-based approach and the risk-based approach had the potential to lead to a stalemate in creating a KPI that had acceptability from most stakeholders.

As shown in Figure 16.4, the situation represented a type of thesis–antithesis conflict between the hazard- and risk-based approaches. After much trial and error, the TSC team believed a solution to the conflict would be to create a synthesis of these two approaches (Poole et al., 2000) by including a third dimension of product safety that the two approaches had not explicitly considered. TSC staff sought some type of authoritative, existing framework that could be used as an undeniable standard that should be aspired to.

At that time, the National Research Council (NRC), a part of the US National Academy of Sciences, had just published a set of recommendations to the US Environmental Protection Agency (EPA) and other federal agencies on how to do rigorous safety assessment (NRC, 2009). In their framework, they indicated that both hazard and risk analysis were essential. Additionally, they identified the principle of product stewardship as key, where the company formulating and producing the chemically based product has a responsibility to collect market-based data on product safety and seek

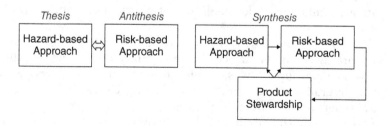

Figure 16.4 Creating a Solution Through Synthesis

ways to continuously learn the risk profile of the product that they are selling and improve their product safety processes.

By combining this principle of product stewardship with the principles of hazard identification and risk assessment, the three components of a KPI were formulated. While many stakeholders were not completely satisfied with the outcome, it was hard to argue against recommendations from the National Academy of Sciences. In that regard, as in the previous case, science served as a mediator to the conflict.

Case 3: Making a Big Deal of the Small Stuff

Many products are made small on purpose. Small products have the advantage of being convenient to carry or travel with, they are less likely to end up creating product or food waste, and they allow consumers to buy small amounts of product at a time, which can be important to the cash flow of more economically stressed consumers. Small products also have the benefit of having a smaller amount of packaging, which means, per unit, that less packaging must be produced.

The wicked issue that faced TSC's stakeholders was that small packaging is not deemed to be curbside recyclable in the US. The Association of Plastic Recyclers defines anything under two inches in two or three dimensions is considered unrecyclable. The reason for this is that if small plastic packaging is put into the recycling stream, it will drop out of the recycling flow along with the glass that gets crashed at the beginning of the process. Subsequently, the glass is further cleaned, and the small plastic and other items in the pile are separated and sent to landfill.

This problem was brought to TSC's attention by several consumer goods companies who were members of TSC. At that time, many consumer goods companies were making pledges to have 100 percent reusable, recyclable, or compostable packaging by 2025. For companies that had a significant amount of small format packaging in their packaging portfolio, these types of pledges were not feasible. TSC convened these stakeholders and created a goal statement aimed to make small format plastic packaging curbside recyclable.

For governance, TSC recruited an industry member to co-lead the working group. Perhaps more importantly, the first project that the working group did was a 9-month (two-semester) project with an undergraduate class from Arizona State University. The class had students from engineering, industrial design, graphic design, business, and sustainability. As the corporate members had time to work together with the students in a relatively casual way, it helped build trust among competitor companies, which was important for the group to act as a collective.

In this project, since there was little available science to draw from, TSC staff had to design, conduct, and outsource research projects. The purpose of the research program was to collect the data needed to make a business case for any technological solution, and to secure a top research lab to begin to innovate solutions. In this role, the engaged university partner is acting as an investment hub, where moneys from donors or sponsors can be collected to fund a singular activity, as well as a project manager. TSC commissioned waste and recycling bale audits from waste management consultants, and commissioned R&D at a top US university.

This data turned out to be useful in a mediating role, as the US Plastic Pact had put small format packaging on its list of "unnecessary and problematic" packaging types. TSC's research was able to show that in many cases, small format packaging is necessary, because of product waste issues, and that different types of small format packaging should be differentiated when it comes to assessment of their sustainability. Thus, as in the other two cases, science was able to be used to mediate a multi-stakeholder conflict.

Summary

A summary of the three cases is shown in Table 16.1.

There are many commonalities and some differences between the three cases. The critical problem being addressed was either shared agreement on business standards or shared collective action on business challenges. Having identified a critical problem, TSC then convened a wide range of relevant stakeholders. For example, in creating the Sustainability Index, corporate, NGO, academic, and government stakeholders had to be identified, recruited, and engaged across multiple industry sectors. The project to create a priority chemical KPI was an example of a project embedded within one of those sector working groups. In the case of small format plastic, it was the consumer goods companies who came to TSC with the identification of the packaging challenge.

For a third party, such as TSC, to effectively coordinate such a multi-stakeholder group and drive action, it was necessary to create governance structures which involved representatives from each type of stakeholder group. The projects that best succeeded were the projects that were co-led by TSC staff and industry volunteers. All three cases created science as part of the project action research project. In developing the Sustainability Index, existing science was synthesized to create business tools. In the case of developing the priority chemical KPI, an authoritative scientific body and their

Table 16.1 Summary of Action Research Projects

	Creating Index	Creating Chemical KPI	Small Format Plastic
Critical problem	Shared agreement on hotspots, KPIs	Shared agreement on product safety, KPI	Make small packaging curbside recyclable
Convene stakeholders	Corporate, NGO, academic, and government; across multiple sectors	Led by Home and Personal Care sector working group	Industry brought problem to TSC
Create governance	Boards, working groups, operating standards	Balance corporate and NGO input	Co-led by industry
Create science	Synthesized over 5000 research articles	Interpreted various chemical safety standards	Did original research and outsourced research
Mediate	Used operating standards and effective working group managers to manage conflicts within the group	Used the authoritative voice of the National Academy of Sciences to create an aspirational framework as a synthesis	Used research to inform decisions within US Plastics Pact
Project manage	Managed over 400 projects as part of the index development program	Created special process outside normal development process to accommodate more discussion	Provided a hub for collective R&D investment
Communicate	There were multiple rounds of stakeholder feedback for each category that was developed	Provided safe platform for retailers, brands, chemical suppliers, and NGOs to discuss issues	Brought waste management and recycling stakeholders into TSC work

aspirational framework was used to create a synthesis that overcame the conflict between hazard and risk-based approaches. In small format plastic project, TSC performed primary research and planned other research that was then outsourced to other third parties, providing an investment hub where participants could pool their financial resources toward a shared research program.

Project management was key to the success of these projects, and dedicated project managers were critical to provide those skills. In all three projects, communication between TSC and stakeholders, and between stakeholders themselves, facilitated in a safe environment, helped develop trust among participants which led to constructive conversation and subsequent action.

In summary, universities should be encouraged to engage in action research, especially when their expertise in developing, interpreting, synthesizing, representing, and communicating science is a critical part of making progress on critical problems. Historically, many researchers engaged with external partners or practitioners in a transactional manner. Research projects are often designed so that minimal coordination between industry and the research lab is required, as this can create efficiencies.

However, for society to reach its sustainable development goals, universities will have to play a more active role in external engagement toward real action (Crow & Dabars, 2015). Academia is often considered a trustworthy broker of the truth, independent, and scientifically objective. For that reason, it can play a role as a convener, a creator, and an advocate for science-based, fact-based decision making and deliberation. In that sense, this type of engagement might be referred to not so much as *action research*, but rather *research-driven action*.

Acknowledgments

Thanks to all the TSC staff and stakeholders engaged in these projects. Thanks to Drs. Jon Johnson, Sarah Lewis, Carole Mars, and Christy Slay in Case 1; to Dr. Christopher Helt in Case 2; and to Jennifer Park and Myriam Fessi in Case 3.

References

ANSI (American National Standards Institute). (2021). *ANSI Essential Requirements: Due Process Requirements for American National Standards*. ANSI, New York. https://www.ansi.org/essentialrequirements

Argyris, C., & Schon, D. (1989). Participatory action research and action science compared: A commentary. *The American Behavioral Scientist* (Beverly Hills), 32(5), 612–623. https://doi.org/10.1177/0002764289032005008

Crow, M., & Dabars, W. B. (2015). *Designing the New American University* (1st ed.). John Hopkins University Press.

Dooley, K. J. (2014). The whole chain. *Science*, 244(6188), 1108.

Dooley, K. J. (2021). Engaging Change: Andrew H. Van de Ven. In D. Szabla, W. Pasmore, M. Barnes, A. Gipson(Eds.), *The Palgrave Handbook of Organizational Change Thinkers*. Palgrave Macmillan, Cham. https://doi.org/10.1007/978-3-319-49820-1_61-1

Dooley, K. J., & Johnson, J. (2015). Product category-level sustainability measurement: The Sustainability Consortium's approach to materiality and indicators. *Journal of Industrial Ecology*, 19(3), 337–339.

Friedberg, S. (2013). Calculating sustainability in supply chain capitalism. *Economy and Society*, 42(4), 571–596. https://doi.org/10.1080/03085147.2012.760349

Hoffman, A. J. (2021). *The Engaged Scholar: Expanding the Impact of Academic Research in Today's World*. Stanford, CA: Stanford University Press.

Johnson, J., Dooley, K. J., Hyatt, D., & Hutson, A. (2018). Cross-sector relations in global supply chains: A social capital perspective. *Journal of Supply Chain Management*, 54(2), 21–33. https://doi.org/10.1111/jscm.12166

NRC (National Research Council). (2009). *Science and Decisions: Advancing Risk Assessment*. Washington, DC: The National Academies Press. https://doi.org/10.17226/12209

Poole, M. S., Van de Ven, A., Dooley, K. J., & Holmes, M. (2000). *Organizational Change and Innovation Processes: Theory and Methods for Research*. Oxford: Oxford Press.

Scott, S. A., Mabey, N., Berkhout, F., Williams, C., Rose, C., Jacobs, M., Grove-White, R., Scoones, I., & Leach, M. (1999). Precautionary approach to risk assessment. *Nature* (London), *402*(6760), 348–348. https://doi.org/10.1038/46413

Van de Ven, A. (2007). *Engaged Scholarship: A Guide for Organizational and Social Research*. Oxford: Oxford University Press.

Van de Ven, A. (2018). Academic–practitioner engaged scholarship RICK section of Information & Organization. *Information and Organization*, *28*(1), 37–43. https://doi.org/10.1016/j.infoandorg.2018.02.002

17 Building Holistic, Integrated Partnerships for Broader Impact
Case Study

Sandra Crocker

In February 2020, Carleton University launched a "holistic integrated partnership (HIP)" team as a collaboration between the offices of University Advancement and the Vice-President (Research and International) to co-ordinate industry engagement across the two units. This paper explores the process of refining the on-campus partnership model and will illustrate the approach in practice by tracing the life cycle of a particular case, with an emphasis on measurement and impact.

Establishing the Team and Narrative

Corporations are increasingly moving away from pure philanthropy towards investing their grant or foundation dollars in more detailed proposals, complete with milestones and outcomes. As a result, proposals have become more specific, often providing direct benefit to the partner, raising the question whether a contribution meets the definition of a gift or charitable donation. Departments of university advancement do not generally write detailed proposals for funding, this expertise is found with the professional grant writers in the vice-president research team. While research has expertise in working with industry and on writing detailed proposals, it does not have the same history or expertise in stewardship and building professional dossiers found in advancement or development offices. Bringing these two teams together to forge a new on-campus collaboration is intended to recognize the expertise in these units, and to co-ordinate submissions to external partners.

The early expressions of the benefits of the collaborative approach reflected elements more commonly seen by advancement in its philanthropic pitches, using language such as "helping to build an inclusive workforce", "amplifying brand", and "creating social impact". Furthermore, the holistic approach initially attempted to simultaneously address community partners, corporate partners, and individuals. It became evident that the language

DOI: 10.4324/9781003459217-19

being proposed by advancement to describe the benefits of partnering was not on target for the corporate audience.

As we gained more experience with the model, and received feedback on the needs of the various partners, the HIP began to distinguish itself with a team of people focused on corporate engagement while those that focused on community and individuals remained under the purview of the department of advancement directly.

The HIP is now a multi-faceted and mutually beneficial relationship that offers the highest return for an organization looking to achieve multiple objectives on campus. The HIP team has expanded beyond research and advancement, to engage all units across campus that are suited to a particular partnership.

Organizations look to the university to help design solutions for research, for talent acquisition, or corporate social responsibility needs. These engagements are often limited and transactional in nature. The HIP initiative takes a more collaborative approach to developing and deepening a partnership. Together, Carleton and partners develop long-term objectives, identify opportunities for integration, and achieve more sustainable outcomes. New partnerships focus on four pillars:

- Research, product development & testing (undergraduate, graduate, and post-graduate).
- Talent development & acquisition (courses, co-ops, interns, and recruitment).
- Corporate social responsibility (philanthropy, inclusion, diversity, equity and accessibility, and sponsorship), and
- Increased brand awareness, reputation, and regional impact through on-campus labs, events, and external communications.

In the past three years, we have implemented five holistic integrated partnerships involving different levels of engagement across the four pillars.

A Strategic Partnership Life Cycle Case Study: 5G Wireless Technology

In today's rapidly evolving technological landscape, partnerships between universities and multinational companies have become instrumental in driving innovation, research, and economic growth. This collaboration on 5G wireless technology represents a visionary alliance aimed at harnessing the transformative potential of 5G. This partnership embodies the university's commitment to fostering technological advancements, providing experiential learning opportunities for students, and contributing to the regional ecosystem's economic development.

Stage 1: Exploration and Identification

Initial conversations between the parties were limited to senior leadership, to establish resource requirements and to articulate a shared set of objectives and goals for the overall relationship.

It is important to note that not all sectors seek the same objectives in a university partnership. In this case, we are working within a technology and IT sector which often seeks to support research collaboration, talent recruitment, and open innovation. These objectives might be markedly different if the partner was from the pharmaceutical, consumer goods, or aerospace sectors. Therefore, it's essential for academic institutions and industry partners to establish clear communication channels and tailor their collaborations to meet the specific needs and objectives of both parties. Five broad objectives were established to guide this partnership:

- Research Excellence: Foster collaborative research endeavours that explore the full potential of 5G technology across various domains, such as healthcare, transportation, smart cities, and more.
- Experiential Learning: Provide students with hands-on experience and exposure to 5G technology, enhancing their readiness for future careers in the technology sector.
- Talent Development: Establish courses and seminars at the university to address technological expertise needed by graduates to engage fully in the 5G economy.
- Enhanced Reputation: Actively promote the partnership as a hub for technology and innovation, attracting top-tier talent, and fostering international collaborations.
- Regional Development: Contribute to the economic growth and competitiveness of the regional ecosystem by attracting investment, creating jobs, and supporting local businesses.

Strong leadership at both organizations has proven critical in setting the initial tone, in ensuring continuity of commitment throughout the implementation of the program and in rapidly troubleshooting issues that arise.

Stage 2: Partnership Formation

Broader stakeholders then convened to initiate discussions on the feasibility and potential benefits of the collaboration, and to explore specific activities that could be conducted in fulfilment of the objectives. This broader group engaged relevant deans, chairs, and recruitment and communication specialists whose departments directly benefit from the funding, but who also share ownership in the success of these activities. This shared ownership is a major factor in ensuring that momentum continues throughout the course of program delivery.

The parties created a framework agreement that governs the overall collaboration and allows for subagreements or appendices to be developed to govern specific activities. This is essential because not all parameters and contractual terms apply equally to all types of activities under the partnership. Terms surrounding confidentiality, publication, and intellectual property will necessarily differ depending on, for example, if we are launching a graduate course or conducting a project relying on proprietary research. Building in this flexibility, based on the activities undertaken, enables the partnership to be more dynamic in adding and subtracting program elements and establishing terms and conditions more appropriate to the specific activity. The agreement's purpose is to establish a strategic relationship, whereby the parties can collaborate in an organized fashion, under the guidance of the agreement, to continuously identify, discuss, and explore at a high level, the potential activities and opportunities that align with the vision, goals, objectives, and strategies of the strategic partnership.

The framework agreement also establishes a joint governance, with approximately equal representation from both parties. The governance is structured to capitalize on the expertise required to implement the specific activities identified by the stakeholder group. Subcommittees were established to oversee curriculum development, research project selection, lab infrastructure implementation, the activities of a named research chair, selection and recruitment of international research fellows, communications, and budget. These committees meet monthly (or as needed) to make decisions regarding activities in their domains. The chair of each subcommittee reports as a standing agenda item to the steering committee.

A steering committee comprising of the chairs of each of the subcommittees, representatives of the Office of the Vice-President, representatives of partner executive leadership, human resources, and engineering meets monthly. An executive of the steering committee that meets biweekly was constituted to deal with emerging business issues, such as contractual matters, budget, timing of activities, renewal, and sustainability.

Stage 3: Implementation and Execution

Through a series of planning meetings with the subcommittees, the program elements were debated, refined, and brought forward for approval at the steering committee. Once the activities were approved, the subcommittees transitioned to be the implementation teams for the activities under their committee.

First, a named industrial research chair in 5G networks was established to provide an anchor for the program in the form of a senior academic leader. The chair is responsible for mentorship and leadership and for overseeing the physical lab space in which the stand alone 5G network is housed. The chair supports six independent research projects covering a wide variety of topics. Second, we established a prestigious international fellowship competition. Each candidate applies both to the university and to the fellowship and is adjudicated first on academic merits and then on fit with the industrial partner. Both organizations agree on the fellowship awardees. These are funded at $50,000 per year for up to two years. As part of their program, each fellowship recipient provides a "tech talk" in the form of a joint symposium. The first symposium took place over three days with presentations from both the faculty supervisors and fellows. More than one hundred participants from our strategic partner tuned in to hear the talks. The third element of the program is to foster leading edge research projects. The industry engineering teams establish "challenge statements" and present these to our faculty. Faculty are invited to submit project proposals to address the challenge statements. Each project must include milestones, resource implications, and have an identified partner champion within the company. Twenty-three projects are on-going under this program to date.

As much as possible, the program activities are designed to maximize the return on investment. Each principal investigator awarded research grant funding, that is eligible to be matched with government funding, is obligated to apply for match funding. This leverage has resulted in an additional $2 million to the university in support of the activities of the partnership. This increased investment allows the program to sponsor significant additional activity and provides a compelling proof point for our partner.

The fourth program element falls under the umbrella of talent development. Under this stream, we support a new graduate course in 5G wireless (with guest speakers from our partner providing insights as well as lab tours at the partner research and development site), we support capstone projects, and a series of events designed to facilitate recruiting with our co-op and careers offices. The final element of the program addresses the strong desire to raise awareness and reputation. We have undertaken significant joint events, presentations, newspaper articles, op-ed pieces, sponsorship, and other related activities to ensure the visibility of the program and its impacts both to the internal and external audiences.

Stage 4: Evaluation and Monitoring

The subcommittee chairs provide a brief overview of the status of the projects underway at each steering committee meeting. In some cases, challenges are readily addressed by the steering committee and, in others, they may be referred to the originating subcommittee with advice or are taken to the executive committee. For example, if the fellowship subcommittee raised a concern regarding low application rates, the steering committee may suggest other venues to advertise or offer to utilize their personal networks. The resolution, however, rests with the subcommittee. If the research chair brings forward a challenge to the steering committee that would result in downtime, or additional expense, the issue would be referred to the executive committee for resolution.

In addition to the reports of subcommittees, the leadership team may bring forward issues that are more fundamental, such as intellectual property or confidentiality concerns. In these cases, without a subcommittee structure, a senior member of the steering committee is tasked to liaise with the intellectual property (or other relevant groups) of both organizations to resolve the issue and report back.

The university management team also updates steering at each meeting on the matters of over or under expenditure. On budgets of this magnitude, over this time frame, budget reallocations are almost an inevitability. The management approach to this potential was to be proactive in identifying areas for reinvestment prior to any surplus being specifically identified. Approximately halfway through the funding cycle, potential underspending was added to the agenda for the steering committee. Following discussion, the committee voted that in this eventuality, reinvestment would be best allocated towards new or extended individual research projects. When underspending occurred in one program area, the funds were reallocated without further discussion.

Stage 5: Impact Assessment

Valuing university–industry partnerships is not a one-size-fits-all process, and the specific factors to consider may vary depending on the nature of the partnership and its goals. It's important to approach the valuation process with a holistic perspective and consider both quantitative and qualitative aspects to make informed decisions and optimize the value of the partnership for all parties involved.

The university prepares a comprehensive impact assessment at the end of each year. The document is extremely well received and serves as a communication tool across many platforms. It is, however, a significant amount of work and must be weighed against the allocation of both human and financial resources. The data for the impact report comes from many sources. A specific survey to capture relevant individual publication, patent, and financial data is distributed to all faculty and student participants each year. The survey also seeks self-assessments of other less tangible talent readiness factors of students. For example, 85 percent of the students said they were better prepared for the labour market and 88 percent of students reported that they had a better industry understanding, as a result of being engaged in the partnership.

Course information is gathered from instructors, co-op and internship numbers from co-op and career services, communication statistics from a variety of sources, and new hires from our partner's human resources team. The survey results, testimonials, graphs, statistics and photos, and insights are compiled in a twelve-page full colour impact report that provides both qualitative and quantitative outcomes. The report is produced as a dynamic online document.

Leadership from both the partner organization and the university provide compelling statements as to the impact the partnership has on the respective organizations. Our industry partner states:

> The Carleton partnership stands as a momentous achievement. As we reflect on three years of collaboration, there is much for us to celebrate. From ground-breaking research successes to the development of exceptional young leaders, this partnership has had a profound impact on our community and industry as a whole.

The 2022–2023 impact report was produced in Q4 and includes the following statistics:

I. Chair Research Outcomes

11 refereed IEEE conference papers accepted.
3 refereed IEEE conference papers submitted/under review.
4 refereed journal publications submitted/under review.
1 patent filed in collaboration with partner.

II. Research Outcomes from Other Research Projects

16 accepted publications.
15 pending publications.
10 presentations conducted.
2 patents filed.
53 graduate students participated in research projects.

III. Talent Development

552 co-op work terms completed by Carleton students to date.
7 students recruited by the industry partner.
67 students completed the 5G course.
2 lab tours at partner site.
11 industry partner guest lectures.

IV. Communications/Visibility Outcomes

5 stories published by Carleton University.
1 joint media release.
80 media pickups.
221 engagements on partnership social media posts.
11,461 web site views developed for this partnership.
3 advertising campaigns – print and online.

Feedback and Lessons Learned

An initial successful university–industry partnership represents a significant achievement, but it is just the beginning of a journey toward greater collaboration and impact. As the partnership moves beyond its initial phase, there are valuable lessons to be learned and strategic steps to take in order to continue growing and thriving.

The case study described above is perhaps one of the most complex to implement. Because of the many program elements, there is significant administrative overhead for the university. Managing the overall budget, supporting the individual research project proposals, selecting fellows, ensuring the lab and chair have the required resources, planning events, writing communication pieces, and preparing the impact report engages a broad range of university personnel. There are fifteen people on campus that devote some (or a substantial) portion of their time to this partnership. In future iterations, we will need to think carefully about the resource implications and streamline operations or budget for a full-time dedicated program manager, specifically for this partnership.

Like many major project implementations, there was a ramp-up period, however, this was not accommodated in a budget that allocated equal amounts across all years. In future agreements, we will adjust the funding timing to meet the realities of the academic schedule and will build in a final (unfunded) year of the agreement to complete projects and expend budgets. In addition to timing of the budget, the university research financial accounting department needed to revise practices to handle a large central budget, that funded a broad variety of teams and activities. Furthermore, while it is in the best interests of the partnership to be flexible in budget allocations, this sometimes conflicts with the terms and conditions of the contract which research finance implements. Ensuring there is budget flexibility in the contract terms going forward will enable better and quicker decision making by the steering committee.

Lastly, given the nature of the partnership (cutting edge, proprietary research) intellectual property and confidentiality management requires extra consideration. Each participant must be informed and agree to the terms in writing. This requires the intellectual property management group at the university to be proactive in identifying when new students or others join a research team, despite there being no established way for this to automatically happen.

Reflecting on the first three years of implementing this partnership, these lessons learned will help us improve practices in our future partnerships, whatever the complexity. While there are some things we will adapt, there are some things that will be core to initiating any new partnership.

Identifying and maintaining the engagement of senior leadership, ideally at the vice-president level or equivalent, of both organizations is critical. Implementing new models often challenges the status quo and having the support to suggest new ways of doing things requires leadership engagement. Leaders can also be a strong external advocate with governments and other potential partners, generating profile and setting up positive conditions for future partnerships.

Early and regular communication with all affected parties on campus to help shape the program elements and achieve buy-in has proven essential. Beyond the initial consultations, ensuring there is a voice at the subcommittees or steering committee has facilitated problem solving and idea generation that would not be possible without a common forum. These committees would not be effective if they were campus only, and equal representation has enabled greater participation and commitment.

The communication structure established keeps the key objectives at the forefront of the partnership. The subcommittees are based on the program elements, and the program elements are based on the key objectives. In this way, each meeting of the steering committee reminds the participants of the key objectives and the progress made against them.

Finally, celebrating the successes at each turn. This requires a budget for writers, for public and private events, for stories or ads in local business journals or national papers and reflects one of the university key objectives in engaging in a HIP, that of enhancing reputational excellence.

Conclusion

Innovative academic–industry partnerships are characterized by a mutual commitment to shared goals, open communication, and a willingness to embrace the dynamic and evolving nature of the collaboration. These partnerships can push the boundaries of academic research and lead to transformative outcomes with tangible regional and national impacts. That being said, we have concluded that some elements of the program, as designed, have been more successful than others. The fellowship program, for example, has underperformed compared to other program elements. It is possible, however, that this is the type of program that takes more than a few years to build significant brand recognition to ensure we are receiving the very best applicants. Some of the partnership activities have a more immediate impact than others and following the outcomes beyond the term of the agreement will be informative.

Both organizations are currently reflecting on the value and impact of the partnership and how we can ensure its success beyond the first phase. To promote sustainability, consideration is currently being given to extending the partnership to other international corporate R&D sites; to diversifying the funding sources with government, philanthropic, and commercialization activities; to expanding partnerships across the ecosystem; and to exploring the next generation of wireless technologies beyond 5G.

18 ENLIGHT

Towards an Impact-Driven University

Glória Nunes Rodrigues, Igor Campillo, and Iñigo Puertas

ENLIGHT is one of the fifty European universities supported by the European Commission Erasmus+ and Horizon 2020 programmes. It is a European-wide alliance composed of ten research-intensive universities[1] committed to raise their potential to transform themselves and the European education and research landscape, as well as to become key players in the promotion of equitable quality of life and sustainability. Explicit in its mission statement is the intention of ENLIGHT to be defined as a transformative and impact-driven university. But what is an impact-driven university? What efforts is ENLIGHT university deploying in this sense? What are the main driving forces and the challenges faced in this process? And what is the strategy ahead?

In this chapter, we will: first, set the scene, introducing why impact is becoming a key priority in higher education, sharing ENLIGHT understanding of impact and of impact-driven university concepts; second, present ENLIGHT efforts to transform itself as an impact-driven university and the key actions undertaken in this sense; and third, discuss the primary challenges encountered throughout this process, the main success factors, and the strategy ahead.

1. The Growing Importance of Impact

From Knowledge Producers and Transmitters to Impact-Driven Universities

Universities have been around for about a thousand years, and their job throughout the time has been, in various ways, to do with knowledge transmission, production, transfer, and application [1]. Traditionally, universities have been focused mainly in two different missions. On the one hand, teaching, i.e., the transmission of knowledge, educating new generations of workers and citizens; and, on the other hand, research, i.e., the production of new knowledge. The symbiosis of these two missions has given rise to what is known as the Humboldtian university [2], which was consolidated

DOI: 10.4324/9781003459217-20

throughout the 19th and 20th centuries. It is the model representing the research university, which is segmented into disciplinary silos, and a generally very self-centred institution, stratified into different layers of academic hierarchy.

However, in recent decades, universities have been increasingly opening up to society and taking on innovation, social, and cultural related activities (technology transfer, dissemination of knowledge, social interventions, etc.), which become part of their portfolio, in what it is usually called the third mission of universities. The growing relationship with society, in particular with companies and public administrations within the so-called triple helix innovation approach [3], has giving rise to what has been called the "entrepreneurial university".

In the European context, it is important to highlight that universities operate as part of national systems of higher education, as well as the so-called European Education Area. These multi-level systems of higher education (regional, national, and European) are composed of many types of institutions subjected to global competition and rankings, but also to the pressing demands and challenges of their immediate local communities (unemployment growth, loss of an industrial base, urban regeneration, etc.).

In more recent years, we are witnessing an additional turn of the screw in that exercise of academic opening. The growing orientation of education and research towards local demands and global challenges driven by UN Sustainable Development Goals agenda, promotes active participation of external stakeholders, both in the identification and definition of challenges, as well as in the research itself and in the learning processes. This represents the "civic university" model [4], in which universities couple their inherent commitment to knowledge with social purposes. Starting about two decades ago on scientific research practice, there is an increasing emphasis about the societal impact of universities [5]. This means that universities cannot be "ivory towers" anymore, and that they need urgent renewal to pay attention to the long-term effects of their activity and stimulate new modes of operation that ensure a positive societal impact [6].

The universities move from "mere knowledge producers and transmitters towards untapping the potential of knowledge as a transformative force to tackle the complex challenges of our societies, by co-creating with societal stakeholders and becoming globally engaged change players" [6] represents our understanding of an impact-driven university.

Understanding "Impact" and "Impact Assessment" in Higher Education

At ENLIGHT, we define *impact* as "the effects or changes that we can see (demonstrate, measure, capture) *on* and *beyond* academia, which happen because of an activity/intervention in the higher education environment";[2] *on*: on learners, academics, support staff, leaders, structures, processes; and *beyond*: on society, economy, environment, etc. *Impact* is thus intrinsically linked to *transformation* and to transformative initiatives, programmes, projects, and activities. In this conceptualisation process, it is important to differentiate *impact* from *impact assessment*, which is the exercise of identifying, capturing, evaluating these effects, and the extent of those on different stakeholders over time.

In parallel to the move towards the model of impact-driven universities, we observe that impact assessment is becoming a practice that is growing in relevance worldwide. More and more organisations (not only universities) are analysing their impact(s) with the objective of getting evidence, and understanding and demonstrating the value of their contributions to society [7]. This movement is accompanied by an increase in the number of methodological approaches and tools developed to assess the impact of organisations or programmes, and to move towards an impact-directed management [8], i.e., managing to maximise and minimise desired and undesired impacts, respectively.

In the higher education context, impact assessment has been mainly associated with the impact of the scientific and research activity. Evaluations, assessments, and indicators have become widespread in the academic world and an integral part of scientific practice at all levels, from individuals and research groups to faculties, universities, funding agencies, and policymakers [9]. At the European level, the "Pact for Research and Innovation in Europe",[3] recognises "value creation and societal and economic impact" as a major value and principle for EU research and innovation (R&I). Impact is a key evaluation element of project proposals in Horizon Europe R&I programme,[4] as relevant as the excellence and implementation evaluation criteria. Worldwide, there are also research policies, programmes, and practices aiming to promote impactful research. Mainly implemented by national research councils, funding agencies, and science policymakers, we should mention the Research Excellence Framework (REF)[5] in the United Kingdom, Research Impact Canada,[6] National Alliance for Broader Impacts (NABI)[7] in the United States, and Engagement and Impact Assessment[8] Australia, for example.

However, the impact assessment of universities in relation to their comprehensive mission (education, research, innovation, and service to society) is still in its infancy [10]. It is in this scenario that the ENLIGHT university stands out, in its efforts to adopt a comprehensive approach to impact assessment and establish itself as an impact-driven university.

2. The ENLIGHT Pathway to Impact

As an impact-driven university, impact is reflected in ENLIGHT's mission, and strategic and operational objectives. More specifically, ENLIGHT accounts for "European university network to promote equitable quality of life, sustainability and global engagement through higher education transformation".[9] Explicit in this headline is the intention of ENLIGHT to be defined as a transformative alliance. Indeed, ENLIGHT is a truly transformative endeavour at three different levels. The ENLIGHT university intends to bring about structural change in the ten partner universities (first level) necessary to become a role-model alliance contributing to the transformation of the larger European Education Area (second level). Furthermore, this transformative effort is intrinsically connected to the claim that universities are key players enabling equity, sustainability, and well-being for Europe and globally (third level).

Consequently, *impact* is a key dimension of the ENLIGHT work programme. Funded by the Erasmus+ 2020 Call[10] and the Horizon 2020 ENLIGHT RISE project,[11] the alliance focuses its impact action in the framework of two work packages, addressing two different but complementary objectives:

- To create a comprehensive methodology and tools for measuring the long-term impact of ENLIGHT on people, communities, institutions, and systems at large, in such a way that the addressed and accomplished transformations may be monitored, measured, and communicated transparently.
- To explore the frontiers of a common impact-driven R&I agenda.

Taking as reference the three different levels of ENLIGHT's transformative endeavour, as highlighted above, these two operational objectives address the first two levels, since they are focused on the transformation of the ENLIGHT partner universities and their major stakeholders (learners, academics, and support staff), and eventually on the European Education Area.

Developing a Comprehensive Methodology and Tools for Measuring the Long-Term Impact of ENLIGHT

In the context of the first objective, ENLIGHT has developed a methodological framework and toolkit for the impact assessment of higher education activities.[12] The ENLIGHT methodology for the assessment of higher education activities was designed as a sequential process, structured in six major phases which are inter-related and retrofitting the next phases in a circular approach. Figure 18.1 illustrates the six different phases of the ENLIGHT methodology for impact assessment.

For each of the six phases, the ENLIGHT methodology proposes a set of specific actions and decisions to be taken in order to proceed to the next phase. Tested through the performance of three pilot case studies, covering different action lines considered to be the most relevant and representative of ENLIGHT potential impact on the transformation of higher education,[13] the ENLIGHT methodology includes the lessons learnt throughout the impact assessment exercise. It is important to highlight that the pilot case studies involved a truly co-creative process between the ENLIGHT Impact

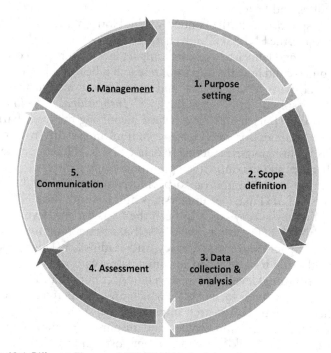

Figure 18.1 Different Phases of ENLIGHT Methodology for Impact Assessment of Higher Education Initiatives

Task Force, the action leaders in charge of the implementation of the selected ENLIGHT actions, and the affected stakeholders, in order to capture the impact on students, academic and non-academic staff, institutions, and systems.

In alignment with the ENLIGHT methodology, the ENLIGHT *online toolkit for impact assessment*[14] provides the tools and guides the users to run these types of exercises.

The ENLIGHT university expect that its methodology, the toolkit and the lessons learnt from the pilot case studies are shared, transferred, and of use beyond the ENLIGHT context. For that purpose, it is organising biennial impact conferences, such as the one held in Bilbao (Spain) in March 2023, and leading the thematic group of European universities alliances on impact matters (FOREU2 impact thematic group).[15]

Exploring the Frontiers of a Common Impact-Driven Research Agenda

In parallel to the development of ENLIGHT methodology and toolkit for impact assessment, ENLIGHT has been focusing its efforts on the promotion of impact-driven research agendas at its universities and beyond.

More specifically, in the context of the Horizon 2020 ENLIGHT RISE project, the ENLIGHT university has first performed a landscaping exercise and launched a research impact literacy survey, in order to better understand how the impact of research is being addressed in the ENLIGHT partner universities and how impact literate they are. Largely inspired in Phipps-Bayley's *Institutional Healthcheck Workbook* [11], its results have helped identifying the main barriers and opportunities for developing common impact-driven research agendas.[16] This analysis is serving to define ENLIGHT action to tackle these barriers and maximise the opportunities offered.

With the overall ambition to promote an impact-based culture within ENLIGHT partner universities and beyond, the ENLIGHT impact literacy survey has also been the basis for the development of the ENLIGHT toolkit for the self-assessment of universities research impact awareness, literacy, and readiness.[17] This toolkit is a self-reflection tool designed for universities who wish to explore, at an institutional level, their research impact potential. The toolkit guides users through focus areas, which are considered as relevant for universities to be research impact-driven, such as clarity, context, commitment, competencies and resources, connectivity, and co-creation. The toolkit provides a diagnostic aid to identify areas of strength and weaknesses, and where there is space for improvement in the research impact environment (Figure 18.2).

Figure 18.2 Different Elements of the ENLIGHT Toolkit for the Self-assessment of Universities' Research Impact Awareness, Literacy, and Readiness

In this context, and with the objective of promoting a model of good practice of impact-directed management and the integration of impact across higher education, research, and innovation activities, ENLIGHT has launched a repository of international good practices on research impact.[18] It has also launched the ENLIGHT Impact Awards,[19] to recognise and give visibility to research endeavours at the partner universities that are exemplars in planning for and achieving impact. The representatives of the awarded teams have been identified as Impact Ambassadors[20] and are engaged in outreach, training, and mutual learning activities. At the time of drafting this chapter, ENLIGHT is designing a training programme for academics, early-career researchers, and research-support staff on impact pathways in research projects, impact in project funding, and societal engagement.

Raising Impact Awareness, Literacy, and Readiness

Overall, both through the pilot case studies' co-creative process that led to the development of the methodology for impact assessment, and the ENLIGHT RISE actions to promote common impact-driven research agendas, ENLIGHT is provoking a *shift in the way of thinking, acting,* and *being* at our universities.

As the ENLIGHT own pathway towards impact shows (Figure 18.3), there are three immediate outcomes we aim at:

- To raise *Impact Awareness*, which provokes *a shift in our way of thinking,* i.e., understanding and internalising the importance of impact, the mission, and position of universities in relation to society, highlighting the transformative role of higher education and research.
- To acquire *Impact Literacy*, which provides us the knowledge, competencies, and skills, with background concepts and methods, and tools necessary to systematically self-assess our impact.

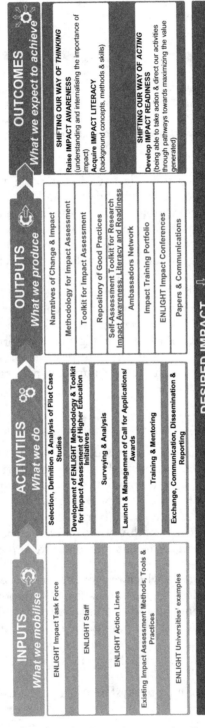

Figure 18.3 ENLIGHT Pathway to Impact

- To develop *Impact Readiness*, which provokes *a shift in our way of acting*, enabling us to direct our activities through pathways, towards maximising the value generated by our teaching and research activities for different stakeholders.

Eventually, we expect that the ENLIGHT impact-action will provoke a shift in our way of *being*, promoting and institutionalising a culture of impact: *towards an impact-driven university*. This will mean the adoption of impact-directed strategy thinking and impact-driven management by higher education institutions in the European Education Area. Ultimately, it is a radical change in the mission of universities, moving from mere knowledge producers and transmitters towards untapping the potential of knowledge as a transformative force to tackle the complex transitions of our society.

3. Challenges, Driving Forces, and Future Outlook

Challenges

The ENLIGHT pathway towards an impact-driven university has not been exempt of difficulties that have been challenging to the university alliance's approach to impact. But rather than hindering it, the process of responding to these challenges has led to further reinforcing of the robustness of its approach.

One of the main challenges faced by the ENLIGHT Impact Task Force has been the confusion around the concept of impact. Impact of higher education is usually confused with quality assurance. However, whilst quality assurance is directed to ensure the efficiency of the process and the effectiveness in the delivery of the results, i.e., it is linked to performance, impact assessment is aimed at capturing the transformative dimension of the different activities carried out in the context of a project or by an organisation. In the research field, research impact is often associated with scientific excellence, measured in terms of scientific publications in high-impact journals and citations, for example. In other cases, research impact is directly linked to "economic valorisation" of research, through business agreements, commercialisation of research results, patents and/or spin-offs. And, in others, impact is confused with communication and societal engagement.

Directly related with the confusion around the impact concept, we have observed a few concerns that the pilot case studies would add an extra layer of assessment of ENLIGHT activities beyond the project commitments. There was an overall concern that the ENLIGHT Impact Task Force would make a comparative performance analysis between action lines and partner universities, whilst the main objective was using the pilot case studies for the development of the ENLIGHT methodology for impact assessment.

In this sense, the multiple working meetings the Impact Task Force has held with the different action lines' representatives and stakeholders, as well as the evidence provided by the results of its work, have been crucial for addressing the different misunderstandings and concerns, contributing thus to raise impact awareness and to acquire impact literacy within the ENLIGHT community.

Another major challenge faced by the ENLIGHT Impact Task Force has been the conception that ENLIGHT is an "internationalisation project", rather than as an "institutional undertaking". The focus on preparing project deliverables contrasts with the ambition of driving the transformative changes at the institutional and systemic levels. This a common challenge across the ENLIGHT community and not only specific to the Impact Task Force. The strong commitment level of the partner universities' top management teams, coupled with the trust links fostered over time across the ENLIGHT community, are helping to overcome the pure project logic.

Driving Forces

As previously highlighted, there is a growing "momentum" for impact and impact assessment practices that helps ENLIGHT positioning as an impact-driven university. The greater prioritisation impact is having at international, national, and regional policies and programmes is being reflected in universities' strategies, which are increasingly focusing their efforts in addressing and capturing the effects of their activities on societal, environmental, and digital transitions.

In parallel, ENLIGHT, composed of ten excellent, research-intensive universities from very different regional contexts and diverse trajectories, creates a critical mass on which the Impact Task Force can capitalise. Coupled with the strong engagement and commitment levels of the different universities' management teams, academics, administrative staff, and students, the ENLIGHT ambition to become a truly transformative university is fully aligned with an impact-driven university vision.

In this context, the support of the ENLIGHT coordination team has been fundamental, as well as the leadership capacity, dedication, and critical review of the ENLIGHT Impact Task Force and the different action leaders.

Another key driving force in the ENLIGHT pathway towards an impact-driven university is the attention to and the involvement of stakeholders in most of its impact-related activities. Either in the framework of the pilot case studies, where stakeholders were consulted on both the expected and desired impacts and on the observed impacts, or through the ENLIGHT Impact Literacy survey, the Impact Task Force has taken into consideration the views of the major stakeholders (students, academics, support staff, university management teams, and societal stakeholders) in the design of its activities. Through the leadership of the FOREU2 Impact Thematic Group, the organisation of the ENLIGHT Impact Conference, and the participation in different international fora, ENLIGHT university has also been in direct contact with international impact experts.

Besides, "rapid prototyping", through the performance of pilot exercises and sequential versions (for example, with different versions of the methodology for impact assessment), has been defined as a key operational principle of the ENLIGHT Impact Task Force. This operational principle is considered to be good practice, allowing advancement in the execution of activities and avoiding limitations of "analysis paralysis".

Overall, ENLIGHT's own comprehensive and integral approach to impact, looking at the university alliance in its full dimension (higher education, research and innovation, and service to society), is not only innovative but it facilitates ENLIGHT Impact Task Force's action.

4. Future Outlook

Looking ahead, in its efforts to move towards an impact-driven university, ENLIGHT intends to promote and institutionalise a culture of impact, both within and beyond the alliance, extending it to other universities and alliances, becoming thus a role model in the European Education Area.

For that, and thanks to the support of European Commission funding for the period 2023–2027, ENLIGHT will focus its action in further reinforcing impact literacy and readiness. It will organise specific training and mentoring for academics and early-career researchers, helping them build robust impact pathways for both education and research and innovation. In addition to assessing the immediate impact of ENLIGHT actions on and beyond academia, it will put its methodology and toolkit for impact assessment to the test, in cooperation with other peer alliances, in their joint effort of capturing their impact in the European Education Area. Keeping the leadership of the FOREU2 Impact thematic subgroups and the organisation of biennial international impact conferences would be essential for this objective.

Looking beyond the strategy defined up to 2027, becoming an impact-driven university is a long-term endeavour that ENLIGHT intends to keep working on beyond the funding periods and as a key distinctive feature of the ENLIGHT university.

Notes

1 University of the Basque Country, University of Bern, University of Bordeaux, Comenius University Bratislava, University of Galway, Ghent University, University of Göttingen, University of Groningen, University of Tartu, and Uppsala University.
2 Definition adapted from Bayley, J. & Phipps, D. (2019). "Institutional Healthcheck Workbook". Emerald Publishing.
3 https://eur-lex.europa.eu/legal-content/EN/TXT/PDF/?uri=CELEX:52021 DC0407
4 https://research-and-innovation.ec.europa.eu/strategy/support-policy-making/shaping-eu-research-and-innovation-policy/evaluation-impact-assessment-and-monitoring/horizon-europe-programme-analysis_en
5 https://ref.ac.uk/
6 https://impact.canada.ca/en
7 https://researchinsociety.org/
8 https://www.arc.gov.au/evaluating-research/ei-assessment
9 https://enlight-eu.org/
10 Grant Agreement N° EAC-A02-2019-1.
11 Grant Agreement N° 101035819.
12 ENLIGHT Deliverable 81: Methodology and Toolkit 2.0 for HEI Impact.
13 The three pilot case studies cover the following ENLIGHT action lines: ENLIGHT Challenge-based Education, ENLIGHT Mobility: Increased, Flexible, Inclusive and Green Mobility, and ENLIGHT Regional Academies.
14 Available at https://impact.enlight-eu.org/toolkit
15 Forum of European University Alliances selected under the Erasmus+ Call 2020.
16 ENLIGHT RISE Deliverable 39: Report on the different workshops, encounters, webinars, surveys, interviews, etc. collecting and analysing the barriers, challenges, and opportunities to implement impact-driven R&I agendas.
17 Available at https://impact.enlight-eu.org/self-assessment
18 Available at https://impact.enlight-eu.org
19 https://enlight-eu.org/index.php/landing-research-and-innovation/impact/1017-enlight-impact-award
20 https://impact.enlight-eu.org/ambassadors

References

[1] Temple, P. (Ed.). (2012). *"Universities in the knowledge economy"*. Routledge.
[2] Bongaerts, J. C.,. (2022). "The Humboldtian Model of Higher Education and its Significance for the European University on Responsible Consumption and Production". *Berg- und Hüttenmännische Monatshefte. 167*(10).

[3] Etzkowitz, H. (2008). *"The tripe helix: University-industry-government innovation in action"*. Routledge.

[4] Goddard, J., Hazelkon, E., Kempton, L., & Vallence P. (Eds.). (2016). *"The civic university: The policy and leadership challenge"*. Edward Elgar Publishing.

[5] Wilsdon, J. (2016). *"The metric tide: Independent review of the role of metrics in research assessment and management"*. Sage Publications Ltd.

[6] Campillo, I., Nunes, G., & Puertas, I. (2023, 15 March). "Defining impact: As shift in thinking, acting and being". *Times Higher Education*.

[7] Nicholls, J. & Richards, A. (Eds.). (2021). *"Generation impact: International perspectives on impact accounting"*. Emerald Publishing.

[8] Maas, K. & Liket, K. (2011). *"Social impact measurement: Classification of methods. environmental management accounting and supply chain management"*. Springer Netherlands.

[9] Smit, J. P. & Hessels, L. K. (2021). "The production of scientific and societal value in research evaluation: A review of societal impact assessment methods". *Research Evaluation, 30*(3), 323–335.

[10] Jonkers, K., Tijssen R. J. W., Karvounaraki, A., & Goenaga, X., (2018). *"A Regional Innovation Impact Assessment Framework for Universities"*; EUR 28927 EN; Publications Office of the European Union. https://doi.org/10.2760/623825

[11] Bayley, J. & Phipps, D. (2019). *"Institutional Healthcheck Workbook"*. Emerald Publishing.

19 How Can Business Schools Increase External Orientation and Business Connect Through Executive Management Education Programs?

Rajagopalan Jayaraman

Introduction: Why Executive Management Education (EME)

The first EME program was started in the University of Chicago in 1943 (Petit, 2011). There were many reasons why EMEs were designed and run for industrial clients. Educating company employees, knowledge transfer to industry from academia, and vice versa, and developing synergies between industry and the EME provider, are some of the points mentioned by Bektaş and Tayauova (2014). Sharma et al. (2022), propose a co-creation between academics and industrial employees as a reason for EME. Conger and Xin (2000) add three more reasons for EME: 'to build awareness and support for strategic transitions, to facilitate large scale organizational change necessary to realize new strategic directions, and to build depth of leadership talent'.

The Impact of EME on Industry

In her essay in *Management Learning*, Antonacopoulou (2009) argued for 'impact' to be included as an additional dimension for the journal's articles. She defined impact as: I = Influential, M = Memorable, P = Practical, A = Actionable, C = Co-created and T = Transformational. She argued that impact is necessary for management and organisation learning. In the current context for EME programs, that impact should focus on sustainability (Tiberius et al., 2021, Williams et al., 2017, Teh & Corbitt, 2015). Thus, the *raison*

DOI: 10.4324/9781003459217-21

d'être for EME programs, is to address the industry needs, create an impact and drive toward sustainability (see Figure 19.1).

Growth of EME Programs

The period up to about the 1990s was one of continuous growth for EME (Farris et al., 2003), due to the impact it was able to create on corporates. However, while initial enrolments were high and increasing, the trend turned negative later. According to the 2010 Executive MBA Council Program Survey (quoted by Petit, 2011, and https://www.topmba.com/why-mba/executive-mba-future-trends), just 30 percent of students enrolled in executive MBA programs received full tuition reimbursement from their employers, down from 44 percent in 2001, to 37 percent in 2005, to 35 percent in 2006 to 32 percent in 2009. In more recent times, American EME providers have innovated by offering variants of the part-time EME programs, such as, short term, two-year part time, online, etc. (Bisoux, 2002; Byrne, 2019; Stotlinger, 2021). Evidently, EME programs started off well, but, after some years, started losing ground with their main customer – the corporates.

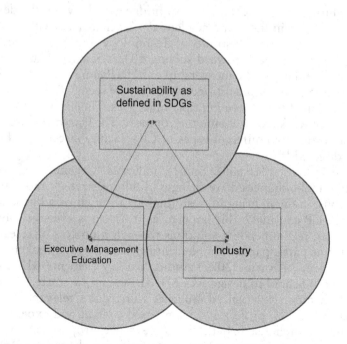

Figure 19.1 The Sustainability Triple Helix for Executive Management Education

Source: Author

Role of Capstone Projects (CP) in EME

To address the 'impact' requirements mentioned by Antonacopoulou (2009), and the various other factors which enable EME to serve the corporate, CPs were introduced as a part of the EME curriculum. This was started in SP Jain Institute of Management and Research (SPJIMR) in 2000, along with the EME program. Over the years, CPs have played a key role in strengthening the utility and close association between corporates and EME institutions, as both benefited. These aspects are covered in the ensuing sections.

CP as an Instrument for Greater Industry – Academia Connect

Universities and colleges run CP for achieving different objectives. Indian Institute of Technology, Kanpur, runs a two semester CP, with the objective to 'Enable a student to not only implement function specific techniques and knowledge, but also to learn the integrative skills where knowledge across specific streams can be applied to a real-life problem', among other things, as a part of its two-year MBA program.[1] LabourNet and Christ University, Bengaluru, have launched a CP, 'to bridge gaps between the development sector in India and academia'.[2] An eight-week CP is being offered by the Birla Institute of Technology and Science, India, 'where you will work toward solving a Data Science related business problem under the mentorship of BITS Pilani faculty members and senior industry practitioners'.[3] As can be seen, CP is a versatile tool, designed to achieve multiple objectives. Timelines can vary – from eight weeks to two semesters, or more. The Harvard Extension School offers two different types of CP – faculty directed and student directed.[4]

Research by Myrsiades (2001), indicates 'Organisations need EME to make changes/drive changes in culture, strategy and market positions, in them, bring in fresh thinking through new knowledge intake'. CP can make this happen, as it develops skills in solving problems, recommending solutions through a process of research, and trains participants in implementing these through 'stakeholder engagement'. Thomas (2007) studied the key elements which can enable a B School to design its EME curriculum, 'a greater number of older, more experienced students will require relevant professional education; project and team-based content and experiential learning is emphasised'. In the five forces model proposed by Iñiguez de Onzoño and Carmona (2007) for introducing changes in EME to keep pace with the changes in the environment, CP can play a significant role in the 'measures to anticipate environmental changes', as the topics chosen by the participants for CP reflect current realities of business. Amdam (2016) has traced the history of the evolution of EME at Harvard, and explains the origins of the Advanced Management Development (AMD) of Harvard, which has served as a model for part time EME. Inamdar and Roldan (2013) 'conducted an empirical study to determine to what extent capstone strategy courses are teaching the following four skills that prepare students to meet business job demands: theoretical, practical, applied, and reflective. We conclude that providing students with the four skills will go a long way toward ensuring that future managerial decisions are grounded on thoughtful iterative analyses that take into account ambiguities, multiple perspectives, and long-term, systemic implications'. The CP at SPJIMR internalises the first three skills.

The EME Program at SP Jain Institute of Management and Research

In India, the first MBA schools were established in Calcutta and Ahmedabad, in 1961 and '62, under collaboration arrangements with Stanford and Harvard respectively. They started their Executive MBA (EMBA) journeys in the late'70s, and, today, offer more than 200 varieties of EME course. These include one and two-year courses, as well as several short duration, customised and open programs, and online programs for sectors of industries (Wood et al., 2012; Joshi, 2019; Jethva & Pithadia, 2022). SPJIMR began its EME journey in 2000, under the label PGEMP (Post Graduate Program in Executive Management).

Some of the considerations that went into the design of the course were similar to those enumerated by Rizvi and Aggarwal (2005):

- Increasing criticality of human competence in creating and sustaining competitiveness of the organisations
- Shift in management paradigm of business schools from earlier academic models to revenue based models
- Increasing interdependence between academia and industry to satisfy need for sustenance and innovation in their respective areas.

Objectives of the CP Course in PGEMP (EME) at SPJIMR

Our CP is designed to enable participants to use a research-oriented methodology – primary and secondary research – to systematically solve organisational problems, using a guided and continuously facilitated approach. Participants are guided by a parter company (PC) mentor (we typically work with PCs who send pre-screened participants, sponsored by the organisation, who are admitted to the EME program after written tests and group discussions) and a faculty guide (FG), during the tenure of the CP, which is of a duration of 21 months. The second objective is to enable participants to get familiar with data collection from various sources, generate original data through stakeholder surveys, studies of industry, Delphi discussions and academic papers. Thirdly, we expect our participants to solve an industrial problem in their organisations, using all the knowledge, tools and techniques taught to them during the duration of the EME. We also expect that all CP are implemented in the organisation, and the mentor and other senior management team members endorse the usefulness of the CP to the company. Finally, we expect all participants to learn and hone their leadership qualities, so that they can advance in their careers and bring benefits to themselves and their organisations. The context of the PGEMP at SPJIMR is shown in Figure 19.2.

The CP at SPJIMR – Design, Implementation and Results

The pillars of the design of our CP is shown in Figure 19.3. The process flow chart for the CP course in shown in Figure 19.4. The course duration of PGEMP is 21 months, with seven contacts, for a total of 63 days. The CP begins in contact 1, and ends with contact 7, lasting for 18 months, although participants become aware of CP upon entry. With the ascending course work and interactive pedagogy, participants are guided through a purposeful journey of self-discovery, application exercises, solving of a real-life problem in their organisation and interaction with stakeholders to strengthen the ropes of team work in the development of recommendations for solving the problem as well as implementation of decisions. The

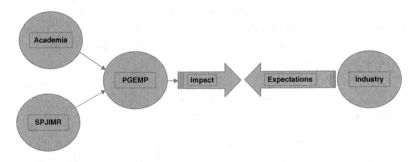

Figure 19.2 The Context of the PGEMP at SPJIMR

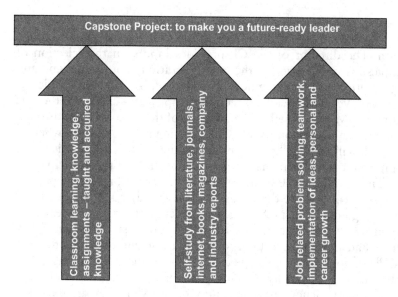

Figure 19.3 The Framework of the CP Course at PGEMP, SPJIMR

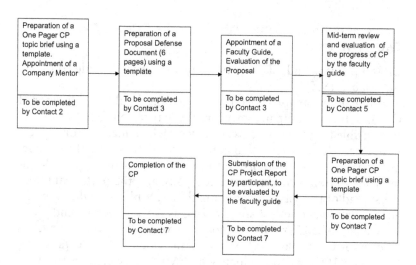

Figure 19.4 Flow Sheet of the CP Process at PGEMP

involvement of the FG and the in-company mentor through the process continuously propels the learning and doing cycle. While in-company mentors work to identify the problem as well as provide continuous encouragement and support from within the company, the FG provides academic and theoretical inputs.

The CP is accomplished in three stages – planning, research and implementation, which is aligned with the model proposed by

Inamdar and Roldan (2013). In each stage, activities are specified, and lectures from faculty (12 in all) provide the support and direction. The director of the CP provides inputs on the selection of topics, is in charge of the administration, course design, and appointment of faculty guides. The first step – selection of topic – is crucial. We recommend a three-point approach – check whether the topic is SMART, whether the contents of the topic will run through at least eighteen months of useful learning and doing, and whether the CP will create a 'good' impact on the organisation. This last is important to the personal career advancement of the participants.

The success of the CP is based on the work done by the participants in each of the three stages. CP is largely a self-driven effort. While guidance is provided, we expect participants to learn on their own, as they are more professionals than students. Since they have had experience in a corporate environment, they need to learn skills of applying knowledge to solve problems and thinking about the future strategically. Well-planned execution of corporate asset creation, efficiency improvement, etc. are what they are expected and trained to imbue.

A Check on the Results of Running the CPs for Over Twenty Years

CP is a process, and, like any other process, has a simple construct (see Figure 19.5)

While inputs are provided by the teaching faculty, the director of CP and the in-company mentor, the participants are primarily responsible for the in-process activities – which include, topic selection, research, problem solving, recommendations and their implementation – the outputs include management approval for implementation, benefits to the company and the participant, and the spread of the 'CP way' of doing things. While a feedback mechanism for each course of study exists, as per the recommendations of AACSB, AMBA, we also conduct surveys to find out the overall efficacy of CP. Tables 19.1 and 19.2 provide the brief details of a survey of 100 past participants of EME, conducted in the year 2022 on the efficacy of CP.

Figure 19.5 Inputs, In-process and Outputs of a Process

Table 19.1 Details of the Survey/Research Methodology

Survey Activity	Duration	Purpose	Remarks
Discussions on what and how to conduct the research, how to develop a questionnaire	6 months	To define the research questions, design the questionnaire	Two faculty members from PGEMP were involved in the exercise
Define the population, find out the number of participants who can be administered the questionnaire	2 months	We decided that those participants who had completed at least three years at work after completing the CP should be considered	There were 1,200 such participants. We did a initial search for the addresses, phone numbers, etc. from our records and tried contact by email and phone calls. It was found that only 300 participants could be reached
Circulate the designed questionnaire through Google sheets	2 months	To obtain responses. Two pilot surveys were conducted, one with past participants, the other with selected mentors. Based on the feedback, the questionnaire was modified (minor)	Follow-up was done through emails only. Six rounds of emails were sent out. We finally received 106 responses out of which we used 100, as they were complete in all respects
Analyse the responses using ANOVA, SPSS tools	3 months	To analyse the results from the survey, to identify areas for improvement, to check whether the course has been well accepted by the student community	ANOVA results are reported

Table 19.2 Structure of the Questionnaire

Part Number of the Question-aire	Heading	Number of Questions Included	Purpose	Remarks
I	Personal details of the past participants, including salary increases, promotions, role changes in the period post CP	15	To get details of career progression, influence in the organisation, benefits to participant and organisation post CP	The idea was to connect the enablers in the Parts II, III and IV with the outcome variables

(Continued)

Table 19.2 (Continued)

Part Number of the Question- aire	Heading	Number of Questions Included	Purpose	Remarks
II	CP planning	28	For any project, planning is a critical activity, as per Project Management Institute. So we asked the participants whether they were satisfied with the planning for CP	The questions were detailed and covered all the aspects needed for the study
III	CP execution	23	Execution is the longest part of CP, which, if done well, leads to satisfaction of participant, mentors and their organisations	The questions were designed to elicit whether the execution was well done and well facilitated
IV	CP, career progression and the organisation	25	Post CP, we expect the participants to spread the culture of CP in the organisation, benefit in their careers by using the way of CP	This is a crucial part of the CP; it enables the institute to get repeat participants

In the survey of 100 past participants, with a five-point response, the scores were found for the top twelve items (Table 19.3).

A scrutiny of table reveals that the CP course has been well appreciated by the cohorts. The areas that need improvements are given in Table 19.4.

Actions have been initiated on some of these areas, and will continue. Table 19.5 shows the actions taken so far.

Table 19.3 The Top 12 Mean Scoring Response Items from the Survey

		Minimum	Maximum	Average	SD	Coefficient of Variation
1	You could appreciate how projects can be done systematically, with greater assurance of better results	2.00	5.00	4.31	0.61	0.14
2	Capstone Project equipped me to be more skilled at the following: Practical problem solving	1.00	5.00	4.32	0.76	0.18
3	You could appreciate how projects can be done systematically, with greater assurance of better results	3.00	5.00	4.33	0.82	0.19
4	Capstone Project equipped me to be more skilled at the following: Becoming data oriented	1.00	5.00	4.34	0.87	0.20
5	Capstone Project Topic: The selected topic was directly related to your work responsibility	2.00	5.00	4.35	0.63	0.14
6	Capstone Project Topic: The CP topic was to your liking	2.00	5.00	4.37	0.65	0.15
7	I found the following Capstone Project elements most valuable in doing my project: Self study	1.00	5.00	4.39	0.71	0.16

(Continued)

Table 19.3 (Continued)

		Minimum	Maximum	Average	SD	Coefficient of Variation
8	Capstone Project Topic: The topic is an area you wanted to work on or learn more about or a problem you had identified	2.00	5.00	4.39	0.68	0.15
9	Overall working on Capstone Project during PGEMP was a good learning experience	1.00	5.00	4.39	0.67	0.15
10	Having a mentor for Capstone Project is a good idea	2.00	5.00	4.44	0.67	0.15
11	I have found the following Capstone Project elements most relevant & applicable in my work in the long term: Data collation & analysis	1.00	5.00	4.45	0.69	0.15
12	Capstone Project equipped me to be more skilled at the following: Structured approach to problem solving	1.00	5.00	4.48	0.74	0.17

Table 19.4 The Bottom 12 Mean Scoring Response Items from the Survey

		Minimum	Maximum	Average	SD	Coefficient of Variation
1	My promotions and increments are largely due to CP	1.00	5.00	3.16	0.92	0.29
2	I send business magazine and industry articles to my bosses for their reference	1.00	5.00	3.47	0.94	0.27

(Continued)

Table 19.4 (Continued)

		Minimum	Maximum	Average	SD	Coefficient of Variation
3	Capstone Project has helped me in my career progression	1.00	5.00	3.53	0.87	0.25
4	I found the following Capstone Project elements most valuable in doing my project: Reading Business magazines	1.00	5.00	3.65	0.92	0.25
5	I have found the following Capstone Project elements most relevant & applicable in my work in the long term: Reading Business magazines	1.00	5.00	3.72	0.91	0.24
6	My company values my CP experience	2.00	5.00	3.78	0.77	0.20
7	My CP has had a deep impact on how I work professionally	2.00	5.00	3.79	0.74	0.19
8	The selected topic was given to you by your organisation/ mentor as a problem to solve	1.00	5.00	3.80	1.06	0.28
9	I regularly ask my teams to use the CP methodology in their day to day work	2.00	5.00	3.85	0.74	0.19
10	The CP helped me to identify areas of growth for the organisation	2.00	5.00	3.86	0.74	0.19
11	I am now in the habit of reading trade journals, research papers, business magazines, financial newspapers and follow business news	2.00	5.00	3.87	0.82	0.21
12	My presentations to the management are made using the CP methodology	2.00	5.00	3.89	0.77	0.20

Table 19.5 Improvement Actions Undertaken in CP over the Years

Number	What was the Change	What was the Basis for the Change	From When the Change was Made, (mm/yy) Approximate Dates	What is the Current Status
1	Best Practices reporting in the CP report	To include 'reflection/reflecting' as a facet of CP. To be introduced from Batch 85. Reflection is to promote the 'CP Way' in participants organisations	07/23	To be introduced in November 2023
2	New course outline, to align with the new PGEMP taxonomy, prepared and adopted	To align with the new PGEMP and SPJIMR vision, mission and values	05/23	Completed
3	Points allocation for faculty guides changed. Eligibility of points for faculty finalised and implemented	To ensure availability of faculty guides, to plan for empanelment of faculty guides as the load on the program after Covid is increasing, and new programs in Delhi are being added	04/23	Currently in use
4	Three videos prepared to explain One Pager and Proposal Defense (PD) document, as supplementary materials for viewing by participants introduced	To provide reading materials to participants which they can view at their convenience before finalising their One Pager and PD document	04/23	In use by cohorts, in faculty
5	Environmental, social and governance (ESG) introduced as a new area to address in CP	The PGEMP took a call to address the ESG issues in the curriculum. Hence, CP also aligned with this initiative of the program	01/23	In use, gaining maturity

6	Changes made in the One Pager template and discussions	The One Pager template had to be modified to include ESG. The format for the One Pager discussion was modified to enable easier allocation of projects to faculty guides	01/23	In use currently
7	Changes made in PD template and evaluation rubrics	The PD template had to be modified to include ESG. The format for the PD evaluation was modified to track progress in ESG during project execution	01/23	In use currently
8	Study done on the performance on CP of batches 73 to 82	To identify areas for improvement	01/23	It has been found that the facilitation for One Pager and PD need improvement. Hence, three videos, as 'supplementary sessions', each of about 25 minutes duration, have been prepared, uploaded on eKosh, and all participants informed of the same
9	Survey conducted of past participants to identify areas for improvements	In order to keep current with the emerging of CP education in PGEMP, it was necessary to get feedback from past participants, as to what worked, what did not, and what further needs to be done	12/22	Areas identified and actions initiated; more actions in the pipeline
10	Introduction of 'Readings for Mind Expansion' in eKosh	Based on the feedback that business magazines should be read, it was decided to facilitate this process by providing copies of some articles from Business Magazines in eKosh for specific reading	06/22	Ongoing. The Capstone Board is currently being used, in addition to the eKosh uploads, to provide additional reading materials

(Continued)

Table 19.5 (Continued)

Number	What was the Change	What was the Basis for the Change	From When the Change was Made, (mm/yy) Approximate Dates	What is the Current Status
11	Draft report changed to Report, the word and the practice of submission of a draft report discontinued.	To avoid delays in project report submission	06/22	In practice
12	New business magazines procured for reading in campus	To improve reading habits of participants	06/22	In practice
13	New evaluation sheets designed and introduced	The basis for evaluation underwent a change. More details were added through the introduction of the rubrics. The sheets were shifted from a Word file format to EXCEL-based file format. The end-to-end journey of a CP was captured in one EXCEL file	03/22	Evaluation sheets format has been changed since, to reflect the inclusion of ESG. Some more changes are being tried out, to improve the comment writing by faculty guides, to improve the quality of the feedback. This will be implemented in the next two months, after discussions
14	Introduction of sessions by alumni	Based on feedback given by participants	02/22	Being followed currently
15	Exercise done to study the performance of CP over the years from Batch 32 to 62 (Years 2015 to 2019)	To select the top 5 CPs from each batch, in each team	12/21	Completed

16	New rubrics for evaluation of CP were written and adopted	While evaluations of CP were done, rubrics were not used. This was a gap which needed to be closed	08/21	Being followed. More changes were made in 2022, to accommodate program requirements. In 2023, the rubrics to evaluate ESG practices in companies were added
17	New course outline prepared and rolled out	Number of sessions increased from 12 to 13. New session on presentation by an alumus was added. Contents of the sessions on Introduction to CP and Report Writing were revised and updated	07/21	Being followed. The contents of the Introduction session have been further changed, by the addition of two slides on brief overview of the batch profiles
18	Study done on FG loading, and new pattern of allocating to faculty decided and implemented	To ensure availability of faculty guides, to plan for empanelment of faculty guides as the load on the program after Covid is increasing, and new programs in Delhi are being added.	06/21	Completed. Done periodically.

(Source: Author)

Conclusion

EME began as an instrument of connection between industry and academia, and continues to be so even today. The impact it has created on the industry has been up and down, but the relevance of EME is still quite strong. CP, as a prime enabler of the 'impact', and also driving the academia–industry connect, has been a major contributor. Most EME courses include CPs of various durations. However, the CP in the EME of SPJIMR is a 21 months, comprehensive effort. Involvement of the partner company mentor is a highlight. The EME in SPJIMR and the CP course are serving the needs of the academia and Indian industry, with the feedback from the participants being quite favourable. Our working method of actioning feedback has stood us in good stead. We hope to continue on this path.

Notes

1 https://iitk.ac.in/ime/capstone/, accessed on 16 Feb 2023
2 https://www.aninews.in/news/business/business/labournet-launches-capstone-project-in-collaboration-with-christ-university-bengaluru2023 0119135044/ accessed on 16 Feb 2023
3 https://bits-pilani-wilp.ac.in/certification-programmes/pgp-ai-ml.php accessed on 16 Feb 2023
4 https://extension.harvard.edu/for-students/degree-candidate-academic-opportunities/capstone-projects/ accessed on 16 Feb 2023

References

Amdam, R. P. (2016). Executive education and the managerial revolution: The birth of executive education at Harvard Business School. *Business History Review*, 90(Winter), 671–690.

Antonacopoulou, E. P. (2009). Impact and scholarship: Unlearning and practising to co-create actionable knowledge. *Management Learning*, 40(4), 420–430.

Bektaş, Ç., & Tayauova, G. (2014). A model suggestion for improving the efficiency of higher education: University–industry cooperation. *Procedia - Social and Behavioral Sciences*, 116, 2270–2274.

Bisoux, T. (2002). What trends are shaping business education? *AACSB Insights*. https://www.aacsb.edu/insights/articles/2022/02/what-trends-are-shaping-business-education

Byrne, J. (2019, August 20). It's official: The MBA degree is in crisis. *Forbes*.

Conger, J. A., & Xin, K. (2000). Executive education in the 21st century. *Journal of Management Education*, 24(1), 73–101.

Farris, P. W., Haskins, M. E., & Yemen, G. (2003). Executive education programs go back to school. *Journal of Management Development*, 22(9), 784–795.

Inamdar, S. N., & Roldan, M. (2013). The MBA Capstone Course: Building theoretical, practical, applied, and reflective skills. *Journal of Management Education*, 37(6), 747–770

Iñiguez de Onzoño, S., & Carmona, S. (2007). The changing business model of B-schools. *Journal of Management Development*, 26(1), 22–32.

Jethva, H., & Pithadia, V. (2022). Management education in India v/s world. *International Journal of Advanced Research in Commerce, Management & Social Science*, 5(1), 250–257.

Joshi, P. L. (2019). An EMBA programme is catching up fast. *Journal of Business-to-Business Marketing*, 2(12), 6–12.

Myrsiades, L. (2001). Looking to lead: A case in designing executive education from the inside. *Journal of Management Development*, 20(9), 795–812.

Petit, F. (2011). Rethinking executive MBA programs. *MIT Sloan Management Review* Fall, 53(1), 19–20.

Rizvi, I. A., & Aggarwal, A. (2005). *Enhancing student employability: Higher education and workforce development*. In *Proceedings of the 9th Quality in Higher Education Seminar*, Birmingham, UK.

Sharma, G., Greco, A., Grewatsch, S., & Bansal, P. (2022). Cocreating forward: How researchers and managers can address problems together. *Academy of Management Learning & Education*, 21(3), 350–368.

Stotlinger, B. (2021). *Covid-19 and executive education trends in 2021*. https://executiveacademy.at/de/

Teh, D., & Corbitt, B. (2015). Building sustainability strategy in business. *Journal of Business Strategy*, 36(6), 39–46.

Thomas, H. (2007). An analysis of the environment and competitive dynamics of management education. *Journal of Management Development*, 26(1), 9–21.

Tiberius, V., Hoffmeister, L., & Weyland, M. (2021). Prospective shifts in executive education: An international Delphi study. *The International Journal of Management Education*, 19, 100514.

Williams, A., Kennedy, S., Philipp, F., and Whiteman, G. (2017). Systems thinking: A review of sustainability management research. *Journal of Cleaner Production*, 148, 866–881.

Wood, V. R., Rangan, N., & Gopalakrishna, P. (2012). Higher education in the Middle East and India: Overview and two programs created to educate global business leaders in emerging markets. *China-USA Business Review*, 11(1), 143–159.

20 Commercialization of Research

Managing the Transition from Academia to Business

Einar Rasmussen

From Research to Impact

Knowledge developed through academic research is undoubtedly one of the most important driving forces for social development. Studies at the macro level show a clear correlation between investments in academic research and innovation (Mansfield, 1998; Salter and Martin, 2001). Research also plays a key role in solving other societal challenges, for example related to health and diseases, national security, food security, and quality of life, as well as sustainability and the environment (Bush, 1945; Fini et al., 2018). The handling of the corona pandemic is a good example of the importance of various disciplines and research efforts to solve societal challenges (Brem et al., 2021).

There is also a clear connection between the establishment of universities in a region and increased value creation and innovation (Valero & van Reenen, 2019). The effects are related to both education and research and are largely geographically conditioned. A classic study by Audretsch and Feldman (1996) showed that in industries where knowledge investment and research were important, innovation activity was geographically concentrated. Recent studies have confirmed such links between investments in academic research and, for example, the creation of innovative start-ups in a region (Ghio et al., 2016; Baptista et al., 2011; Fritsch and Aamoucke, 2013). Several studies also show that the establishment of new universities has a greater effect on innovation and start-ups than investments in regions that already have a high level of research activity (Andersson et al., 2009; Cowan and Zinovyeva, 2013).

Commercialization of Research

Academic research is more complex and less adapted to the needs of business than practical knowledge, and therefore, more difficult for companies to adopt (Cohen and Levinthal, 1989). Hence,

DOI: 10.4324/9781003459217-22

commercialization of research is an important mechanism for developing practically applicable solutions based on research. Commercialization of research can be defined as the process of transforming research-based knowledge into new or improved products and services available in the market (Fini et al., 2018). The terms technology transfer and commercialization are often used interchangeably to describe the process from research results to industrial application. For example, most universities have set up technology transfer offices (TTOs) to contribute to increased commercialization.

The concept of knowledge transfer (and Knowledge Transfer Office) has increasingly been adopted as an alternative to technology transfer, with the aim of also including non-technological research results and channels for knowledge transfer (Zhou and Tang, 2020). It can also be discussed whether the terms technology transfer and knowledge transfer indicate a too simple and linear understanding of the process. It is rare for technology or knowledge from research to be in a format that can be 'transferred' directly to application, as it is often required to 'translate' and 'transform' this knowledge before it can be used by industry (Carlile, 2004; Hayter et al., 2020).

How Does Commercialization Contribute to Value Creation?

Commercialization is an important activity seen both from the research side and from the business side. From a research perspective, commercialization contributes to the application and usefulness of research-based knowledge and results in society. Commercialization can be seen as a dissemination activity and thus, an important part of the research process. Commercialization can also be seen as an important source of business development, especially at the regional level. Two well-known examples are Silicon Valley in California and Cambridge in England, where a significant part of the local industry originates from universities in the region (Saxenian, 1994). Indeed, some industries are largely based on the commercialization of research, such as biotechnology (Pisano, 2006), where 60 percent of biotechnology companies being listed in Europe are research-based start-ups based on university research (Bonardo et al., 2010).

Value creation based on research implies that the knowledge is being used and entails communication between the research institutions and industry. Value creation can take place both directly in commercialization projects, for example through profitability and jobs, or indirectly through the projects contributing to increased value creation in other ways, such as:

- make available new products, processes, and services that can solve social, cultural, or environmental challenges.
- spread technology that other companies can make use of and use for innovation and their own value creation.
- spread knowledge and expertise that is put to use by other actors in society.
- lay the foundation for the development of new innovations that, in turn, can be a source of new commercial activity, for example through established spin-off companies being the source of new spin-off companies. (Leitch and Harrison, 2005)

Challenges Related to Commercialization

Successful commercialization requires, in most cases, close interaction between research institutions and commercial actors. The literature points to two particular challenges and distinctive features related to the commercialization of research results from academic research (Fini et al., 2019). First, the knowledge to be commercialized must be transferred – or reshaped – from an academic to a commercial context. Second, the commercialization process involves many different interests and goals that must be reconciled. We will discuss these in turn.

Transition from Academia to Business

A fundamental challenge in the commercialization of research is the lack of market mechanisms that contribute to an effective transfer of knowledge between academic research and commercial application (Dasgupta and David, 1994). Commercialization of research, therefore, entails bridging the gap between academia and industry so that knowledge and technology from research can provide the basis for products and services in the market. Hence, creating a link between research and business is difficult and time-consuming because it requires collaboration between actors who are fundamentally different. The research system has a different purpose and functioning than the business sector. Researchers are motivated by academic interest and are relatively free to choose their research topic. They build their careers by contributing to general knowledge development and the results are evaluated by other researchers through peer review and referee schemes that determine funding and publication. A basic attitude in the research world is that the results have been obtained jointly and therefore, should be dedicated to society (Merton, 1973).

Because scientific results are publicly available, and thus available for testing and further development, they are generally accepted as credible and based on accumulated knowledge. This is often cited as the reason why the research system has proven to be very effective in generating new discoveries (Nelson, 2004). The reward system based on recognition encourages the dissemination and use of research results. In simple terms, researchers are motivated by academic interest, prestige, and the prospect of financial reward if they succeed (Stephan and Levin, 1996). Economic models for explaining the research system are, therefore, considered to be less relevant (Stephan, 1996).

In contrast, commercial success is often the result of specific applications of knowledge in which the protection of intellectual property rights (IPR), speed of development, and other ways of taking ownership of values are important. Table 20.1 provides an overview of how the academic system for knowledge production differs from commercial activities on some key dimensions. However, there are large variations both between academic environments and within business, so this presentation is somewhat simplified. The distinctive characteristics of the universities are not so pronounced in the research institute sector and the health trusts, but the academic values are central to all basic research activity.

These differences between academia and industry form a unique starting point for developing new innovations and drawing on complementary knowledge. Greater differences in the frame of reference between companies and alliance partners increase the likelihood of developing something innovative (Nooteboom et al., 2007), and

Table 20.1 Fundamental Differences in Academic and Commercial Logic

Dimension	Academic Logic	Commercial Logic
Economic system	Public/non-commercial	Commercial
Method of work	Basic research with the purpose of new knowledge and contributions to scientific debates	Applied research with the purpose of applying knowledge to problem solving and developing solutions
Decision on tasks	Based on personal freedom and scientific curiosity	Coordinated in hierarchy
Use of results	Unrestricted disclosure	Applied to innovations often with protection or confidentiality
Reward of individuals	Scientific recognition in the field	Recognition in the organization

(Based on Perkmann et al., 2019: Table 20.1).

companies that cooperate with universities are more likely to succeed with new products and services in the market (Aschhoff and Schmidt, 2008). However, it is demanding to exchange technology and knowledge between actors who are very different. For companies, innovation projects in collaboration with research communities will more often fail (Lhuillery and Pfister, 2009), but lead to increased sales from highly innovative innovations (Gómez et al., 2020). The same pattern recurs for spin-off companies from universities, that often have a very high degree of innovation, but encounter significant barriers when entering the market (Colombo and Piva, 2012). Furthermore, licenses from university research are often related to technologies at an early stage of development (Jensen and Thursby, 2001).

Unification of Different Interests and Goals

Knowledge exchange between academia and industry means that different goals and results must be reconciled. The literature has traditionally emphasized the direct commercial results of technology transfer, such as the number of patents, licenses, and spin-off companies, as well as licensing revenues and ownership in spin-offs. However, the commercialization of research can have a number of other effects, related to teaching and research, industrial and regional development, as well as technological and societal changes (Fini et al., 2018).

The tensions that arise between the academic and commercial context seem to be a greater challenge at the individual level than at the organizational level (Ambos et al., 2008). At the individual level, researchers' involvement in commercialization is driven by various factors, such as the dissemination of knowledge, the development of technology, financial motives, social benefits, and valuation from colleagues (Lam, 2011; van Rijnsoever and Hessels, 2020). Both individual preferences (Roach and Sauermann, 2015) and goals (Bercovitz and Tyler, 2014), as well as norms in the academic community and the field (Rasmussen et al., 2014), affect how researchers involve themselves in commercialization. A study of universities in Norway, Italy, and the UK showed that both legislative changes and the establishment of TTOs resulted in the establishment of more spin-offs, but that the quality of these firms was lower (Fini et al., 2017). This shows that the researchers are responding to incentives. In this case, by establishing new companies, but it does not necessarily lead to more commercial successes.

For universities, commercialization may constitute a possible source of income, but, perhaps even more importantly, an activity that can strengthen the institution's attractiveness and role in society.

Studies have also begun to look at the connection between different activities. A study of universities in the UK shows that the indirect effect of spin-off companies in the form of increased research revenues to the universities is far greater than the direct revenues from commercialization (Pitsakis et al., 2015).

Different Channels for Interaction Between Research and Application

Knowledge transfer between research communities, on the one hand, and society and business, on the other hand, can take place both directly and indirectly, and involve a number of both commercial and non-commercial channels (Cohen et al., 2002). The commercialization of research is often measured by the number of patents, licenses, and start-ups. This entails a relatively narrow understanding of how research is applied. Studies by researchers show that formal channels, such as patenting, licensing, and start-ups, occur much less frequently than other channels, based on personal contact and direct problem solving (Hughes and Kitson, 2012). Although licensing and start-ups account for a relatively small proportion of technology transfer, these forms of commercialization may be the most effective or, in some cases, the only way to commercialize an invention.

An important characteristic of knowledge exchange is that it usually involves several different channels interacting with each other over time. Establishing spin-off companies and collaborating with industry are complementary activities (Pitsakis et al., 2015; van Looy et al., 2011), and most researchers use several different channels to interact with business (D'Este and Patel, 2007). Studies of knowledge exchange between academia and industry usually study the individual channels separately. Case studies of successful technologies and researchers show how both formal and informal channels interact over time and that value creation is the result of a complex interaction between the different channels (Azagra-Caro et al., 2017; Schaeffer et al., 2020). These findings may explain why public policy instruments based on stimulating a single channel, such as spin-off companies, often fail if the surrounding ecosystems are not taken into account (Brown et al., 2016).

Recently, several new channels have emerged with the potential to change or improve the exchange of knowledge between academia and industry. For example, many companies and universities have adopted open research strategies where new knowledge is published instead of patented (Hayter and Link, 2018), for example in partnerships between companies and universities for sharing open data (Perkmann and Schildt, 2015). There are also examples of new channels, made possible by the internet and social media, where a large number of actors, regardless of location, contribute to research, such as crowd science or citizen science (Franzoni and Sauermann, 2014). Another new mechanism for research funding is crowdfunding, where users can contribute directly to the funding of specific research projects (Stanko and Henard, 2017). In addition to the financing itself, crowdfunding can be a useful mechanism for identifying user needs and getting feedback from the market (Da Cruz, 2018), which in turn can make commercialization easier. These new channels show that the interaction between research and industry is changing and that the understanding of how knowledge exchange takes place in practice must be constantly updated.

A final point is that many of the channels for knowledge exchange are informal and thus more difficult to assess than the more formal channels. Taken together, these points make it difficult to make a precise mapping of how knowledge exchange between academia and industry takes place and, thus, also the role of commercialization of research in ensuring that research is used and contributes to value creation.

Important Elements for Successful Commercialization of Research

The most important prerequisite for successful commercialization of research is competent and motivated people who can develop the projects. At an early stage, this often means that the researchers themselves must take a leading role, but the tensions between academia and industry will affect who engages in commercialization (Ambos et al., 2008). Previous own experience and networks with researchers who have commercialization experience make it more likely for academics to participate (Ding and Choi, 2011). However, there is a need for different competencies in a commercialization process, which means that it can be an advantage to have a team consisting of both researchers and people with other backgrounds (Rasmussen et al., 2011).

At the organizational level, there are significant differences in commercialization activity across universities, and the list of high-performing universities is relatively stable over time (O'Shea et al., 2005). There is a connection between scientific quality and commercialization activity through, for example, spin-off companies (Di Gregorio and Shane, 2003). Links to the research institution may also be important for success in the further commercialization process (Bolzani et al., 2021).

There are increasingly actors who have a mediator role or act as intermediary organizations to link research and commercial application (Clayton et al., 2018). Examples of such intermediaries are TTOs, incubators, accelerators, entrepreneurship centers, and research centers (Villani et al., 2017).

Policy and Policy Implications

This overview of the research provides a good basis for discussing how to facilitate the commercialization of research and thereby increase value creation based on academic research. Here are some key points to consider when designing policies to improve the links between academia and business:

- The transition from an academic context to business presents some particular challenges for the commercialization of research that differ from other forms of innovation and entrepreneurship. This indicates that dedicated instruments are needed to promote the commercialization of research, especially in the early phases of the commercialization process.
- Differences in both the size and orientation of research institutions and the regions where they are located indicate that policy instruments and their organization must be adapted to local conditions.
- Researchers and research communities play a key role in succeeding with commercialization. Hence, incentives and framework conditions should be provided so that researchers and academic communities become actively involved.
- The commercialization of research interacts with many other channels for knowledge exchange between academia and industry. Hence, it is important that these are seen in connection with each other so that the benefits to society are maximized.
- It takes a long time to build up expertise and infrastructure to work on commercialization in connection with the research communities, so the continuity of policy instruments is important.
- The commercialization of research can be an important tool for addressing societal challenges, for example related to the UN Sustainable Development Goals. This corresponds well with the goals of many academics and their research project. Hence, focusing on social impacts can contribute to increased interest in commercialization within the academic communities.

References

Ambos, T. C., Mäkelä, K., Birkinshaw, J., & D'Este, P. (2008). When does university research get commercialized? Creating ambidexterity in research institutions. *Journal of Management Studies*, 45(8), 1424–1447.

Andersson, R., Quigley, J. M., & Wilhelmsson, M. (2009). Urbanization, productivity, and innovation: Evidence from investment in higher education. *Journal of Urban Economics*, 66(1), 2–15.

Aschhoff, B., & Schmidt, T. (2008). Empirical evidence on the success of R&D cooperation—happy together? *Review of Industrial Organization*, 33(1), 41–62.

Audretsch, D. B., & Feldman, M. P. (1996). R&D spillovers and the geography of innovation and production. *American Economic Review*, 86(3), 630–640.

Azagra-Caro, J. M., Barberá-Tomás, D., Edwards-Schachter, M., & Tur, E. M. (2017). Dynamic interactions between university–industry knowledge transfer channels: A case study of the most highly cited academic patent. *Research Policy*, 46(2), 463–474.

Baptista, R., Lima, F., & Mendonça, J. (2011). Establishment of higher education institutions and new firm entry. *Research Policy*, 40(5), 751–760.

Bercovitz, J. E. L., & B. B. Tyler. (2014). Who I am and how I contract: The effect of contractors' roles on the evolution of contract structure in university–industry research agreements. *Organization Science*, 25(6), 1840–1859.

Bolzani, D., Rasmussen, E., & Fini, R. (2021). Spin-offs' linkages to their parent universities over time: The performance implications of equity, geographical proximity, and technological ties. *Strategic Entrepreneurship Journal*, 15(4), 590–618.

Bonardo, D., Paleari, S., & Vismara, S. (2010). The M&A dynamics of European science-based entrepreneurial firms. *Journal of Technology Transfer*, 35(1), 141–180.

Brem, A., Viardot, E., & Nylund, P. A. (2021). Implications of the coronavirus (COVID-19) outbreak for innovation: Which technologies will improve our lives? *Technological Forecasting and Social Change*, 163, 120451.

Brown, R., Gregson, G., & Mason, C. (2016). A post-mortem of regional innovation policy failure: Scotland's Intermediate Technology Initiative (ITI). *Regional Studies*, 50(7), 1260–1272.

Bush, V. (1945). *Science, the endless frontier: A report to the President*. United States Government Printing Office.

Carlile, P. R. (2004). Transferring, translating, and transforming: An integrative framework for managing knowledge across boundaries. *Organization Science*, 15(5), 555–568.

Clayton, P., Feldman, M., & Lowe, N. (2018). Behind the scenes: Intermediary organizations that facilitate science commercialization through entrepreneurship. *Academy of Management Perspectives*, 32(1), 104–124.

Cohen, W. M., & Levinthal, D. A. (1989). Innovation and learning: The two faces of R&D. *Economic Journal*, 99(397), 569–596.

Cohen, W. M., Nelson, R. R., & Walsh, J. P. (2002). Links and impacts: The influence of public research on industrial R&D. *Management Science*, 48(1), 1–23.

Colombo, M. G., & Piva, E. (2012). Firms' genetic characteristics and competence-enlarging strategies: A comparison between academic and non-academic high-tech start-ups. *Research Policy*, 41(1), 79–92.

Cowan, R., & Zinovyeva, N. (2013). University effects on regional innovation. *Research Policy*, 42(3), 788–800.

Da Cruz, J. V. (2018). Beyond financing: Crowdfunding as an informational mechanism. *Journal of Business Venturing*, *33*(3), 371–393.

Dasgupta, P., & David, P. A. (1994). Toward a new economics of science. *Research Policy*, *23*(5), 487–521.

D'Este, P., & Patel, P. (2007). University–industry linkages in the UK: What are the factors underlying the variety of interactions with industry? *Research Policy*, *36*(9), 1295–1313.

Di Gregorio, D., & Shane, S. (2003). Why do some universities generate more start-ups than others? *Research Policy*, *32*(2), 209–227.

Ding, W., & Choi, E. (2011). Divergent paths to commercial science: A comparison of scientists' founding and advising activities. *Research Policy*, *40*(1), 69–80.

Fini, R., Fu, K., Mathisen, M. T., Rasmussen, E., & Wright, M. (2017). Institutional determinants of university spin-off quantity and quality: A longitudinal, multilevel, cross-country study. *Small Business Economics*, *48*(2), 361–391.

Fini, R., Rasmussen, E., Siegel, D., & Wiklund, J. (2018). Rethinking the commercialization of public science: From entrepreneurial outcomes to societal impacts. *Academy of Management Perspectives*, *32*(1), 4–20.

Fini, R., Rasmussen, E., Wiklund, J., & Wright, M. (2019). Theories from the lab: How research on science commercialization can contribute to management studies. *Journal of Management Studies*, *56*(5), 865–894.

Franzoni, C., & Sauermann, H. (2014). Crowd science: The organization of scientific research in open collaborative projects. *Research Policy*, *43*(1), 1–20.

Fritsch, M., & Aamoucke, R. (2013). Regional public research, higher education, and innovative start-ups: An empirical investigation. *Small Business Economics*, *41*(4), 865–885.

Ghio, N., Guerini, M., & Rossi-Lamastra, C. (2016). University knowledge and the creation of innovative start-ups: An analysis of the Italian case. *Small Business Economics*, *47*(2), 293–311.

Gómez, J., Salazar, I., & Vargas, P. (2020). The role of extramural R&D and scientific knowledge in creating high novelty innovations: An examination of manufacturing and service firms in Spain. *Research Policy*, *49*(8), 104030.

Hayter, C. S., & Link, A. N. (2018). Why do knowledge-intensive entrepreneurial firms publish their innovative ideas? *Academy of Management Perspectives*, *32*(1), 141–155.

Hayter, C. S., Rasmussen, E., & Rooksby, J. H. (2020). Beyond formal university technology transfer: Innovative pathways for knowledge exchange. *Journal of Technology Transfer*, *45*(1), 1–8.

Hughes, A., & Kitson, M. (2012). Pathways to impact and the strategic role of universities: New evidence on the breadth and depth of university knowledge exchange in the UK and the factors constraining its development. *Cambridge Journal of Economics*, *36*(3), 723–750.

Jensen, R., & Thursby, M. (2001). Proofs and prototypes for sale: The licensing of university inventions. *American Economic Review*, *91*(1), 240–259.

Lam, A. (2011). What motivates academic scientists to engage in research commercialization: 'Gold', 'ribbon' or 'puzzle'? *Research Policy*, *40*(10), 1354–1368.

Leitch, C. M., & Harrison, R. T. (2005). Maximising the potential of university spin-outs: The development of second-order commercialisation activities. *R&D Management*, 35(3), 257–272.

Lhuillery, S., & Pfister, E. (2009). R&D cooperation and failures in innovation projects: Empirical evidence from French CIS data. *Research Policy*, 38(1), 45–57.

Mansfield, E. (1998). Academic research and industrial innovation: An update of empirical findings. *Research Policy*, 26(7–8), 773–776.

Merton, R. K., The normative structure of science. (1973). In R. K. Merton (Ed.), *The sociology of science. Theoretical and empirical investigations*, (pp. 267–278). University of Chicago Press.

Nelson, R. (2004). The market economy, and the scientific commons. *Research Policy*, 33(3), 455–471.

Nooteboom, B., Van Haverbeke, W., Duysters, G., Gilsing, V., & Van den Oord, A. (2007). Optimal cognitive distance and absorptive capacity. *Research Policy*, 36(7), 1016–1034.

O'Shea, R. P., Allen, T. J., Chevalier, A., & Roche, F. (2005). Entrepreneurial orientation, technology transfer and spinoff performance of US universities. *Research Policy*, 34(7), 994–1009.

Perkmann, M., McKelvey, M., & Phillips, N. (2019). Protecting scientists from Gordon Gekko: How organizations use hybrid spaces to engage with multiple institutional logics. *Organization Science*, 30(2), 298–318.

Perkmann, M., & Schildt, H. (2015). Open data partnerships between firms and universities: The role of boundary organizations. *Research Policy*, 44(5), 1133–1143.

Pisano, G. P. (2006). *Science business: The promise, the reality, and the future of biotech*. Harvard Business Press.

Pitsakis, K., Souitaris, V., & Nicolaou, N. (2015). The peripheral halo effect: Do academic spinoffs influence universities' research income? *Journal of Management Studies*, 52(3), 321–353.

Rasmussen, E., Mosey, S., & Wright, M. (2011). The evolution of entrepreneurial competencies: A longitudinal study of university spin-off venture emergence. *Journal of Management Studies*, 48(6), 1314–1345.

Rasmussen, E., Mosey, S., & Wright, M. (2014). The influence of university departments on the evolution of entrepreneurial competencies in spin-off ventures. *Research Policy*, 43(1), 92–106.

Roach, M., & Sauermann, H. (2015). Founder or joiner? The role of preferences and context in shaping different entrepreneurial interests. *Management Science*, 61(9), 2160–2184.

Salter, A. J., & Martin, B. R. (2001). The economic benefits of publicly funded basic research: A critical review. *Research Policy*, 30(3), 509–532.

Saxenian, A. (1994). *Regional advantage. Culture and competition in Silicon Valley and Route 128*. Harvard University Press.

Schaeffer, V., Öcalan-Özel, S., & Pénin, J. (2020). The complementarities between formal and informal channels of university–industry knowledge transfer: A longitudinal approach. *Journal of Technology Transfer*, 45(1), 31–55.

Stanko, M. A., & Henard, D. H. (2017). Toward a better understanding of crowdfunding, openness and the consequences for innovation. *Research Policy*, 46(4), 784–798.

Stephan, P.E. (1996). The economics of science. *Journal of Economic Literature*, *34*(3), 1199–1235.

Stephan, P. E., & Levin, S. G. (1996). Property rights and entrepreneurship in science. *Small Business Economics*, *8*(3), 177–188.

Valero, A., & van Reenen, J. (2019). The economic impact of universities: Evidence from across the globe. *Economics of Education Review*, 68, 53–67.

van Looy, B., Landoni, P., Callaert, J., van Pottelsberghe, B., Sapsalis, E., & Debackere, K. (2011). Entrepreneurial effectiveness of European universities: An empirical assessment of antecedents and trade-offs. *Research Policy*, *40*(4), 553–564.

van Rijnsoever, F. J., & Hessels, L. K. (2020). How academic researchers select collaborative research projects: A choice experiment. *Journal of Technology Transfer*, *46*(6) 1917–1948.

Villani, E., Rasmussen, E., & Grimaldi, R. (2017). How intermediary organizations facilitate university–industry technology transfer: A proximity approach. *Technological Forecasting and Social Change*, 114, 86–102.

Zhou, R., & Tang, P. (2020). The role of university Knowledge Transfer Offices: Not just commercialize research outputs! *Technovation*, 90, 102100.

21 A Scorecard for Designing and Evaluating University Partnerships

Chris J. Barton, Derrick M. Anderson,
Leah R. Gerber, Candice Carr Kelman,
and Martha Arízaga

Introduction

Since the introduction of the Balanced Scorecard framework in the 1980s, formal performance measurement and management strategies have become widely adopted in private, government, and non-profit settings. Although an abundance of conceptual frameworks have been developed, there are few which are designed to evaluate the unique collaborative efforts undertaken by universities. In this paper, we propose a scorecard tool for use by universities in managing and evaluating their collaborative partnerships with external organizations.

The scorecard design is the result of a literature review on existing research on why and how universities partner with other organizations, as well as what makes these partnerships successful. The core of the tool is based on several papers which themselves were systemic reviews of various subsections of the literature (Al-Ashaab et al., 2011; Amabile et al., 2001; Ankrah & AL-Tabbaa, 2015; Philbin, 2008a; Rybnicek & Königsgruber, 2019). Each of the papers which constitute the backbone of the scorecard tool reviewed dozens, sometimes hundreds, of other articles. The tool also incorporates the findings of other articles which were discovered during our literature review but were not included in the main review articles.

As noted above, a literature-based, broadly applicable partnership scorecard framework is useful for two reasons. The first is that such a tool allows for direct comparison of partnerships which might otherwise be difficult to compare. An effective scorecard will be able to assess all partnerships, regardless of what organization the university is partnering with, the formality or scale of the partnership, the time frame the partnership operates under, or the stage of operation the partnership is currently in. The second benefit of a

DOI: 10.4324/9781003459217-23

scorecard is its ability to provide guidance to those building or operating partnerships. If a partnership scores low on a particular metric, they should be encouraged to improve in that area, so that if they are reassessed, they will score above an acceptable threshold. The scorecard can be used to identify both areas of improvement for individual partnerships and areas of success, which can then lead to the identification of best practices.

The proposed scorecard contains a diverse set of performance measures designed to evaluate the effectiveness of collaborations. The tool contains 144 indicator variables classified within three categories (institutional factors, team factors, and goals and outcomes) and across three phases of the partnership (initiation phase, operation phase, and delivery phase), as well as 12 quantitative metrics. The scorecard's modular design makes it applicable to a wide range of university partnership models. The scorecard is designed to help universities in two ways: (1) by providing guidance to individuals engaged in partnerships on how to structure and operate the partnership, based on literature-backed best practices, and (2) by giving university administrators a tool to assess the effectiveness of partnerships and compare diverse partnerships along standardized metrics. This tool will allow universities to improve the effectiveness of their existing partnerships and also make better-informed decisions regarding their larger partnership strategy.

Similar projects have been attempted before. The existing work generally falls into three categories: articles that review specific cases of collaboration between universities and industry; articles that review these cases and extract best practices; and a handful which attempt to operationalize these best practices in a tool to measure or improve the effectiveness of university–industry partnerships. Two commonalities among the literature are important to note, as our project differentiates itself from those which came before it in these ways. First, most of the literature takes as its audience the private sector, and therefore, the criteria of what makes a successful partnership are based on what is best for a firm partnering with a university, rather than for the university itself. A notable exception to this is Ankrah & AL-Tabbaa (2015), in which the authors view partnerships from the perspective of both universities and companies.

Our work takes universities as its audience, and specifically those people within universities who are administering partnerships. Therefore, our scorecard is designed to record metrics that are of interest to universities that are engaged in partnerships.

Second, the literature is almost entirely focused on partnerships that revolve around research and development. However, this is just a subset of the kinds of partnerships that a university might engage in. For example, our home institution (Arizona State University, ASU) partnered with Starbucks, a publicly-owned firm, to provide education services to Starbucks' employees (Arizona State University, n.d.), and with the Ministry of Education in China to offer ASU degrees out of Hainan University in Hainan, China (*Hainan University—Arizona State University Joint International Tourism College*, 2018). Both of these partnerships are significantly different in both form and function from an R&D-based partnership, and therefore need to be assessed differently. Our tool is designed to be useful for all university partnerships, regardless of whether they are focused on R&D, delivering education, or something else entirely.

Defining University Partnerships, Collaborations, and Teams

Partnerships between universities and other organizations—private companies, NGOs, public entities, or other universities—have proliferated in recent decades (Hagedoorn et al., 2000; Poyago-Theotoky, 2002; Rybnicek & Königsgruber, 2019). Government funding for higher education has long been unsteady, but took a sharp downward turn during the Great Recession of 2008—and those revenue streams have not returned (American Academy of Arts and Sciences, 2016). Many universities across the country have pursued alternative revenue streams by increasing tuition and fees and by exploring partnerships with private, nonprofit, and other public organizations. According to Perkmann and Walsh (2007), this development is a result of three key shifts in what they call the "academic capitalistic landscape":

- Federal policies/legislation aimed at increasing research that would result in more patenting and licensing
- Decreases in federal funding; increased need for private investment
- Increased importance of the technology industry as a catalyst for innovation and economic growth

Since the 1980s, universities have had to navigate reductions in public investment in higher education, coupled with an uptake of federal policies aimed at improving industry competitiveness. Reduced government funding has pressed universities to explore partnerships as an effective means to source new revenues for research activities; accompanying this shift has been a significant rise in industry investment in university research (Poyago-Theotoky,

2002). Collaboration in research has broadened and diversified stakeholder involvement in the knowledge creation process (Bozeman et al., 2013). The shift has generally been applauded because it allows universities to continue driving the innovation process while distributing costs and increasing industry talent in research activities. Private and public organizations and universities have come together to capitalize on knowledge-based innovation that would not be possible by the actions of each institution alone.

There are many reasons why a university might enter into a partnership, including pooling resources, influencing information flow, and improving competitive advantage (Hagedoorn et al., 2000). Motivations for collaborating and forms of engagement differ in each partnership arrangement. University partnerships may take many forms and can be formal or informal. Some examples include a single academic researcher working with another researcher at another university, a firm contracting with a university to conduct R&D on its behalf, universities licensing their technology to companies for commercialization, and universities entering into strategic partnerships with other universities (Ankrah & AL-Tabbaa, 2015; Bozeman et al., 2013; Hagedoorn et al., 2000; Poyago-Theotoky, 2002).

For this project, we draw inspiration from a Council on Competitiveness (1996) report on R&D partnerships to define a *university partnership* as any cooperative arrangement engaging a university with another university, a company, and/or a government agency in various combinations to pool resources in pursuit of a shared objective. A significant departure from the original is that our definition includes partnerships with objectives other than R&D. We also differentiate a partnership from a collaboration, in that we follow Bozeman et al. (2013) in defining a collaboration as "social processes whereby human beings pool their human capital to achieve shared objectives" (p. 3). A partnership is an official relationship under which one or more collaborations may occur. A partnership implies collaboration between members of the partner organizations, but the degree to which these members collaborate may vary significantly from partnership to partnership. Also, the form of the collaboration may differ significantly; a partnership between a university and a company might result in scientists collaborating on a specific area of research, while a partnership between two universities might result in collaborations between administrators working on recruiting into each other's programs or publicizing a shared research project. We define the group of people engaged in collaboration as the partnership team. The team may change in size as the partnership progresses, though it can be assumed that key members remain engaged throughout the lifespan of the partnership.

Partnership Scorecard Background and Literature Review

Performance Management

The transformation in the private sector from family-owned single businesses to multifunction enterprises in the late 19th century required companies to expand and subdivide their activities into specialized departments. The specialization and diversification of units introduced administrative challenges that demanded the creation of the business manager role to coordinate efforts and outcomes from the multidivisional structure (Chandler, 1990). In business administration, performance management allows an organization to assess its progress toward its objectives, highlight its strengths and weaknesses, and support decision-making for future initiatives. Project management can expand the executive officer's analysis beyond cost-control measures toward long-term strategic directives and sustained economic value creation for stakeholders and employees at all levels (Cokins, 2009).

Performance management uses different methods and tools to integrate operational, technological, social, and financial data. The Balanced Scorecard (BSC) is one popular performance management tool. Developed by Drs. Robert S. Kaplan and David Norton in the '90s, the BSC was based on a study of performance management in companies whose products were dependent on intangible assets. According to Kaplan and Norton, in order to derive the maximum value from the company's work, the intangible assets should be measured alongside tangible ones (Niven, 2014). As a result, the BSC analyzes organizational performance and improves the alignment between the corporation's mission and the operational activities, showing the value of the unique aspects of the organization to support its final goal (Kaplan, 2009). This strategic approach also provides feedback on internal business processes and external outcomes, continuously contributing to organizational awareness (Lin, 2015).

However, the BSC is designed for use with private firms. It is of limited use when assessing partnerships, which—unless they are formalized in independent organizations, such as joint ventures—are difficult to fit into the BSC framework. The BSC is also of limited use when analyzing partnerships from the perspective of a university, which has significantly different priorities and obligations than a private firm. Private firms are interested largely in producing market value, whereas universities must also consider their ability to deliver public value (see Bozeman, 2002). In fact, Anderson and Taggart (2016) have noted that "the normative environment of higher education sometimes stands in sharp contrast with the logic of corporatism and/or the profit goal orientation" (p. 780). The unique needs and obligations of a university require a purpose-built assessment tool.

It is worth noting the work of Al-Ashaab et al. (2011) and their attempt to adapt the BSC to assess university–industry partnerships. Their framework was designed to measure success using metrics relevant to industry, and "identify the opportunity areas when managing open innovation research activities in collaboration with universities and other research institutes" (Al-Ashaab et al., 2011, p. 569). Their approach is useful in that it helps identify each partner's main characteristics, how they deal with innovation, and how aligned their goals are, which is important for the planning phase of a partnership. The information gathered from this exercise can aid industry leadership in deciding whether to engage in a partnership, communicating the importance of the collaboration to company staff, establishing the rules and goals for the partnership, and determining how the project fits into the larger strategy of their organization. The Al-Ashaab et al. scorecard can be used in all stages of the partnership as a monitoring and evaluation tool throughout the life of the collaboration.

Al-Ashaab et al.'s tool is useful and effective in its own right— however, it assesses from primarily an institutional (rather than an interpersonal) perspective, with its core objectives focused on measuring how innovative a specific organization is. Considering how many partnerships are based on personal relationships, this is a large flaw. The tool also does not capture the collaborative behavior of both partners, focusing instead on the firm. The authors also retain the BSC framework and, thus, create a tool that is of more use to firms assessing partnerships with universities than to universities assessing partnerships with other organizations. A new tool is needed. Our project takes inspiration from the BSC as a model for performance management, but we have attempted to build a university partnership scorecard in the style of the BSC, rather than based on the BSC.

Motivations For and Structure of Collaborations

Partner motivations are unique to the participating organizations and highly influential on the nature of the relationship. Evidence from the literature highlights a range of potential benefits of research collaboration for both research partners (academia and industry) as well as society. According to Ankrah and AL-Tabbaa (2015), there are three primary types of benefits that motivate the universities and industry to collaborate: economic benefits, institutional benefits, and social benefits.

Economic Benefits

Universities are motivated to share research costs, capitalize on business opportunities that generate revenue, and contribute to the local economy. Collaboration allows industry to improve product quality, build market competencies, and benefit from universities' access to public research funding (Ankrah & AL-Tabbaa, 2015; Lee, 2000). Partnership outcomes also have an impact on community and economic development. For instance, the increase in the research collaboration of Korean physicists with American universities since the 1990s enriched the knowledge base in Korea. In fact, the great majority of the first-generation Korean physicists completed their doctorate degrees in the United States (US), which helped Korean industries to innovate, develop at unexpected speed, and experience benefits from the technological advancement in the US. In turn, this industry development had positive impacts on the economy of the Korean Republic (Kim, 2006). Moreover, collaborations can help companies maintain competitive positions and profit margins in the national market as well as increase international market share and profitability (Hanel & St-Pierre, 2006).

Institutional Benefits

Universities benefit from collaborations which connect students and faculty to practical industry problems, provide a testbed for ideas, maintain channels for the practical application of university research as well as training and employment pipelines for students, and continue the university's outreach prerogatives (Ankrah & AL-Tabbaa, 2015; Lee, 2000). For industry partners, collaboration can provide access to new knowledge and leading-edge technologies, offer opportunities to hire talented graduates, and accelerate the commercialization of technologies (Ankrah & AL-Tabbaa, 2015). Furthermore, firms are increasingly engaging in collaboration as a means to explore solutions for product design, product development, quality improvement, product patents, and other R&D agenda items. Additionally, universities and industries stand to strengthen their reputation and build on each other's brands by engaging in collaboration (Ankrah & AL-Tabbaa, 2015). Advantages like these motivate industries not only to engage more with education institutions, but also to develop sustainable long-lasting relationships with universities (Lee, 2000).

Social Benefits

Knowledge production and technology innovations are the main two social benefits (common pool goods) of research collaboration (Bozeman et al., 2013). In the highly competitive innovation space countries are eager to assert the originality of citizens' contributions to knowledge platforms. In some cases, collaboration was found to boost the novelty of these outcomes. Hanel and St-Pierre's (2006) findings suggest that outcomes from collaborative relationships have a higher degree of originality as opposed to non-collaborative innovation outcomes. For instance, nearly 22 percent of collaborating firms introduced what's considered "world first" innovation while only 10 percent of non-collaborative companies did the same. Additionally, half of the collaborative firms introduced "Canada-first" innovations compared to just 25 percent of non-collaborative companies. The distribution of benefits varies based on the contributions from each partner and how outcome ownership is negotiated. However, there is a consensus that the practice of collaboration is overall beneficial for industries and universities and will continue to be used as an effective means to drive innovation and deliver services (Lee, 2000). "The flow of developmental, educational ideas, of the need to cultivate intellectual capital and innovation, runs between the university and industry in both directions" (Slotte & Tynjälä, 2003, p. 446).

Collaboration Process

The majority of the literature in this area is focused on the concept of university–industry collaboration (often shortened to UIC), which refers to "the interaction between any parts of the higher education system and industry, aiming mainly to encourage knowledge and technology exchange" (Ankrah & AL-Tabbaa, 2015, p. 387). This reflects the bias in the literature for studying only the partnerships universities make with private firms. Although this is only one type of potential university partnership, many of the insights gleaned from studying UICs are applicable to other types of university partnerships as well. Even within the limited scope of UICs, partnerships vary in terms of structures and collaborations differ in their formality, duration, scope, management, partner proximity, and desired outcomes.

Despite the popularity of collaborative ventures, not all outcomes and services need to be achieved through collaboration (Hilvert & Swindell, 2013). If collaboration is determined to be an optimal strategy, then partners must work closely to develop a formal relationship. The literature suggests that following a framework for partnership execution creates a solid foundation for a healthy and successful partnership (Philbin, 2008a).

The success or failure of collaborations is related to the form of collaboration (Amabile et al., 2001) and collaboration motivations (Ankrah & AL-Tabbaa, 2015). Decisions in the formation phase may lead to several different partnership forms; some may benefit from rigid collaboration structures while others have flexible collaboration structures. An important initial consideration is establishing trust between partners and setting a clear direction for the partnership. One study (Philbin, 2008b) proposed a five-step framework to use for the design and management of partnerships. In this study, researchers interviewed key stakeholders (academic staff, professional services staff, and business contacts in external technology companies) and identified familiarity, trust, common understanding, access to social networks, social interactions, and commitment as the major factors that have a bearing on the formation and management of partnerships. Based on these findings, Philbin (2008b, p. 496) proposed a 5-step linear process for the formation and management of partnerships:

1. Terrain Mapping—evaluate opportunity landscape for collaboration
2. Proposition—review partner values and assets, align research offerings of the research organization with the strategies/objectives of the external company
3. Initiation—the initial formation of collaboration
4. Delivery—operational management stage
5. Evaluation—a review of the post-delivery outcomes

Numerous studies make a similar case for differentiating levels of collaboration progression and assigning various objectives and tasks at each stage. Kraut et al. (1987) outlined a simpler process format which includes three stages: the initiation stage (planning), the execution stage (implementation), and the public presentation stage (reporting). We use this model to structure our scorecard and to illustrate how collaborators can shape and manage successful partnerships.

Planning

In the initiation and planning stage, the partners must articulate well-defined goals and objectives and establish ground rules early in the process, so stakeholders are clear on all expectations and guiding principles that will govern the partnership (Rybnicek & Königsgruber, 2019). The leadership of all partner institutions should communicate the importance of the collaboration to the organizational staff in general, so they are mentally ready to provide the required support to the collaboration-related activities when needed (Amabile et al., 2001). In addition to researchers, the team should include people with business experience (Siegel et al., 2003) for expert insight on the marketability of the intended project/service from the initial stages. The project manager for the collaboration project should have in-depth knowledge of the technology needs in the field, be inclined to networking across functional and organizational boundaries, and make connections between the research and the final product application (Pertuzé et al., 2010).

UICs work best when the collaboration supports the mission of each collaborator (University–Industry Demonstration Partnership, n.d.). Organizations looking to collaborate with a university should have a clear understanding of the project's outcomes in reference to its own strategic context. This can be done by determining what the collaboration opportunities are, defining the partnership's output, and identifying the user of the partnership's output (Pertuzé et al., 2010). Evidence suggests that universities should select for the collaboration team researchers who understand and appreciate the practices, technology goals, and project strategy of the partnering organization. The partnering organization should also share information with the university researchers, so the collaborators may help the organization to achieve its vision (Pertuzé et al., 2010). Moreover, partners need to understand each other's capabilities, commitments, roles, responsibilities, expectations, resources, and interests from the initial stages of the collaboration (Amabile et al., 2001). A lack of clear understanding in the beginning can result in mission confusion, create mistrust among the partners, and sometimes seriously delay the work.

Implementation

During the implementation stage, the regular, clear, documented, and effective communications among the partners are the most critical determinant of success (Bozeman et al., 2016; Philbin, 2008a). Partnership agreements that emphasize networking between individuals and collaboration among research groups are vital for rapid knowledge dissemination (Abramo et al., 2009). Increasing the frequency of communication allows individuals and organizations to advance relationships, develop trust, and build strong networks. In addition to regular team meetings, collaborations benefit when the partner organizations build broad awareness of the project within the organizations. Success is also related to partners' ability to communicate feedback on project design between the organizations. The team's feedback on product design increases the marketability of the final product (Pertuzé et al., 2010).

The effective use of research members' capabilities and the establishment of conflict resolution mechanisms are also essential tools for a successful collaboration (Amabile et al., 2001). The team and partner organizations should embrace changes in technology that happen during the collaboration process, as no single technology is likely to fit the needs of all team members at all times (Kraut et al., 1987). Parties should be open to considering any changes in the collaboration process and strategy, as long as changes provide added efficiencies or capabilities, not already provided with existing practices.

Reporting

In the third and final stage of public presentation (reporting) of collaboration, Kraut et al. (1987) express the need for credit allocation and urges organizations to give team members the opportunity to be recognized for their contributions to the work. This can be done by implementing a reward system that recognizes team efforts, risk-taking, personal relationships, and building networks as part of the collaboration process (Siegel et al., 2003). Ideally, neither organization should end the partnership when the collaboration ends, but the partner organizations should instead invest in a long-term relationship with a multi-year time frame. The main reason for this is that personal relationships take years to develop, and the creation and maintenance of personal relationships is what holds collaborative research efforts together (Kraut et al., 1987).

Partnership Forms

The forms of university partnerships have been discussed from different points of view in the literature, and emphasize the level and types of engagement in the collaboration from beginning to end. One of the more widely-discussed frameworks groups university collaborations with industry into four forms: joint ventures, networks, consortia, and alliances (Barringer & Harrison, 2000). Other classification approaches include Santoro and Gopalakrishnan's (2000) topology, which suggests four forms of UIC: research support, cooperative research, knowledge transfer, and technology transfer. Bonaccorsi and Piccaluga's (1994) framework considers six forms of UIC: personal informal relationships, personal formal relationships, third parties, formal targeted agreements, formal non-targeted agreements, and the creation of focused structures. Of the classifications, Bonaccorsi and Piccaluga's (1994) has the broadest scope and is used by Ankrah and AL-Tabbaa (2015) as a framework to analyze different forms of UIC in their literature review. According to Ankrah and AL-Tabbaa (2015), the six forms show an increasing level of organizational involvement, which can be understood from three dimensions: university resource involvement, agreement length, and collaboration formalization. Our discussion of collaboration form focuses on Bonaccorsi and Piccaluga's (1994) framework.

Of the six forms proposed by Bonaccorsi and Piccaluga (1994), "formal targeted agreements" are perhaps the most common. The form can manifest as contract research, patenting and licensing agreements, cooperative research projects, equity holding in companies by universities or faculty members, exchange of research materials, joint curriculum development, joint research programs, and training programs for employees (Ankrah & AL-Tabbaa, 2015). One example of this collaboration type is between the California Institute of Technology (Caltech) and the Boeing Company, a partnership called the Caltech Boeing Strategic Agreement. To aid their development of technology, Boeing has signed long-term agreements with nine research universities, Caltech being one of them. Boeing has provided significant investment in Caltech via research funding, technology transfer and patenting, student internships and career pathways, faculty engagement, and employee/faculty exchange programs (University–Industry Demonstration Partnership, n.d.). This highly integrated form of collaboration involves many formal activities between the two parties and requires both parties to work closely with each other.

However, a high-engagement form of UIC can sometimes devolve into a lower-engagement form of UIC, or the collaboration may end entirely. That is, merely building an engaging form of UIC does not guarantee a long-term and successful collaboration. An example of this is the case of Syracuse University and JPMorgan Chase. In 2007, the university and bank started working together toward shared objectives (Syracuse School of Information Studies, 2007). The four initial objectives for collaboration included building a sustainable UIC model that would transform the approaches by which technologists are trained in the classroom and on the job, promote innovation in university education and financial services technology, and create long-term value to the university, bank, and broader community. In order to achieve these objectives, Syracuse University and JPMorgan Chase launched joint applied research projects. The bank also opened an information security research center at the university. These research collaborations influenced the university's curriculum design and engaged students and faculty members in applied research. JPMorgan Chase recruited many students from these collaborative programs. Although the two parties made efforts to build a long-term collaborative relationship, most of their collaborative projects ended in 2015 (Moriarty, 2015). For now, the partnership relies primarily on personal informal relationships among faculty and bank personnel, with the student recruitment and employment pipeline program being the only remaining formal arrangement. Partners rarely expect to engage in collaborations which start with a high level of engagement but end up with a low level of engagement, like the partnership between Syracuse University and JPMorgan Chase; the desire is to sustain a high level of engagement. Other collaborations start with a low level of engagement which shifts to a high level of engagement. This low-to-high engagement indicates a sustainable collaboration that is beneficial to both parties.

Determinants of Successful Collaborations

The literature identifies many determinants of successful partnerships between universities and industry. Several studies have tested hypotheses regarding the impacts of different partner dynamics, such as previous links, commitment, the reputation of organizations, intellectual capital, and resources (Bozeman et al., 2013). We considered these factors and others in developing a scorecard framework. Discussed here are five common themes found in the literature: goals, degrees of formalization, trust between partners, duration, and proximity to partners.

Goals

In terms of goals and outcomes, the research highlighted a distinction between knowledge-focused partnerships and property-focused partnerships (Bozeman et al., 2013). These two perspectives are significant to the activities and management of collaborative relationships. While the former is focused on expanding basic knowledge and often involves producing measurable deliverables in the form of co-authorship or patents, the latter has a broader focus on how partnerships can make meaningful contributions to the innovation process and produce economic value. Property-focused efforts can serve to produce significant gains in systems optimizations, increased citation rates on publications from researchers, and cost savings both for the university and partner organizations (Bozeman et al., 2013). However, knowledge-focused efforts are less encumbered by output measures for success—instead focused on research for the sake of producing new knowledge—and this has proven highly relevant and beneficial to the innovation process (Welsh et al., 2008). While one might assume that industry is primarily motivated by property-focused outcomes such as patents or profitable products, Caloghirou et al. (2003) show that industry partners often are motivated by less targeted work aimed at generally enriching the knowledge available to them.

Formalization

The degree of formalization can be interpreted by the institutionalization of official policies and how the relationship links are maintained. The more rules, administrative procedures, and regulations present in the cooperative agreement the more formal it is (Mora-Valentin et al., 2004). While some partnerships are developed in an ad hoc manner with loose management structures, those that dedicate more attention to planning and the organizational structure of partnerships have demonstrated better results during technology transfer (Geisler, 1995).

Trust

Research on collaboration consistently finds that the value of partnerships increases at the speed of trust. Mora-Valentin et al. (2004) studied ten organizational and contextual factors and found that trust and commitment were the most outstanding features in determining the success of research and development agreements. In their study, individual researchers were more likely to be satisfied and seek to evolve the relationship if there was trust and commitment between partners. Establishing trust is fundamental to the health of the partnership and can be achieved by fostering high levels of engagement, establishing clear protocols around protecting the interests of each partner and team member, as well as providing equitable access to partnership resources.

The chances of success in partnerships increase when issues of knowledge appropriation are addressed head-on (Caloghirou et al., 2003). While it is common for companies to protect proprietary information, sometimes these efforts can result in a loss of trust with university partners. Finding a balanced approach to knowledge appropriation should deemphasize the importance of raising revenue, and instead focus on the potential to commercialize and further develop the product (Welsh et al., 2008). Collaborators can do this by proactively creating policies on resolving conflicts of interest and disputes as well as establishing property protection mechanisms to safeguard researchers' work from opportunistic behaviors (Welsh et al., 2008).

Duration

The motivations and goals of the partnership have a heavy bearing on the length of the cooperative agreement. Bozeman et al. (2013) found that industries are less likely to partner with universities if projects are designed to be short term. However, that does not mean short term collaborations are impossible; sometimes they make sense for the goals of the project. For example, if an organization is seeking to create a new patent or publish a paper then it is likely that the partnership will come to a natural end shortly after the outcome is achieved. Regardless of the formal endings of these associations, partners should invest in the continuation of their relationships into the foreseeable future. Pertuzé et al. (2010) argue that this is a best practice for UICs. They suggest that companies should invest in long-term relationships with universities and plan for multi-year collaboration. Similarly, relationships between individual researchers should also be long-term and focus on strengthening relationships (Pertuzé et al., 2010).

Proximity

Proximity can describe physical distance as well as "distance" between the bodies of knowledge brought to bear on the collaborative projects. Partnerships that reach across fields and geographical boundaries have been shown to positively impact the collaboration process. However, too much deviation between the focus of collaborative research and the core competencies of the partner organizations can cripple the collaboration process (Caloghirou et al., 2003). When distance is a factor, studies highlight that face-to-face communication between teams is essential for the success of the project. Amabile et al. (2001) reported that increased physical distance could be a barrier to success and highlighted the importance of physical presence/proximity in the collaboration process.

The University Partnership Design Scorecard

Scorecard Framework

Based on our literature review, we developed a new partnership scorecard designed to fit the needs of a university. This scorecard is designed to help practitioners to monitor, evaluate, and improve the university's partnerships and collaborations. The scorecard consists of three separate surveys, one for each stage of the partnership: the establishment phase, the operation phase, and the delivery phase (Kraut et al., 1987). Each survey consists of a distinct set of questions, which should ideally be considered during the corresponding phase of the partnership. However, the surveys can be completed retroactively; a partnership that is well into the operation phase can take both the establishment and operation phase surveys, and each will offer unique guidance on how to improve the effectiveness of the partnership.

Within each of the surveys, questions are grouped into three areas: institutional factors, team factors, and goals and output. These three groupings emerged from the literature, and are similar to the three main attribute categories found in the literature by Bozeman et al. (2013, p. 6):

1. collaborator attributes—corresponds to the team factors
2. attributes about the collaboration in general—corresponds to goals and outputs
3. specific organizational or institutional attributes— corresponds to institutional factors

Since the goal of this scorecard is to be actionable, an attempt was made to develop groups which correspond to domains of possible action—if, say, a partnership's overall score is brought down by low scores in the institutional factors groups of questions, then the partnership team knows they need to focus their efforts on improving how the two partner institutions act.

The questions are all phrased as positive statements of best practice (e.g., "the partnership provided valuable training opportunities for students"), and responses are given on a seven-point scale, ranging from "strongly agree" to "strongly disagree." What is being measured is essentially the extent to which the partnership adheres to best practices. Not all questions are applicable to all partnerships, though it is expected that most questions will be answerable. The partnership's score is calculated by adding up the numerical value of all the answers given (strongly agree = 6; strongly disagree = 0), and dividing by the number of questions which had been answerred, and multiplying by 16.67. This gives a score between 1 and 100. From initial tests, it is expected that most partnerships will score an initial score between 50 and 85, which indicates that the scorecard does identify room for improvement. The minimum score that indicates overall alignment with best practices is a 66, which results from answering at least "somewhat agree" to all questions. However, attention should be paid to a partnership's score per section: for example, a high score in institutional factors could balance out a low score in team factors, thereby leading to a passible overall score but obfuscating possible areas of improvement.

The scorecard also includes a shortlist of quantitative metrics, which are assessed during or after the delivery phase (e.g., "number of peer-reviewed journal articles which resulted from the partnership"). These metrics are less useful for assessing the effectiveness of the partnership because there are many reasons why, say, one partnership might lead to more journal articles or tech transfer

Table 21.1 The Structure of the Proposed Partnership Scorecard

	Establishment Phase	Operation Phase	Delivery Phase	Quantitative Metrics
Institutional Factors				
Team Factors				
Goals & Output				

contacts than another. Nonetheless, these metrics are useful for assessing the university's overall partnership strategy.

The general form of the scorecard is shown in Table 21.1.

Scorecard Use—Consultant Model

The tool is simple to use and easy to access, and so it could be made available to partnership teams for use in self-assessment. However, if the results are to be used to compare and assess a university's many partnerships, there must be some degree of standardization in how the tool is administered. If the answers are self-reported, it is possible that the results will be skewed by team members not wishing to report on problem areas, or by the team member who fills out the scorecard having a different perspective than the rest of the team. Results could also be skewed by variation in how individuals judge their adherence to best practices—one person's "somewhat agree" could be comparable to another person's "strongly agree."

Therefore, our suggestion is that the scorecard be administered by a single individual (or group of individuals, if need be) who uses the scorecard to assess all partnerships within the university. For our purposes, we will call this person a consultant. When it is decided that a particular partnership will be assessed, the consultant imbeds themselves within the partnership for a few days to a week (not necessarily concurrently), interviewing team members and observing the partnership's operations. The consultant then fills out the scorecard for the partnership and compiles a report for the partnership team, which includes the partnership's score and suggestions for how to improve the effectiveness of the partnership (based on areas where the partnership scored poorly). Once the consultant has compiled several of these reports, they will begin to build a body of knowledge about what makes a successful partnership. At that point, the consultant will be able to work directly with struggling partnerships on improving their operations.

The scorecard assessment could be made available as an optional service for partnerships that wish to improve their operations, or it could be required as a pre-requisite for the partnership to advance or be formally recognized by the university. For example, a policy could be put in place to require that a partnership score at least a 70 in order to receive funding through the university. Ideally, the partnership team would have the support of the consultant in ensuring that they are able to achieve this minimum score, which would help the scorecard assessment be seen as a useful way to ensure the partnership's success instead of unnecessary red tape.

Another important role of the consultant is to document university-specific best practices and incorporate them into the scorecard. Successful partnerships should be acknowledged and probed for insights that can be used to improve the scorecard. Although the scorecard tool is based on our extensive literature review, the literature does have gaps (for example, little is said about university–university partnerships), and each university environment is unique. In order for the scorecard to be as effective as possible, it needs to be constantly improved to better fit the needs of the university where it is being applied.

Conclusion

Due to the decrease of government funding for higher education in recent decades, as well as new policies which encourage universities to be more active in the market (largely by patenting and licensing technologies), universities have increasingly engaged in partnerships with other organizations (Ankrah & AL-Tabbaa, 2015; Hagedoorn et al., 2000; Perkmann & Walsh, 2007; Poyago-Theotoky, 2002). At the same time, performance management trends have been embracing the value of diversity in the innovation process. Collaboration efforts are increasingly transdisciplinary, involving actors from other areas of study and other geographic areas. Partnerships between universities and other organizations have been recognized for their ability to reduce costs for both partners, increase enrollment, achieve research outcomes, and advance the commercialization of technologies.

There are many factors related to successful partnerships. The most common themes that emerged from our study related to establishing thoughtful goals, pursuing formalization of the partnerships, establishing trust, aiming for long-term partnerships, and creating teams based on proximity (both physical proximity and disciplinary proximity). Additionally, how an evaluative procedure is designed and executed, and whether the metrics are reviewed regularly, can impact the success of the partnerships. It should be noted that other potentially critical factors exist that have yet to be addressed in the literature. For example, studies have not widely explored the effects of external resource providers on the outcomes of university partnerships. We have built our scorecard based on the best practices identified in the literature, but it is and always will be incomplete. We intend this scorecard to be a living tool—as it is used, it will be improved, and it will hopefully become more useful as time goes on.

Acknowledgments

Taylor Reimann, Ahmad Saleem, ChiaKo Hung, and Soraya Jennings contributed significantly to early research. Their work is excellent and was much appreciated.

This work was supported by a Science of Science Innovation Policy NSF Award (#1661406) to Leah Gerber and Derrick Anderson.

Table 21.2 Partnership Scorecard Framework

	Scorecard		
	Initation Phase	**Operation Phase**	**Delivery Phase**
Institutional Factors	The partner institutions share similar institutional goals	The team has the institutional support necessary to seize opportunities should they arise	The partnership's outcomes advanced the organizational strategy of both partner organizations
	The partner organizations understand each other's institutional goals	The partner institutions are willing to adjust priorities as project evolves	Students and faculty involved in the partnership were exposed to practical problems and new ideas
	The partner institutions share similar institutional visions	The team has access to adequate resources	Problems / ideas from the partnership were incorporated into the curricula taught at ASU
	The partner organizations understand each other's institutional visions	The team has the institutional support necessary to take advantage of outside resources should they become available	The partnership provided valuable training opportunities for students
	The partner institutions have compatible interests	The team is able to access necessary equipment	The partnership provided valuable professional development opportunities for ASU staff and faculty
	The partner institutions understand each other's interests	The team is able to access necessary expertise	Non-ASU partner's ability to innovate was improved by engaging in this partnership

(*Continued*)

Table 21.2 (Continued)

Scorecard		
Initation Phase	**Operation Phase**	**Delivery Phase**
The partner institutions understand each other's reasons for engaging in the partnership	The project retains the support of top management / leadership of both partner organizations	ASU's ability to innovate was improved by engaging in this partnership
The partner institutions are aware of each other's pre-existing relationships with other organizations	All team members are incentivized to contribute to the project	The partnership improved the public's opinion of both partner organizations
Partner institutions are aware of each other's political context	Sensitive information is treated similarly by both partner organizations	
Partner institutions are aware of each other's social context	Confidentiality agreements have NOT hindered the necessary dissemination of knowledge	
Partner organizations are aware of each other's economic context	Senior leaders of both collaboration partners (i.e. company board or senior academic faculty) interact regularly	
The partnership's organizational structure is well-defined	Partner organizations inform each other of relevant developments within a reasonable time frame	
The partnership's organizational structure was established with input from both institutions	Partner organizations communicate with each other openly and honestly	
Administrative responsibility for the partnership is clearly defined	Academic integrity and research ethics are respected by both partner organizations	
Administrative responsibility for the partnership was established with input from both institutions		
The interests of both partners are protected by contractual safeguards		
Official Intellectual Property agreement was signed before work began		
Communication between partner institutions is open and honest		

(Continued)

Table 21.2 (Continued)

Scorecard		
Initation Phase	Operation Phase	Delivery Phase
Partner institutions engage in frequent and regular communication		
Partner organizations are transparent about their goals for the partnership		
Partner organizations are transparent regarding intellectual property policies		
Partner organizations are transparent regarding knowledge sharing policies		
The partnership's resource needs were estimated before work began		
The partnership's resource needs were acknowledged by both institutions before work began		
Resources required for the partnership were allocated before work began		
The expected resource contribution of each partner institution is clearly defined		
The expected resource contribution of each partner institution was established with input from both institutions		
Responsibilities of each partner institution are clearly defined		
Responsibilities of each partner institution were established with input from both institutions		
Senior leaders of both collaboration partners (i.e. company board or senior academic faculty) interact regularly		
The role of each partner institution is clearly defined		

(Continued)

Table 21.2 (Continued)

	Scorecard		
	Initation Phase	**Operation Phase**	**Delivery Phase**
	The role of each partner institution was established with input from both institutions		
Team Factors	The partnership team is willing to adopt formal rules	Team leadership is able to manage instability and change	All team members would feel comfortable attending events hosted by either partner organization
	Team members understand and accept cultural differences between industry and academia	Team leaders are able to adapt leadership style to fit the needs of the team	Strong personal relationships were built between team members from different partner organizations
	Team members are open to utilizing approaches they are not familiar with	Team leadership is able to manage the interests of both partner organizations	The partnership built trust between academic researchers and industry practitioners
	Team members bring diverse, complementary skills to the project	All team members follow through on promises	The partnership provided team members with access to a useful professional network
	Team members share a common core of knowledge	All team members feel that they can trust each other	
	Team members have the capacity to engage in collaboration without sacrificing the quality of their work in other areas	All team members have compatible values	
	Team members bring intrinsic motivation to the project	Team members have interpersonal familiarity	
	Team members have experience working as part of a collaborative team	All team members respect each other	
	There is a clearly established team leader	Team members communicate with each other openly and honestly	
	Team members possess compatible problem-solving styles (Kirton Adaption Innovation Inventory)	Academic integrity and research ethics are respected by all team members	
	An official conflict resolution process was put in place before work began	The unique capabilities of each team member are acknowledged and utilized	

(Continued)

Table 21.2 (Continued)

Scorecard		
Initation Phase	**Operation Phase**	**Delivery Phase**
There is agreement among the team about how conflicts will be resolved	Team meetings are held regularly	
Team members are aware of project's political and economic context	Relevant information and agendas are distributed to all team members before each meeting and event	
Team members are aware of all intellectual property or knowledge-sharing agreements established between partner institutions	Team effectiveness is examined on a regular basis	
Core team members reside in the same geographic area	Conflicts within the team are dealt with professionally	
	Team members do NOT attempt to impose their own conventions and approaches on other team members nor on the team as a whole	
	Projects engage with the communities that they are embedded within	
The team is highly knowledgeable about about the field in which the partnership will be working	Roles and responsibilities of each team member are clearly defined and articulated	The team became more knowledgeable about the fields in which the partnership did work
The purpose of the partnership is clearly defined	Benchmark goals are realistic	Partnership deliverables met time, cost, and quality requirements
The purpose of the partnership was established with input from both institutions	Tensions between academic rigor and industrial/commercial relevance are noted and are resolved	Partnership outcomes will have a positive effect on ASU's operations
The goals of the partnership are clearly defined	Technologies are advanced toward commercialization at a speed acceptable to both partner institutions	Partnership outcomes will have a positive effect on the non-ASU partner organization's operations
The goals of the partnership were decided with input from both institutions	Team members feel comfortable reporting failures and negative results	The partnership led to the creation of new or improved products / processes

(The rows in the "Goals and Outcomes" group are labeled vertically at left: Goals and Outcomes)

(Continued)

Table 21.2 (Continued)

Scorecard		
Initation Phase	**Operation Phase**	**Delivery Phase**
The goals of the partnership are realistic		The partnership produced use-inspired research
Specific project milestones have been agreed upon		The team was able to openly and honestly report all research results
Measures/indicators of the partnership's success have been agreed upon		Research results advance fundamental knowledge about the world
Ownership of any patents which result from partnership was decided before work began		Research results are useful for solving real-world problems
Both partners' expectations regarding knowledge ownership are clearly articulated		Proprietary information remained under control (was not leaked)
Both partners' intentions regarding the application of project results are clearly articulated		All technology transfer processes were completed
It has been decided under what conditions results will not be published in academic journals / publishing will be postponed (i.e. until patent is awarded)		The partnership provided a 'test bed' for refining academic ideas/theories
		The partnership stimulated research activities
		The partnership stimulated the development of new technologies
		The partnership served the commuinty
		The partnership contributed to local/regional economic developemnt
		What best practices were developed during this partnership that could assist future ASU partnerships?
		What factors contributed most to this partnership's success?
		How could this partnership have been improved?

References

Abramo, G., D'Angelo, C. A., & Di Costa, F. (2009). Research collaboration and productivity: Is there correlation? *Higher Education, 57*(2), 155–171.

Al-Ashaab, A., Flores, M., Doultsinou, A., & Magyar, A. (2011). A balanced scorecard for measuring the impact of industry–university collaboration. *Production Planning & Control, 22*(5–6), 554–570. https://doi.org/10.1080/09537287.2010.536626

Amabile, T. M., Patterson, C., Mueller, J., Wojcik, T., Odomirok, P. W., Marsh, M., & Kramer, S. J. (2001). Academic–Practitioner Collaboration in Management Research: A Case of Cross-Profession Collaboration. *The Academy of Management Journal, 44*(2), 418–431. https://doi.org/10.2307/3069464

American Academy of Arts and Sciences. (2016). *Public Research Universities: Serving the Public Good* (p. 20). https://www.amacad.org/sites/default/files/publication/downloads/PublicResearchUniv_PublicGood.pdf

Anderson, D. M., & Taggart, G. (2016). Organizations, policies, and the roots of public value failure: The case of for-profit higher education. *Public Administration Review, 76*(5), 779–789.

Ankrah, S., & AL-Tabbaa, O. (2015). Universities–industry collaboration: A systematic review. *Scandinavian Journal of Management, 31*(3), 387–408. https://doi.org/10.1016/j.scaman.2015.02.003

Arizona State University. (n.d.). *Starbucks College Achievement Plan.* Retrieved December 12, 2019, from https://starbucks.asu.edu/

Barringer, B. R., & Harrison, J. S. (2000). Walking a tightrope: Creating value through interorganizational relationships. *Journal of Management, 26*(3), 367–403.

Bonaccorsi, A., & Piccaluga, A. (1994). A theoretical framework for the evaluation of university–industry relationships. *R&D Management, 24*(3), 229–247.

Bozeman, B. (2002). Public-value failure: When efficient markets may not do. *Public Administration Review, 62*(2), 145–161. https://doi.org/10.1111/0033-3352.00165

Bozeman, B., Fay, D., & Slade, C. P. (2013). Research collaboration in universities and academic entrepreneurship: The-state-of-the-art. *The Journal of Technology Transfer, 38*(1), 1–67. https://doi.org/10.1007/s10961-012-9281-8

Bozeman, B., Gaughan, M., Youtie, J., Slade, C. P., & Rimes, H. (2016). Research collaboration experiences, good and bad: Dispatches from the front lines. *Science and Public Policy, 43*(2), 226–244. https://doi.org/10.1093/scipol/scv035

Caloghirou, Y., Hondroyiannis, G., & Vonortas, N. S. (2003). The performance of research partnerships. *Managerial and Decision Economics, 24*(2-3), 85–99.

Chandler, A. D. (1990). *Strategy and structure: Chapters in the history of the industrial enterprise* (Vol. 120). MIT Press.

Cokins, G. (2009). *Performance management: Integrating strategy execution, methodologies, risk, and analytics* (Vol. 21). John Wiley & Sons.

Council on Competitiveness. (1996). *Endless frontier, limited resources: US R&D policy for competitiveness.* Council on Competitiveness. https://nii.nist.gov/coc.html

Geisler, E. (1995). Industry–university technology cooperation: A theory of inter-organizational relationships. *Technology Analysis & Strategic Management, 7*(2), 217–229.

Hagedoorn, J., Link, A. N., & Vonortas, N. S. (2000). Research partnerships. *Research Policy, 29*(4–5), 567–586.

Hainan University—Arizona State University Joint International Tourism College. (2018, February 12). Watts College of Public Service and Community Solutions. https://publicservice.asu.edu/content/hainan-university-arizona-state-university-joint-international-tourism-college

Hanel, P., & St-Pierre, M. (2006). Industry–university collaboration by Canadian manufacturing firms. *The Journal of Technology Transfer, 31*(4), 485–499.

Hilvert, C., & Swindell, D. (2013). Collaborative service delivery: What every local government manager should know. *State and Local Government Review, 45*(4), 240–254.

Kaplan, R. S. (2009). Conceptual foundations of the balanced scorecard. *Handbooks of Management Accounting Research, 3*, 1253–1269.

Kim, K.-W. (2006). Measuring international research collaboration of peripheral countries: Taking the context into consideration. *Scientometrics, 66*(2), 231–240.

Kraut, R. E., Galegher, J., & Egido, C. (1987). Relationships and Tasks in Scientific Research Collaboration. *Human-Computer Interaction, 3*(1), 31. https://doi.org/10.1207/s15327051hci0301_3

Lee, Y. S. (2000). The sustainability of university–industry research collaboration: an empirical assessment. *The Journal of Technology Transfer, 25*(2), 111–133. https://doi.org/10.1023/A:1007895322042

Lin, H.-F. (2015). Linking knowledge management orientation to balanced scorecard outcomes. *Journal of Knowledge Management, 19*(6), 1224–1249.

Mora-Valentin, E. M., Montoro-Sanchez, A., & Guerras-Martin, L. A. (2004). Determining factors in the success of R&D cooperative agreements between firms and research organizations. *Research Policy, 33*(1), 17–40.

Moriarty, R. (2015, April 4). *JP Morgan Chase to close Syracuse tech center, cut 91 jobs.* Syracuse. https://www.syracuse.com/news/2015/04/jp_morgan_chase_to_close_syracuse_tech_center_cut_91_jobs_1.html

Niven, P. R. (2014). *Balanced scorecard evolution: A dynamic approach to strategy execution.* John Wiley & Sons.

Perkmann, M., & Walsh, K. (2007). University–industry relationships and open innovation: Towards a research agenda. *International Journal of Management Reviews, 9*(4), 259–280.

Pertuzé, J. A., Calder, E. S., Greitzer, E. M., & Lucas, W. A. (2010). Best Practices for Industry– University Collaboration. *MIT Sloane Management Review, 51*(4), 10.

Philbin, S. (2008a). Measuring the performance of research collaborations. *Measuring Business Excellence, 12*(3), 16–23. https://doi.org/10.1108/13683040810900368

Philbin, S. (2008b). Process model for university–industry research collaboration. *European Journal of Innovation Management, 11*(4), 488–521. https://doi.org/10.1108/14601060810911138

Poyago-Theotoky, J. (2002). Universities and fundamental research: Reflections on the growth of university–industry partnerships. *Oxford Review of Economic Policy, 18*(1), 10–21. https://doi.org/10.1093/oxrep/18.1.10

Rybnicek, R., & Königsgruber, R. (2019). What makes industry–university collaboration succeed? A systematic review of the literature. *Journal of Business Economics, 89*(2), 221–250.

Santoro, M. D., & Gopalakrishnan, S. (2000). The institutionalization of knowledge transfer activities within industry–university collaborative ventures. *Journal of Engineering and Technology Management, 17*(3–4), 299–319.

Siegel, D. S., Waldman, D. A., Atwater, L. E., & Link, A. N. (2003). Commercial knowledge transfers from universities to firms: Improving the effectiveness of university–industry collaboration. *The Journal of High Technology Management Research, 14*(1), 111–133.

Slotte, V., & Tynjälä, P. (2003). Industry–university collaboration for continuing professional development. *Journal of Education and Work, 16*(4), 445–464.

Syracuse School of Information Studies. (2007, December 5). *JPMorgan Chase in partnership with Syracuse University Selects Site for New Technology Center in Upstate New York*. School of Information Studies I Syracuse University. https://ischool.syr.edu/articles/news/view/jpmorgan-chase-in-partnership-with-syracuse-university-selects-site-for-new/

University–Industry Demonstration Partnership (UIDP). (n.d.). *UIDP: 10 Case Studies of High-Value, High-Return University-Industry Collaborations*. https://www.uidp.org/wp-content/uploads/documents/Case-Studies-pre-20141.pdf

Welsh, R., Glenna, L., Lacy, W., & Biscotti, D. (2008). Close enough but not too far: Assessing the effects of university–industry research relationships and the rise of academic capitalism. *Research Policy, 37*(10), 1854–1864.

Part III

The Impact Academic

22 Becoming an Impact Academic

Jane McKenzie

Engineering Bridges Across Divides

For many academics, ensuring their scholarly endeavours have impact is an increasingly important aspiration. Greater focus on the value creation activities of academic institutions has put impact high on the agenda. The universities employing them occupy privileged positions as 'repositor[ies] of clever minds' (Moscardini et al., 2022, p. 822) and so are expected to contribute to the intellectual wealth of society (Kogut and Zander, 1992; Grant, 2002). They expect academics to be both effective knowledge producers, through research with impact, and efficient educators capable of transferring existing scientific knowledge into learning programmes that develop other members of society. The skills and abilities of a generative researcher are different from those that make a good educator and communicator, yet, to make a difference to business and management practice in organisations and wider society, the impact academic needs to be capable of fulfilling both these roles well. In other words, they need to be ambidextrous (Markides, 2007) – exploring the new and exploiting the known for value.

The associated requirement to ensure research is both rigorous and relevant is challenging. First, academics have to bridge 'two types of gap – the "lost in translation" gap (where managerially relevant research fails to reach practitioners) and the "lost before translation" gap (where managerially relevant research is not undertaken by academics)' (Markides, 2007 p. 762). Then, in a practice arena like business and management, a bridge that spans the knowing–doing gap (Ahmadi and Vogel, 2022; Hulme, 2014) is also required: simply generating and disseminating relevant knowledge is not enough, it has to transform practice, if it is going to help commercial and public sector organisations to deliver better value from intellectual capital. Hence, the impact academic also needs ways to help practitioners transform what they learn in an educational setting into practice in their organisations.

This chapter explores what it takes to bridge these gaps and develop research and educational activities that translate into

DOI: 10.4324/9781003459217-25

changed practice, so that valuable knowledge is neither lost before or in translation and does not fall into the knowing–doing gap.

For the individual and the university, rigorous and relevant knowledge production, timely and meaningful knowledge transfer and the process of translating knowledge into practice is complex and fraught with tensions and paradox (Bartunek and Rynes, 2014) that shape the way academics connect theory to practice. These play out in the process of creating effective working relationships with the people who ultimately transform academic knowledge (know-what) into practically useful business and management know-how (Carlile, 2004; Blackler, 1995). As Bartunek and Rynes highlight, epistemologically, the academic demands of rigour and relevance may not seem comfortable allies, when rigour relies on depth of knowledge, logical abstract reasoning that generalises across contexts but takes time to produce, and is communicated in precise technical language with methodological transparency to assure its scientific merit, whereas relevance often demands broad, multi-disciplinary application of knowledge and theory to issues that have all the attributes of 'wicked' problems (Skaburskis, 2008) and are situated in particular contextual conditions surrounding the phenomenon (Gibbons et al., 1994). Solutions have to be communicated in a manner that is credible to practitioners; the application in practice usually requires multi-level, interpersonal and socio-material activity and expects relatively quick results. Despite arguments that this rigour relevance gap is unbridgeable (Kieser and Leiner, 2009), others offer fellow academics some hope that it is possible to achieve both. There are three main bridge building considerations. First, how to overcome some of the tensions and gaps by researching in paradigms, where the 'onto-epistemological assumptions' (Sandberg and Tsoukas, 2011, p. 339) underlying the research design and the logic of inquiry are more attuned to the connection between theory and practice (Sandberg and Tsoukas, 2011; Van De Ven and Johnson, 2006; Van de Ven, 2007; Aram and Salipante Jr, 2003); second, how collaborative methodologies can bridge the gaps during the research activities (Sharma et al., 2022; Sharma and Bansal, 2019; Coghlan, 2011); third, how establishing multi-modal means of connecting and relating across the divide can keep relevance to the fore for academics and foster appreciation of rigorously generated theory for improving business and management practice, so that knowledge translates into action. Let us now consider each of these in turn.

Crossing Paradigmatic Bridges

Historically, considerations of what constitutes rigorous science drew heavily on objectivist ontological assumptions of reality as 'being' – that natural and social phenomena have an existence in entities, themes, concepts, constructs and variables that can be defined, measured and evidenced by a detached observer adopting robust, epistemological and methodological principles to produce knowledge and generate abstract theory about a reality. This is not to exclude the accommodations for researcher subjectivity that qualitative methodologies allow for, in order to generate rich and nuanced understanding of informants meaning in context. However, in principle, whether research is qualitative or quantitative, the search still involves some form of rational science where researchers are 'spectators of practice' and 'impose a representational logic on practice' which neglects the situationally specific conditions and activity 'in favor of generic propositional statements' (Sandberg and Tsoukas, 2011, p. 342).

Some researchers adopt the so called 'weaker' ontologies that assume reality is a complex, contextually relative, dynamic process of 'becoming'. These are *relatively* recent developments in the history of business and management research (Tsoukas and Chia, 2002; Chia, 1995; Langley et al., 2013; Langley and Tsoukas, 2017). They have the advantage of acknowledging that in practice settings, change is a constant, and managers live in the flux of interdependent and contradictory activity. Thus, researchers adopting a process ontology, pay attention to considerations of temporality, activity and flow, driven by human responses to tensions and contradictions (Smith and Lewis, 2011) that surface in relationships and interactions within the social system (Langley et al., 2013). Such problems of contextual relativism and dynamism tend to raise concerns about undermining the rigour of theorising, so may discourage traditional academics from engaging with this form of research, despite arguments that researchers can assume a 'flat ontology' (Schatzki, 2016; Schatzki, 2006) that views reality as no more that the socio-material unfolding of events produced by material structures and agent activities, combined in the practical process of organising. Nevertheless, we have seen a growing interest in legitimising the studying of many business disciplines through an 'as practice' lens e.g., strategy, (Golsorkhi et al., 2010; Jarzabkowski, 2005), leadership (Carroll et al., 2008; Raelin, 2007, 2016), project management (Blomquist et al., 2010), management accounting (Ahrens and Chapman, 2007), sustainability (Silva and Figueiredo, 2017). From an impact perspective, this has the advantage of focusing the research process on relevant 'doings' in organisations (Raelin, 2007); thus, the knowledge produced may be closer to the experience of business and management practitioners and, hence, more plausible and easier to communicate and translate into action. This may go some way to addressing both the 'lost before translation' gap, and the 'lost in translation' gap. Nevertheless, by implication, grasping the logic of practice demands two changes in orientation for the impact academic. The first is a change in focus, from entities to relationships, time and space within whole systems of socio-material practices; the second, is to move from 'theoretical detachment to involved thematic deliberation (namely focusing our research attention on temporary breakdowns)' (Sandberg and Tsoukas, 2011, p. 346).

Some academics may be uncomfortable with weaker ontologies, resisting any move away from realist principles of theoretical abstraction and detachment simply to gain impact; they may consider idiographic routes to theorising about contextually relative dynamic activities unsatisfactory and inconclusive. One alternative is to adopt more complex and demanding realist positions, such as those espoused in Bhaskar's Critical Realism (Bhaskar and Hartwig, 2016; Bhaskar, 1979) or Campbellian realism (McKelvey, 1999; McKelvey, 2003). Both hold objectivity as the goal of science, but argue that a progressive and critical integration of dualist epistemic positions is essential to the evolution of theorising, which can move beyond either imperfect conceptual descriptions of observable reality that each produce in isolation.

Bhaskar challenges researchers to design studies that probe beneath the transitive world of knowing and the entangled interactions between actual events and empirical diversity. To probe the depth of reality, it is necessary to focus research on the causal mechanisms of emergence through a metatheoretical lens that acknowledges both entitative and process ontologies, values both theory and practice orientations, yet combines them by examining the interdependence between structures and agency. To achieve this, a researcher would use a creatively critical process of abductively inferring (Sætre and Van de Ven, 2021b) the nature of real but hidden mechanisms and their generative powers and tendencies (Lichtenstein, 2014), retroductively examine the verisimilitude of that inference in the light of existing theory (Sætre and Van de Ven, 2021a), often using interdisciplinary research teams, then retrodictively confirming the existence of these mechanisms of emergence through further investigation (Danermark, 2019; Danermark et al., 2019). This mix of different logics of inquiry, critical and interdisciplinary theoretical dialogue and subsequent testing, epistemologically takes the researcher from the concrete to the abstract and back to the concrete during the research process, integrates the idiographic and the nomethetic, accounting for apparent contradictions via critical reasoning, then theorises their integration. This is argued to produce research about the deeper reality of the organising experience. Cambellian realism deals with the complexity and unpredictability of the real world in similar ways, but apparently without the depth ontology that Bhaskar espouses. Both paradigms are too complex to explore here in detail; suffice it to say that they have the characteristics of strong methodological rigour, allow theoretical detachment and maintain objectivity through a critical and progressive approach to knowledge generation, whilst still acknowledging a relativist epistemology and incorporating the dynamics of activity and practice.

Unfortunately, this makes them time consuming, expensive – since interdisciplinarity is resource intensive – and methodologically demanding; hence, for an impact academic, they fail to meet expectations for prompt solutions to problems in practice, which inevitably delays impact from the research. Further, their technicality makes communication harder, so the impact academic needs greater translation skills. Nevertheless, since they achieve depth, for certain complex problems the long-term impact may be greater.

Abduction as a logic of inquiry is peculiar to an alternative paradigmatic position, namely pragmatism. In this instance, the assumption that agency and knowing are inseparable and language, theory and action are simultaneously implicated in the process of producing knowledge goes some way to bridging the knowing–doing gap. Researchers may feel less constrained by apparent incommensurability arguments (Czarniawska, 1998) that divide researchers who need both qualitative and quantitative tools to surface solutions to complex problems. With careful reasoning and ethical reflection, it is argued that the impact academic can translate results from 'one place and time and put it into another – an act which changes both the translator and what is translated' (Czarniawska, 1998, p. 275). As Czarniawska argues, this may be a useful way to bridge the dichotomies that separate 'them' as practitioners and 'us' as academics.

This process of translation can also take place through collaborative methodologies as practitioners and academics work together to co-create knowledge that is useful in both settings.

Building Methodological Bridges

Collaborative methodologies (Shani et al., 2008) and action/intervention methodologies, both encourage the researchers to co-create knowledge <u>with</u> those who own and/or have direct involvement with the problem in practice. This has the dual advantages that theory and practice, academics and practitioners, unite with purpose around a shared concern to combine their expertise. Each elicits different value from their participation, but, through their joint work and the rhythm of interactions over time, the knowledge products of research become impactful because a) the process of knowing is situated in, rather than abstracted from, the context where it can deliver value, b) it is mediated through social interactions in meaningful relationships between the communities who separately have different priorities, which are the source of tension between them (Bartunek and Rynes, 2014), and c) its utility can be contested among the different groups of experts and progressively transformed into something pragmatically useful (Blackler, 1995).

Collaborative methodologies involve insider/outsider research teams (Bartunek and Louis, 1996) studying an organisational problem together, which brings diversity into the knowledge generation process. They will be informed by existing research, so theory meets practice, and the teams jointly interpret its utility, so that insiders can incorporate that knowledge into the self-design of solutions (Mohrman et al., 2001), and outsiders can advance knowledge about the phenomenon. By dint of the fact that in any considerations and discussions, the outsider researchers uphold the foundations of rigour and the insiders, who own the problem, uphold demands for relevance, the dialogue involved in analysing and interpreting becomes a safe 'container' where both sets of interests can combine to developing impactful answers. The joint interpretation processes can surmount the differences in perspective that divide theory and practice, academics and practitioners, and simultaneously unite researchers' knowledge with the lived experience of the manifest problem. Thus, abstract domain specific theoretical knowledge travels across the academic–practitioner boundary and is transformed into something usable and applicable to the specifics of concrete contextual conditions (Carlile, 2004). Partnering that is problem focused, builds social capital (Adler and Kwon, 2002; Nahapiet and Ghoshal, 1998) and the shared understanding and trust supports the bridge across the lost in translation gap. It creates fertile conditions for bridging the knowing–doing gap, as well; through the process, those responsible for action become invested in applying knowledge into their organisational designs, so are more likely to realise some impact through their actions in the practice setting. The impact academic engages in the collaborative process with the intention of furthering their research agenda around a topic. For example, Ed Lawler's Centre for Effective Organisation in the Marshall School at University of Southern California (Mohrman, 2018), Laura Empson's Centre for Professional Service Firms at Bayes Business School in London (Empson, 2018) and the Henley Forum for Knowledge and Learning at Henley Business School, University of Reading (McKenzie and Van Winkelen, 2018) each have their dedicated areas of research, and their partnership activities further that academic agenda.

Although, action/intervention methodologies (Chandler and Torbert, 2003; Reason and Bradbury, 2006; McNiff, 2009; Coghlan, 2011) also work collaboratively, their agenda is different, in that they start with the specific purpose of creating change to practice. Consequently, the research knowledge selected and the research questions that guide the study are dictated by the needs of the problem rather than the impact academic's research aims and objectives; in these settings, the academic becomes an insider in the practice context, applying their knowledge with the deliberate intent to generate action for change to support the insider problem owners. Together, they act into the setting on a moment by moment basis, in order to facilitate change. Change emerges in the moment through the collective activities and action research methodologies study that emergence process.

Being more deeply embedded in a specific setting clearly creates limits as to the transferability of the findings, and, unfortunately, due to the apparent similarities to consultancy work (Coghlan 2011), impact academics who use these methodologies have historically faced criticisms about whether they are engaged in 'real research' (Shani and Coghlan, 2019, p. 13) that is unbiased and rigorous. Nevertheless, as Shani and Coghlan highlight, even though action research takes place in settings of practice, rigour and quality can be embedded in the process (Coghlan and Shani, 2014) through evidence of reflection on the choices made at each stage of an action research project: viz. 'contextual analysis, design, purpose, degrees of collaboration, planning implementation and review' (Shani and Coghlan, 2019, p. 14), as well as reflexivity on the ethics and positionality of the researcher in creating the narrative (Cunliffe and Ivaldi, 2020; Ripamonti et al., 2016). The advantage of action research is that it completely circumvents the lost before translation gap, and, by engaging the owners of the problem in both generating and applying the actionable insights that emerge in the process, it also avoids the knowing–doing gap. However, the downside of this approach is that it can be hard to publish action research in the higher quality journals that have become the evaluation criteria in many institutional recruitment and performance assessments.

One route to overcoming the publication problem seems to be to identify a metatheoretical position to which the action researcher can contribute, since metatheory is 'unconstrained by particular contexts, variables or methods' (Lewis and Smith, 2014, p. 129), and relies on concepts and assumptions that pertain much more generally across theoretical domains. For example, paradox and sensemaking (Lüscher and Lewis, 2008), transformative learning, education and development (Hoggan, 2016; Soh et al., 2023) and complexity in the process of management (Tsoukas, 1994; Tsoukas and Dooley, 2011; Anderson and Meyer, 2017; Burnes, 2005; Boisot and McKelvey, 2010).

As such, both collaborative and action/intervention methodologies are powerful ways to bridge the lost in translation gaps the knowing–doing gap, and, in the latter case, the lost before translation gap. Based on philosophies of practical knowing (Coghlan, 2011), such approaches immerse the researcher in the tensions identified by Bartunek and Rynes (2014), such that the act of working together allows academics and practitioners to work through their different priorities before the gaps become unbridgeable (Jarzabkowski et al., 2018).

Constructing Educational Bridges

Executive education, learning and development is the third way to bridge some of the gaps (Tushman et al., 2007). Just as 'research can inform teaching ... teaching can enlighten our research' (Burke and Rau, 2010, p. 132); the opportunity to build relationships with people in practice settings provides a crucial opportunity to avoid the lost before translation gap. Furthermore, teaching does not only happen in the classroom. Learning and development can occur in many ways: in professional networks and communities of practice (Lave, 1996; Van Winkelen et al., 2008) that offer opportunities to make the connection between the pervasive epistemic cultures (Van Winkelen and McKenzie, 2012) in settings and with people involved with knowledge production (Van De Ven and Johnson, 2006), and the settings and people who use that knowledge. Such interplay can also occur through organising and presenting at conferences at which both academics and practitioners are present and interested in learning; action learning activities in the classroom (Berggren and Söderlund, 2011), designed to help students apply theoretical knowledge to their organisational problems and unlearn some of the practices that hinder improvement (Brook et al., 2016); supervising doctoral students (Collins and McBain, 2018; Van de Ven, 2007) and even adopting a temporal rhythm of working inside and outside of academia in different phases of your career. Indeed, some impact academics adopt a deliberate strategy of 'intersectoral mobility' to bridge the knowing–doing gap. As Dame Jessica Corner, Executive Chair of Research England highlights 'porosity is key'. Her own career 'straddled academia, the NHS, national charities, organisations and public bodies' (National Centre for Universities and Business, 2023). The punctuation of careers, where individuals have one foot in each camp, allow scholars to remain connected to the language, concerns and realities of practice, whilst at the same time holding true to the rigorous onto-epistemological, methodological and ethical requirements of academia.

Professional doctorates like the DBA (Banerjee and Morley, 2012; Kalika and Platt, 2022) are a particularly impactful way of bridging the gaps. An individual doctoral candidate spends four to six years deliberately engaged in developing scholarship which they expect to be beneficial in practice (Stevens-Long et al., 2011), whilst at the same time being supervised and developed in the standards for rigour expected for publishable research (Spencer et al., 2022, Tushman and O'Reilly, 2007). On completion of such a doctorate, they may choose not enter academia, but they still become impact academics or engaged scholars, who populate the higher echelons of business and management with a sound understanding of how to connect theory and practice in both rigorous and relevant ways (Wellington and Sikes, 2006). During the time that their doctoral journey takes, they learn to work through the discomfort created by the contradictory demands of the two worlds of academia and practice, as they punctuate their time in the class room and supervision meetings, with time in the business world and with peers in their cohort who are experiencing the same dissonance. (Hay and Samra-Fredericks, 2016; McKenzie and Collins, 2021). Granted the crossing the threshold to 'doctorateness' can be an unsettling process for apprentice scholars (Irving et al., 2019; Keefer, 2015; Hawkins and Edwards, 2015; Trafford and Leshem, 2009), but, in fact, experiencing this liminal space between the two different worlds of academia and practice does not stop even for experienced impact academics (Empson, 2013). However, these scholars all develop a deeper understanding of the mechanisms for connecting rigour and relevance, theory and practice, to create impact. Andrew Van de Ven's (2007, 2022)) critical realist model of the mechanisms of engaged scholarship formalises some of the structured pathways for doctoral level educators, whether on PhDs or DBAs, to build bridges for creating impact, demonstrating that a rigorous and relevant knowledge production process is inherently possible.

Conclusion

Becoming an impact academic, capable of working with the different priorities of academia and business and management practice, has become increasingly important for performance in universities, which are both engines of rigorous and relevant knowledge production and educational institutions required to deliver value back to society.

To avoid loss of value, the impact academic has to avoid knowledge being either lost in translation between themselves and the context in which it is used, lost before translation because research produces the right answer to the wrong problem (Mitroff and Featheringham, 1974), or lost somewhere in the knowing–doing gap, when cognitive understanding fails to produce a difference in practice. This requires the know-how to engineer bridges that adequately support a capacity to integrate theory into practice and practice into theory. Transcending the paradigmatic divides in knowledge creation, connecting the academic and practice communities through collaborative and action/intervention methodologies in research, and constructing educational bridges that translate existing theoretical knowledge into transformative practice, are three key considerations that demand the impact academic's attention. It's a question of taking a both/and mindset to bridge the natural dualities that differentiate the world of research from the world of practice, and make impact hard to achieve. By giving equal attention to integrative mechanisms, metatheoretical positions, knowledge co-creation and educational partnerships, impact is more likely to be achieved.

References

Adler, P. & Kwon, S.-W. 2002. Social capital; Prospects for a new concept. *Academy of Management Review*, 27, 17–40.

Ahmadi, A. & Vogel, B. 2022. Knowing but not enacting leadership: Navigating the leadership knowing-doing gap in leveraging leadership development. *Academy of Management Learning & Education*, 22(3).

Ahrens, T. & Chapman, C. S. 2007. Management accounting as practice. *Accounting, Organizations and Society*, 32, 1–27.

Anderson, P. & Meyer, A. D. 2017. Complexity theory and process organization studies. In: Langely, A. & Tsoukas, H. (eds.), *The Sage Handbook of Process Organization Studies*. Sage Publications.

Aram, J. D. & Salipante JR, P. F. 2003. Bridging scholarship in management: Epistemological reflections. *British Journal of Management*, 14, 189–205.

Banerjee, S. & Morley, C. 2012. Professional doctorates in management: Toward a practice-based approach to doctoral education. *Academy of Management Learning & Education*, 12, 173–193.

Bartunek, J. M. & Louis, M. R. 1996. *Insider/outsider team research*. Sage Publications.

Bartunek, J. M. & Rynes, S. L. 2014. Academics and practitioners are alike and unlike: The paradoxes of academic–practitioner relationships. *Journal of Management*, 40, 1181–1201.

Berggren, C. & Söderlund, J. 2011. Management education for practicing managers: Combining academic rigor with personal change and organizational action. *Journal of Management Education*, 35, 377–405.

Bhaskar, R. 1979. *Philosophy and the human sciences: A philosophical critique of the contemporary human sciences. The Possibility of Naturalism.* Harvester Press.

Bhaskar, R. & Hartwig, M. 2016. *Enlightened common sense: The philosophy of critical realism.* Routledge.

Blackler, F. 1995. Knowledge, knowledge work and organizations: An overview and interpretation. *Organization Studies,* 16, 1021–1046.

Blomquist, T., Hällgren, M., Nilsson, A. & Söderholm, A. 2010. Project-as-practice: In search of project management research that matters. *Project Management Journal,* 41, 5–16.

Boisot, M. A. X. & Mckelvey, B. 2010. Integrating modernist and postmodernist perspectives on organizations: A complexity science bridge. *Academy of Management Review,* 35, 415–433.

Brook, C., Pedler, M., Abbott, C. & Burgoyne, J. 2016. On stopping doing those things that are not getting us to where we want to be: Unlearning, wicked problems and critical action learning. *Human Relations,* 69, 369–389.

Burke, L. A. & Rau, B. 2010. The research–teaching gap in management. *Academy of Management Learning & Education,* 9, 132–143.

Burnes, B. 2005. Complexity theories and organizational change. *International Journal of Management Reviews,* 7, 73–90.

Carlile, P. R. 2004. Transferring, translating and transforming: An integrative framework for managing knowledge across boundaries. *Organization Science,* 15, 555–568.

Carroll, B., Levy, L. & Richmond, D. 2008. Leadership as practice: Challenging the competency paradigm. *Leadership,* 4, 363–379.

Chandler, D. & Torbert, B. 2003. Transforming Inquiry and Action: Interweaving 27 flavors of action research. *Action Research,* 1, 133–152.

Chia, R. 1995. From modern to postmodern organizational analysis. *Organization Studies,* 16, 579–604.

Coghlan, D. 2011. Action research: Exploring perspectives on a philosophy of practical knowing. *Academy of Management Annals,* 5, 53–87.

Coghlan, D. & Shani, A. 2014. Creating action research quality in organization development: Rigorous, reflective and relevant. *Systemic Practice and Action Research,* 27, 523–536.

Collins, C. & Mcbain, R. 2018. Learning the Craft: Developing apprentice scholars with the capacity to integrate theory and practice. In: Bartunek, J. M. & Mckenzie, J. (eds.) *Academic practitioner research partnerships: Developments complexities and opportunities.* Routledge.

Cunliffe, A. L. & Ivaldi, S. 2020. Embedded ethics and reflexivity: Narrating a charter of ethical experience. *Management Learning,* 52, 294–310.

Czarniawska, B. 1998. Who is afraid of incommensurability? *Organization,* 5, 273–275.

Danermark, B. 2019. Applied interdisciplinary research: A critical realist perspective. *Journal of Critical Realism,* 18, 368–382.

Danermark, B., Ekström, M. & Karlsson, J. C. 2019. *Explaining Society: Critical realism in the social sciences.* Taylor & Francis.

Empson, L. 2013. My Affair with the "other": Identity journeys across the research–practice divide. *Journal of Management Inquiry,* 22, 229–248.

Empson, L. 2018. My liminal life. Perpetual journeys across the research practice divide. In: Bartunek, J. M. & Mckenzie, J. (eds.) *Academic practitioner research partnerships: Developments complexities and opportunities.* Routledge.

Gibbons, M., Limoges, C., Nowotny, H., Schwartzman, S., Scott, P. & Trow, M. 1994. *The new production of knowledge: The dynamics of science and research in contemporary societies.* Sage.

Golsorkhi, D., Rouleau, L., Seidl, D. & Vaara, E. 2010. *Cambridge Handbook of Strategy as Practice.* Cambridge University Press.

Grant, R. M. 2002. The knowledge-based view of the firm. In: Choo, C. W. & Bontis, N. (eds.) *The strategic management of intellectual capital and organizational knowledge.* Oxford University Press.

Hawkins, B. & Edwards, G. 2015. Managing the monsters of doubt: Liminality, threshold concepts and leadership learning. *Management Learning,* 46, 24–43.

Hay, A. & Samra-Fredericks, D. 2016. Desperately seeking fixedness: Practitioners' accounts of 'becoming doctoral researchers'. *Management Learning,* 47, 407–423.

Hoggan, C. D. 2016. Transformative learning as a metatheory: Definition, criteria, and typology. *Adult education quarterly,* 66, 57–75.

Hulme, P. E. 2014. EDITORIAL: Bridging the knowing–doing gap: Know-who, know-what, know-why, know-how and know-when. *Journal of Applied Ecology,* 51, 1131–1136.

Irving, G., Wright, A. & Hibbert, P. 2019. Threshold concept learning: Emotions and liminal space transitions. *Management Learning,* 50, 355–373.

Jarzabkowski, P. 2005. *Strategy as practice: An activity based approach.* Sage Publications.

Jarzabkowski, P., Lewis, M. & Smith, W. K. 2018. Practices for leveraging the paradoxes of engaged scholarship. In: Bartunek, J. M. & Mckenzie, J. (eds.) *Academic practitioner research partnerships: Developments complexities and opportunities.* Routledge.

Kalika, M. & Platt, S. (eds.) 2022. *The doctor of business adminstration: Taking your professional practice to the next level.* Ideas for Leadership Publishing.

Keefer, J. M. 2015. Experiencing doctoral liminality as a conceptual threshold and how supervisors can use it. *Innovations in Education and Teaching International,* 52, 17–28.

Kieser, A. & Leiner, L. 2009. Why the rigour–relevance gap in management research is unbridgeable. *Journal of Management Studies,* 46, 516–533.

Kogut, B. & Zander, U. 1992. Knowledge of the firm, combinative capabilities, and the replication of technology. *Organization Science,* 3, 383–397.

Langley, A., Smallman, C., Tsoukas, H. & Van De Ven, A. H. 2013. Process studies of change in organization and management: Unveiling temporality, activity, and flow. *Academy of Management Journal,* 56, 1–13.

Langley, A. & Tsoukas, H. (eds.) 2017. *The Sage Handbook of Process Organization Studies.* Sage Publications Ltd.

Lave, J. 1996. Situated learning in communities of practice. In: Resnick, L. B., Levine, J. M. & Teasley, S. D. (eds.) *Perspectives on socially shared cognition.* American Psychological Association.

Lewis, M. W. & Smith, W. K. 2014. Paradox as a metatheoretical perspective: Sharpening the focus and widening the scope. *The Journal of Applied Behavioral Science*, 50, 127–149.

Lichtenstein, B. B. 2014. *Generative emergence. A new discipline of organizational, entrepreneurial and social innovation.* Oxford University Press.

Lüscher, L. S. & Lewis, M. W. 2008. Organizational change and managerial sensemaking: Working through paradox. *Academy of Management Journal*, 51, 221–240.

Markides, C. 2007. In search of ambidextrous professors. *Academy of Management Journal*, 50, 762–768.

Mckelvey, B. 1999. Toward a Campbellian realist organization science. In: Baum, J. A. C. & Mckelvey, B. (eds.) *Variations in Organization Science: In honor of Donald T Campbell.* Sage Publications.

Mckelvey, B. 2003. From fields to science: Can organization studies make the transition? In: Westwood, R. & Clegg, S. (eds.) *Debating organization: Point counterpoint in organization studies.* Blackwell.

Mckenzie, J. & Collins, C. 2021. Transitioning from expert practitioner to apprentice scholar: Journeys through liminality. In the *proceeding of the 11th Developing Leadership Capacity Conference (DLCC)*, 13 July 2021.

Mckenzie, J. & Van Winkelen, C. 2018. Sustaining the interaction: The Henley Forum for organizational learning and knowledge strategies. In: Bartunek, J. M. & Mckenzie, J. (eds.) *Academic practitioner research partnerships: Developments complexities and opportunities.* Routledge.

Mcniff, J. 2009. *You and your action research project.* Routledge.

Mitroff, I. I. & Featheringham, T. R. 1974. On systemic problem solving and the error of the third kind. *Behavioral Science*, 19, 383–393.

Mohrman, S. A. 2018. Partnering to advance sustainable effectiveness at the centre for effective organisations. In: Bartunek, J. M. & Mckenzie, J. (eds.) *Academic practitioner relationships: Developments, complexities and opportunities.* Routledge.

Mohrman, S. A., Gibson, C. B. & Mohrman, A. M. 2001. Doing research that is useful to practice: A model and empirical exploration. *The Academy of Management Journal*, 44, 357–375.

Moscardini, A. O., Strachan, R. & Vlasova, T. 2022. The role of universities in modern society. *Studies in Higher Education*, 47, 812–830.

Nahapiet, J. & Ghoshal, S. 1998. Social capital, intellectual capital and the organizational advantage. *Academy of Management Review*, 23, 242–267.

National Centre for Universities and Business. 2023. *Diverse researcher career pathways will power UK innovation and growth, say business and university leaders - National Centre for Universities & Business (ncub.co.uk)* [Online]. Available:https://www.ncub.co.uk/insight/diverse-researcher-career-pathways-will-power-uk-innovation-and-growth-say-business-and-university-leaders/#:~:text=The%20Taskforce%20has%20shown%20that%20businesses%20and%20universities,the%20experiences%20they%20need%20to%20develop%20impactful%20innovations. [Accessed October 19 23].

Raelin, J. A. 2007. Toward an epistemology of practice. *Academy of Management Learning & Education*, 6, 495–519.

Raelin, J. A. 2016. *Leadership-as-practice: Theory and application.* Routledge.

Reason, P. & Bradbury, H. (eds.) 2006. *Handbook of Action Research.* Sage.

Ripamonti, S., Galuppo, L., Gorli, M., Scaratti, G. & Cunliffe, A. L. 2016. Pushing action research towards reflexive practice. *Journal of Management Inquiry*, 25, 55–68.

Sætre, A. S. & Van De Ven, A. H. 2021a. Abductive theorizing is more than Idea Generation: Disciplined imagination and a prepared mind. *Academy of Management Review*.

Sætre, A. S. & Van De Ven, A. H. 2021b. Generating theory by abduction. *Academy of Management Review*.

Sandberg, J. & Tsoukas, H. 2011. Grasping the logic of practice: Theorizing through practical rationality. *Academy of Management Review*, 36, 338–360.

Schatzki, T. R. 2006. On organizations as they happen. *Organization Studies*, 27, 1863–1873.

Schatzki, T. R. 2016. Practice theory as flat ontology. In: Spaargaren, G., Weenink, D. & Lamers, M. (eds.) *Practice theory and research: Exploring the dynamics of social life*. Taylor and Francis.

Shani, A. B. & Coghlan, D. 2019. Action research in business and management: A reflective review. *Action Research*, 19(3), 1–24.

Shani, A. B. R., Mohrman, S. A., Pasmore, W. A., Stymne, B. & Adler, N. (eds.) 2008. *Handbook of collaborative management research*. Sage Publications.

Sharma, G. & Bansal, P. 2019. Cocreating rigorous and relevant knowledge. *Academy of Management Journal*, 63, 386–410.

Sharma, G., Greco, A., Grewatsch, S. & Bansal, P. 2022. Cocreating forward: How researchers and managers can address problems together. *Academy of Management Learning & Education*, 21, 350–368.

Silva, M. E. & Figueiredo, M. D. 2017. Sustainability as practice: Reflections on the creation of an institutional logic. *Sustainability*, 9, 1839.

Skaburskis, A. 2008. The origin of "wicked problems". *Planning Theory & Practice*, 9, 277–280.

Smith, W. K. & Lewis, M. W. 2011. Toward a theory of paradox: A dynamic equilibrium model of organizing. *Academy of Management Review*, 36, 381–403.

Soh, W. G., Antonacopoulou, E. P., Rigg, C. & Bento, R. 2023. Embedding a "reflexive mindset": Lessons from reconfiguring the internal auditing practice. *Academy of Management Learning & Education*, 22, 88–111.

Spencer, L., Anderson, L. & Ellwood, P. 2022. Interweaving scholarship and practice: A pathway to scholarly impact. *Academy of Management Learning & Education*, 21(3), 422–448.

Stevens-Long, J., Schapiro, S. A. & Mcclintock, C. 2011. Passionate scholars: Transformative learning in doctoral education. *Adult Education Quarterly*, 62, 180–198.

Trafford, V. & Leshem, S. 2009. Doctorateness as a threshold concept. *Innovations in Education and Teaching International*, 46, 305–316.

Tsoukas, H. 1994. What is management? An outline of a metatheory. *British Journal of Management*, 5, 289–301.

Tsoukas, H. & Chia, R. 2002. On organizational becoming: Rethinking organizational change. *Organization Science*, 13, 567–582.

Tsoukas, H. & Dooley, K. J. 2011. Introduction to the special issue: Towards the ecological style: Embracing complexity in organizational research. *Organization Studies* 32, 729–735.

Tushman, M. L., Fenollosa, A., Mcgrath, D. N., O'Reilly, C. & Kleinbaum, A. M. 2007. Relevance and rigor: Executive education as a lever in shaping practice and research. *Academy of Management Learning & Education*, 6, 345–362.

Tushman, M. L. & O'Reilly, C. A., III. 2007. Research and relevance: Implications of Pasteur's quadrant for doctoral programs and faculty development. *Academy of Management Journal*, 50, 769–774.

Van De Ven, A. H. 2007. *Engaged scholarship: A guide for organizaational and social research*. Oxford University Press.

Van De Ven, A. H. 2022. *Theory building and research design* [Online]. University of Minnesota. [Accessed October 20 23].

Van De Ven, A. H. & Johnson, P. E. 2006. Knowledge for theory and practice. *Academy of Management Review*, 31, 802–821.

Van Winkelen, C., Birchall, D. & Mckenzie, J. 2008. Exploring relevance: A case study of an interactive research method within the context of an inter-organizational community of practice. Bristish Academy of Management, 9-11 September, Harrogate.

Van Winkelen, C. & Mckenzie, J. 2012. An Exploration of epistemic culture as a barrier to knowledge flows. *European Conference on Knowledge Management*, Cartagena Spain, September.

Wellington, J. & Sikes, P. 2006. 'A doctorate in a tight compartment': Why do students choose a professional doctorate and what impact does it have on their personal and professional lives? *Studies in Higher Education*, 31, 723–734.

23 The Early Career Researcher

A Science and Innovation Perspective

Paul J. Woodfield, Erling Rasmussen,
and Rafaela Costa Camoes Rabello

Introduction

New Zealand (NZ) universities have seen significant changes over the past three decades and have restructured considerably recently. This restructuring included many scientists leaving to work overseas or in industry, as Crown Research Institutes and other government agencies merged or devolved (Crawford, 2021; MBIE, 2020). This prompted a reaction through emphasising science, technology, engineering, and maths (STEM) areas and forums, including the Catching the Knowledge Wave project, which further spurred universities, government, and industry to rethink potential economic benefits through the science and innovation sector (New Zealand Herald, 2001).

Why are we now thinking about early career researchers (ECRs)? Increasingly, NZ universities are becoming managerial and entrepreneurial and expected to generate additional revenue, including by offering technological solutions to address societal challenges (Ferreira et al., 2018; Guerrero et al., 2016). Coupled with an emphasis on STEM, such expectations add pressure to ECRs in the science and innovation areas to adapt to new academic settings. ECRs are more prone to career uncertainty and precarity than senior colleagues as confirmed by a recent White Paper:

> Many submissions also highlighted the constrained opportunities for early to mid-career researchers and the challenging and precarious work environment in which they operate.
>
> (MBIE, 2022c, p. 4)

Thus, this volatile scenario poses concerns for both ECRs and their mentors, since they are constantly pressured to reconsider the fundamental role of ECRs, and also places some urgency on finding ways to cultivate and maintain a pipeline of ECRs. We find that countries are now thinking more deeply about science, technology, and knowledge in general, with a focus on generating more action in these

DOI: 10.4324/9781003459217-26

areas (OECD, 2023). Unfortunately, there is a lack of research investigating the different knowledge bases and multiple role expectations between generations of researchers (Park et al., 2023). Our empirical research focuses on science and innovation teams. Understanding the landscape for ECRs in science and innovation is vital in establishing relevant capacity development.

Background

In this section, we address why ECRs are of particular importance to NZ, what we are currently doing to address the precarity of ECRs (MBIE, 2021, 2022c), and what insights could possibly come from better understanding the landscape for ECRs in science innovation.

Early Career Researchers (ECRs) in Science and Technology Teams

The Science for Technological Innovation (SfTI) National Science Challenge is a 10-year (2014–2024) research programme, and one of the 11 National Science Challenges in NZ (MBIE, 2023). SfTI has 11 large spearhead projects and 86 small seed projects, with 687 researchers from 58 organisations (SfTI, 2023b). The programme aims to advance technology challenges in Aotearoa-New Zealand, to build sustainable economic growth and prosperity through physical sciences and engineering. SfTI focuses on developing cutting-edge science and technology that offer feasible applications for NZ industries. This chapter presents research from the SfTI's Building New Zealand's Innovation Capacity (BNZIC) spearhead project (SfTI, 2023a), examining the move from the laboratory to industry and related soft and networking skills within the national innovation ecosystem (SfTI, 2022).

Although ECR pathways and structures are well-established globally, NZ has not got a mature ECR culture. In recent years, there have been academic career advancement programmes established in some universities (e.g., University of Auckland, 2023). However, these are still relatively nascent and limited in their capacity and structure.

Knowledge Sharing in Science and Technology Teams

We adopt a knowledge-based view (Grant, 2015) to frame the relationship between senior researchers and ECRs. Knowledge is considered the most important resource under the resource-based view and, although we are exploring research teams, not firms, the knowledge-based view allows us to understand different knowledge bases between generations of researchers (Felin & Hesterly, 2007; Grant, 2015; Woodfield & Husted, 2017). We can also speculate upon the types of knowledge – tacit and explicit – each generation possesses, and how each researcher generation shares knowledge (Faith & Seeam, 2018), borrowing from concepts in employer–employee and intergenerational knowledge sharing (Husted & Michailova, 2002; Ritala et al., 2015). This knowledge sharing extends to Māori knowledge (Mātauranga), where Vision Mātauranga (VM) is embedded in NZs' government science policy framework, particularly its funding (SfTI, 2023c).

Research Location, Focus, and Methodology

Our case study represents data from science innovation teams within SfTI. BNZIC, a social science team, sought insights regarding the researchers' capacity to co-innovate. This study revolves around a multi-method, longitudinal (seven-year), grounded, and exploratory research approach. BNZIC used a multi-method, longitudinal research methodology based on an inductive insider–outsider technique (Woodfield et al., 2021). Primary data were gathered from 40 group and individual semi-structured and open-ended interviews, spanning 20 to 90 minutes. These interviews were from two diverse spearhead projects (Spearhead 5 – Additive manufacturing and 3D and/or 4D printing of bio-composites; and Spearhead 6 – Adaptive learning robots to complement the human workforce), involving researchers from different generations and disciplines. The interviewees were from universities, industry, research institutes, and government agencies. The interviewee quotes in the Findings section below are referenced with respect to the spearhead project, researcher interviewee number, and interview year. Thus SP6-R2, 2018 refers to Spearhead project 6, researcher interview number 2, and interview year being 2018.

In the analysis, we identify the overlapping themes permeating the scientists' expectations of ECRs. Through the elements unpicked by our thematic analysis, we mapped the multiple expectations in our case study, indicating which direction ECR mentors choose to share and create knowledge with their respective ECRs.

Findings

Our findings indicate that ECR mentors hold multiple expectations for ECRs, which include being technical experts and intermediaries (boundary spanners). These expectations feed into ECRs being the future of science in NZ.

ECR as Technical Experts

ECRs are seen to be technical experts, given the proclivity to new knowledge they have gained through their undergraduate, master's, or PhD studies. This brings new explicit knowledge to projects. However, as the analogy below shows, ECR knowledge can be treated more as a commodity or a resource that needs to be managed, rather than developed and nurtured.

> Look at the end of the day, researchers are farmers, and PhDs are cows, and you milk them. If you can't milk your cow the town dies because nobody can drink milk... You've got to have your cows to milk... if I'm paid .15 EFT (effective full time) on a project there's probably seven of those that I'm doing anyway, at the moment, and then you've got to do your day job. You've got to understand that part of that .15 is mentoring those younger researchers to do a lot of their heavy lifting... The fundamental doing stuff is still your PhDs.
>
> (SP6-R2, 2018)

Being technical experts was reflected by senior researchers on the one hand, but equally speculated on the lack of appropriate ECRs in NZ. With attrition rates for NZ trained researchers being reasonably high, researchers are sought from overseas. This can be helpful for growing capacity in NZ, but the timeframe and lead time to get these researchers into the country includes barriers like visas, relocation costs, or family considerations.

> I think it's more of a wider problem, where researchers need to be able to tap into PhD students, and people that actually do the projects. In a lot of cases, we're relying on getting people from overseas, and we have to work on visas and all sorts of other [stuff] before they even get here. Then, because they're on a project, and the time frame's two years, but it takes a year to get a PhD, and then they take about six months to get up to running... and then three months later they're still doing lit reviews, because that's what you have to do. Then, by the time we actually start getting going, the project's over. Then, you have to do it all over again... There's plenty of leaders... but not enough actual doers.
>
> (SP6-R12, 2016)

Moreover, the retention of ECRs – be they PhD or post-doctoral – can be difficult. There can be a lot of down time and knowledge being lost as new ECRs come and go:

PhDs come and go, so you never build a core base of people that know how to do things, so you're having to re-teach or re-learn... same mistakes over and over... You get a new team basically every project... Because we can't afford post-docs, because they're too expensive. I think they say you can get four or five PhDs for the cost of one post-doc, but you want to be bringing these people into post-doc positions, so that they can then come through to earlier research.

(SP6-R12, 2016)

One ECR reflected on how they are used for their knowledge and still, they are in an insecure position careerwise. While having a position as a PhD or a post-doc "buys time", it does not provide job security. Moreover, the credit tends to go to the senior researchers who have their name on the project, but do not carry out the actual work:

... a lot of people get insecure PhD students to... actually do the work, and a lot of the professors [and] the less new researchers like me, who nowadays, they've got 20 different projects they're named on. They're not actually working on any of those projects; they're not programming, [developing, and] not actually doing any research. So, when they're named on this project, and they don't have their PhD, nothing actually gets done.

(SP6-R12, 2018)

The scarcity of PhD candidates has meant senior researchers have employed undergraduates. Referring to a senior researcher, a mid-career researcher commented on the reality that senior researchers are unlikely to be able to carry out the research. This can be due to a lack of knowledge in a specific area but could be interpreted as being unable to navigate newer technology, techniques, or instruments used:

They're not going to work on [the project]. They're so far beyond actually doing research, they don't know how to do it anymore, [and] they don't have time... It's not a leadership thing or criticism; it's just hard to get PhDs... I don't know why universities don't dig into their 20-thousand-odd students and dig them out more... Which is why I'm using a lot of funding to generate – I've got four undergrad students working for me, now.

(SP6-R12, 2018)

Senior researchers suggested that having ECRs was fundamental to them being productive, given their time allocation on projects is limited. Their reflection rhymes with that of the mid-career researchers' observation that senior researchers do not always have the skills and are time poor. They also have budget constraints reducing their time:

> … part of the reason stuff feels like it's not progressing is because we don't have someone who's actually 100 per cent on the project doing it… I'm .14 EFT, so if I don't have my PhD student (and the four Ras [research assistants] I managed to find), there's sweet bugger-all I can do on this project…
>
> (SP6-R12, 2018)

There is a hierarchy. ECRs at a post-doctorate level act as an intermediary between the professor, who may be named on the project, and the other ECRs, who do the day-to-day tasks. They are important for the running of research projects as they are technical experts with advanced knowledge:

> Post-docs actually run the projects. Professors do the professor stuff, but they have dedicated post-docs for basically the projects, and they coordinate the PhDs, and do the day-to-day activities, and they're the ones actually in charge of it…
>
> (SP6-R12, 2016)

As this mid-career researcher notes, capacity development is important. SfTI builds capacity development in as a compulsory component, however, this is not necessarily compensated for (to the same extent) by universities. In summary, ECRs are important to the functioning of teams. They have technical knowledge that allows them to run projects with guidance from senior researchers who are time poor in terms of their allocation to the research.

ECRs as Boundary Spanners

ECRs can be viewed as intermediaries across teams, with stakeholders, and, sometimes, for their indigenous Māori background. Given there are numerous large spearhead projects and smaller seed projects, there is considerable cross pollination between universities research institutes, government, and industry. One researcher commented on the "two degrees of separation" in NZ and how relationships can be a proxy for expertise that cannot be accessed due to a conflict of interest, cost, or availability:

> … there's two degrees of separation. [One] of the project partners is my [previous] doctorate student, and he's doing a post-doc with [a professorial colleague]. [Although] we would like

[our professorial colleagues'] expertise into the project, it didn't really make sense to employ [them, as it would be] a huge conflict of interest [as a leader in the wider National Science Challenge]. [As a post-doc, my previous PhD student] is very much skilled to do the job... therefore it made sense to have that linked to [our professorial colleague through them]. So, we've got that expertise channel.

(SP6-R1, 2018)

Another researcher commented on the acceleration the project has taken place over the first couple of years and how a collaborative culture is being built between different discipline areas:

[We are getting horizontal movement] that's coming at just the right time... entering the third year. We've got four master students coming in for their final year, so that actually puts us ahead of what we had anticipated... So growing that collaborative research culture is really beginning to happen... it's science/design collaboration. We're talking different languages.

(SP5-R10, 2018)

This collaborative research culture between senior researchers and ECRs suggests that researchers become "interpreters" across disciplines. ECRs can be well placed to straddle different domains with their knowledge being malleable. Moreover, taking time out for a sabbatical on a project as a ECR was seen as beneficial to a senior researcher for gaining and sharing knowledge from another setting:

... we had the summer scholarships which were speculative, and 'blue-sky' in thinking. [Some] came back with a material that potentially might have applications in those areas... and [another master's student suggested going] on an internship... and understanding the process that [the colleague] goes through in order to actually formulate and print material... it was great that there was that sabbatical type of opportunity there.

(SP5-R16, 2019)

From a different angle, mutual respect was garnered where each party can play to different strengths. Again, the ECR can be an intermediary between research teams, or indeed industry, or government:

... that closer way of working is really good because both parties understand what each needs. [What's] been working really well with [my colleague], is our respect for him as to what he does, and his respect for us as to what we're trying to do with it. [Neither] party would be as strong without the other. Each party gives validity to each other. So, I think that's really important. [For example] a student [goes to another organisation] and works with them...

(SP5-R16, 2019)

Where finding PhDs is difficult, it is even harder to incentivise Māori ECRs who are invaluable for bringing their knowledge to projects in fulfilment of Vision Mātauranga (VM). One suggestion for encouraging more Māori researchers is summer scholarships:

The one thing we are struggling with [regarding] VM and Māori engagement is finding Māori doctorate students, and that's simply because a Māori engineer will have done four years of study, racked up X-thousands of dollars of debt. Any engineer is a very sought-after commodity. Anybody can command $60-$70k salaries. Why would you take a doctorate on $25-$30k? It is difficult to find home-grown doctorate students, and when you put a premium on the Māori skills and the Māori relationships, which a lot of companies do... we're not favoured. [We need to] get people interested in our research through summer scholarships... leading onto master's and [PhDs, so] we might stand a chance... dollar for dollar, we can't cope.

(SP6-R1, 2018)

Moreover, building a "railroad" and concentrating on embedding the right people is important, rather than treating VM as a tick-box exercise:

I think it works well when it's done on a basis of what is the science. [The] summer project we've got going; it is almost incidental that it is a Māori student doing this project. We want to build a railroad; we want to do this – how do you do this – how can you influence this – how does that go? ... I think VM, when it becomes a tick-box exercise – an artificial one, it stops working.

(SP6-R1, 2018)

These expectations shape the type of knowledge shared and how ECRs are prepared for their academic career. We find that ECRs have a different knowledge base than their senior colleagues. While senior researchers have built tacit knowledge over their career from their experience, and sometimes by trial and error, ECRs are exposed to new knowledge that they can share. There are various reasons for this, including their education and experiences, which shape their knowledge base. For example, ECRs will invariably have up-to-date knowledge based on current curriculum and events, alongside their own research – particularly at PhD and post-doctoral levels – where they make their own contribution to knowledge.

Moreover, ECRs may bring different experiences from other institutions and countries, contributing to solving problems and engaging with colleagues and external stakeholders. As such, they can be drivers of the external relationships as ECRs serve as intermediaries, crossing the boundaries of current knowledge toward new scientific and technological discoveries. Although there is a difference between generations of researchers, we find that knowledge sharing is bidirectional in nature. That is, there is a mentoring relationship from the senior researchers to the ECR, and vice versa.

The role and usefulness of the next generation researchers may differ depending on their mentorship and whether they have gathered experience on other projects, other universities, government, or other research institutes. This can have impact on the knowledge they are able to share. Moreover, depending on how they have been mentored, they may be either of the mind to openly share ideas in new settings or hoard or hold back knowledge.

Discussion

Senior researchers may be more "T" shaped with a depth of knowledge in their discipline (Madhavan & Grover, 1998), and with experiences of "learning by doing" over time which cultivates tacit knowledge. These researchers would have an ability to collaborate across disciplines and with different stakeholders. One could argue that ECRs develop "A"-shaped skills where they have expertise in more than one discipline with an ability to integrate insights in a synergistic way from multiple sources of knowledge (Leonard-Barton, 1995; Madhavan & Grover, 1998; Tsai & Huang, 2008). A question may be whether ECRs are gravitating toward or are expected to have "A"-shaped skills, where this may not have been a prerequisite for senior researchers. Additionally, this also begs the question whether ECRs bring a knowledge base and capabilities which, as they progress their careers, would appear more advanced than the senior researchers at the same career stage.

Our findings concur with sentiments from the science and innovation community, who contributed to a green paper on the research, science, and innovation (RSI) sector (MBIE, 2021), followed by a consultation process in 2021-2022 with key actors across the sector, including SfTI (MBIE, 2022a, 2022b). The green paper also revealed that NZ "...currently trains many more PhDs than there are academic positions available, often driving talent to low value jobs or overseas" and with overhead calculations perpetuating these issues by making "postdoctoral involvement in research teams significantly more expensive than PhD students" (MBIE, 2022a, p. 10). The report suggested measures NZ needs to consider matching modern research systems in other small, advanced economies that have:

> a serious approach to talent development, resourcing, attraction, and retention, with a strongly international mindset. Many systems support early to mid-career researchers with pathways to establish programmes and teams, and have dedicated schemes for attracting and retaining outstanding international researchers to establish research groups and programmes.
>
> (MBIE, 2021, p. 20)

In other words, NZ first needs to move away from treating ECRs like "cows" that get "milked", toward a structured, incentivised system. The system needs to attract the best ECRs to NZ, and go further, by supporting and developing them, including more postdoc positions being available. Beyond this, senior researchers need to adopt a knowledge-sharing environment that is bidirectional across generations (Woodfield & Husted, 2017). That is, not just mentoring the ECRs, but nurturing an environment where ECRs can and will share knowledge based on their new education and experiences. Importantly, more support and incentives for a pipeline of Māori scholars are needed, as highlighted by the recent white paper (MBIE, 2022b).

Setting priorities will provide opportunities for long-term career pathways, supporting new researchers through their early- and mid-career stages (MBIE, 2022c). With generations of researchers having different knowledge bases, we need to be mindful of the expectations and realities of the different roles of senior researchers and ECRs. Where senior researchers build relationships with colleagues, industry, and other stakeholders over time, this cannot be expected to be the same for ECRs. However, evidence shows that ECRs bring new perspectives to the nature of engagement internally and externally within a research project. They serve as an intermediary between research teams, industry, and other stakeholders with a level of technical expertise that meets current industry demands.

Conclusions and Implications

The empirical study was conducted to provide a better understanding of the different expectations and knowledge bases of ECRs in science and innovation. The research findings suggest that mitigating ECRs' career precarity and providing them with appropriate career paths and capacity development will benefit both them and their organisations. Since this is initial research of career pressures, there is a need to develop further in-depth understanding of career issues faced by ECRs. Future research could include a micro-foundational approach to how knowledge is shared in interdisciplinary research teams. This could extend to investigating bidirectional knowledge sharing through the different stages of a research career, and thereby recognising ECRs knowledge base and malleability through learning and navigation of new technology, techniques, or instruments. Moreover, further studies could explore the role trust plays with knowledge sharing in intergenerational research teams, or how entrepreneurial research teams are developed through engaging or recruiting ECRs. Finally, how ECRs impact external relationships with industry and other stakeholders could be explored.

References

Crawford, R. (2021). *Focused innovation policy: Lessons from international experience: Working paper 2021/03.* New Zealand Productivity Commission. https://www.productivity.govt.nz/assets/Documents/focused-innovation-policy/Focused-innovation-policy.pdf

Faith, C. K., & Seeam, A. K. (2018). Knowledge sharing in academia: A case study using a SECI model approach. *Journal of Education, 9,* 53–70.

Felin, T., & Hesterly, W. S. (2007). The knowledge-based view, nested heterogeneity, and new value creation: Philosophical considerations on the locus of knowledge. *Academy of Management Review, 32*(1), 195–218.

Ferreira, J. J., Fayolle, A., Ratten, V., & Raposo, M. (2018). *Entrepreneurial universities.* Edward Elgar Publishing.

Grant, R. M. (2015). Knowledge-based view. In C. L. Cooper (Ed.), *Wiley Encyclopedia of Management* (3 ed., Vol. 12, Strategic Management). John Wiley & Sons. https://doi.org/10.1002/9781118785317.weom120172

Guerrero, M., Urbano, D., Fayolle, A., Klofsten, M., & Mian, S. (2016). Entrepreneurial universities: Emerging models in the new social and economic landscape. *Small Business Economics, 47*(3), 551–563. https://doi.org/10.1007/s11187-016-9755-4

Husted, K., & Michailova, S. (2002). Diagnosing and fighting knowledge-sharing hostility. *Organizational Dynamics, 31*(1), 60–73. https://doi.org/10.1016/S0090-2616(02)00072-4

Leonard-Barton, Dorothy (1995). *Wellsprings of knowledge: Building and sustaining the sources of innovation.* Harvard Business School Press.

Madhavan, R., & Grover, R. (1998). From embedded knowledge to embodied knowledge: New product development as knowledge management. *Journal of Marketing, 62*(4), 1–12. https://doi.org/10.1177/002224299806200401

MBIE – Ministry of Business Innovation & Employment. (2020). *Te Pae Kahurangi: Positioning Crown Research Institutes to collectively and respectively meet New Zealand's current and future needs.* New Zealand Government. https://www.mbie.govt.nz/assets/te-pae-kahurangi-report.pdf

MBIE – Ministry of Business Innovation & Employment. (2021). *Research, science and innovation: Te Ara Paerangi Future Pathways Green Paper 2021.* New Zealand Government. https://www.mbie.govt.nz/dmsdocument/ 17637-future-pathways-green-paper

MBIE – Ministry of Business Innovation & Employment. (2022a). *Te Ara Paerangi: Future Pathways Summary of Submissions - Part 1 - All Submissions and Engangement.* New Zealand Government. https://www.mbie.govt.nz/ assets/te-ara-paerangi-future-pathways-summary-of-submissions-part-1- summary-of-all-submissions.pdf

MBIE – Ministry of Business Innovation & Employment. (2022b). *Te Ara Paerangi: Future Pathways Summary of Submissions - Part 2 - Summary of Māori Engagements and Submissions.* New Zealand Government. https:// www.mbie.govt.nz/assets/te-ara-paerangi-future-pathways-summary-of- submissions-part-1-summary-of-all-submissions.pdf

MBIE – Ministry of Business Innovation & Employment. (2022c). *Te Ara Paerangi: Future Pathways White Paper 2022.* New Zealand Government. https://www.mbie.govt.nz/assets/te-ara-paerangi-future-pathways-white- paper-2022.pdf

MBIE – Ministry of Business Innovation & Employment. (2023). *National Science Challenges.* Retrieved 30 October 2023 from https://www.mbie.govt. nz/science-and-technology/science-and-innovation/funding-information- and-opportunities/investment-funds/national-science-challenges/

New Zealand Herald. (2001). *Helen Clark: Catching the Knowledge Wave.* Retrieved 31 October 2023 from https://www.nzherald.co.nz/nz/ihelen-clarki- catching-the-knowledge-wave/IAKLRFHXR62QMJ7ZCKJVFRMDCA/

OECD. (2023). *OECD Science, Technology and Innovation Outlook 2023.* https://doi.org/10.1787/0b55736e-en

Park, W., Cullinane, A., Gandolfi, H., Alameh, S., & Mesci, G. (2023). Innovations, challenges and future directions in nature of science research: Reflections from early career academics. *Research in Science Education.* https://doi.org/10.1007/s11165-023-10102-z

Ritala, P., Olander, H., Michailova, S., & Husted, K. (2015). Knowledge sharing, knowledge leaking and relative innovation performance: An empirical study. *Technovation, 35,* 22–31. https://doi.org/10.1016/j.technovation.2014.07.011

SfTI – Science for Technological Innovation. (2022). *He hiringa hangarau, he oranga tangata: Building New Zealand's Capacity for Science-based Open Innovation.* https://www.sftichallenge.govt.nz/assets/Uploads/BNZIC2022- FINAL-VERSION-13122022.pdf

SfTI – Science for Technological Innovation. (2023a). *Building New Zealand's innovation capacity.* Retrieved 31 October 2023 from https://www. sftichallenge.govt.nz/our-research/projects/spearhead/building-new-zealands- innovation-capacity/

SfTI – Science for Technological Innovation. (2023b). *The Science for Technological Innovation National Science Challenge.* Retrieved 31 October 2023 from https://www.sftichallenge.govt.nz/

SfTI – Science for Technological Innovation. (2023c). *Vision Mātauranga.* Retrieved 31 October 2023 from https://www.sftichallenge.govt.nz/for-researchers/vision-matauranga/

Tsai, M. T., & Huang, Y. C. (2008). Exploratory learning and new product performance: The moderating role of cognitive skills and environmental uncertainty. *Journal of High Technology Management Research, 19*(2), 83–93. https://doi.org/10.1016/j.hitech.2008.10.001

University of Auckland. (2023). *Academic Career Advancement Programme.* Retrieved 30 October 2023 from https://www.auckland.ac.nz/en/students/academic-information/postgraduate-students/doctoral/doctoral-opportunities/acap.html

Woodfield, P. J., & Husted, K. (2017). Intergenerational knowledge sharing in family firms: Case-based evidence from the New Zealand wine industry. *Journal of Family Business Strategy, 8*(1), 57–69. https://doi.org/10.1016/j.jfbs.2017.01.001

Woodfield, P. J., Ruckstuhl, K., & Rabello, R. C. C. (2021). Charting a course of action: An insider-outsider approach. *Technology Innovation Management Review, 11*(7/8). https://doi.org/10.22215/timreview/1456

24 The Early Career Academic

Engaging with Business

Rebecca Beech

Introduction

In this chapter, I provide an early career academic perspective towards the opportunities and barriers for early careers that engage with businesses when holding a position at a business school – be that engaging with a business when teaching or undertaking and/or delivering their research. I highlight my own experiences and reflections throughout, in the hope to empower early career academics in considering the pursuit of liaising with businesses, as well as understanding what would motivate them to do such an activity. I provide a few lessons learnt from my own experience and reveal why the activity of engaging with businesses enriched my career so far, and how I encountered such opportunities. To summarise, I reveal five golden rules for an early career academic who is considering engaging with a business or is at the start of their journey, along with caveats to be mindful of when engaging with a business. It is important to acknowledge that my own experiences and reflections shared in the chapter demonstrate one person's journey; in your own journey as an early career academic, or as a mentor/supervisor/manager to an early career, it is important to recognise that you may have different experiences that reveal other caveats and/or benefits of engaging with a business. The main purpose of this chapter is to start that conversation among early career academics in a business school, and foster a sense of curiosity and enthusiasm to understand how there are benefits in liaising with businesses in order to support their own thinking, research interests, academic progression via networking or promotion and personal satisfaction.

First, I will discuss the benefits of engaging with a business as an early career academic based in a business school, the importance for your academic journey and warrants from business schools to foster engagement. Second, exploring the barriers for early career academics when liaising with a business, I will shed light on internal and external factors that prohibit the academic in collaborating with external engagement and guidance to overcome hurdles that may arise. Third, I will offer lessons learnt from my personal

DOI: 10.4324/9781003459217-27

experience as an early career academic and how I started to engage with businesses via my network. Last, I provide five golden rules for a curious early career academic, or an academic that wishes to motivate early carer academics, to consider when engaging with businesses, to support their intentions and drivers to engage, and caveats are provided to be mindful of when engaging.

In order to understand why I share such perspectives and experiences in this chapter, here is brief summary of my academic journey to date. I identify as an early career academic, as I am three years post-PhD. I hold two elected positions at the British Academy of Management to promote, foster and support early career academic development, these are: an early career academic position on the Marketing and Retail Special Interest Group, and co-lead of the Early Career Academic Network which supports all early career academics across the association. I was granted a full-time PhD studentship by the Centre for Business in Society at Coventry University in 2016. I was awarded my PhD in Marketing in July 2020, following a viva in April 2020 which achieved minor corrections. It is important to note, that my PhD topic 'Understanding Knowledge Sharing on Twitter: Within the Context of Green Clothing' was from a consumer perspective and did not entail engagement with a business. During my PhD, I was an active doctoral researcher at the research centre, collaborating in conference organising, research projects, teaching and external activities. The latter I will expand on during the chapter, as this was when I started to engage with a business. My first full-time appointment was as Lecturer in Business Management at Coventry University. After two and half years at the prestigious institute, where I received the opportunity to develop in my academic career, I was appointed as Lecturer in Marketing at Oxford Brookes University. In my current institution, a university that holds high regard for business engagement and is a prominent university in the sector for business collaboration, I have been able to continue my engagement and grow my network.

The Importance of Engaging With Businesses For Early Career Academics

In current literature, there still seems to be a disconnect between academics in business schools and external engagement with the business world (Scandura and Iammarino, 2022). A recent report from the *Times Higher Education* (2022), points out that academics on the one hand see engaging with businesses as a 'chore', whilst on the other hand do not understand the significance of collaborating. This demonstrates two hindrances as to why academics would not engage with businesses, and suggests that the relationship between external engagement and academia is purely one way for academics that wish to engage, which is often due to the nature of their research. Such examples of collaboration are selling or licensing intellectual property, and joint research projects to produce new knowledge (De Silva et al., 2023). Whilst this is not an exhaustive list, there is potential for academics to engage via many channels. I explore further avenues when recalling from my own engagement later in the chapter.

Engaging with businesses can add to an academic's career, the process can build an academic's ability to relate to people – these 'people' may be stakeholders that they work with in their study or prospective collaborators. As a result, engaging with external businesses can foster an academic's proficiency in making strong successful professional relationships (*Times Higher Education*, 2022), which can be seen as a pivotal tool that underpins an academic's career progression (Cairney and Oliver, 2020). For instance, such a tool is required for interdisciplinary collaborations, leading research or teaching groups, and working with colleagues in teams at the business school. There are significant benefits to an academic's reach, in terms of their outputs making valuable impact and substantial outcomes, getting out of their 'ivory tower' and bridging the gap to make real change (2019). Therefore, adhering to the 'Research Excellence Framework', a prominent benchmark for academics in the UK, and the requirement for 'pathways to impact' which can lead to securing funding from noteworthy national and international funders (Boswell and Smith, 2017: 2). The caveat here, is that researchers must be aware of their audience when writing and/or delivering outputs, to make the valuable impact warranted (see Cairney and Oliver's 2020 paper for guidelines on how to make real impact considering your research audience).

Light has been shed on the importance of engaging, but without the Business School's vision and support for academics to engage with businesses, the opportunity is lost. There is a glimmer of hope, as business schools in the UK do demonstrate the endeavour to bridge academia and industry, by showcasing events for academics to collaborate, funding opportunities and having administrative teams to support academics. To date, studies evidence the pressure on academics to diversify their outputs and activities by engaging with practitioners (Cairney and Oliver, 2020).

Present studies show a plethora of barriers and reasons for academics, in general, to engage with business. However, there is a warrant to understand what the barriers are for early career academics in a UK business school in the present day and requirements for those academics to prosper.

Barriers For Early Career Academics in UK Higher Education When Engaging With a Business

During my academic journey so far, as an early career academic engaging with businesses, I have received immense support and encouragement at my past and current institutions. However, from conversations with early career academics in my elected positions at the British Academy of Management and during conferences, barriers to their engagement have been revealed. In this section, I share the barriers that I am aware of from past conversations with peers in the early career academic arena and from observations. These are in no way criticisms of UK institutions, nor to be seen as reasons that have failed the early career academic community, but tools in which to complement existing processes to make engagement easier and, ultimately, successful for an early career academic.

First, let's consider the words of Rosalynn Carter, a celebrated author and activist, 'A leader takes people where they want to go. A great leader takes people where they don't necessarily want to go, but ought to be' (Forbes, 2018). A barrier which may prohibit early career academics is the lack of guidance and exemplar of how to initiate a collaboration with a business. It is noteworthy that leaders at the business school are a role model for their early career academic colleagues, be this the dean, associates or programme leaders; but in particular, the dean who has the ability to make changes. An example of being a role model includes showcasing their business engagements in the business school newsletter, to evidence how academics can contribute to business projects and the benefits of doing so. The style may be written in a way that describes their collaboration and the impact, as well as a reflection on the challenges that they overcame and the advantages in sharing knowledge. The aim of doing this would be to lead to by example and, hopefully, with a snowball effect, other colleagues would proceed to collaborate with businesses and showcase their efforts and reflections in the business school newsletter. If the newsletter additions grew in popularity, potentially there could be a sub-set newsletter with an industry focus, which would act as a repository for academics to turn to for advice before collaborating with a business and/or to overcome any challenges they face during the process.

Second, an early career academic is often told that they are at a fantastic time of their career as they can experience 'a bit of everything' in academia, to see what truly fits their interests and ambitions. The barrier is the time limitation in their working day, to contribute to business engagement. In order to grasp the benefits of such an advantageous experience and beneficial activity to one's career, an early career academic's workload (and other colleagues also) should reflect their engagement with business. In doing so, this allocates time, if time is warranted, to engage with businesses and be able to do so in their working hours. Considering past reports (WONKHE, 2017) that evidence the rising mental health issues and burnout among academic staff in UK higher education, by managing workload to encompass activities, such as a collaboration with a business, this could reduce signs of ill health amongst academic staff as they are not working outside of their paid working hours. However, this is a contentious statement, as some may argue that this takes away autonomy from the academic (WONKHE, 2023). It is important to note that if the activity was added as workload, it would be discussed between the early career academic and their line manager to provide a rationale as to why the workload hours were given and if they are required.

Third, a barrier for early career academics is the opportunity to meet businesses that require their expertise and practical support during a collaboration. Business schools should consider organising events and workshops that, (1) showcase businesses that require support from academics, (2) offer best practice sessions that enable experienced academics to share their experiences, both good and bad, (3) invite industry representatives to share what a business would require from an academic and how they support an academic, and (4) provide networking events for academics to meet with businesses to share their expertise and knowledge to understand how they could collaborate. The four initiatives would help to advocate engagement between early career academics at the business school and businesses, and create an encouraging environment to take up the opportunity of collaboration.

Lessons Learnt as An Early Career Academic When Liaising with Businesses

I have had the privilege to work with businesses nationally and internationally as an early career academic. The first lesson learnt is that you should never underestimate the power of your network and the significance of networking. During my PhD, I had my first experience of liaising with a business when working as a consultant for a branding agency in London. I was invited by my professor to share my expertise on the project, who was one of their extended networks. The experience enriched my understanding of how businesses benefit from academic input, and the short-time turnarounds of delivering insights and results for the client. Going forward, when working as a consultant, it is important that the academic is clear about what they are expected to do and what they must deliver in terms of outcomes, as well as not overpromising to the business and/or client. Transparency is key during the role of consultancy, which in turn builds rapport between the academic and business and leads to a successful working relationship.

Similarly, 'networking' created an international opportunity during my role as lecturer at my past institution, which boasted a wide range of international partnerships. I took on the role of leading a collaboration with a European university as part of a summer school for students to work on real-life consultancy projects, and as coach to a student group which was working with a European government collaborator. As part of the collaboration, I was required to invite a company to be a part of the project, which led to reaching out to the university's knowledge exchange unit to understand what business partnerships the university held. This activity opened my eyes to another key lesson. I would encourage an early career academic to locate their knowledge exchange team at the university that liaise with businesses. In doing so, an early career academic can obtain information on how the university works with businesses, training for academics and opportunities to meet with businesses.

For the last two academic years, whilst working with the European university's summer school, I have worked closely with UK-based companies that I provided to the summer camp, and a European government collaborator when coaching a student team. The business encounters provided me with an in-depth understanding of the benefits for students who had the opportunity to take part in the project during their studies, and how they may contribute their knowledge. A lesson learnt from the experience entailed how I can use my experiences with businesses to benefit my students learning, and the importance of students working with businesses. The latter is fitting with the pressure for UK higher education institutions to provide students with opportunities to boost their employability, such as via experiential learning, learning goals that are work-related and delivering curriculum that aligns with required skills in graduate jobs (*Times Higher Education*, 2022). Therefore, demonstrating a lesson learnt, that the early career academic's engagement with business can provide not only career progression in terms of knowledge acquirement, but also delivering meaningful content from their experiences, to provide students with a curriculum and experience that is warranted in the present day. Potentially, leading to job progression via activities that improve student experience and curriculum redesign.

As well as international collaborations being a beneficial prospect for engaging with a business and collaborating, inviting guest speakers from your network, your colleagues and the university's network can deliver interesting avenues for collaboration – my final lesson learnt. Benefits include bouncing ideas around with someone from industry to aid your curriculum, developing your research ideas by speaking to industry experts to understand managerial implications or how a concept is understood in business terms, and sharing expertise with a business on areas for development.

Golden Rules and Caveats to Consider

To conclude, here are five golden rules for early career academics to consider prior to collaborating with a business or during their engagement. The following guidance is a summary of my own experiences and thoughts expressed in the chapter.

1. Build meaningful professional relationships.

   A consistent element that is revealed throughout my experiences when liaising with a business, is the importance to build professional relationships that are meaningful. Meaningful meaning that the academic keeps in touch with the person over email, social media platforms and events/workshops, in order to keep up to date with the business and their developments or needs for collaboration. You may wish to sign up to a newsletter from the business to learn of key news and collaborators that they are working with, or topics of business that they are progressing in, e.g., sustainability. A surface-level professional relationship would not create the rapport and trust that is built during a meaningful professional relationship, where you can build trust in terms of knowledge exchange and working on projects that potentially require anonymity.

2. Learn from senior academics in the business school.

   In order to gain experience and insight, early career academics are encouraged to reach out to colleagues who have engaged with businesses. Academics can be identified, via the knowledge exchange unit at the university, that work with businesses, or by undertaking research about business active academics via the institution's portals/intranet. An informal conversation over coffee would be beneficial in understanding the key challenges and advantages of their collaborations, as well as potential to expand your network to support on future projects. Every journey is different, so experiences may differ, which is why speaking to more than one person would be advantageous to build a rounder picture of academic engagement with businesses. If your university offers a mentorship programme, it is recommended that as an early career academic with interest in business collaboration, to sign up and determine that the mentor should hold experience in business engagement; you can further identify disciplines in which you would like to focus on in terms of mentorship.

3. Build rapport with alumni.

Often an area that we overlook as an academic, are the benefits of keeping in touch with our alumni. One invaluable purpose would be to create a professional connection with a past student to keep updated about their industry experience, and potential seeking of academic/industry collaboration in the future.

4. Network, network and network.

Most opportunities are created by your existing network. You should never underestimate the importance of a network, made from past institutions, conference attendance, and via social media platforms. It is important to note that in order to build a successful network, you must have meaningful conversations so that you know who does what and vice versa – have your elevator speech ready at events.

5. Work with like-minded people.

What makes collaborations and the engagements personally enjoyable and interesting, is working with like-minded people who are enthusiastic about the topics you are passionate about. Often these are the best collaborations as they are mentally stimulating, and you get to learn so much more about an area that will progress your own research understanding and/or teaching. Similarly, work with like-minded peers, in terms of values and ethics, to build a respectful working relationship that is supportive of your work–life balance.

Caveats to be mindful of include, 'be true to yourself' which entails being transparent about what you can contribute and where your expertise lies in. This leads to another, 'do not over promise', prioritise where you want to develop as an early career academic and how you can engage with a project and deliverables. An important skill is 'reflection', following collaborations, networking and engagements, reflect on the process and collaboration. Going forward, what did you learn? What would you change? What went well? Would I like to work with them again?

References

Boswell, C. and Smith, K. (2017). Rethinking policy 'impact': Four models of research-policy relations. *Palgrave Communications*, 3(1), p. 44.

Cairney, P. and Oliver, K. (2020). How should academics engage in policymaking to achieve impact? *Political Studies Review*, 18(2), pp. 228–244.

De Silva, M., Al-Tabbaa, O. and Pinto, J. (2023). Academics engaging in knowledge transfer and co-creation: Push causation and pull effectuation? *Research Policy*, 52(2), p.104668.

Forbes. (2018). Great leaders take people where they may not want to go. [online]. Available from https://www.forbes.com/sites/karagoldin/2018/10/01/great-leaders-take-people-where-they-may-not-want-to-go/ [17 October 2023].

Forbes. (2019). How to ensure more business schools research is relevant to business. [online]. Available from https://www.forbes.com/sites/andrewstephen/2019/01/08/how-to-ensure-more-business-school-research-is-relevant-to-business/?sh=63f7335fbd85 [21 September 2023].

Scandura, A. and Iammarino, S. (2022). Academic engagement with industry: The role of research quality and experience. *Journal of Technology Transfer*, 47(4), pp. 1000–1036.

Times Higher Education. (2022). External engagement in academia: Lessons from the business world. [online]. Available from https://www.timeshighereducation.com/campus/external-engagement-academia-lessons-business-world [21 September 2023].

WONKHE. (2017). The rise of academic ill health. [online]. Available from https://wonkhe.com/blogs/the-rise-of-academic-ill-health/ [23 October 2023].

WONKHE. (2023). A beginners' guide to academic workload modelling. [online]. Available https://wonkhe.com/blogs/a-beginners-guide-to-academic-workload-modelling/ [23 October 2023].

25 Spanning Boundaries Through Intersectoral Mobility

Jenny Bäckstrand and Malin Löfving

1. Introduction

This chapter focuses on temporary intersectoral mobility positions and presents a checklist, with activities, that can be a support for both individuals and host organisations before, during, and after the mobility position. This chapter is relevant for universities, non-academic organisations, and individual academics that are interested in intersectoral mobility. However, we have taken the university perspective in this chapter.

In this chapter, we have studied academics with a PhD degree working at either a university or in an organisation in another sector. However, the individuals can also be non-academics, working at a university or in an organisation in another sector.

2. Why Intersectoral Mobility?

Universities have three missions: education, research, and public outreach. The outreach activities often focus on external engagement. External engagement aligns universities and society and, as it is a two-way approach, it aims at collaboration to develop and apply knowledge to address societal needs. External engagement emphasises the mutually beneficial exchange of knowledge and resources.

The interaction between universities and society has been referred to as 'knowledge transfer' or 'knowledge sharing'. This can be done in a distant and adversarial way, by the use of impersonal carriers of knowledge, such as written text, or by overbridging the border between these two instances in a closer way. A joint sharing and mutual access of knowledge to create common meanings can enable mutual benefits between academia and society. This is called 'knowledge translation' and will link academia to society and vice versa. The linking or bridging activities between academia and society are called 'boundary spanning'. Boundary spanning can be viewed both from individual and organisational levels. At the organisational level, boundary spanning refers to broader

DOI: 10.4324/9781003459217-28

institutional strategies to engage with external organisations and can be viewed as multiple types of relationships with external organisations.

At the individual level, boundary spanners at universities are academics or non-academics, who are interested in interacting and engaging with external non-academic organisations. These individuals are one of the most important factors for boundary spanning between universities and organisations in other sectors. The individual academic transfers knowledge and experience between sectors. In this chapter, the focus is on intersectoral mobility, where individuals span boundaries between university and organisations and spend time in another sector. Intersectoral mobility is defined as '*the physical mobility of researchers between sectors (e.g., academia/industry/govt. agency/research institutes) in both directions*'. (Melin et al., 2019, p. 3). 'Both directions' here means both from university to external organisation, and from external organisation to university.

Mobility between universities and organisations are often ad hoc occasions, derived from individuals who are interested in spending time in another sector. The interest from universities and funding agencies regarding intersectoral mobility is increasing due to the requirement to contribute to the so-called third mission, public outreach.

In literature about intersectoral mobility, the focus has so far been on international mobility in academia (see e.g., Guthrie et al., 2017; Netz et al., 2020), permanent mobility between universities in a country (see e.g., Abramo et al., 2022), permanent mobility decisions: work in industry or academia (see e.g., Millard, 2018), PhD students or postdocs mobility (see e.g. Alfano et al., 2021), or individual incentives for mobility (see e.g., Nordforsk, 2014).

Nordforsk (2014, p. 24–25) furthermore writes about benefits with mobility:

> researchers will be able to work better together if they spend an extended period of time with each other. Efficiency in research collaborations is largely based on shared understandings of what will be done, on established procedures and on trust in each other's competencies and ways of working.

Even though this refers to 'intra-academic mobility', shared understandings, established procedures, and trust in each other are also potential benefits of intersectoral mobility.

Studies on the process and success factors of intersectoral mobility are, however, scare to nonexistent. Moreover, the role of the host organisation is rarely mentioned in literature. The host organisation is affected by intersectoral mobility, as the organisation will host an academic researcher (or industry representative) for an extended period and needs to have structures to manage this.

Due to this, the purpose of the chapter is to increase the likelihood of successful mobility by presenting a checklist for the process of intersectoral mobility.

3. Intersectoral Mobility in this Chapter

Intersectoral mobility can be divided into two different kinds of mobility:

Permanent intersectoral mobility. When an individual changes sector permanently. An example is an academic that begin to work in industry.
Temporary intersectoral mobility. When an individual takes on a temporary position for a defined period.

This chapter focuses on temporary intersectoral mobility by academics. We take the perspective of the university and differentiate between incoming academics and outgoing academics. An incoming academic is, hence, employed in industry and spend their mobility at a host university. An outgoing academic is employed by a university and spend their mobility at a host organisation, see Figure 25.1.

There is, of course, also intersectoral mobility carried out by non-academics, but these positions are usually either permanent or very temporary, for example, when an industry expert conducts a guest lecture.

3.1 Content of Mobility

The tasks and activities for temporary intersectoral mobility positions need to be decided and agreed on by the host organisation and the individual academic. The incoming academic can, for example, take on teaching responsibilities or supervision that align education and industrial needs.

Figure 25.1 Outgoing Academics from University and Incoming Academics from Non-Academic Organisations in Other Sectors

4. Intersectoral Mobility Position Process

The temporary mobility position process can be viewed in terms of a project management process, as they have similar characteristics. Both are one-time temporary tasks with defined start and end and include human resources. The aim of a project is to create something new. In the temporary mobility positions, new or deepened collaborations as well as mutual benefits are created. The temporary mobility position processes could, hence, benefit from being managed and reported as projects.

The project management process generally includes four stages: initiating, planning, executing, and closing. In this chapter, three phases that resemble the project management process stages are used:

The **pre-mobility** phase focuses on initiation and planning of the mobility positions. The **execution** phase manages activities and information needed while the mobility project runs, and **the post-mobility** phase focuses on closing the position and the activities after the closure, illustrated in Figure 25.2.

5. Factors Affecting the Intersectoral Mobility Position Process

A study was conducted to understand the factors influencing the temporary intersectoral mobility positions. First, a literature review was conducted to identify factors in literature. Then, six academics holding temporary intersectoral mobility positions, were interviewed. Two of these were outgoing academics while four were incoming academics. All six academics had a PhD degree. One contact person at a university and one contact person at a host organisation were also interviewed. The empirical data was analysed and compared with literature. The result of this study is presented in this subchapter.

The factors are described in the three different phases of the process, see Sections 5.1–5.3 and Tables 25.1–25.3. We have studied the factors from both an individual and organisational perspective and have identified factors that can have positive or/and negative effects of the mobility position.

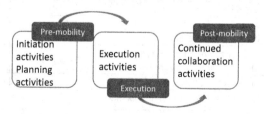

Figure 25.2 The Three Phases of a Temporary Intersectoral Mobility Position Process

Table 25.1 Factors Affecting the Pre-mobility Phase

Pre-mobility Factors	Individual	Organisation
Initiation: interest from individual	+	
Initiation: interest from both organisations		+
Strategic decision in both organisations		+
Identification of individual benefits	+	
Planning: Development of project plan with pre-defined activities	+	+
Identification of mentor at the hosting organisation	+	
Clear objectives	+	+
Mutual commitment (identification of steering committee)	+	+

Table 25.2 Factors Affecting the Execution Phase

Execution Factors	Individual	Organisation
Introduction at the host organisation and meeting the co-workers at the host organisation	+	
Employed by one organisation	+	
Continuous dialogue with mentor	+	
Project plan with clear activities and objectives	+	+
Project plan that are followed up and reviewed on annual basis with mentor and steering committee	+	+
Personal capacity building through meeting new people and network building	+	
Access to systems and e-mail, and a place to sit at the host organisation	+	
Invitations and participation in meetings at the host organisation	+	+
Continuous mutual commitment		+
Disruptions (such as Covid-19)	-	-
Cultural differences	-	-
Lack of clear objectives	-	
Lack of defined activities	-	
Too well-defined activities	-	
Change of mentor	-	-
Follow ups (too few or to many)	+ and -	+ and -
Belonging to several departments at the host organisation ('*Where do I belong?*')	-	-
No clear working tasks ('*I need to find my own working tasks and people I can work with.*')	-	
Duration of the mobility position	+ and -	+ and -
Lack of opportunities to engage in empirical research	-	

Table 25.3 Factors Affecting the Post-mobility Phase

Post-mobility Factors	Individual	Organisation
New collaboration projects	+	+
New job tasks	+ and -	
Continued and deepened collaboration between the organisations		+
No plan for exit	-	-
Mobility position might not be an academic merit as industry does not focus on publications	-	
New structures for collaboration		+

5.1 Pre-mobility Phase

Before the temporary intersectoral mobility position begins, the position needs to be initiated and planned properly. The initiation decision can derive from the university, the organisation, or an individual academic. The position can be initiated to support a long-term collaboration between strategic partners or on an individual level as part of competence development. In the study, it was most common that the initiative derived from the individual as part of competence development. Often, the individual had an existing relationship with the host organisation and wanted to deepen the relationship. In other cases, the initiation of a temporary mobility position was a strategic decision from the organisation or the university.

All parties involved in the temporary intersectoral mobility position need to be informed and involved as soon as possible in the process, for mutual understanding and mutual commitment. If the initiation derives from an organisation, benefits for the individual carrying out the mobility needs to be identified. For a successful temporary mobility position, the individual needs to identify or be aware of the potential benefits at the individual level. If there is a lack of identified benefits for all involved parties, or there are only benefits for one of the parties, it will have a negative effect on the mobility.

After the initiation decision, the position needs to be planned. Important factors in this phase are the identification of clear objectives, defined activities, and a designated mentor. Depending on how these activities are managed in the pre-mobility phase, they can have positive or negative effect on the following execution phase. During this phase, it is vital that all parties have a dialogue to understand both the requirements and responsibilities of the individual and the host organisation. If not handled during the pre-mobility phase, this could negatively affect the parties during the mobility period.

In Table 25.1, the factors influencing the pre-mobility phase are listed together with the potential positive (+), negative (-) or neutral (=) effect on the individual and the host organisation.

5.2 Execution Phase

In the execution phase, the factors affecting the mobility position are more focused toward the individual than the host organisation. Factors in this phase focus on belonging, participation, and involvement at the department in the host organisation. For example, we could see positive effects when the individual academic received the same introduction as new employees at the host organisation and had access to an office space, e-mail, and systems at the host organisation.

A factor that was associated with negative effect in the execution phase derived from a feeling of '*Where do I belong?*' This is somewhat related to the duration of the position. In this study, the individuals spent 20–50 percent of full time at the host organisation for 2–3 years. After a longer period, the academics felt a belonging to both organisations, and sometimes needed to take different roles depending on situation. Another negative effect can be derived from the position being viewed as a temporary project, but, after spending an extended time in another organisation, the tasks can become permanent. This might increase the confusion of where to belong. Moreover, this is also related to what extent the individual is invited to and participate in university or organisation meetings. Place of employment was also identified as an affecting factor. The place of employment of the academics in the study differed, but the most satisfactory solution was to be employed solely by one organisation, due to current tax and pension regulations.

In the literature, the lack of opportunities for the incoming academics to engage in empirical research was identified as a factor that had negative effects. However, in our study we did not see this negative effect. Previous reports and studies write about incentives for intersectoral mobility. However, for an academic that wants to work part-time in a non-academic organisation, the temporary intersectoral mobility is not always recognised, as academic merit still derives from publication and lecturing, and less on collaboration.

A factor that could have negative effects on the position is cultural differences between the organisations and related to the resource efficiency of the individual. The non-academic organisations might not want their employees to spend more than one day per week at the university. However, in academia, teaching is, for example, often scheduled not for only one day a week, but rather spread over the whole week. Individuals acting as teachers are, furthermore, assumed to be able to answer e-mails from students expeditiously and on any day of the week. Here, there is a trade-off between resource efficiency of the individual and the ability to follow the culture at the university or non -academic organisation.

We also found that disruptions have a negative effect on the mobility. In this case, most of the individuals in the interview study were affected by the Covid-19 pandemic and the associated restrictions. They were, in some cases, not allowed to be present at the host organisation for a long period and that affected the feeling of belonging as well as pre-made plans and working tasks. Even though the Covid pandemic was an unprecedented event, we can conclude that when planning the positions, it is important to identify risks and carry out a risk analysis to be aware of how disruptions can affect the position.

5.3 Post-mobility Phase

In the post-mobility phase, and directly after the position has ended, factors identified for a successful mobility focused on continued collaboration between the parties.

The closing of and exit from the temporary mobility position can have negative effects, as both incoming and outgoing academics get new job tasks at the end of the mobility. If the new job tasks do not include work towards a deepened collaboration with the host organisation, this will affect the organisations and their collaboration negatively. The mobility position might not be seen as worthwhile, neither in academia nor at the organisation and this might negatively influence the career for the academics with a mobility position. In our study, only some of the outgoing researchers talked about conducting research in the industry where they had held their temporary position. They did, however, talk about the mutual benefits for university and industry and how they could translate their academic knowledge to the host organisation.

6. Checklist

A checklist based on the enablers and challenges previously described are summarised in Table 25.4. The checklist includes activities crucial for success in each phase of the temporal intersectoral mobility. The intended users of the checklist are the organisations and the individuals involved in the mobility and the checklist can be used as a base for dialogue between the organisation and the individual to understand what is expected for each party.

Table 25.4 Checklist for Successful Temporary Intersectoral Mobility Positions

Activity	Who is Responsible?	Done
PRE-MOBILITY PHASE		
Initiation		
1. Who initiates the mobility position?		
Planning		
2. Identification of funding opportunity		
3. Write a project proposal and anchor it within each organisation/department		
4. Reading of the funding agencies requirements for application		
5. What are the (mutual) benefits for industry, academia, and individual		
6. Identification of clear objectives		
7. Write project plan with clear working tasks		
8. Identify project manager and host department		
9. Identify mentor		
10. Identify steering committee		
11. Duration and extent of mobility position?		
12. Employment? (100% in one organisation)		
Execution		
13. Introduction at the host organisation		
14. Where to sit, access to needed systems		
15. Internal competence development?		
16. Dialogue with mentor		
17. Working tasks		
18. Annual report		
POST-MOBILITY PHASE		
Closing		
19. Plan post-mobility for the individual 6 months before the position ends.		
20. Plan continued collaboration between the organisations		

7. Conclusion

Temporary intersectoral mobility positions can contribute to both organisations and universities and can increase the collaboration between them. The individual academic is the key to span boundaries between universities and non-academic organisations. This chapter has focused on describing temporary intersectoral mobility positions and the factors affecting this process on both individual and organisational level. Depending on how the factors are managed, they can have either positive or negative effects on the mobility. Here, the checklist presented in Table 25.4 can be a support for both the organisation and the individual when planning and implementing mobility and can be a help to avoid the negative effects that can ensue.

We can conclude that the non-academic organisations, university, and individual academics will benefit from temporary intersectoral mobility in different ways:

- The benefits for the **non-academic organisation** are that they receive the latest research and can get help to solve their challenges in new innovative ways in close collaboration with an outgoing academic or they will receive the latest research from an employee acting as an incoming academic.
- The benefits for **the university** are the possibilities to better understand the requirements and challenges from industry and to deepen the relation.
- The benefits for the **individual academic** are that they can try new working tasks and individual development depending on the individual objectives. They can also create a strong base for collaborative research projects.

References

Abramo, G., D'Angelo, C. A., & Di Costa, F. (2022). The effect of academic mobility on research performance: The case of Italy. *Quantitative Science Studies*, 3(2), 345–362.

Alfano, V., Gaeta, G., & Pinto, M. (2021). Non-academic employment and matching satisfaction among PhD graduates with high intersectoral mobility potential. *International Journal of Manpower*, 42(7).

Guthrie, S., Lichten, C., Harte, E., Parks, S., & Wooding, S. (2017). *International mobility of researchers*. RAND Europe.

Melin, G., Bengtsson Jallow, A., Kuritzén, S., & Sundgren, K. (2019). *Analysis of mobility*. Technopolis Group. https://www.technopolis-group.com/wp-content/uploads/2020/06/SSF_Intersectoral-Mobility_Final-Report-191002.pdf

Millard, D. (2018). Blended and co-existing worlds in intersectoral mobilities of European PhD graduates in the social sciences and humanities. *Globalisation, Societies and Education*, 16(2), 224–240.

Netz, N., Hampel, S., & Aman, V. (2020). What effects does international mobility have on scientists' careers? A systematic review. *Research Evaluation*, 29(3), 327–351.

Nordforsk, (2014). Crossing borders – Obstacles and incentives for research mobility.

26 Publishing in Practitioner Journals

Pamela Sharkey Scott

This chapter is intended to be a practical guide to support academics wishing to publish in practitioner journals, so it is written in a non-academic, practitioner-friendly style.

Introduction

Many academics are consciously aware of the need for our research to address emerging management challenges, if only for the reason that these 'hot topics' are likely to catch the interest of journal editors and reviewers alike. Most of our research is read by academics, who write like us so can absorb our message, or who need to make an effort to read us for specific goals, such as exams or citation. Few of these academic journals are read by the audience they are potentially most useful for, practitioners. If we are to achieve meaningful economic and social impact as academics, we must make our work accessible to a wider audience.

A key means of increasing the accessibility of our work and achieving greater impact is through writing for practitioner journals (online and hardcopy), magazines, blogs and websites. Writing for this audience is not like writing for academics. Indeed, writing for practitioners demands a shift in mindset. The purpose of this chapter is to examine why we, as academics, may want to write for practitioner journals, to give guidance on identifying how our work can be made interesting to practitioners and to provide some concrete suggestions on the process of writing a paper for a practitioner journal. This chapter is not intended to be a comprehensive guide to writing for practitioners, and is not written with particular reference to any one practitioner journal. It is, however, intended to stimulate you to think about how your academic work can reach a wider audience and increase its economic and societal impact.

Why Write for Practitioners?

Why would academics wish to write for practitioners? First, engaging with practitioners demonstrates that our work makes a valuable

DOI: 10.4324/9781003459217-29

contribution to business or society at large and is not just esoteric or irrelevant except to elite or rarefied circles! Second, establishing that our work is of practical relevance and importance allows our schools and universities to access support from this broader audience. Such support includes endowments, professorial chairs, contracts for the provision of executive education, research projects and media profile and attention. For the individual, practitioner impact can provide a calling card for organizations and senior executives, enabling great research access and triggering new research questions. Publishing in practitioner journals also builds individual researcher's personal media profiles, consultancy portfolios or can be a differentiator in promotion. A third reason is that, even for well published academics, writing for practitioners is a different skill set so it adds another competency to your resume or career portfolio. Last but not least, writing in practitioner journals can be fun! Writing for academic journals is a formal process, rigorous and time consuming. Writing a short (maybe 3000 words) paper about something that you are really familiar with and involved with, in more everyday language, is not without effort, but it is more straightforward and creative, and can even be inspirational!

What Makes Papers Interesting?

If, having decided that writing for practitioners is something that you want to do, it is then necessary to identify what you can write about. This involves identifying a topic that is interesting for a practitioner audience. Much work (for example, Corley and Gioia, 2011; Magnani and Gioia, 2023; Sutton and Staw, 1995), has established what makes theory papers relevant and interesting to their target audience. Applying similar ideas to practitioner papers, and having read many, in my view, the better papers challenge existing management practices, are counterintuitive and the message is contrary to management expectations. They are intended to provide a definite 'aha moment', a revelation for the reader.

The importance of new ideas and innovative findings does not imply that academic rigor in the underlying research is not important. Both academics and practitioners are trying to make sense of what happens in a 'buzzing, blooming, confusing world' (Van de Ven, 1999), so the value of the message in your paper will still depend on the quality of your research. To demonstrate this quality, just as well-crafted theory and sophisticated methodology are required in the leading academic journals, the better practitioner publications demand well-crafted stories presented by credible authors. Often, the track record of the authors provides a measure of support for their findings and recommendations. Some journals require a succinct description of the methodology or provision of research design details in supporting documentation. The message of the paper needs to be underpinned by a new study or new perspective, as rehashing old views won't make it into the leading practitioner journals. At the same time, just as academic research joins existing conversations and extends what has gone before, practitioner interest in an area needs to be established and/or emerging. Just look at the emerging number of papers on how to cope with AI in recent times, while the concerns of remote/hybrid work are becoming more normalized!

Importantly, in addition to being of strong practitioner interest, the style of writing must be easily accessible to the practitioner audience. This demands a strong hook to capture a busy business reader and clear and engaging, well-structured content. Rather than presenting new theory, a practitioner paper is expected to provide new insights into how an existing or emerging problem can be approached in a new way, or how old solutions can be reformulated to be relevant to the 'real world'. Just one example of how this can be achieved is provided by Bova et al. (2023) in their recent publication in *Sloan Management Review* highlighting the potential of quantum computing in transforming drug development pipelines to benefit millions worldwide. Presenting new ideas that will allow practitioners to engage with such 'real world' challenges grabs attention and increases the recognition for and impact of our work.

In sum, while journals vary in their style, writing for practitioner journals demands a shift from theory to focusing on providing succinctly presented interesting insights, engaging and broadly relatable illustrations of key points, and upfront and impactful key takeaways.

The Three Steps of Writing for Practitioners

Writing for practitioners demands a different mindset to writing for academic papers. I propose that the first step is to look at your data and to ask, what can I write about bearing the above comments on what is interesting to practitioners in mind. You can then ask yourself: What is new for managers in my research, what new dimension can I contribute? What is new must be topical, of the moment, and is not likely to be as relevant to managers in five years' time. For example, following changing work patterns during Covid, there was an emerging acceptance that innovation may be negatively impacted by the drive in remote working. This prompted my collaborators and I to write about our research findings, that both conflict and collaboration are needed to drive remote innovation (Tippmann et al., 2021a). This topic was timely but not necessarily timeless!

Other approaches to identifying a topic is to ask: What is evolving in industry, what might happen, what is on the cusp of happening, what are the new ways of doing business, new impacts of technology, workplace practices, organizational structures that my work can shed light on? One way of identifying interesting topics is to ask managers what they are just starting to worry about, as this can prompt inspiration (for an example see Tippmann et al., 2021b). Another approach is to attend practitioner conferences and listen to the practitioners' conversations and the questions being asked. Engaging with leading practitioner journals is not without work!

It is important that what you write about sparks interest in the journal gatekeepers and editors, as well as practitioners. This may be a part of your study that is of most relevance to them *now*, rather than when your theoretical contribution will be published. Remembering that practitioner conversations move quicker than academic theory development is critical. Unfortunately, it is not just the speed of conversation change but it is unlikely that a practitioner journal will accept a paper that relates to a conversation which has moved on, no matter how well the paper is written. For example, a quick review of the topics of practitioner journals will see the movement of conversation from wellbeing to remote working to Equality, Diversity and Inclusion and then to AI ....

It is important to remember that your topic may grow from a germ of an idea that emerged from a research project that can be expanded and made relatable to practitioners. This requires a shift of mindset and a move from the meticulous building blocks of theory development approach. Examining what you do and identifying the most forward looking and new ideas, that are grounded in your expertise and research and publications in a particular area, is likely to offer fertile ground for practitioner insight.

In my view, identifying what is interesting is probably the greatest challenge of writing for practitioners. As authors, we are confronted with the 'novelty paradox'; on one hand, if you confirm all of the intended audience's assumptions, your work is obvious and boring as it doesn't offer anything new. On the other, if your work disconfirms all of their assumptions, it will not be credible and is likely to be rejected out of hand!

Having identified what is interesting, the second step is to ask who should I write with. Collaboration is accepted as critically important in our academic research and, similarly, collaborating is essential for practitioner publications, not just to boost the credibility of our papers but to stimulate new ideas and novel, often interdisciplinary thinking. In addition, collaborating with a senior practitioner or consultant boosts the credibility of the authors for the readers and journal editors, as it confirms the relevance of the piece to business leaders.

The third step in writing for practitioners, is to learn how to write in the style of the target journal. Remembering that the practitioner journal will not change their approach to accommodate your paper, no matter how interesting you believe it to be, is essential. Similarly to academic journals, each practitioner journal has a target audience and a particular approach to engaging with this specific audience. There is also a need to be aware of the level of manager or business leader your target journal is engaging with, as this will also determine your approach to the topic.

Getting an understanding of the journal's style may require you to read multiple papers published there, to examine the standard format and structure of their articles and to understand the dynamics of their papers. The importance of the title for engaging interest cannot be underestimated. For example, many titles ask leading questions on emerging issues (for example, Which hybrid model works best for your business?) or offer a number of solutions to current challenges (for example, 4 Phrases that Build a Culture of Curiosity). Understanding the norms of your target journal may require you to take a micro approach to analyzing a number of its papers. I suggest that these include identifying the number of sections in a 'standard' paper, number of paragraphs in a section, number and style of sentences in a paragraph, words in a sentence and the type of language adopted. Even more, the dynamics of the language and the type of verbs utilized need to be understood, so that you can adopt a similar approach. Rather than the serious and more considered, even ponderous language of academia, practitioner journals enjoy a more informal, relaxed and enthusiastic conversation with their readers.

One of the key differences between academic and practitioner journals is the use of illustrations and examples. A review of your target journal will identify how that particular publication utilizes illustrations to emphasize key points. You will need to emulate their approach in three main ways as outlined below: first to emphasize the importance of your topic and hook the reader into reading your paper, second to make complex ideas more relatable, and thirdly, to demonstrate that there is a puzzle or problem to be solved.

In emphasizing the importance of your topic, you may choose an illustration to show how your area of interest is of general importance. Taking examples of successful organizations who utilize your particular approach is often useful. For example, Anthony et al. (2023) use Amazon as an exemplar to illustrate how the tool described in their paper can be adopted for increasing the quality of discussions:

> Amazon is a great example of a company that holds data-informed dialogues. The beginnings of important meetings at Amazon are characterized by a strange sound: silence.

The second purpose of using illustrations is to make complex ideas easily and quickly relatable. For example, Hult (2023) explains marketing systems and coevolving using Starbuck's expansion into India as an illustration:

> For example, Starbucks varies its approach to global expansion depending on the marketing ecosystem it's operating within. Because India is a heavy tea market, Starbucks opted to not develop its offering within the coffee market. It relied on its joint venture partner's (Tata's) supply chain, distribution, fulfilment networks, and market-specific resources. Starbucks focused on leveraging its brand and resource complementarity with Tata in the growing Indian metro markets.

The third approach is to use illustrations to show the importance of the puzzle or problem to be solved by your paper.

> BCG research has found that 15% of companies outperform their industry in more than 80% of crises
>
> (Reeves et al., 2020)

Vivid, up-to-date illustrations can be used to bring your practitioner paper to life and to engage the editor and the reader.

In sum, writing for practitioners is an accessible means of increasing the impact of our research, but it does require a shift in mindset from publishing in academic journals. By examining what aspects of our research is interesting from a practitioner perspective and presenting our ideas in a relatable way, in the style of the target journal, we can open our work to a new and increasingly recognized audience. And sometimes, it can also be fun!

References

Anthony, S., Painchaud, N. and Parker, A. 2023. Building consensus around difficult strategic decisions. *Harvard Business Review*, Digital Article, Oct.

Bova, F., Goldfarb, A. and Melko, R. 2023. The business case for quantum computing. *MIT Sloan Management Review*, 64(3), pp. 31–37.

Corley, K.G. and Gioia, D.A. 2011. Building theory about theory building: What constitutes a theoretical contribution? *Academy of Management Review*, 36(1), pp. 12–32.

Hult, G. Tomas M. 2023. 8 best practices for creating a compelling customer experience. *Harvard Business Review*, (March).

Magnani, G. and Gioia, D. 2023. Using the Gioia Methodology in international business and entrepreneurship research. *International Business Review*, 32(2), p. 102097.

Reeves, M., Nanda, S., Whitaker, K., and Wesselink, E. 2020. Becoming an all-weather company. [online article] BCG. https://www.bcg.com/publications/2020/how-to-become-an-all-weather-resilient-company

Sutton, R.I. and Staw, B.M. 1995. What theory is not. *Administrative Science Quarterly*, pp. 371–384.

Tippmann, E., Sharkey Scott, P. and Gantly, M. 2021a. Driving remote innovation through conflict and collaboration. *Sloan Management Review*, (April).

Tippmann, E., Sharkey Scott, P. and Gantly, M. 2021b. Which hybrid work model is best for your business? *Harvard Business Review*, (August).

Van De Ven, A.H. 1999. The buzzing, blooming, confusing world of organization and management theory: A view from Lake Wobegon University. *Journal of Management Inquiry*, 8(2), 118–125.

27 Generating Applied Impact Through Executive Doctoral Programs in Business and Management

John A. Parnell

Business schools navigate two distinct worlds. Academically, they seek to develop, extend, and refine theories by employing advanced and sophisticated research methods. Professionally, they strive to understand what drives organizational success in an increasingly complex, interconnected, and politicized world. These tasks appear compatible on the surface. As Kurt Lewin (1945) counseled, "There is nothing so practical as a good theory." However, the domains we call theory and practice often collide.

The overlap and discontinuity of theory and practice inform a rigor–relevance challenge that has confounded the field for decades (Hughes et al., 2011; Simon, 1967; Van de Ven, 1989; Worrell, 2009). Proponents of theory development promote methodological rigor as a prerequisite to relevance, while advocates of practice underscore timely, real-world relevance (Mintzberg & Waters, 1985). Ideally, research is both rigorous and relevant, but executing studies that excel in both realms is an arduous task. Efforts to find common ground are legion and span decades (e.g., Clinebell & Clinebell, 2008; Paterson et al., 2018), but no consensus has emerged.

Against this backdrop, stakeholders—governments, accreditors, organizations, and even students—want to understand better how institutions *impact* their constituencies and help solve pressing problems in organizations. These stakeholders may not be conversant with the rigor–relevance debate. Still, they inherently favor relevance because they are more familiar with business and social problems than with the methods academics employ to evaluate them. The demand for more impact does not necessarily translate into more relevance at the expense of rigor, but at a minimum, it requires academics to think more clearly about the value of their work. Focusing on impact means engaging in academic debates and publishing articles is not enough. The onus is on business schools to explain how their work impacts the profession and society.

DOI: 10.4324/9781003459217-30

The metrics used to demonstrate impact can vary based on a business school's mission, which is often embedded in how they understand the theory–practice and rigor–relevance quandaries. The mission invariably includes a teaching component, although its value vis-à-vis research varies substantially across institutions. Business schools that award the Ph.D. degree tend to focus more on research and emphasize methodological rigor. In contrast, those that award only master's and baccalaureate degrees focus more on teaching and emphasize more practical, relevant, or "applied" research. The theory–practice and rigor–relevance distinctions in business schools create a foundation for *theoretical and applied impact*.

There is no silver bullet for delivering impact, but Doctor of Business Administration (DBA) and other executive-oriented programs emphasizing applied research can foster it in unique ways if they are designed and implemented correctly. For parsimony, the term "DBA" is used in this chapter to connote any doctoral program designed to promote an advanced understanding of business and organizations by emphasizing both research and practice. Such programs focus on business practice, teach research methods, and require a dissertation. Some students pursue a DBA to transition from industry to academia, while others seek greater expertise as practitioners or consultants. Further, the discussion of DBAs in this chapter includes programs that go by other names, such as EDBA, Doctor of Management, or Doctor of Leadership. Some Ph.D. programs espouse applied goals and, arguably, resemble a DBA program, and vice versa. However, a detailed discussion about degree nomenclature is beyond the scope of this chapter.

Research on applied doctoral programs in business is limited, although distinctions between DBA and Ph.D. programs have been chronicled (MacLennan et al., 2018; Sarros et al., 2005; Tushman et al., 2007). Most DBA programs have been launched by Ph.D.-granting institutions seeking to expand a research orientation to the applied space and MBA-granting institutions seeking to expand a practice orientation to the research space. If one views rigor and relevance simplistically as a continuum, the proliferation of DBA programs can be understood as an effort by business schools on either end to address a void in the middle, by supporting research that balances rigor and relevance in ways that produce impact. Table 27.1 compares Ph.D., DBA, and MBA programs. DBA programs occupy the middle column because they typically retain some characteristics of MBA programs while transitioning to a research context. Placing the DBA between the MBA and Ph.D. is not intended to position it as an advanced MBA or a lightweight alternative to the Ph.D.

Table 27.1 Graduate Programs in Business

Characteristic	Traditional Ph.D.	Executive DBA	Master's (MBA)
Emphasis	Rigor	Rigor–relevance	Relevance
Interest	Theory development	Application of theory	Immediate practice
Program Focus	Depth	Depth–breadth	Breadth
Focus	Constructs	Constructs–context	Context
Goal	Exhaustive	Informed judgment	Timely, rule-of-thumb
Impact Opportunity	Theoretical impact: Progress toward comprehensive understanding	Applied impact: Enhance and leverage existing understanding	N/a

Understanding how DBA programs can foster impact begins with understanding how DBA and traditional Ph.D. programs are similar and different in ways that extend beyond rigor and relevance. Both programs seek to help students develop a deeper understanding of organizations and business. Theory is an important part of achieving this goal in any doctoral program, but the DBA views theory as foundational to the process, not an output per se. In this respect, the DBA is qualitatively different from a traditional Ph.D. program.

Managing rigor and relevance in DBA programs begins with program design. An applied doctoral experience cannot prepare students to deliver impact unless it teaches them how to consume and critique research from different genres. It should also include sufficient content that teaches students how to design and execute a quality research project. Such programs can provide the foundation for students to deliver *applied impact* by making a measurable difference appropriate for practice.

Rigor requires precision and depth, so traditional Ph.D. programs usually require an intense focus on a specific discipline or sub-discipline. Relevance requires a greater understanding of how disparate parts should work together, so content coverage in DBA programs tends to be more generalist. For example, a Ph.D. student interested in strategic management might take numerous seminars on the economic foundations of strategy, organizational theory, capabilities, collaborative strategy, corporate strategy, corporate governance, nonmarket strategy, and so on. A DBA student or "scholar-practitioner" (Hay, 2004; Wolfberg, 2017) interested in strategic management might take one or two strategy seminars complemented by coursework in other functional business areas. A successful Ph.D. student obtains extensive knowledge about academic research in the strategy field. In contrast, a successful DBA student receives broader academic exposure in the strategy realm.

The extent to which a DBA student augments this training with high-level organizational experience provides them with a potential for impact that differs from that of traditional Ph.D. students in ways that are difficult to calculate.

DBA and Ph.D. programs tend to approach writing differently. Tourish (2020) provided numerous examples of academic writing that is unnecessarily verbose, confusing, or tautological. Indeed, all doctoral students should be taught to write clearly and in ways that practitioners, not just other academics, can understand. DBA students are in a unique position to tackle this problem. Whereas traditional Ph.D. students are taught to emphasize precision and acknowledge all the shortcomings of their studies and arguments, DBA students often and instinctively write more authoritatively but from a broader perspective. Indeed, DBA programs are often distinguished by a focus on writing for a generalist business audience. Because of their bent toward practice, preference for more immediate applications, and a shared disdain for academic prose, the DBA's path to accessible writing may be fraught with fewer obstacles.

The DBA Distinction: Constructs vs. Context

Another way of thinking about how DBA and traditional Ph.D. programs can drive different types of impact is to consider how context and constructs provide unique, complementary perspectives on business problems. Context refers to the circumstances, surroundings, and background of a study. It provides a framework for implementing the project. Constructs refer to phenomena that cannot be measured perfectly. We identify and measure proxies for constructs, such as profits for business performance or income for poverty status. A deep understanding of both context and constructs is a prerequisite for impactful research.

Traditional Ph.D. students are taught to focus on constructs. For example, they might be interested in how one's concerns about safe and healthy work environments influence job satisfaction and organizational commitment. They emphasize accurate construct measurement and warn against extrapolating findings from one study across many nations, sectors, and cultures. They focus on theory development and execute their studies for highly ranked academic journals (Hambrick, 2007; Tourish, 2020). However, because they lack a deep understanding of a specific sector or type of organization—a context—they might struggle to provide straightforward advice for practitioners. Instead, their practical recommendations are brief and lack particular action. They often suggest that companies and managers "consider" a trend or "reevaluate" their environments, leaving the details to the reader. Their focus is on advancing knowledge about the construct, so limited attention to context is not a concern.

DBA students often focus on context. They typically understand how things work in their organization and industry because of their experience. They are less concerned with delineating constructs, developing theories, and testing models and focus more on identifying solutions within their enterprises. DBA students see practitioner advice, not theory building, as the desired ends of a research study and are more susceptible to bias in their work. The lack of contextual knowledge is the traditional scholar's greatest challenge. Because they are conscious of the gaps in their knowledge caused by their research constraints, many traditional academics experience anxiety and doubt what they really know.

The contextual focus, grounded in experience, is the DBA's greatest asset and liability because they can see how research might address significant problems and enhance their organizations. It also enables them to fill the gap between academics and practitioners and offer relevant, evidence-based guidance for managers. However, the Dunning-Kruger effect can be a problem (see Kruger & Dunning, 1999). Because they "don't know what they don't know," they often overestimate their capacity to transfer their familiarity and comprehension of one situation to another. Scholar-practitioners are prone to overgeneralize. They fail to recognize how their study relates to other situations. In contrast, traditional scholars tend to undergeneralize because they do not understand the significance of context.

Leveraging DBA Programs for Applied Impact

The construct–context distinction is linked to differences in program goals. Ph.D. students seek a comprehensive understanding of the field and are often taught that a good study identifies more research questions than it answers. In contrast, to a DBA student, a good study answers a question, which permits policy-makers and practitioners to wield informed action and scholars to move on to another question. As scholar-practitioners, DBA students can promote impact by closing the loop.

At the extremes, some DBA students prefer to "skip practice and play the game," while some Ph.D. students are content to stay on the sideline. In other words, DBA students are inclined to launch a research endeavor or pontificate about a topic with limited knowledge and learn as they go. As a result, they are prone to oversights and avoidable mistakes. In contrast, Ph.D. students are trained to plan their studies meticulously and identify all the limitations in advance. They view each project as part of a "research stream" with little or no intent to resolve a problem. *Both extremes limit potential impact.* The former produces studies that are not grounded in a clear understanding of the literature or practice, while the latter often generates more questions than answers.

Given the distinctions of DBA scholarship, there are several ways a DBA program can contribute to institutional impact. First, DBA programs can facilitate cultural change inside and outside of the classroom. Because DBA students often have extensive contextual knowledge, they can contribute to faculty conversations, especially about current issues and challenges. Business schools can leverage this by promoting a "give and take" environment with DBA students. Doing so not only helps students see the world from other industrial and organizational contexts but can provide a "reality check" for faculty and help change the culture of an institution detached from practice. Traditional scholars often pursue impact by explaining what ought to happen, while scholar-practitioners pursue impact by identifying what works.

Second, DBA programs provide unique opportunities for research collaboration, especially when most faculty members in a business school were trained in traditional Ph.D. programs. Traditional scholars are often trained to research non-controversial, narrow, discipline-specific topics, where data is easily obtained and the prospects for journal publication are high. As a result, they might overlook important business problems that are controversial, cross-disciplinary, and otherwise difficult to study and publish. Such problems might pique the interest of engaged scholars who have experienced them. Moreover, DBA students who work with faculty on research projects can often provide access to data and can help interpret the findings. The impact potential is excellent when scholar-practitioners steeped in context work with faculty who understand research design and the literature.

Third, DBA faculty can encourage impact by promoting development and activities specific to DBAs, such as publishing in practice-oriented journals (e.g., *Engaged Management Review*) and presenting their work at conferences that focus on applied research (e.g., Engaged Management Scholarship). Such venues can reinforce a healthy balance of rigor and relevance and promote applied impact.

Finally, business school faculty can encourage and celebrate the scholarly contributions of their DBA students. The research they do—individually or under the direction of a faculty member—contributes to institutional impact. Moreover, DBA faculty can help students develop dissertations iteratively and balance rigor and relevance (Mathiassen, 2017). High rigor is typically required by traditional Ph.D. programs, even at the expense of a more relevant study. But many DBA students want to create an engaging and pertinent study that uses their thoughts and experience. Without a solid research design that can answer research questions, an intriguing and relevant study is useless. Business faculty are in a unique position to provide this expertise.

Challenges for Delivering Applied Impact

The "constructs versus context" dilemma helps explain some common challenges DBA students experience. First, they frequently emphasize earlier research less because they highly value recent experience. Scholar-practitioners may read several articles to understand what others have done, but they may already have ideas about organizing a study. They undervalue the significance of specific research objectives, construct definitions, legitimate and trustworthy metrics, and similar factors. Faculty should be aware of this tendency and mentor their students accordingly.

Second, scholar-practitioners frequently fail to explicitly articulate their notions of interest early because they are more interested in context. Because they tend to think in contextual terms, they might not define a problem well. For example, a DBA student with two decades of management experience in the fast-food industry is well acquainted with turnover challenges. Resolved to reduce turnover once and for all, she might focus her research attention on reasons fast-food workers quit their jobs. However, the insight required to design and carry out a study on the topic involves knowledge about turnover in other industries and potential drivers of turnover, such as job satisfaction, economic conditions, and even immigration. Scholars with traditional training are better qualified to foresee these issues early on and help students shift their attention accordingly. A DBA student with extensive experience and interesting ideas cannot wield impact without the appropriate guidance from mentors who can help them frame problems and design executable studies.

Third, most DBA students lead busy lives and study part-time. They approach their studies to complement their ongoing careers. They are successful in industry in part because they have learned to multitask, engineer shortcuts, and cull salient takeaways from large swaths of data and literature expediently. They might not see the need to develop familiarity with the academic literature by completing an extensive literature review before launching a study. Convinced they already understand an issue well, they are susceptible to confirmation bias and content to peruse a few studies that reinforce their mindset. Moreover, many DBA students have mixed views about academic research partly because it emphasizes rigor over relevance. They might lack the patience required to digest large volumes of literature.

These challenges can be curtailed when faculty in a business school understand the fundamental differences between traditional and applied doctoral programs and oversee their programs in several ways. First, a DBA program should be treated as a distinct entity, not a lesser version of a Ph.D. Some faculty with traditional research backgrounds misunderstand the purpose of DBA programs. Professors who work with DBA students should explain to their colleagues how DBAs can help address the rigor–relevance challenge and create a different type of impact.

Second, business schools should promote faculty-student engagement. Many DBA programs are designed with part-time, weekend, hybrid, or online formats. Students in such programs can easily be overlooked, but they can be valuable resources.

Third, business schools should take DBA dissertations seriously. An applied perspective is appropriate for important, cross-disciplinary, hands-on topics like crisis management (Parnell, 2021). Moreover, acknowledging a rigor–relevance tradeoff does not mean rigor is unimportant. Compromises related to rigor are appropriate when they promote greater relevance. Put another way, a DBA student might enjoy more flexibility in rigor when carrying out a dissertation, but only if it helps address a complex problem in a more timely or productive way. Appropriate tradeoffs increase the burden on students to explain the relevance and, ultimately, demonstrate practical impact.

An applied dissertation that balances rigor and relevance is not a superficial version of a traditional dissertation. Any sacrifices in rigor must be reasonable and balanced with a heightened emphasis on relevance. For example, suppose a student wanted to investigate how workers responded to changes in the workplace associated with Covid early on during the pandemic. A rapid data collection would likely include newly developed survey items, and a cross-industry sample might be necessary to measure ongoing responses. Such an approach would help the student analyze the results and craft insights for organizations as early as possible but might be more susceptible to common method bias (Jordan & Troth, 2020). The compromise in rigor might be warranted, but the tradeoff requires the student to focus more intently on relevance—how organizations should interpret the changes and respond decisively. Understanding the managing the tradeoff is fundamental to helping the student leverage a dissertation for impact.

Conclusion

The demands by stakeholders for impact are changing how business schools think about, carry out, and report their research activities. Faculty and DBA students engaged in applied scholarship are in a unique position to generate research that makes a significant impact in ways stakeholders can understand.

Like traditional Ph.D. students, scholar-practitioners can only contribute to impact if they execute their craft well. DBA programs should not be viewed and managed as advanced MBA programs. The context with which MBA students are familiar is valuable and can lead to impact but is ancillary to constructs. Organizational experience can provide a doctoral student with keen insights, but it is most useful in concert with an understanding of academic literature on constructs of interest. A proper balance of rigor and relevance is appropriate for applied impact, but students in applied doctoral programs can deliver impact through high relevance only if they maintain reasonable rigor.

References

Clinebell, S. K., & Clinebell, J. M. (2008). The tension in business education between academic rigor and real-world relevance: The role of executive professors. *Academy of Management Learning & Education*, 7(1), 99–107. doi:10.5465/AMLE.2008.31413867

Hambrick, D. C. (2007). The field of management's devotion to theory: Too much of a good thing? *Academy of Management Journal*, 50, 1346–1352.

Hay, G. W. (2004). Executive PhDs as a solution to the perceived relevance gap between theory and practice: A framework of theory–practice linkages for the study of the executive doctoral scholar-practitioner. *International Journal of Organizational Behavior*, 7(2), 375–393.

Hughes, T. I. M., Bence, D., Grisoni, L., O'Regan, N., & Wornham, D. (2011). Scholarship that matters: Academic–practitioner engagement in business and management. *Academy of Management Learning & Education*, 10(1), 40–57. doi:10.5465/AMLE.2011.59513272

Jordan, P. J., & Troth, A. C. (2020). Common method bias in applied settings: The dilemma of researching in organizations. *Australian Journal of Management (Sage Publications Ltd.)*, 45(1), 3–14. doi:10.1177/0312896219871976

Kruger, J., & Dunning, D. (1999). Unskilled and unaware of it: How difficulties in recognizing one's own incompetence lead to inflated self-assessments. *Journal of Personality & Social Psychology*, 77(6), 1121–1134. doi:10.1037/0022-3514.77.6.1121

Lewin, K. (1945). The research center for group dynamics at Massachusetts Institute of Technology. *Sociometry*, 8, 126–135.

MacLennan, H., Piña, A., & Gibbons, S. (2018). Content analysis of DBA and PhD dissertations in business. *Journal of Education for Business*, 93(4), 149–154. doi:10.1080/08832323.2018.1438983

Mathiassen, L. (2017). Designing engaged scholarship: From real-world problems to research publications. *Engaged Management Review, 1*(1), Article 2.

Mintzberg, H., & Waters, J. A. (1985). Of strategies, deliberate and emergent. *Strategic Management Journal, 6,* 257–272.

Parnell, J. A. (2021). An ounce of prevention: What promotes crisis readiness and how does it drive performance? *American Business Review, 24*(1), 90–113.

Paterson, T. A., Harms, P. D., & Tuggle, C. S. (2018). Revisiting the rigor–relevance relationship: An institutional logics perspective. *Human Resource Management, 57*(6), 1371–1383. doi:10.1002/hrm.21911

Sarros, J. C., Willis, R. J., Fisher, R., & Storen, A. (2005). DBA examination procedures and protocols. *Journal of Higher Education Policy & Management, 27*(2), 151–172. doi:10.1080/13600800500046446

Simon, H. A. (1967). The business school: A problem in organizational design. *Journal of Management Studies, 4,* 1–16.

Tourish, D. (2020). The triumph of nonsense in management studies. *Academy of Management Learning & Education, 19*(1), 99–109. doi:10.5465/amle.2019.0255

Tushman, M. L., Fenollosa, A., McGrath, D. N., O'Reilly, C., & Kleinbaum, A. M. (2007). Relevance and rigor: Executive education as a lever in shaping practice and research. *Academy of Management Learning & Education, 6*(3), 345–362. doi:10.5465/AMLE.2007.26361625

Van de Ven, A. H. (1989). Nothing is quite so practical as a good theory. *Academy of Management Review, 14*(4), 486–489. doi:10.5465/AMR.1989.4308370

Wolfberg, A. (2017). Narrowing the dissemination gap: Genres for practitioner scholarship. *Engaged Management Review, 1*(1), article 1.

Worrell, D. L. (2009). Assessing business scholarship: The difficulties in moving beyond the rigor–relevance paradigm trap. *Academy of Management Learning & Education, 8*(1), 127–130. doi:10.5465/AMLE.2009.37012187

28 Unleashing Organisational Potential

Paul Jones and Keith Schofield

For any organisation, harnessing the latent potential of its workforce will help maximise current and future success. Within higher education, the demands placed on employees are increasing (Naidoo-Chetty & Du Plessis, 2021) with competition to excel in league tables, rankings, and student attraction growing year on year, and the way that society interacts with education changing (Kaplan, 2021).

> **Question: How do we make the most of employee potential within an organisation?**

Within higher education, two broad employee groups exist, i.e., academic (those focused on the delivery of teaching, research, and/or knowledge exchange) and professional services (those who support those activities and operate core organisational functions). Both groups are important for organisational success in higher education, particularly their interaction and mutual influence (Gibbs & Kharouf, 2022; Briody et al., 2021; Kallenberg, 2020; Gornitzka & Larsen, 2004). We cannot continue to rely on asking staff to work more hours, working them harder and faster. Rather, we need to raise efficiency, effectiveness, and energy levels, and avoid excessive workload and under-resourcing (a cause of low engagement, increased stress, and poor work–life balance) (Mudrak et al., 2018; Melin et al., 2014; Rothmann & Jordaan, 2006). This chapter will explore ways in which we can better understand staff that work in universities, utilise motivational theory (for ourselves and others), and develop an environment in which employees can thrive.

> **Reflect: Questions are provided throughout the chapter to enable the reader to reflect on their own practices and to help drive future success in universities.**

DOI: 10.4324/9781003459217-31

Measuring Performance

Organisational performance is complicated. It is difficult to comprehend and can be measured in lots of different ways. For instance, you can take a results-based approach to measuring performance, which can take the form of a balanced scorecard (Kaplan & Norton, 1992). This approach has received a lot of positive attention as well as a lot of criticism (Cokins, 2010; Watson, 2021). A well-established approach is to use behaviourally anchored rating scales, each scale representing a different job dimension (Pounder, 1999). In practice, there are usually 5-10 of these scales used, and they are decided consensually by all employees. More recently, an updated version of this, known as the 'behavioural observation scale', provides an idea of frequency. While this behavioural approach is considered both reliable and accurate, managers often struggle with the sheer volume of data available, which can lead to bias (Bohlander & Snell, 2010). These methods, among others, demonstrate the difficulty and variance in measuring performance. What they do have in common though, is the idea that measuring performance will lead to increased activity. Therefore, it is easy to imagine that all organisations will have some form of performance measurement that has been agreed upon, though they may vary considerably. In hgher education, that could take the form of league tables, the quality and quantity of research, teaching, and knowledge exchange, the ability to develop societal impact, or increasing customer and stakeholder satisfaction, amongst many others (Abadi et al., 2019; Abubakar et al., 2018). The act of providing a target alone does not mean people will behave as you expect, and it is important to understand the influences that can affect behaviour, and, therefore, performance.

Understanding Drive and Motivation

Understanding people, their behaviours, motivations, and the factors that influence them is a complex task. As far back as 1890, it was suggested by William James (1890) that his 'instinct theory' could explain human behaviour and motivation. He believed that innate, automatic behaviours (instincts) were triggered by stimuli (particularly basic survival needs) and could explain a wide range of human activities. This was the first psychological theory on motivation; however, philosophers have been debating the reason why people act in the way they do for a lot longer. For instance, social contract theory (Rousseau, 1762), idealism (Kant, 1785), nihilism (Nietzsche, 1886), and determinism (Spinoza, 1677), as well as the thinking of many other philosophers, have all contributed towards our understanding of people and are the basis for many motivational theories.

The hierarchy of needs (Maslow, 1943, 1954, 1970) is one of the more popularised theories on motivation. It provides a clear structure, and takes a holistic approach to understanding human needs. At its core is a positive view of people, where it focuses on the ability of humans to grow, each with an underlying need to self-actualise (i.e., for individuals to become everything they can become). The theory is, however, not without its detractors. It has been shown to be culturally biased, with a focus on Western cultural values (Fallatah & Syed, 2018) and it overemphasises self-actualisation and individualism (Ryan & Deci, 2000a). Generally, there is a lack of empirical evidence to back up this theory, and more modern psychological research has shown these relationships to have greater complexity, to be more nuanced, and to demonstrate non-linearity. More recent theories include:

Flow Theory (Csikszentmihalyi, 1975, 1990, 1997) relates to the idea there is a state of 'flow' achievable when an individual becomes fully engaged and immersed in an activity. When the challenge of the task matches the skill level of an individual, it can lead to a sense of absorption, enjoyment, and motivation.

Goal-Setting Theory (Locke & Latham, 1990, 2002, 2006) relates to the impact of setting specific and challenging goals on motivation and performance. They suggest that clear and ambitious goals can lead to increased effort and persistence. This, in turn, relates to enhanced performance.

Expectancy-Value Theory (Atkinson, 1957; Eccles & Wigfield, 2002; Eccles, 2009) relates to cognitive psychology and focuses on the interplay between their beliefs about their ability to achieve success (expectancy) and the perceived value or importance of the goal. Both the expectation of success and its perceived significance influence the motivation to engage in a task.

For understanding the needs of individuals the focus, in this chapter, will be on **Self-Determination Theory** (Deci & Ryan, 1985; Ryan & Deci, 2000a, 2000b). Their theorising is based on the idea that performance is influenced by a person's sense of three key areas:

Autonomy: This is about matching the internal desire to have a sense of freedom, to be the director of one's own destiny.

Competence: This is about being able to control the outcome, to become a master of one's art, and to demonstrate expertise.

Relatedness: This is about a desire to interact with others, to feel a connection, and to look after and nurture those around them.

These three areas constitute an individual's basic psychological needs. Those who have these needs met are more likely to be intrinsically (internally) motivated rather than extrinsically (externally) motivated. Their theorising has been investigated, validated, and developed further by others (Ryan & Deci, 2000a; Gagné & Deci, 2005; Van den Broeck et al., 2008; Chen & Jang, 2010; Wentzel & Brophy, 2014), and, while the theorising suggests a self-determination continuum, which can provide more nuance, the focus here is on intrinsic motivation as fuel for increased performance. Those central ideas of autonomy, competence, and relatedness are fundamental for success, but how can this be applied within hgher education (see the questions below to help with reflective practice)?

Autonomy

1. **Allow for choice and decision-making:** Provide employees with opportunities to make decisions related to their work tasks, schedules, and projects.

     As *a leader, ask yourself... are employees (academic and professional services) currently involved in decision-making processes, or do decisions come from top–down directives?*

     As *an employee, ask yourself... how can I get more involved in decision-making and how can I work with management to generate opportunities to get involved?*
2. **Encourage ownership:** Let employees take ownership of their projects and initiatives.

     As *a leader, ask yourself... do employees feel a sense of ownership and responsibility for their work, or do they feel micromanaged (and does this differ between academic staff and professional services)?*

     As *an employee, ask yourself... how do I feel about the way I am managed and have I communicated to others how to get the best out of me?*
3. **Flexible work arrangements:** Offer flexibility in work hours or remote work options while also maintaining the right engagement, culture, and collaboration.

     As *a leader, ask yourself... where are the opportunities for employees (both academic and professional services) to have control over when and where they work and to identify when working together is important (and how that is going to be achieved)?*

     As *an employee, ask yourself... how do I stay productive, motivated, and connected in the workplace contributing to the development of the organisation in the broadest sense?*

Competence

1. **Clear expectations**: Set clear expectations and provide employees with well-defined goals and tasks.

   As a leader, ask yourself... do employees understand their roles and responsibilities, and are they aware of what is expected of them?

   As an employee, ask yourself... do I understand what accountability means for me in my role and am I clear on expectations from others?

2. **Skill development**: Provide opportunities for skill development and training.

   As a leader, ask yourself... are employees given the chance to enhance their skills and knowledge (and how do academic staff and professional services differ)?

   As an employee, ask yourself... how do I take responsibility for, and actively engage in, activities that are there to help my own development?

3. **Feedback and recognition**: Offer regular feedback and recognition for a job well done.

   As a leader, ask yourself... how often are employees provided with constructive feedback and acknowledgement of their contributions?

   As an employee, ask yourself... how often I have asked for feedback, and when provided, how have I embedded that into the way I work, think, or behave?

Relatedness

1. **Team-building activities**: Organise team-building activities and events to foster connections among team members.

   As a leader, ask yourself... how well do employees know and interact with their colleagues (and what barriers exist)?

   As an employee, ask yourself... what have I done to integrate myself into the team, department, or organisation and how have I built collaborations?

2. **Collaborative projects**: Encourage collaboration on projects that require employees to work together.

   As a leader, ask yourself... are there opportunities for employees to collaborate across departments or teams?

   As an employee, ask yourself... what am I working on that will allow me to work with others and how do I communicate my interest in working with them?

3. **Open communication**: Promote open communication channels and a supportive environment.

As a leader, ask yourself... do employees feel comfortable sharing their ideas, concerns, and feedback?

As an employee, ask yourself... how effective am I at sharing my ideas and concerns, and at providing feedback, and how do others perceive me in this process?

These questions highlight how self-determination theory can be applied across the three key areas. The reflections made through considering these questions can form the basis of an action plan, both at an individual level as an employee and as a leader in the organisation. However, it should be remembered that everyone is different, and we should pay attention to people as individuals. Therefore, using other techniques to gather information, and inform developments, is particularly important.

For instance, one could use **employee surveys** (to gather feedback on employee satisfaction, perceived autonomy, competence, and relatedness), embed these core constructs into **one-on-one conversations** (to understand the needs, challenges, and aspirations of individuals and groups), and **observe** team dynamics and work interactions (to identify any gaps in autonomy, competence, or relatedness).

The information gathered through these types of processes can help identify issues, patterns, or trends, that relate to motivation and engagement. The output from your reflections and data gathering, could be a tailored plan that addresses the specific needs of individual staff members, and the organisation more generally, and that processes are put in place to regularly assess the impact of any changes. It is a challenge to develop a robust plan, to ensure consistency (across different areas), and select outputs that are both meaningful and measurable. The importance of developing internal expertise to do this successfully, or indeed hiring external expertise, becomes an important consideration.

> **Question: How will you develop staff members so that they can take a lead on developing a plan, that they ensure consistency, can agree objectives that are meaningful and measurable, and have the ability to motivate and mobilise staff?**

Developing a Strength-based Approach

Another approach that has received positive attention is identifying and utilising the strengths of individuals. The Positive Organizational Scholarship movement (Cameron & Spreitzer, 2012) promotes building on strengths rather than focusing solely on weaknesses. It builds on the theory of appreciative inquiry (Cooperrider & Srivastva, 1987) that advocates strength-based organisational development. This type of thinking encourages organisations to uncover what is going well and to promote its amplification. It could be thought of as helping people to bloom, releasing their full potential.

> **An Idea to Try...**
>
> **Strengths showcases** where employees present information about the strengths they have and how they have utilised these in the workplace. It can be a way to inspire others to reach new heights with their own strength skillset and can encourage a culture of utilising individual talents. It relates back to the basic psychological needs of competence – being able to develop mastery of an art and showcasing competence to others.
>
> *As a leader, ask yourself... do you know the full range of strengths that members of your team have (and not limited to their current job)?*
>
> *As an employee, ask yourself... do I understand what my biggest strengths are and have I correctly communicated these with others?*

This idea could be developed further when thinking about the creation of roles in organisations (Wrzesniewski & Dutton, 2001). Traditionally, job analysis techniques have been used to understand roles, develop job descriptions, and specify work tasks. However, fundamental errors and bias exist in those processes, including how job-related data is collected, interpreted, and used (Furnham, 2005). It may be better to empower employees to mould their roles according to their strengths, potentially leading to higher job satisfaction and performance (Tims et al., 2012). One could liken this to building a sports team where a holistic view is taken of how the players fit together and what their strengths are. From this point of view, a person's strengths should be celebrated, and they should be encouraged to develop them further. This contrasts with the traditional view of identifying weaknesses in an individual and asking them to develop in the areas that are lacking.

Positive organisational scholarship and strength-based job design has been shown to link back to some key benefits for the workplace, including:

- Enhanced engagement of employees
- Higher levels of innovation and creativity
- Reduced levels of burnout

- Increases in productivity
- The retention of organisational talent

However, to maximise the potential for these positives, other areas need consideration. An organisation may need to reconsider its employee-related standard operating practices. For recruitment and selection, there may need to be a change from a traditional person specification to a **strengths-based needs analysis** of the team. Though given the size and complexity of universities, the redesign of work packages around employee strengths, could be a difficult and time-consuming process. It may be easier to consider reshaping the way training and development opportunities are identified and delivered. Rather than bringing people with the same skills gap together (which is a traditional development approach), those who have the same strengths could come together to find ways to enhance their strengths further and build **communities of excellence**. For this to work, there would have to be a focus on helping employees recognise their strengths (this does not always come naturally), the promotion of self-awareness as a key skill for the workplace, and a general focus on personal growth and development. It makes sense to encourage individuals to take ownership of their developmental journey, so that they are enthused about their potential and that they receive positive feedback (through an appreciation of their strengths).

> Self-development is personal development, with the person taking primary responsibility for their own learning and for choosing the means to achieve this. Ultimately, it is about increasing your capacity and willingness to take control over, and be responsible for, events.
>
> Pedler et al., 2013, p. 5

Done well, and encouraged effectively, personal development (whether you are an academic or professional services member of staff) can meet all three of the psychological needs outlined by Deci and Ryan (1985): autonomy, competence, and relatedness.

Cultivating a Fertile Culture for Growth

The motivational aspects of performance are clearly articulated above, particularly their link to the psychological needs of employees. To release potential, we need to do more than understand and harness individual drivers. Organisational culture has an important influence on employee behaviour, decision-making, and goal achievement. It is described as the shared values, beliefs, norms, and practices that shape the identity of, and the behaviours within, an organisation (Cameron & Quinn, 2011). Schein (2010) suggested that culture can be understood at three levels: symbols and behaviours; explicitly stated beliefs; and unconscious beliefs. Denison (1990) preferred to describe four elements: mission; adaptability; involvement; and consistency. Whichever model is chosen, and there are others available, they all provide a framework to identify an organisation's culture and to critique how the values, beliefs, and behaviours can be improved and how it can lead to enhanced performance.

As an example, it has been shown that higher levels of innovation and customer satisfaction are generated when a culture emphasises employee engagement, open communication, and adaptability

10 Strategies for Measuring and Developing Organisational Culture

(Cooke & Rousseau, 1988; Schein, 2010; Cameron & Quinn, 2011; CIPD, 2011, Goffee & Jones, 2013)

- **Conduct Cultural Assessment**: Initiating a comprehensive cultural assessment, by using a validated tool (e.g., organizational culture assessment), will help an organisation understand its current cultural baseline and plan future development.
- **Define Core Values**: Values act as a compass for desired behaviours and cultural norms, forming the foundation of an effective culture. Employees at all levels must be engaged in defining and refining the organisation's core values. It is essential that these align with the organisation's mission and strategy.
- **Foster Leadership Alignment**: It is crucial for leaders and their teams to align with the desired culture. Additional training and support will help leaders model the cultural values and behaviours effectively, reinforcing organisational consistency.
- **Establish Feedback Mechanisms**: To ensure effectiveness, it is crucial to conduct regular employee surveys and feedback mechanisms to measure cultural alignment and monitor progress. This enables organisations to continuously refine their cultural journey and critique different forms of initiative.
- **Encourage Inclusion and Diversity**: Develop initiatives that promote diversity and inclusion. Embrace diversity of thought, background, and perspective to create a culture that values and leverages differences.
- **Empower Employee Engagement**: Create opportunities for employees to contribute ideas and solutions empowering them to take ownership of their work and encourage active participation in decision-making processes.

- **Recognise Cultural Champions**: Identify and celebrate employees who embody the desired culture. Recognising and rewarding them reinforces cultural values and encourages others to follow.
- **Implement Ongoing Training**: Offer regular training programmes focused on enhancing cultural awareness, emotional intelligence, and cross-cultural competence. These programmes will help develop a more inclusive and adaptable culture.
- **Align HR Practices**: Ensure that human resource policies, procedures, and practices align with the desired culture. From recruitment and onboarding to performance evaluations, every aspect of HR should reinforce culture.
- **Monitor and Adjust**: Regularly monitor cultural indicators and evaluate performance metrics. Make necessary adjustments to cultural development initiatives to align with evolving organisational needs.

(Cameron & Quinn, 2011; O'Reilly & Chatman, 1996). Conversely, when the culture has high levels of toxicity, distrust, and rigidity, it can hinder creativity, collaboration, and other positive markers (Schneider et al., 2013). To create an effective culture, leaders in the organisation must model positive behaviours, make informed decisions, and adopt a leadership style that aligns with the company's values (Schein, 2010). Additionally, the organisation's values must be clear, communication consistent, and HR practices must align with the cultural goals set (Cooke & Rousseau, 1988).

Universities have an opportunity to leverage culture as a strategic advantage for success through its measurement and development. The many factors that can influence the release of potential have not all been covered here, such as communication techniques, effective leadership styles, and utilising emotional intelligence. This is the start of developing university environments that encourage change, understand individual drivers, and where employees are encouraged to become agents of innovation, growth, and success.

Reflect on These Final Questions to Unlock Your Full Potential and Inspire Others:

- How can your university's culture impact the willingness of employees to express their potential?
- What are the bureaucratic barriers that exist within your organisation and how can they be overcome?
- What strategies can your leaders adopt to encourage open and transparent communication within their teams?

- In what ways can cross-functional collaboration enhance your university's ability to tap into its hidden potential?
- How might your university balance the preservation of its core values with the need for cultural adaptation?
- How can the insights from motivational theories and organisational culture shape strategies for releasing potential in your university?
- How can you foster a culture of innovation and enhanced performance through utilising the strengths of staff?
- How can your university's HR team design learning and development programmes that cater to individual needs, fostering skill growth and personal potential?
- What specific steps can your leaders take to encourage job crafting and support employees in aligning their roles with their strengths?
- What practical approaches can your university adopt to create an inclusive leadership style that embraces diverse perspectives and maximises potential?
- How does the leadership style within the university foster a culture of potential and growth within their teams?
- What strategies can the leaders in the university use to enhance their emotional intelligence and effectively connect with their employees, promoting a sense of belonging and unleashing potential?

References

Abadi, S., Widyarto, S., & Shukor, N. S. A. (2019). Customer and Stakeholder Perspective Using Analytical Hierarchy Process Method for Evaluation Performance of Higher Education. *International Journal of Supply Chain Management*, 8(3), 1057–1064.

Abubakar, A., Hilman, H., & Kaliappen, N. (2018). New Tools for Measuring Global Academic Performance. *Sage Open*, 8(3), doi: 10.1177/2158244018 790787

Atkinson, J. W. (1957). Motivational Determinants of Risk-Taking Behavior. *Psychological Review*, 64(6), 359–372.

Bohlander, G. W., & Snell, S. A. (2010). *Managing Human Resources*. South-Wester Cengage Learning.

Briody, E. K., Rodriguez-Mejía, F. R., & Berger, E. J. (2021). Professional Staff Making a Difference: Cultural Change in Higher Education. *Innovative Higher Education*, 47, 297–325.

Cameron, K. S. & Quinn, R. E. (2011). *Diagnosing and Changing Organizational Culture: Based on The Competing Values Framework*. John Wiley & Sons.

Cameron, K. S. & Spreitzer, G. M. (eds.). (2012). *The Oxford Handbook of Positive Organizational Scholarship*. OUP USA.

Chen, B. & Jang, S. J. (2010). Motivation in Online Learning: Testing a Model of Self-Determination Theory. *Computers in Human Behavior*, 26(4), 741–752.

CIPD. (2011). *Developing Organisation Culture: Six Case Studies*. Chartered Institute of Personnel and Development. Available at: https://www.cipd.org/uk/knowledge/reports/organisational-culture-report/ (Accessed 21 October 2023).

Cokins, G. (2010). The Promise and Perils of the Balanced Scorecard. *Journal of Corporate Accounting & Finance*, 21(3), 19–28.

Cooke, R. A., & Rousseau, D. M. (1988). Behavioral Norms and Expectations: A Quantitative Approach to the Assessment of Organizational Culture. *Group & Organization Studies*, 13(3), 245–273.

Cooperrider, D. L., & Srivastva, S. (1987). Appreciative Inquiry in Organizational Life. *Research in Organizational Change and Development*, 1(1), 129–169.

Csikszentmihalyi, M. (1975). *Beyond Boredom and Anxiety: Experiencing Flow in Work and Play*. Jossey-Bass.

Csikszentmihalyi, M. (1990). *Flow: The Psychology of Optimal Experience*. Harper & Row.

Csikszentmihalyi, M. (1997). *Finding Flow: The Psychology of Engagement with Everyday Life*. Basic Books.

Deci, E. L., & Ryan, R. M. (1985). *Intrinsic Motivation and Self-Determination in Human Behavior*. Springer.

Denison, D. R. (1990). *Corporate Culture and Organizational Effectiveness*. John Wiley & Sons.

Eccles, J. S. (2009). Who Am I and What Am I Going To Do With My Life? Personal and Collective Identities as Motivators of Action. *Educational Psychologist*, 44(2), 78–89.

Eccles, J. S., & Wigfield, A. (2002). Motivational Beliefs, Values, and Goals. *Annual Review of Psychology*, 53, 109–132.

Fallatah, R. H. M., & Syed, J. (2018). A Critical Review of Maslow's Hierarchy of Needs. In: *Employee Motivation in Saudi Arabia*. Palgrave Macmillan, pp. 19–59.

Furnham, A. (2005). *The Psychology of Behaviour at Work: The Individual in the Organisation*. Psychology Press.

Gagné, M., & Deci, E. L. (2005). Self-Determination Theory and Work Motivation. *Journal of Organizational Behavior*, 26(4), 331–362.

Gibbs, T., & Kharouf, H. (2022). The Value of Co-Operation: An Examination of the Work Relationships of University Professional Services Staff and Consequences for Service Quality. *Studies in Higher Education*, 47(1), 38–52.

Goffee, R., & Jones, G. (2013). Creating the Best Workplace on Earth. *Harvard Business Review*, 91(5), 120–128.

Gornitzka, Å., & Larsen, I. M. (2004). Towards Professionalisation? Restructuring of Administrative Work Force in Universities. *Higher Education*, 47, 455–471.

James, W. (1890). *The Principles of Psychology*. Holt and Company.

Kallenberg, T. (2020). Differences in Influence: Different Types of University Employees Compared. *Tertiary Education Management*, 26, 363–380.

Kant, I. (1785). *Groundwork of the Metaphysics of Morals*. (H. J. Paton, Trans.) Harper & Row.

Kaplan, A. (2021). *Higher Education at the Crossroads of Disruption: The University of the 21st Century*. Emerald Publishing Ltd.

Kaplan, R. S., & Norton, D. P. (1992). The Balanced Scorecard: Measures that Drive Performance. *Harvard Business Review*, 70(1), 71–79.

Locke, E. A., & Latham, G. P. (1990). *A Theory of Goal Setting and Task Performance*. Prentice-Hall.

Locke, E. A., & Latham, G. P. (2002). Building a Practically Useful Theory of Goal Setting and Task Motivation: A 35-year Odyssey. *American Psychologist*, 57(9), 705–717.

Locke, E. A., & Latham, G. P. (2006). New Directions in Goal-Setting Theory. *Current Directions in Psychological Science*, 15(5), 265–268.

Maslow, A. H. (1943). A Theory of Human Motivation. *Psychological Review*, 50(4), 370–396.

Maslow, A. H. (1954). *Motivation and Personality*. Harper & Row.

Maslow, A. H. (1970). *Motivation and Personality* (2nd ed.). *Harper & Row*.

Melin, M., Astvik, W., Bernhard-Oettel, C. (2014). New Work Demands in Higher Education. A Study of the Relationship between Excessive Workload, Coping Strategies and Subsequent Health among Academic Staff. *Quality in Higher Education*, 20(3), 290–308.

Mudrak, J., Zabrodska, K., Kveton, P., Jelínek, M., Blatny, M., Šolcová, I. P., Machovcova, K. (2018). Occupational Well-being Among University Faculty: A Job Demands-Resources Model. *Research in Higher Education*, 59, 325–348.

Naidoo-Chetty, M., & Du Plessis, M. (2021). Job Demands and Job Resources of Academics in Higher Education. *Frontiers in Psychology*, 12, 1–13.

Nietzsche, F. (1886). *Beyond Good and Evil*. (W. Kaufmann, Trans.) Vintage Books.

O'Reilly C. A., & Chatman J. A. (1996). Culture as Social Control: Corporations, Cults, and Commitment. *Research in Organizational Behavior*, 18, 157–200.

Pedler, M., Burgoyne, J., & Boydell, T. (2013). *A Manager's Guide to Self-Development*. McGraw Hill Education.

Pounder, J. S. (1999). Organisational Self-Assessment in Higher Education: Experimenting with the Competing Values Model and Behaviourally Anchored Rating Scales. *Research in Post-compulsory Education*, 4(1), 39–57.

Rothmann, S., & Jordaan, G. M. E. (2006). Job Demands, Job Resources and Work Engagement of Academic Staff in South African Higher Education Institutions. *SA Journal of Industrial Psychology*, 32(4), 87–96.

Rousseau, J. J. (1762). *The Social Contract*. (G. D. H. Cole, Trans.) The Macmillan Company.

Ryan, R. M., & Deci, E. L. (2000a). Self-Determination Theory and the Facilitation of Intrinsic Motivation, Social Development, and Well-Being. *American Psychologist*, 55(1), 68–78.

Ryan, R. M., & Deci, E. L. (2000b). Intrinsic and Extrinsic Motivations: Classic Definitions and New Directions. *Contemporary Educational Psychology*, 25(1), 54–67.

Schein, E. H. (2010). *Organizational Culture and Leadership*. John Wiley & Sons.

Schneider, B., Ehrhart, M. G., & Macey, W. H. (2013). Organizational Climate and Culture. *Annual Review of Psychology*, 64, 361–388.

Spinoza, B. (1677). *Ethics*. (E. Curley, Trans.) Penguin Classics.

Tims, M., Bakker, A. B., & Derks, D. (2012). Development and Validation of the Job Crafting Scale. *Journal of Vocational Behavior*, 80(1), 173–186.

Van den Broeck, A., Vansteenkiste, M., De Witte, H., & Lens, W. (2008). Explaining the Relationships between Job Characteristics, Burnout, and Engagement: The Role of Basic Psychological Need Satisfaction. *Work & Stress*, 22(3), 277–294.

Watson, J. (2021). Balanced Scorecard Improvement. *Global Journal of Technology and Optimization*, 11(2), 1–3.

Wentzel, K. R., & Brophy, J. E. (2014). *Motivating Students to Learn*. Routledge.

Wrzesniewski, A., & Dutton, J. E. (2001). Crafting a Job: Revisioning Employees as Active Crafters of their Work. *Academy of Management Review*, 26(2), 179–201.

29 How High-Impact Academics Can Build Exceptional Academic Incubators by Leveraging Business Partnerships[1]

Victor Schiller

The growth in student demands for experiential learning has driven universities to expand capabilities to meet those demands. This has led to a rise in university-operated entrepreneurial courses along with academic incubator programs and, by implication, academic entrepreneurs. However, there is limited knowledge regarding the specific strategies, tactics, and ideas to accomplish this.

This chapter delves into the prospects for enhanced business partnerships and provides five practical suggestions for initiating, fostering, and managing academic institution relationships with business partners. Also included, is a link to a detailed online twenty-one-component Entrepreneurial Support Processes (ESPs) design canvas, with three essential elements identified and explained. The chapter concludes with twelve actionable insights, strategies, and tactics to improve academic incubator ESP design and operations.

Introduction

In recent years, entrepreneurship has emerged as a viable employment alternative, not only for individuals with considerable skills and experience but also for university students and recent graduates (Belitski and Heron, 2017; Jones et al., 2021). To meet increasing student expectations and demands for experiential learning, alongside traditional classroom sessions, universities have broadened their capabilities. This trend is confirmed by the

DOI: 10.4324/9781003459217-32

escalating rate of new venture launches by students, particularly in the science, technology, engineering, and mathematics (STEM) domains. Concurrently, there has been an elevated demand for entrepreneurial educational courses and support infrastructures, such as academic incubator programs, within global academic institutions (Agarwal et al., 2007; Fiet, 2001; Mele et al., 2022; Peterman and Kennedy, 2003). This interest in entrepreneurship training is also derived from the trend across all academic tracks, including the arts, medicine and social sciences, of increasing student demand for access to the knowledge required for successful entrepreneurship (Wu et al., 2022).

Additionally, these programs foster customer-centric thought processes, which are highly sought after by corporations intent on identifying dynamic employees and promoting innovation internally (Kwong et al., 2012; Robinson and Stubberud, 2014; Stuetzer et al., 2013). To meet student entrepreneurship demands, it is imperative for academics to not only teach business fundamentals through coursework, but also to leverage local businesses when designing and implementing experiential components, such as incubators, essential to developing and reinforcing skills and mindsets (Hausberg and Korreck, 2020). These university–business collaborations are crucial in devising relevant and engaging methodologies, curricula, and structures that adequately equip students for a competitive, dynamic, and demanding entrepreneurial future.

How Can Student Entrepreneurship Incubators Be Designed to Leverage Business Partnerships?

This chapter explores the design, operation, and optimization of student ESPs by tailoring the program to student passions, tapping into the distinct character of the community, and the strategic utilization of community assets, with a particular emphasis on leveraging local business partnerships. This student ESP will form the core of the unique Entrepreneurial Ecosystem (EE) needed to initiate and support entrepreneurial ventures. First, the EE's foundational actors and factors will be examined and clarified, with an emphasis on the critical financial sustainability concept of downward causality, or the ecosystem flywheel.

Ecosystem Actors and Factors – Fuel for Academic Incubators

An academic incubator and ESP are not standalone entities, but instead form the core of a university-centered EE. EEs provide an approach to understanding and theorizing the context and contributing components leading to business establishment and productive entrepreneurship (Amezcua et al., 2020; Antony et al., 2017; Fernandes and Ferreira, 2022; Hakala et al., 2020; Spigel, 2020). EEs consist of interdependent actors and factors, often managed by organizational sponsorship and/or orchestration actors (Isenberg, 2011; Leendertse et al., 2021; Nambisan and Baron, 2013; Pauwels et al., 2016; Stam, 2015; Stam and van de Ven, 2021). In the academic incubator case, the educational institution is the organization sponsor that will guide entrepreneurs from initial idea-search/ sensing to business launch/operation, referred to as *productive entrepreneurship* (Baumol, 1993; Bhave, 1994; Brown and Mawson, 2019; Cohen, 2013; Levie and Lichtenstein, 2010).

As part of a broader entrepreneurial community viewpoint, van de Ven (1993) argued that individual entrepreneurs could not manage all the required resources, institutions, markets, and business functions necessary to develop and commercialize their new entrepreneurial ventures. Instead, it requires both an internal team and a variety of external actors and factors to build and sustain businesses (Stam, 2015; Stam and van de Ven, 2021).

The Stam & van de Ven (2021) ten-element EE model is one example of a theoretical foundation in this study area. See Figure 29.1 from Stam (2018). Successful and sustainable small businesses are a necessary fuel for the essential downward causation or "EE Flywheel", where they feed experience, contacts, mentors, funding, and more back into the EE (Aldrich and Yang, 2014; Mason and Harrison, 2006; Spigel and Vinodrai, 2021). The EE Flywheel may not seem important for a shorter-term academic incubator, but there are two cases to consider: (1) The EE is what exists when the incubator ESP is complete, and students may want to continue their business within the EE; (2) For the academic incubator to operate and deliver maximum benefit, it will rely on actors from the larger ecosystem, such as specialists like lawyers and accountants, angel investors, successful entrepreneurs, and local businesses.

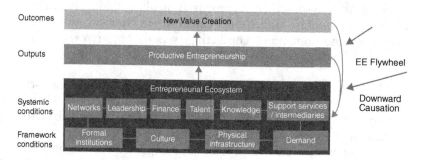

Figure 29.1 Key Elements, Outputs, and Outcomes of the Entrepreneurial Ecosystem

Source: Stam, 2018

Alignment—Managing Actor Conflicting Goals and Objectives

While Stam and van de Ven (2021) focus on visible/measurable EE elements and ecosystem conditions, Adner (2017) adds the additional concept of actor alignment, which takes an activity-centric view of interdependence, with the actor-centric "ecosystem-as-affiliation" approach:

> By starting with a clear definition of "ecosystem"—the alignment structure of the multilateral set of partners that need to interact in order for a focal value proposition to materialize—I am able to be explicit about its implications, its boundaries, and its relationship with alternative perspectives.
> (Adner, 2017, p. 40)

Aligning partner activities, actions, cooperation, and links within the EE is crucial for achieving flywheel financial sustainability. The EE consists of various stakeholders who opt to participate in, disregard, or resist EE activities. When the majority actively participate at some level, it creates the potential for remarkable synergies.

University, Student, Community, and Business Incubator Goals

Reaching alignment between EE stakeholders hinges on the systematic identification, cross-communication, and management of the diverse, and sometimes conflicting, objectives, requirements, and priorities inherent to each stakeholder group. The academic incubator manager should devote time to talk with all EE stakeholders. Pilot study interviews involving seventeen stakeholders in five EEs show that engaging and aligning a broad base of stakeholders can make the difference between a financially sustainable or collapsed effort. Table 29.1 shows the summary elements of that pilot study.

For university-based entrepreneurial incubator initiatives, there may be four primary stakeholder categories to consider, along with a unique, and sometimes conflicting, sets of objectives, requirements, and priorities.

1. **The University:** An entrepreneurship program that provides students with an immersive experiential learning activity, underpinned by formal classroom sessions. Provide an opportunity for students to navigate challenges, make mistakes, build and collaborate within teams, explore and expand professional networks, and engage with mentors.

Table 29.1 Pilot study – Entrepreneurial Ecosystem Alignment and Design

Informants	Organization	Location	Status
8	Community Investment Collaborative (CIC)	Virginia, USA	Self-sustaining – thriving
5	EU-Funded Venture Capitalstartup founders, & government agency representatives	Bulgaria	Mostly non-sustaining – collapsed
2	Bulgarian American Enterprise Fund	Bulgaria	2011 exit with a 10x return
1	Devitaki Plateau EE	Bulgaria	Sustainable – thriving
1	Alive Ventures/SCAN Foundation	California, USA	Collapsed

(Schiller, 2023)

2. **The Student:** A way to experience an entrepreneurship journey while leveraging university resources and the relative comfort of a university "safety net." Benefit from an enriched professional network and acquire knowledge beyond traditional classroom boundaries through mentorship and soft skills improvement.

3. **The Community:** This includes members from both the overarching university sphere as well as individuals from the adjoining non-academic region. This segment also includes service providers—legal practitioners, accountants, and consultants—interested in providing free expertise to student startup groups, thereby fostering entrepreneurship, and establishing a foundation for future prospective professional engagements.

4. **The Businesses:** Businesses surrounding university campuses, providing the input of "real world" stakeholders into academic incubator programs, present many advantages for student participants. Businesses might be motivated to participate for various reasons: continued engagement by university alums, talent acquisition for future staffing, the source of innovative ideas for their businesses, or to meet corporate social responsibility objectives.

Strategies and Tactics for Engaging Businesses in Academia

The inclusion of stakeholders from local businesses in the academic incubator operation framework and process can provide many services and benefits to students along with the educational institution. With the importance of partnerships between academic incubators and businesses presented, along with various methods to capitalize on these collaborations, now let us address pragmatic strategies and tactics for establishing and building these business relationships. This discussion will guide academics and other university representatives in forging crucial business alliances and engaging businesses in the academic incubation process.

1. **Assign an outreach person:** Assign one person on the university team to facilitate building the university–business network. This person will act as the "connector" between the academic incubation participants and individuals from business. Keep a live scorecard to track the growth of the network.

2. **Create a "dream list":** The academic incubator team should work together to create a list of companies and individuals to target for this network-building effort. Then, with these names, reach out to others in the university to assess if there is any current connection to the university, or if someone exists who can make an introduction. The key information element that the outreach connector needs to gather is the answer to this question: "What do they care about?" Once this is added to the individual's contact info, it will be the key to encouraging them to engage.

3. **Manage the "ask":** When people are contacted, they will expect an "ask" of some type. Asking them to commit to a time-consuming mentoring engagement or to sponsor a pitch day prize before building a relationship will most likely be ineffective. Instead, consider asking:

   We are trying to learn more about the local entrepreneurial eco-system, and I have three questions for you. It should not take more than seven minutes. (1) How have you interacted with the university in the past, if at all? (2) If there is one thing the university could do for your business, what would it be? (3) What business issue do you worry about most related to your business?

This initial contact will form the basis of the relationship going forward. The information from these three questions will help curate future engagement with this business.

4. **Create a series of engagement events:** Consider a series of periodic business events. Give businesspeople a reason to visit the university and incubator. Using what was learned from the three questions, categorize them, then create an academic talk on the subject or a panel of other businesspeople to engage and explore the issue. Consider asking the business contact to chair or be a

panel member. *Reverse pitching* by businesspeople can always be interesting. The businessperson has 15 minutes to describe their company, how it offers value, and ask for something, e.g., students who are about to graduate to apply for jobs, university academics' help with a problem, or for people in the audience to brainstorm innovation ideas for the company. Other reverse pitching examples will appear in the final section of this chapter.

5. **Monthly ecosystem-wide meeting**: Regular monthly ecosystem stakeholder meetings are the best way to consistently break down barriers, build networks, and promote a more inclusive ecosystem. A great example is called "Entrepreneurs + Espresso" ("Entrepreneurs & Espresso," 2023), a monthly gathering open to all regional entrepreneurs that includes networking, an experienced entrepreneur's "Near Business Death—Crash & Learn" experience story, a new entrepreneur's pitch, and a new (no more than one year in operation) business founder presenting their business and a current problem to the crowd for possible solutions. This event has been going on for over ten years at the University of Virginia and has helped build a large and resilient network.

A Holistic Approach to Academic Incubator ESP Design

With a strategy for expanded stakeholder engagement, including the university's improved business entity network, this section offers insights on enhancing the functionality and outcomes of an academic incubator's ESP and the resultant wider university-led EE. There are hundreds of process elements available and no one-size-fits-all solution (Amezcua et al., 2020; Audretsch and Belitski, 2017; Bhave, 1994; Cohen et al., 2019; Liguori et al., 2019; Lingens et al., 2021).[2] Amezcua et al. (2020) identify three core mechanisms: buffering, bridging, and curating. Buffering shields new businesses, bridging connects them externally, and curating directs them to the optimal matched resources.

The way these process elements are used for academic incubator ESP design is the key. With so many elements, an academic incubator ESP designer can start by using effectuation principles. In conditions of uncertainty and multiple stakeholders, effectuation logic uses the concept of *"opportunity shaping,"* orchestrating connections among internally and externally available resources, actors, and networks to realize creative opportunities (Roach et al., 2016; Zahra, 2021). Another key dimension is the timing and sequence of these design elements; these and other temporal dynamics can make or break the ESP (Schiller, 2023).[3]

There is a note of caution when selecting the person to lead an academic ESP initiative. Entrepreneurial experience is very important (Burke et al., 2010; Deligianni et al., 2022; Yusuf and Saffu, 2005). As Sarasvathy (2001a, 2001b, 2004) warns related to the use of effectuation, individuals with a broader and deeper experience base had much better results than people with limited experience. The depth and breadth of this entrepreneurial experience can markedly impact academic incubator outcomes. If an adept entrepreneur isn't available, forming an advisory board of seasoned entrepreneurs from local business partners can fill the gap.

Three Essential Academic Incubator ESP Design Elements

A well-formulated academic incubator ESP design, tailored to the university and community EE, executed with aligned community stakeholders, that includes the use of business partnerships, can contribute to consistent, productive student entrepreneurship experience and new business development (Busch and Barkema, 2022; Guerrero and Martínez-Chávez, 2020).

When entrepreneurs design companies, products, or services, they may use a tool like the Lean Startup Canvas or Minimum Viable Product Canvas to focus decision-making (Shepherd and Gruber, 2021). Like similar valuable canvas tools, the Minimum Viable Entrepreneurial Ecosystem (MVEE) Design Canvas, with its detailed twenty-one-components, can engender smarter ESP design decisions.[4] The key is to focus on the three "Must Have!" items: matched mentors; motivated entrepreneurs; and markets. Even with everything else, if these are missing, the ESP will most likely fall short of expectations.

1. **Matched Mentors:** Experienced professionals with skills, talents, and abilities matched to the entrepreneur's startup business requirements. This is the most important thing a university–business partnership can provide to entrepreneurship students (Assenova, 2020; Miller et al., 2023; St-Jean and Tremblay, 2020).[5]
2. **Motivated Entrepreneurs:** At the core of any student ESP initiative is the student's level of motivation. Before starting the university-led ESP, the student's motivation level should be assessed, and if needed, remedial workshops or boot camps should be recommended, similar to attending remedial reading or math classes to get up to speed. One way to assess a student's

readiness for the rigors of an ESP experience is to use interview questions to evaluate them.[6]

3. **Markets:** Access to markets for the potential product or service considered for development by the student entrepreneur. If there is limited or no potential market available—someone who will find value in the offering and pay money for that value—then the student entrepreneur should continue searching for other ideas. A way to find this initial market is to identify local business partners who have needs—a *"pain point"*—for some product or service.

Some Final Strategies, Tactics, and Ideas for Exceptional Academic Incubators

The target outcomes for academic incubators can range from learning how to develop a basic financial business plan to building, pitching, attaining seed funding, and launching a going concern. No matter what the desired outcomes might be, the following strategies, tactics, and ideas could help create an exceptional academic incubator.

1. **Pre-incubator hackathons:** Before the incubator program starts, run quick one- or two-day hackathons to give students a chance to use creative problem-solving techniques and get to know other students in the entrepreneurship community.
2. **Field trips to local startups:** A great way to see how companies operate is to visit a local small company. Schedule this early in the entrepreneurship curriculum so students can build networks for potential summer internships.
3. **Pre-incubator student networking:** In the months running up to the incubator's launch, run a series of university events for students to get to know each other, brainstorm ideas, and build networks. Students can pitch early general business ideas and tell other students what team members they need.
4. **Consider themes:** It will always be best if the student entrepreneurs generate their own business ideas. This assures personal commitment and connection with the effort. If students are struggling to formulate innovative ideas, consider group brainstorming where pain points and business categories can be generated.
5. **Don't forget social ventures:** If the ESP is focused on for-profit ventures, consider a few social enterprises as long as the student entrepreneurs can show a future plan to cover their expenses with donations, grants, or selling a product or service.

6. **A perpetual program:** Allow student entrepreneurs to remain connected to the incubator in some way after the final evaluation and grade.

7. **Local participants:** Consider allowing local non-student participants, either as part of a team or as the entire team. This can add some interesting energy to the incubator.

8. **University innovation commercialization:** If academics within the institution, neighboring universities, research centers, or similar possess innovations, inventions, patented technologies, or nascent ideas with potential as a foundation for a new enterprise, encourage these scholars to present their concepts to student entrepreneurs for potential commercialization. This is known as reverse pitching.

9. **Business partner commercialization:** Similar to the reverse pitch by academics above, business partners from the region could pitch student entrepreneurs on pain points they would like addressed, product ideas, or technology the company owns that could be commercialized.

10. **Inclusion of non-entrepreneurial students on startup teams:** University startups often benefit from the involvement of students across a wide range of disciplines. Recognizing the value of diversity in academic backgrounds, consider opening positions within student startups for those not traditionally aligned with entrepreneurship. Students enrolled in anthropology, music, or foreign language programs, for instance, can significantly enrich the team dynamic. Their specialized knowledge and unique perspectives can be invaluable in shaping the development and enhancement of the final product or service offering. This approach fosters a more inclusive, innovative, and interdisciplinary team environment, ultimately contributing to the startup's success.

11. **Downstream pitching:** The pitch used to communicate the company to investors—an *"upstream pitch"*—is vital. A different pitch will be required to recruit team members, partners, vendors, and mentors. This upstream pitch will emphasize vision and inspiration, instead of financial aspects. If the student entrepreneur can't inspire people to join, partner, or help with the business, it will be difficult to launch the enterprise.

12. **Timing of ESP elements:** In addition to the three "Must Have!" MVEE canvas elements of matched mentors, motivated entrepreneurs, and markets, the timing and temporal aspects of the ESP are important. Strive to execute the ESP process in an efficient order. Two examples of this are: (1) conduct entrepreneur mindset improvement workshops before throwing the students into the full ESP and (2) create a deep list of matched, qualified, and ready to engage mentors before the ESP program begins.

There is no one-size-fits all formula for an instant ESP program. There are too many variables and too many things that can unexpectedly drift. It will take time and partnerships for the ESP to evolve toward maximum potential. The right engaged business partnerships can make the difference.

Notes

1 Selected material in this chapter is drawn from the author's previous paper, "Alternative Design Theories and the Temporal Nature of Top–Down Entrepreneurial Ecosystem Support Processes: Implications for Resource-Constrained Emerging Ecosystems in Transition" (Schiller, 2023).
2 "ESP Development Strategies, Processes, and Procedures" (see: https://bit.ly/ESPDev), illustrates ESP development resources, tools, and processes identified in past research (Cohen, 2013; S. Cohen et al., 2019; Hallen et al., 2020).
3 "Effectuation+ for ESP Design" (see: https://bit.ly/EffESPDesign) shows a process framework to guide ESP designers.
4 Minimum Viable Entrepreneurial Ecosystem (MVEE) Design Canvas is available at: https://bit.ly/MVEE2023
5 This TED Talk provides insights on effective mentorship: https://www.youtube.com/watch?v=sVDgOLLL66o
6 Interview questions can be devised, based on the four-phase Entrepreneurial Mindset Markers, available at: https://bit.ly/EntMindsetMarkers

References

Adner, R., 2017. Ecosystem as structure: An actionable construct for strategy. *J. Manag.* 43, 39–58. https://doi.org/10.1177/0149206316678451

Agarwal, R., Audretsch, D., Sarkar, M.B., 2007. The process of creative construction: knowledge spillovers, entrepreneurship, and economic growth. *Strateg. Entrep. J.* 1, 263–286. https://doi.org/10.1002/sej.36

Aldrich, H.E., Yang, T., 2014. How do entrepreneurs know what to do? learning and organizing in new ventures. *J. Evol. Econ.* 24, 59–82. https://doi.org/10.1007/s00191-013-0320-x

Amezcua, A., Ratinho, T., Plummer, L.A., Jayamohan, P., 2020. Organizational sponsorship and the economics of place: how regional urbanization and localization shape incubator outcomes. *J. Bus. Ventur.* 35, 105967. https://doi.org/10.1016/j.jbusvent.2019.105967

Antony, J., Klarl, T., Lehmann, E.E., 2017. Productive and harmful entrepreneurship in a knowledge economy. *Small Bus. Econ.* 49, 189–202. https://doi.org/10.1007/s11187-016-9822-x

Assenova, V.A., 2020. Early-stage venture incubation and mentoring promote learning, scaling, and profitability among disadvantaged entrepreneurs. *Organ. Sci.* 31, 1560–1578. https://doi.org/10.1287/orsc.2020.1367

Audretsch, D.B., Belitski, M., 2017. Entrepreneurial ecosystems in cities: establishing the framework conditions. *J. Technol. Transf.* 42, 1030–1051. https://doi.org/10.1007/s10961-016-9473-8

Baumol, W.J., 1993. *Entrepreneurship, management, and the structure of payoffs.* London: MIT Press.

Belitski, M., Heron, K., 2017. Expanding entrepreneurship education ecosystems. *J. Manag. Dev.* 36, 163–177. https://doi.org/10.1108/JMD-06-2016-0121

Bhave, M.P., 1994. A process model of entrepreneurial venture creation. *J. Bus. Ventur.* 9, 223–242. https://doi.org/10.1016/0883-9026(94)90031-0

Brown, R., Mawson, S., 2019. Entrepreneurial ecosystems and public policy in action: a critique of the latest industrial policy blockbuster. *Camb. J. Reg. Econ. Soc.* 12, 347–368. https://doi.org/10.1093/cjres/rsz011

Burke, A., Fraser, S., Greene, F.J., 2010. The multiple effects of business planning on new venture performance. *J. Manag. Stud.* 47, 391–415. https://doi.org/10.1111/j.1467-6486.2009.00857.x

Busch, C., Barkema, H., 2022. Align or perish: Social enterprise network orchestration in Sub-Saharan Africa. *J. Bus. Ventur.* 37, 106187. https://doi.org/10.1016/j.jbusvent.2021.106187

Cohen, S., 2013. What do accelerators do? insights from incubators and angels. *Innov. Technol. Gov. Glob.* 8, 19–25. https://doi.org/10.1162/INOV_a_00184

Cohen, S., Fehder, D.C., Hochberg, Y.V., Murray, F., 2019. The design of startup accelerators. *Res. Policy* 48, 1781–1797. https://doi.org/10.1016/j.respol.2019.04.003

Deligianni, I., Sapouna, P., Voudouris, I., Lioukas, S., 2022. An effectual approach to innovation for new ventures: the role of entrepreneur's prior start-up experience. *J. Small Bus. Manag.* 60, 146–177. https://doi.org/10.1080/00472778.2019.1698432

Entrepreneurs & Espresso [WWW Document], 2023. Cville Entrep. Espresso. http://ce2.squarespace.com (accessed September 14.2023).

Fernandes, A.J., Ferreira, J.J., 2022. Entrepreneurial ecosystems and networks: a literature review and research agenda. *Rev. Manag. Sci.* 16, 189–247. https://doi.org/10.1007/s11846-020-00437-6

Fiet, J.O., 2001. The pedagogical side of entrepreneurship theory. *J. Bus. Ventur.* 16, 101–117. https://doi.org/10.1016/S0883-9026(99)00042-7

Guerrero, M., Martínez-Chávez, M., 2020. Aligning regional and business strategies: looking inside the Basque Country entrepreneurial innovation ecosystem. *Thunderbird Int. Bus. Rev.* 62, 607–621. https://doi.org/10.1002/tie.22162

Hakala, H., O'Shea, G., Farny, S., Luoto, S., 2020. Re-storying the business, innovation and entrepreneurial ecosystem concepts: the model-narrative review method. *Int. J. Manag. Rev.* 22, 10–32.

Hallen, B.L., Cohen, S.L., Bingham, C.B., 2020. Do accelerators work? if so, how? *Organ. Sci.* 31, 378–414. https://doi.org/10.1287/orsc.2019.1304

Hausberg, J.P., Korreck, S., 2020. Business incubators and accelerators: a co-citation analysis-based, systematic literature review. *J. Technol. Transf.* 45, 151–176. https://doi.org/10.1007/s10961-018-9651-y

Isenberg, D., 2011. The entrepreneurship ecosystem strategy as a new paradigm for economic policy: principles for cultivating entrepreneurship. *Present. Inst. Int. Eur. Aff.* 1, 1–13.

Jones, P., Maas, G., Kraus, S., Lloyd Reason, L., 2021. An exploration of the role and contribution of entrepreneurship centres in UK higher education institutions. *J. Small Bus. Enterp. Dev.* 28, 205–228. https://doi.org/10.1108/JSBED-08-2018-0244

Kwong, C.C.Y., Thompson, P., Cheung, C.W.-M., Manzoor, H., 2012. The role of environment in fostering conductive entrepreneurial learning: teaching the 'art' of entrepreneurship in boot camps. *J. Gen. Manag.* 38, 45–71. https://doi.org/10.1177/030630701203800103

Leendertse, J., Schrijvers, M., Stam, E., 2021. Measure twice, cut once: entrepreneurial ecosystem metrics. *Res. Policy* 104336. https://doi.org/10.1016/j.respol.2021.104336

Levie, J., Lichtenstein, B.B., 2010. A terminal assessment of stages theory: introducing a dynamic states approach to entrepreneurship. *Entrep. Theory Pract.* 34, 317–350. https://doi.org/10.1111/j.1540-6520.2010.00377.x

Liguori, E., Bendickson, J., Solomon, S., McDowell, W.C., 2019. Development of a multi-dimensional measure for assessing entrepreneurial ecosystems. *Entrep. Reg. Dev.* 31, 7–21. https://doi.org/10.1080/08985626.2018.1537144

Lingens, B., Miehé, L., Gassmann, O., 2021. The ecosystem blueprint: how firms shape the design of an ecosystem according to the surrounding conditions. *Long Range Plann.* 54, 102043. https://doi.org/10.1016/j.lrp.2020.102043

Mason, C.M., Harrison, R.T., 2006. After the exit: acquisitions, entrepreneurial recycling and regional economic development. *Reg. Stud.* 40, 55–73. https://doi.org/10.1080/00343400500450059

Mele, G., Sansone, G., Secundo, G., Paolucci, E., 2022. Speeding up student entrepreneurship: the role of university business idea incubators. *IEEE Trans. Eng. Manag.* 1–15. https://doi.org/10.1109/TEM.2022.3175655

Miller, A., O'Mahony, S., Cohen, S.L., 2023. Opening the aperture: explaining the complementary roles of advice and testing when forming entrepreneurial strategy. *Organ. Sci.* Orsc.2023.1656. https://doi.org/10.1287/orsc.2023.1656

Nambisan, S., Baron, R.A., 2013. Entrepreneurship in innovation ecosystems: entrepreneurs' self–regulatory processes and their implications for new venture success. *Entrep. Theory Pract.* 37, 1071–1097. https://doi.org/10.1111/j.1540-6520.2012.00519.x

Pauwels, C., Clarysse, B., Wright, M., Van Hove, J., 2016. Understanding a new generation incubation model: the accelerator. *Technovation* 50–51, 13–24. https://doi.org/10.1016/j.technovation.2015.09.003

Peterman, N.E., Kennedy, J., 2003. Enterprise education: influencing students' perceptions of entrepreneurship. *Entrep. Theory Pract.* 28, 129–144. https://doi.org/10.1046/j.1540-6520.2003.00035.x

Roach, D.C., Ryman, J.A., Makani, J., 2016. Effectuation, innovation and performance in SMEs: an empirical study. *Eur. J. Innov. Manag.* 19, 214–238. https://doi.org/10.1108/EJIM-12-2014-0119

Robinson, S., Stubberud, H.A., 2014. Teaching creativity, team work and other soft skills for entrepreneurship. *J. Entrep. Educ.* 17, 186.

Sarasvathy, S.D., 2001a. Effectual reasoning in entrepreneurial decision making: existence and bounds. *Acad. Manag. Proc.* 2001, D1–D6. https://doi.org/10.5465/apbpp.2001.6133065

Sarasvathy, S.D., 2001b. Causation and effectuation: toward a theoretical shift from economic inevitability to entrepreneurial contingency. *Acad. Manage. Rev.* 26, 243. https://doi.org/10.2307/259121

Sarasvathy, S.D., 2004. Making It happen: beyond theories of the firm to theories of firm design. *Entrep. Theory Pract.* 28, 519–531. https://doi.org/10.1111/j.1540-6520.2004.00062.x

Schiller, V., 2023. Alternative design theories and the temporal nature of top-down entrepreneurial ecosystem support processes: implications for resource-constrained emerging ecosystems in transition. *New Bus. Models Conf. Proc. 2023* Maastricht Univ. Press.

Shepherd, D.A., Gruber, M., 2021. The lean startup framework: closing the academic–practitioner divide. *Entrep. Theory Pract.* 45, 967–998. https://doi.org/10.1177/1042258719899415

Spigel, B., 2020. *Entrepreneurial ecosystems: theory, practice and futures.* Edward Elgar Publishing.

Spigel, B., Vinodrai, T., 2021. Meeting its Waterloo? recycling in entrepreneurial ecosystems after anchor firm collapse. *Entrep. Reg. Dev.* 33, 599–620. https://doi.org/10.1080/08985626.2020.1734262

Stam, E., 2015. Entrepreneurial ecosystems and regional policy: a sympathetic critique. *Eur. Plan. Stud.* 23, 1759–1769. https://doi.org/10.1080/09654313.2015.1061484

Stam, E., 2018. Measuring entrepreneurial ecosystems, in: O'Connor, A., Stam, E., Sussan, F., Audretsch, D.B. (Eds.), *Entrepreneurial Ecosystems*, International Studies in Entrepreneurship. Springer International Publishing, Cham, pp. 173–197. https://doi.org/10.1007/978-3-319-63531-6_9

Stam, E., van de Ven, A., 2021. Entrepreneurial ecosystem elements. *Small Bus. Econ.* 56, 809–832. https://doi.org/10.1007/s11187-019-00270-6

St-Jean, É., Tremblay, M., 2020. Mentoring for entrepreneurs: A boost or a crutch? Long-term effect of mentoring on self-efficacy. *Int. Small Bus. J. Res. Entrep.* 38, 424–448. https://doi.org/10.1177/0266242619901058

Stuetzer, M., Obschonka, M., Schmitt-Rodermund, E., 2013. Balanced skills among nascent entrepreneurs. *Small Bus. Econ.* 41, 93–114. https://doi.org/10.1007/s11187-012-9423-2

Van De Ven, H., 1993. The development of an infrastructure for entrepreneurship *J. Bus. Ventur.* 8, 211–230. https://doi.org/10.1016/0883-9026(93)90028-4

Wu, L., Jiang, S., Wang, X., Yu, L., Wang, Y., Pan, H., 2022. Entrepreneurship education and entrepreneurial intentions of college students: the mediating role of entrepreneurial self-efficacy and the moderating role of entrepreneurial competition experience. *Front. Psychol.* 12, 727826. https://doi.org/10.3389/fpsyg.2021.727826

Yusuf, A., Saffu, K., 2005. Planning and performance of small and medium enterprise operators in a country in transition. *J. Small Bus. Manag.* 43, 480–497. https://doi.org/10.1111/j.1540-627X.2005.00148.x

Zahra, S.A., 2021. The resource-based view, resourcefulness, and resource management in startup firms: a proposed research agenda. *J. Manag.* 47, 1841–1860. https://doi.org/10.1177/01492063211018505

30 From Purpose to Impact

Time for a New Business School Model?

Nicholas O'Regan

The Changing University Environment

Continuous and rapid change is now facing the university sector, from technology/AI advancements to global and societal challenges. This disruptive change is technology driven and impacts on all sectors of the economy and society, making today's world highly interconnected, interdependent and interrelated in a broad ranging global ecosystem.

The role of universities and business schools has changed from the provision of third-level education to that of being a catalyst for regional regeneration and competitiveness. Indeed, many universities stress their economic and societal roles. However, concerns are now increasing on the ability of the university sector to meet these roles, with a report by the World Economic Forum (Krishnan, 2020) referring to the need to make education more efficient and effective if it is to meet the needs of the current workplace. Hamel (1996:113) contended that 'we are standing on the verge of a new industrial revolution dealing with genetics, materials, and, more than anything else, information'. To address these emerging challenges, he urged radical change.

But, is radical change possible in a sector that is overly bureaucratic, rigidly structured and with significant resource requirements? Or are we at the point where we don't have any choice but to change given that a continuation with business schools in their current design and structure will delay progress in meeting the challenges of the future? Is now the time to develop a new paradigm with new ideas for new structures that provide solutions for business and society. This is a collective action for all business schools – one school making a major change will be seen as a maverick or dissident.

Prof Michael Crow (2016), President of Arizona State University (ASU) referring to the New American University, stresses the need to be entrepreneurial orientated, enterprise managed, rapidly adaptably, democratically engaged and egalitarian, with the

DOI: 10.4324/9781003459217-33

potential to achieve scale. Crow (2008) says that academics are 'part of the most structured, rigid, bureaucratic, non-changing, non-creative, organisations and incapable of altering their institutions trajectory'. He emphasises the need to ask who we are, why we are here, what we are, what we are doing, what our role is and what are the measures of accountability?

In his call for change, Crow uses the analogy of bureaucrats running a 'railroad' made up of science departments, economics departments, mechanical engineering or chemical engineering departments, that are like little railroad stations on a railway network. All tend to be replicative of each other, with all the same stations run by bureaucrats, often called department chairs or school directors, with little or no differentiation. Crow contends that now is the time to think about a new model of a business school – one where the movement from the mindset of manager to that of designing new approaches is unstoppable.

To meet this change, business schools need to prepare the leaders of the future to meet the challenges of a world that will be much different from today's world. This will need a thorough review and redesign of the business school offering. Business schools now need a stronger focus than ever on knowledge transfer and engagement with external stakeholders, from business to government.

Kitchener et al. (2022:3) state *'for business schools and their stakeholders, the goal of purposeful engagement would be to collaboratively tackle real-world problems in commercial, civic and policy spheres'*. They go on to describe an ecosystem where academics and stakeholders co-create shared value. Such an ecosystem provides the foundation for sustainability, arguably for both the business school and its stakeholders. This calls for a change in the way academics think and behave, with the resultant university culture needing to move beyond the traditional teaching and research remit and, in turn, overcome any obstacles to change, as well as embracing social and environmental issues. Tufano (2020) argued that the traditional business school model is looking dated and that change is needed.

Why is this change needed and have business schools lost their way or failed to keep up with the changing times? Business schools have three main roles: teaching, research and stakeholder engagement. While the research function is well honed, can we say the same about teaching and engagement? Given that the main rationale for business schools is to develop the leaders and managers of the future for the future, can we say that this 'is mission accomplished', and, in doing so, continue to focus on maximising/optimising their research output that is targeted to the elite journals and where lower teaching loads are the norm? Elite or highly ranked journals are rarely, if ever, read by business leaders/ managers, while more practitioner-related journals, such as the Harvard Business Review, are shunned by leading academics. While there is abundant evidence of the need for real management training and support for practitioners, some academics tend to pursue esoteric academic paths that have no discernible value outside the academic domain. The current incentive system for academics pushes them in this direction.

Business schools in all universities are successful entities and are often referred to as the 'cash cow' for the university. Criticisms of business schools and their role in both the economy and society are plentiful. A plethora of articles appeared in the last two decades questioning the value of business schools – see for example, Pfeffer and Fong (2002), Bennis and O'Toole (2005). The main criticisms are that both research and teaching are silo based, with a focus on one discipline, and significant amounts of research are conducted to further the academics own career rather than create impact and value creation for business and society. It is not unreasonable to expect that business schools focus on matters relevant to business.

Another criticism relates to the risk in following an interdisciplinary path, given that peer reviews on both grant applications and journal papers are unlikely to accept radical thinking that does not align with the work of established academics, when even intricate challenges require a multidisciplinary approach. This reinforcing senior academic behaviour makes any significant change very difficult.

But what really drives business schools? Apart from the financial achievements, the main drivers are outcomes such as rankings, reputation, accreditation and financial issues, rather than purpose. Yet, the history of many business schools show that they were initially created to address skills and expertise shortfalls within the local employment market. The processes and structures developed over time provide the underpinning for the external orientation ethos. While the local employment market has changed dramatically in the past few decades, many business schools are resistant to change and prefer to retain existing processes and structures, and, thereby, maintain the status quo where research excellence is the institutional goal. Thus, the purpose is substituted by the outcome.

The success of universities and business schools in addressing the consequences of the Covid-19 pandemic showed that academics were quickly able to develop dramatically new working practices. This provides confidence that academics can, equally, adapt to meeting the skills shortfall as well as engage with stakeholders and nurture and leverage that engagement.

Preparing Future Leaders and Managers

A report, published in 2023 by the Chartered Management Institute [CMI] in the UK, found that almost one-third of UK workers leave their jobs because of a negative workplace culture and the quality of management. The CMI also found that over 80 per cent of managers in the UK have no formal training in management or leadership and are in effect 'accidental managers'. Clearly, UK managers need training to enhance economic performance. This would appear to be an obvious task for business schools. However, research and publication take priority, even though the majority of the university's work involves teaching – which also happens to be the major source of funding. This is compounded by the categorisation of universities into research-led and teaching-led. In reality, both categories drive engagement in a highly engaged university.

It could be argued that the lack of purpose is a result of a lack of frequent and beneficial engagement between the business school faculty and stakeholders. It is not that radical to expect such close engagement – as in other disciplines such as law, medicine and engineering. The core purpose of all disciplines is to advance their work to be more effective and fruitful. The ultimate measure of success is the degree to which their discipline has advanced. But to achieve this, business school faculty need to have a clear purpose, like other disciplines have. The CMI finding that over 80 per cent of managers have no formal training would not be accepted in other disciplines such as medicine, dentistry or engineering. The conundrum revolves around the high standing of business schools while, at the same time, the performance of stakeholders, such as businesses, are underperforming. The solution relates to how academic faculty perceive their purpose and roles.

The Engaged Faculty

Recent years have seen a reorientation of universities with a strong emphasis on proactive entrepreneurial behaviour. While a relatively small number of faculty members actively and effectively engage with business and stakeholders, the engagement activity is underdeveloped and is often looked on with a degree of distain. Traditionally, business schools have adopted a casual approach to engagement, with many collaborations arising from personal connections, trial and error or simply serendipity. No longer can business schools avoid having a more professional approach, and there are calls for a new approach where collaborative engagement is the new norm. This points to a need to provide all faculty with the skills to engage and the ability to recognise opportunities and leverage them.

If we are seriously committed to mutually beneficial collaboration, the future is likely to look very different to how engagement operated in the past. The literature sees the role of universities and business schools as central to economic performance. This will depend largely on the support and training available and the incentives to make it happen, as well as the culture of the school. Academic culture has traditionally been defined by publications and research, rather than engagement. In the case of engagement, the emphasis on publications as the means to promotion, particularly for early career researchers, is an issue. Paradoxically, engagement should ideally begin with the doctoral programme, and continue as the academic's career advances. Engagement is, however, often seen as a distraction and poses a risk to academic career advancement. This is particularly the case when senior academics stress the importance of publishing in top-tier journals, both for the university in terms of academic excellence and for the individual in terms of building their career.

Another issue is the lack of incentives, and the likelihood that engagement is disregarded in pay and performance reviews. Effective engagement requires an interdisciplinary mindset, as business issues and challenges are rarely single discipline based, but the silo approach in academia militates against this, as do the difficulties that interdisciplinary researchers face in career advancement.

Strategic Academic Engagement for Competitive Advantage

Engagement is a two-way process and interactions are influenced by a range of factors, from the university and the motivations of its staff to engage, to the propensity of the stakeholders and their staff to respond/be proactive. Interaction tends to be driven by individuals, with engagement seen in many universities as a discretionary activity. Stakeholders also need the resources to enable them to engage with universities.

The literature base on engagement has expanded greatly over the past two decades with engagement widely seen as the key to competitive advantage. Engagement is defined as 'a positive, fulfilling, work-related state of mind that is characterized by vigour, dedication, and absorption' (Albrecht et al., 2023), requiring physical, emotional and cognitive energies. Employee engagement relates to the individual academic and how they see their role in the organisation, their degree of motivation and effort they give to achieving the organisational goals. Other definitions also encompass attributes relating to 'psychological presence' and cognitive focus (Schaufeli & Bakker, 2004; Shuck & Reio, 2011).

Academic engagement involves overseeing an interdisciplinary focus that leads to both real-world solutions and the advancement of the research base. Yet, this may come at a price, as business schools look for trade offs in the form of research funding or additional students. To address this, co-creation, using the capabilities of both the university and the business stakeholders to lead to impact, is needed. However, the right institutional environment is vital, where a culture that supports engagement, taking into account academic autonomy and competencies, is in place.

In short, engagement is a transmission mechanism for ensuring academic research has an impact on the economy and society. To be effective, it must be strategic.

Why Strategic Engagement?

The extant literature strongly emphasises the need to be strategic if competitive advantage is to be achieved. Developing and leveraging relationships with key stakeholders is key. Strategic engagement is defined 'as an intentional set of cognitions, emotions, and behavioural attributes that employees demonstrate in their daily work to help advance organizational goals' (Arif et al., 2023). In short, it is making sense of the organisational strategy by employees to achieve the organisational goals. This means having a clear understanding of where the organisation is going, and the recognition of the best route to achieve this. Strategic behaviours are 'the physical actions employees demonstrate that translate their understanding of the organizational strategy and goals into concrete implementation steps that help achieve competitive advantage' (Arif et al., 2023).

Why Academics Should Engage with Stakeholders

The literature sees engagement as having many benefits that accrue to both the individual academic and their university in aspects such as job satisfaction, adaptivity and creativity. Engagement is a 'positive and fulfilling, work-related state of mind whereby employees feel motivated and enthusiastic, and are actively involved in their work' (Albrecht et al., 2023). The literature outlines other benefits to engagement, e.g. student placement and employability, with resultant feedback into curriculum development. Intangible benefits may include peer recognition. Proactive, engaging academics tend to have the ability to network effectively and pursue opportunity recognition.

To enable effective engagement, it is vital that we understand what motivates academics to engage. Many reasons are given for those academics involved in active engagement with stakeholders, from furthering research to testing new ideas. The modes of engagement can vary from informal to formal relationships, with the main activity being collaboration intended to further the academics own research. The reasons for the relatively low number of academics engaged with stakeholders, arguably, range from lack of awareness of the potential benefits, the absence of engagement champions and a weak knowledge engagement ecosystem. Other reasons include the academics perception of support available and potential risks that may arise.

Arguably, the motivational factors for academics to engage, feature aspects such as academic standing, funding for research and the opportunity to deploy current research/seek input to new research ideas, while financial aspects are way down the list of factors.

This implies that a broad range of incentives are needed to motivate academics to engage, with both the university and its various faculties playing a key role.

Conclusion

The main argument in this chapter is that stakeholder engagement matters and impacts on both teaching and research dissemination. The focus on engagement needs to move from ad hoc and accidental engagement to a professional and committed approach. A focus on an inclusive, collaborative and mutually beneficial approach provides an opportunity to advance and leverage the value of engagement with stakeholders. The reorientation towards a model of co-creation that is mutually beneficial is required. This is a low-cost and high-returns approach that can leverage opportunities in many areas. Seizing these opportunities will mean a dramatic change in academia with a new model of engagement encompassing a coherent infrastructure. Such a step-change will mean the development of new methods to broaden successful academic–business engagement on a major scale, and entails setting programmes, creating incentives and structuring recruitment that will transform effective academic–business engagement.

The movement towards being more entrepreneurial originated in the Uinted States of America (US) with MIT and Stanford focusing on the transfer of knowledge to both the industrial and the non-academic sectors. Interestingly, US universities seem to be actively and effectively involved with stakeholders, possibly due to corporate philanthropy and contract research.

ASU (2024), led by its President Michael Crow, is already working on the future and the New American University. He has introduced nine design aspirations, that are pathways to think about the 'why question' and achieve excellence, access and impact. One of the design aspirations is intellectual fusion – fusing intellectual fields together, rather than keeping them compartmentalised and siloed.

Crow refers to the necessity for change and says that in its absence the output will remain the same. Following design changes at ASU, research activity increased by a factor of 5 – Crow fused disciplines to form outcome-orientated schools, such as Global Sustainability. ASU launched a new school around the faculty of engineering: The Future of Innovation in Society, that is reshaping thinking and is non-disciplinary, but theme and outcome orientated.

The case for change is clear but it cannot be piecemeal. For example, Crow contends that if one wants to produce a new kind of academic who has a fundamentally different view of the way they see the world, then one must step back and look at everything: raison d'etre, design, outcomes, goals and measurements, and hold oneself accountable.

However, it is important to mention that change is not an overnight task, but rather one of a decade-long investment in being truly impactful. ASU embarked on the change journey almost two decades ago. Engagement is not a one-way street and greater involvement and support from business in the research agenda from input to funding could potentially change the way research is conducted.

References

Albrecht, S. L., Furlong, S., & Leiter, M. P. (2023). The psychological conditions for employee engagement in organizational change: Test of a change engagement model. *Frontiers in Psychology*, *14*, 1071924. doi: 10.3389/fpsyg.2023.1071924

Arif, S., Johnston, K. A., Lane, A., & Beatson, A. (2023). A strategic employee attribute scale: Mediating role of internal communication and employee engagement. *Public Relations Review*, *49*(2), 102320.

ASU. (2024). *New American university: Toward 2029 and beyond*. https://president.asu.edu/sites/default/files/2024-03/ASU_Charter_Mission_Goals_2029_Beyond_Final_Feb2024_0.pdf

Bennis, W. G., and O'Toole, J. (2005). How business schools lost their way. *Harvard Business Review*, *83* (5):96–104.

Chartered Management Institute. (2023, October). *Taking responsibility: Why UK Plc needs better managers*.

Crow, M. (2008). A plea for a new kind of academic. *Academe*, *94*(2), 31–35.

Crow, M., (2016). Entrepreneurial Mindset in Higher Education, in a speech to Engineering Unleashed https://www.youtube.com/watch?v=YYm10IriKKU&t=72s

Hamel, G. (1996). In: *Training the fire brigade: Preparing for the unimaginable*. EFMD Publications.

Kitchener, M., Levitt, T., and McKiernan, P. (2022). Business schools and the public good. *Global Focus*, 16(1). https://www.globalfocusmagazine.com/business-schools-and-the-public-good/

Krishnan, K. (2020). *Our education system is losing relevance. Here's how to unleash its potential*. In World Economic Forum, Geneva, Switzerland, https://www.weforum.org/agenda/2020/04/our-education-system-is-losingrelevance-heres-how-to-update-it

Pfeffer, J., & Fong, C. T. (2002). The end of business schools? Less success than meets the eye. *Academy of Management Learning and Education*, 1(1):79–95

Schaufeli, W. B., & Bakker, A. B. (2004). Job demands, job resources, and their relationship with burnout and engagement: A multi-sample study. *Journal of Organizational Behavior*, 25, 293–315.

Shuck, B., & Reio, T. G., Jr. (2011). The employee engagement landscape and HRD: How do we link theory and scholarship to current practice? *Advances in Developing Human Resources*, 13(4), 419–428.

Tufano, P. (2020, March 11). *A bolder vision for business schools*. Harvard Business Review.

Index

Printed in the United States
by Baker & Taylor Publisher Services